*Strategic Management
in Non-Profit Organizations*

STRATEGIC MANAGEMENT IN NON-PROFIT ORGANIZATIONS

AN ADMINISTRATOR'S HANDBOOK

ROBERT D. HAY

Q

Quorum Books

New York · Westport, Connecticut · London

Library of Congress Cataloging-in-Publication Data

Hay, Robert D.
   Strategic management in non-profit organizations : an
administrator's handbook / Robert D. Hay.
      p.   cm.
   ISBN 0–89930–551–2 (lib. bdg. : alk. paper)
   1. Corporations, Nonprofit — Management.   2. Strategic planning.
I. Title.
HD62.6.H39   1990
658.4′012 — dc20   89–24368

British Library Cataloguing in Publication Data is available.

Library of Congress Catalog Card Number: 89–24368
ISBN: 0–89930–551–2

First published in 1990 by Quorum Books

Greenwood Press, Inc.
88 Post Road West, Westport, Connecticut 06881

Printed in the United States of America

The paper used in this book complies with the Permanent Paper Standard issued by the
National Information Standards Organization (Z39.48–1984).

10 9 8 7 6 5 4 3 2 1

Contents

Part IV: Implementation of Strategies

Preface

This book is written as a response to administrators of various non-profit organizations (NPOs) who have expressed a need for information concerning the strategic management of NPOs. These chief executive officers and board members of NPOs feel that they should be practicing truly professional administration in addition to practicing their specialized training in hospitals, churches, educational institutions, civic clubs, and many other types of not-for-profit organizations. The professional approach suggests that there is a body of knowledge that can be mastered, rather than using a hit-or-miss approach in administering the affairs of a non-profit organization.

Certain concepts of administration are fairly universal in nature, but these have to be applied to the unique situations facing each NPO. This book emphasizes these universals, but at the same time it stresses a situational approach which suggests that each NPO has its own unique environment, its own strengths and weaknesses, and its own managerial philosophy which are unlike those of other NPOs.

A special feature of this book is the self-evaluations of various objectives, strategies, and policies related to the functions that each non-profit organization has to perform. These self-evaluations, comparing sound administrative theory to the situations facing each NPO, can aid administrators in making strategic decisions and in evaluating their strengths and weaknesses in order to achieve the NPO's mission and related objectives. These evaluations have been used by the author and his students in making live management audits of many different kinds of non-profit organizations during the past 15 years.

This book is distinctive because it provides a professional strategic managerial approach to administering the functions of any non-profit organization. It stresses the NPO's mission and related objectives, which are determined by a managerial philosophy, by a managerial perception of external environmental factors, and by a managerial perception of internal strengths and weaknesses. Strategies are then suggested to accomplish this mission and related objectives. Thus, Part Two of the book is concerned with this strategy formulation.

Part Three, the second phase of strategic management, is concerned with integrating the overall mission into the operative functions of any NPO — namely, the operations, marketing, personnel, and financing functions. This phase is called strategy integration.

The third phase of strategic management, discussed in Part Four, involves implementing the strategies to accomplish the NPO's mission and related objectives. The major emphasis is on the managerial functions — planning, acquiring, organizing, leading, coordinating, and evaluating — that have to be performed. This phase is called strategy implementation.

Obviously, there are some differences in the management of non-profit organizations and profit organizations. However, there are more similarities than differences. Therefore, while the differences are pointed out, the basic thrust is to emphasize the universal functions of any type of organization as applied to the unique situations facing each non-profit organization. The self-evaluation management approach is the primary tool used to evaluate the strengths and weaknesses relevant to administering the NPO.

This book's audience includes those people who have a vital interest in providing services through non-profit organizations; those who are dedicated to serving the needs of the NPO's clients, employees, managers, and the general public; and those who hope to improve the quality of life through non-profit organizations.

PART I

Introduction

Because this book is about strategic management of non-profit organizations, the first three chapters discuss the nature of non-profit organizations (NPOs), the nature of management, and the nature of strategy. These introductory chapters will provide the background necessary to serve as a framework for formulating, integrating, and implementing strategies to accomplish the NPO's mission and related objectives.

1

The Nature of Non-Profit Organizations

WHAT IS A NON-PROFIT ORGANIZATION?

A non-profit organization (NPO) is one that is formed to provide services and goods for its clientele, with profit being a minor objective. Its primary mission is one of providing services, usually for charitable, religious, educational, scientific, literary, humanitarian, or other non-business purposes. Examples of such organizations include non-profit old age homes, parent-teacher associations, charitable hospitals, alumni associations, schools, chapters of the Red Cross or Salvation Army, animal protection groups, amateur sports clubs, youth groups, churches, and public safety research groups.

To be considered an NPO, (1) the organization must be formed to provide services not for profit; (2) no part of any net earnings can be distributed to its members, trustees, or officers or to other private persons; (3) its assets must be permanently dedicated to its major mission and must not, upon dissolution, be paid to any private person or organization; and (4) it usually cannot engage in developing or disseminating political propaganda to influence the election of a candidate for public office. If there are any questions about the NPO's mission or status, the law of the state where the NPO was created governs.

According to Section 501(c)(3) of the Internal Revenue Code, an NPO may qualify for exemption from federal income tax if it is organized to serve charitable, religious, educational, scientific, or literary purposes; to foster amateur sports competitions; or to prevent cruelty to children or animals.[1] Contributions to these types of NPOs are deductible as charitable contributions on the donor's federal income tax return.

A state or municipal instrumentality may qualify as an NPO if it is organized as an entity separate from the governmental unit that created it. Examples would be a state school, university, or hospital. However, if an organization is an integral part of the local government, it does not qualify as a separate NPO.

WHAT KINDS OF NPOs EXIST?

Perhaps the most useful method of classifying the different kinds of non-profit organizations is that developed by the Internal Revenue Service (IRS).[2] The IRS has classified them by activities as follows:

 1. Religious activities
 2. Schools, colleges, and related activities
 3. Cultural, historical, or other educational activities
 4. Other instruction and training activities
 5. Health services and related activities
 6. Scientific research activities
 7. Business and professional activities
 8. Farming and related activities
 9. Activities of mutual organizations
10. Activities of employee or membership benefit organizations
11. Sports, athletic, recreational, and social activities
12. Youth activities
13. Conservation, environmental, and beautification activities
14. Housing activities
15. Inner-city or community activities
16. Civil rights activities
17. Litigation and legal aid activities
18. Legislative and political activities
19. Advocacy activities
20. Other activities directed to individuals
21. Activities directed to other organizations
22. Other purposes and activities

Each of these general classes of NPOs can be further broken down into specific types of organizations. For example, a religious NPO may be described as one in which the particular religious belief of the organization is truly and sincerely held and in which the practices and rituals associated with the organization's religious belief or creed are not contrary to clearly defined public policy. Examples of NPOs engaged in church activities would be churches and synagogues, associations of churches, religious orders, church auxiliaries, missions, missionary organizations, evangelist groups, and religious publishing companies.

Schools, colleges, and related activities involve the instruction or training of individuals for the purpose of improving or developing their capabilities. Examples of this type of NPO would include schools, colleges, trade schools, faculty groups, alumni associations, parent-teacher associations, fraternities or sororities, student societies, school or college athletic associations, scholarship programs for children of employees, student loan programs, student housing groups, other student aid programs, foreign student exchange programs, and student-operated businesses.

Cultural, historical, or other educational activities would be central to the following types of organizations: museums, zoos, planetariums, libraries, historical site or monument conservators, organizers of commemorative events or fairs, community theatrical groups, singing societies, cultural performance groups, art exhibit sponsors, literary activity clubs, foreign cultural exchange programs, and genealogical research groups.

Other instruction and training activities might consist of the following: publishing, broadcasting radio or television programs, producing films, holding discussion groups, conducting study and research, and providing apprentice training.

One who analyzes the various kinds of NPOs might reach the following generalizations: (1) most NPOs deal with services, rather than products; (2) most NPOs are small when compared to the large size of many profit businesses; (3) the activities and purposes of NPOs are widely diverse; and (4) most people are touched by NPOs in one way or another.

MISPERCEPTIONS ABOUT NPOs

Many people think that NPOs do not try to make a profit. This is not the case. While executives may state publicly that their NPO is not trying to generate enough revenues to offset its expenses, privately they will admit that profit is an objective — perhaps not too much emphasis is placed on profits, but enough cash revenues must be coming in to at least break even and possibly make a small profit. Executives recognize that an excess of revenues over expenses is necessary for the NPO to survive. An NPO has to survive to accomplish its mission, and without profits, the organization has little chance to pursue its reason for existence.

There is no "free lunch" for any organization in the long run. The services produced and consumed by clients must be paid for — either by clients, donors, or taxpayers or by subsidies in one form or another. There is no truth to the notion that the government *prevents* an NPO from making a profit, but the essence of governmental approval is that any profits cannot be distributed to any of the NPO's officers, members, or trustees or to any other private persons. Profits can be made, but not distributed.

Another misperception is that non-profits are all guided by public-spirited altruists who seek only to serve the public interest. Human nature would suggest otherwise. Self-interest is prevalent in all people, including those who manage the activities of non-profit organizations. Admittedly, altruism is more prevalent in NPOs, but altruism also exists in profit organizations.

Further, many people believe that non-profits exist almost solely on the donations of the public. Actually, revenues come primarily from clients or members, from government in the form of taxes, from grants, from private profit organizations, from revenues generated by producing and selling related products/services, and also from private donors.

Another myth is that nonprofits are outside the mainstream of economic

Table 1.1
Number of Active Entities in the Exempt Organizations Master File

	1980	1987
Religious, Charitable, etc.	*319,842	*422,103
Fraternal Beneficiary Societies	137,449	98,979
Social Welfare	129.553	138,485
Labor, Agriculture Organizations	85,774	75,238
Social and Recreation Clubs	51,922	60,146
Business Leagues	48,717	59,981
War Veterans' Organizations	22,247	24,749
Domestic Fraternal Beneficiary Societies	16,178	17,813
Voluntary Employees' Beneficiary Societies	7,738	10,927
Cemetery Companies	5,947	7,942
Credit Unions	5,639	6,652
Titleholding Corp	5,358	5,977
Benevolent Life Insurance Assn.	4,945	5,572
Mutual Insurance Companies	1,140	950
Supplemental Unemployment Benefit Trusts	806	728
Legal Service Organizations	46	210
Corporations Organized Under Act of Congress	42	24
Corp. to Finance Crop Operation	22	18
Teachers' Retirement Fund	12	11
Employee Funded Pension Trust	4	5
Black Lung Trusts	--	21
Religious and Apostolic Organizations	67	88
Cooperative Hospitals	--	80
Farmers' Cooperatives	2,985	2,405
Taxable Farmers Cooperatives	--	3,150
Nonexempt Charitable Trusts	--	36,421
Total	846,433	978,675

    *This figure does not represent a true universe of organizations covered by section 501(c)(3) of the Internal Revenue Code. For example, because of their integrated auxiliaries and conventions or associations, churches need not apply for recognition of exemption unless they desire to receive a ruling. When issued, the ruling letter goes to the central organization, but it covers all of its subordinate units. Only the central organization is established in the exempt organizations master file, where it is counted as one entity in the figures stated above. However, this one ruling may represent a large number of subordinate units, as in the case of larger religious sects. Exceptions are subordinate units considered non-integrated auxiliaries, which are established and included in the above figures because they may be required to file information returns as prescribed under sec. 6033 of the Internal Revenue Code.

Source: Commissioner of Internal Revenue (1980 and 1987) Annual Reports, available at Superintendent of Documents, U. S. Government Printing Office, Washington, D.C. 20402. Published by the IRS, Office of Public Affairs, 1111 Constitution Ave. N.W., Washington, D.C. 20224.

activities in our society. In fact, non-profits are governed by the same marketplace, competitive forces, prices, and all other variables that govern the provision of goods and services for our economy as profit organizations are.

HOW MANY NPOs ARE THERE?

According to the IRS, there were 978,000 active NPOs in the United States in 1987. The classifications and numbers are shown in Table 1.1. Because this IRS list does not include approximately 80,000 governmental units, 25,000 high schools, and individual churches, it would seem that there are well over 1 million NPOs in the United States.

The financial impact of NPOs can be measured by the number of income tax returns they file with the IRS, along with their total receipts, total assets, and total net equity. For example, of the NPOs with annual receipts of more than $10,000, the IRS has made available the information in Table 1.2.

ARTICLES OF ORGANIZATION

Most non-profit organizations are legally organized under the laws of the state in which they reside. They usually have articles of organization, which

Table 1.2
Financial Aspects of NPOs

		1975	1977	1978
1.	Total number of returns filed with IRS of tax exempt organizations with total receipts of more than $10,000 (There are approximately 650,000 active organizations with less than $10,000 annual receipts)	179,052	191,526	215,701
2.	Total receipts of those organizations with $10,000 or more annual receipts	$114,585,998 (000s omitted)	$176,462,097	$238,388,877
3.	Total assets of those organizations	$175,533,077 (000s omitted)	$250,616,142	$346,357,726
4.	Total liabilities of those organizations	$ 75,549,032 (000s omitted)	$100,318,288	$127,068,904
5.	Total equity of those organizations with receipts of more than $10,000 annual receipts	$ 99,984,045 (000s omitted)	$150,297,854	$219,311,822

Source: Statistics of Income Bulletin, Vol. 1, No. 2, published by the Department of the Treasury, Internal Revenue Service, Fall, 1981, 6.

may consist of a corporate charter, articles of association, a trust instrument, or other written instruments by which they are created.

The following is an example of a charter that contains information as to an NPO's mission and related powers:

Draft

Articles of Incorporation of ——— [Name] ———

The undersigned, a majority of whom are citizens of the United States, desiring to form a non-profit corporation under the Non-Profit Corporation Law of ——— [State] ———, do hereby certify:

First: The name of the corporation shall be ———.

Second: The place in this state where the principal office of the corporation is to be located is the city of ———, ——— County.

Third: Said corporation is organized exclusively for charitable, religious, educational, and scientific purposes, including, for such purposes, the making of distributions to organizations that qualify as exempt organizations under Section 501(c)(3) of the Internal Revenue Code of 1954 (or the corresponding provision of any future United States Internal Revenue Law).

Fourth: The names and addresses of the persons who are the initial trustees of the corporation are as follows:

Names   *Addresses*

Fifth: No part of the net earnings of the corporation shall inure to the benefit of, or be distributable to its members, trustees, officers, or other private persons, except that the corporation shall be authorized and empowered to pay reasonable compensation for services rendered and to make payments and distributions in furtherance of the purposes set forth in Article Third hereof.

No substantial part of the activities of the corporation shall be the carrying on of propaganda, or otherwise attempting to influence legislation, and the corporation shall not participate in, or intervene in (including the publishing or distribution of statements) any political campaign on behalf of any candidate for public office.

Notwithstanding any other provisions of these articles, the corporation shall not carry on any other activities not permitted to be carried on (a) by a corporation exempt from federal income tax under Section 501(c)(3) of the Internal Revenue Code of 1954 (or the corresponding provision of any future United States Internal Revenue Law) or (b) by a corporation, contributions to which are deductible under Section 170(c)(2) of the Internal Revenue Code of 1954 (or the corresponding provision of any future United States Internal Revenue Law).

[If reference to federal law in articles of incorporation imposes a limitation that is invalid in a state, the following sentence may be substituted: "Notwithstanding any other provision of these articles, this corporation shall not, except to an insubstantial degree, engage in any activities or exercise any powers that are not in furtherance of the purposes of this corporation."]

Sixth: Upon the dissolution of the corporation, the board of trustees shall, after paying or making provision for the payment of all the liabilities of the corporation, dispose of all of the assets of the corporation in such manner, or to such organization or organizations organized and operated exclusively for charitable, educational, religious, or scientific purposes as shall at the time qualify as an exempt organization or organizations under Section 501(c)(3) of the Internal Revenue Code of 1954 (or the corresponding provision of any future United States Internal Revenue Law), as the Board of Trustees shall determine.

Any such assets not so disposed of shall be disposed of by the Court of Common Pleas of the county in which the principal office of the corporation is then located, exclusively for such purposes or to such organization or organizations as said Court shall determine, which are organized and operated exclusively for such purposes.

In witness whereof, we have hereunto subscribed our names this day of ———— 19————.[3]

Constant reference is made to the IRS Code in this draft because the articles of organization must limit the organization's purposes to those stated in section 501(c)(3) if the NPO wants to remain exempt from paying income taxes. Further, the IRS insists that the purposes be stated in explicit language in the articles now in the bylaws. A statement by the officers that the NPO will operate only for exempt purposes will not satisfy the IRS, nor will the NPO be exempt if its activities are for exempt purposes. The articles of organization have to contain specific language as to the purposes of the NPO. Generalities will not satisfy the IRS. In addition, the articles have to contain provisos on the use of assets and the disposition of assets in case of dissolution, the distribution of earnings, and political campaigning.

THE TAX-EXEMPT STATUS OF NPOs

NPOs have some distinct advantages over profit organizations: (1) non-profit organizations may be declared exempt by the IRS from paying federal income taxes, (2) exempt organizations can receive contributions that are deductible on the donor's federal income tax return, (3) no one owns the right to share in any profit or surplus, and (4) some nonprofits receive a variety of subsidies, such as reduced postage rates, free public service advertising on radio and television, and, in some states, exemption from local property and state sales taxes. These advantages can save an NPO thousands of dollars, and they allow it to raise additional revenues which are necessary for its survival by making donations deductible on income tax returns.

In granting tax-exempt status, the government evidently believes that these organizations should be exempt from federal taxes because, in the organizations' absence, the government would need to perform the services that the organizations are performing. The government is therefore willing to forego the tax revenues in return for the public services rendered.[4]

An organization seeking recognition of exemption from federal income tax must file Form 1023, *Application for Recognition of Exemption*, which is a 13-page form seeking detailed information about the identification, type of entity, organizational documents, activities, operations, and financial functioning of the NPO. This form seeks the specific and general information needed to document the NPO's exempt purpose. Each exempt organization is also required to have an employer identification number, which may be obtained by filing Form 55-4, *Application for Employer Identification Number.*

All the data, documents, lists, financial statements, and the like are made available for public inspection and copying. However, trade secrets, patents, and so forth may be withheld from public inspection by request and permission from the IRS. Once the IRS has determined that an NPO is tax exempt, it will send a determination letter to that effect. If an NPO applies and is turned down, appeal procedures are available to the NPO.

If the NPO is a subordinate of a central organization (e.g., church, Boy Scouts, fraternity), the NPO should check with the central organization to see if it has been issued a group exemption letter. If it has, then the subordinate NPO does not have to file for exemption. To maintain a group exemption letter, the central organization must annually submit information regarding its continued existence and its exemption status and an *Annual Information Return* (Form 990).

Most exempt organizations are required to file various annual returns and reports at some time during or following the close of their accounting period. The basic report is Form 990 or some variation of it.

Even though an NPO is recognized as tax exempt, it may still be liable for tax on its unrelated business income, which is income for a trade or business, regularly carried on, that is not substantially related to the charitable, educational, or other purpose constituting the basis for its exemption. If the NPO has $1,000 or more of unrelated business income, it has to file a form to report that income and pay tax on it.

For more detailed information regarding the tax-exempt status and special reporting requirements, consult *Tax-Exempt Status for Your Organization,* Publication 557 of Internal Revenue Service.

OTHER CLASSIFICATIONS OF NPOs

Some economists have suggested three sectors of economic activity — the profit sector, the government sector, and the not-for-profit sector. The government and not-for-profit sectors are part of the non-profit activities. However, such a three-way classification of organizations can be useful for research purposes to compare similarities and differences among the three types of organizations.

Classification by the Nature of the Product/Service — Collective vs. Individual

Another method for classifying organizations is according to the types of products and/or services they offer. Non-profit organizations that produce public-type services with widely shared benefits are called *collective-type NPOs*, while those that are individually shared or consumed are called *private-type services*. A collective-type is described as having a product/service which is indivisible, that is, the service/product cannot be segregated into separate units for individual consumption. A divisible product/service can be segregated into units of consumption. An example of a collective product is a park or public highway. An individual product is one which is consumable by individuals who can exclude others from consuming it — for example, a water department of a city where products are separated (by gallons) from each other for individual consumption. Other examples would be electricity, sewage, and telephone services. These services have a collective characteristic but can be segregated for individual consumption.

Further, both collective and individual goods and/or services have a cost characteristic which distinguish them. A collective one has a low marginal cost attached to it, that is, the additional cost of providing a good/service to an additional person is very low or minimal. On the other hand, the marginal cost of providing a good/service to an additional person is fairly high in an individual good/service situation.[5]

A collective good/service is usually available to everyone while an individual good/service is available to restricted persons. A collective-type involves a shared consumption, that is, several persons can enjoy the benefits of it at the same time while an individual-type allows an individual to enjoy its benefits by excluding it from other persons. Obviously, some non-profit organizations, classified by the nature of product/service, may be called quasi-collective or quasi-individual. The key characteristic is excludability. If it is fairly difficult to exclude persons from consuming the NPO's products and/or services, then it is called a collective-type. On the other hand, if it is fairly easy to exclude persons from consuming the product/service (usually by price, membership, or other restrictions), then the product/service is called an individual-type.

The characteristics of collective and individual goods and services may be defined by a series of a continua built around (1) divisibility, (2) marginal cost, (3) availability, (4) excludability, and (5) consumption of a product/service.

Collective	Individual
Difficult to Divide the Product/Service into Units	Easy to Divide the Product/Service into Units
Marginal Cost of Adding a Product/Service for an Additional Client is Relatively Low/Minimal	Marginal Cost is Relatively High
Availability of Product/Service is Unrestricted to Potential Consumers	Availability is Restricted by Various Restraints

Collective	Individual
Difficult to Exclude Anyone From Consuming the Product/Service	Easy to Exclude People from Consuming
Consumption is Shared by Several Clients	Consumption is Made by an Individual

For a product/service to be classified as a collective-type, it is necessary for it to pass the five tests on the left side of the continuum.

A unique collective service is one characterized by advocacy organizations whose mission is to promote a cause which is related to a common goal. For example, the National Rifle Association espouses the right to bear arms as guaranteed by the U.S. Constitution. The service that the NRA provides is available to everyone, it is difficult to divide into units, the marginal cost of adding a member is low, its services are shared by all its members, and it would be difficult to exclude people from consuming its services. The NRA would be considered a collective service.

Classification by the Nature of the Market — Homogeneous versus Heterogeneous

The collective/individual product/service classification of NPOs may be further broken down by the nature of demand or the nature of the market which the non-profit organization serves. A homogeneous market or demand is one in which clients of a non-profit organization are members of a group (large or small) which perceive the need for a service or good the same as other members of the group. The homogeneous market has identical characteristics in such areas as age, sex, geography, job, and tastes. These criteria classify the members of a group who have identical preferences for the services or goods.

A heterogeneous market is one in which the clients are members of a group who perceive their needs for a service or product as dissimilar to the needs of other persons. The heterogeneous market varies in such characteristics as age, sex, geography, income, and taste. As a result it becomes difficult for an NPO to segment its market to tailor its goods/services for its clients.

An example of an NPO that serves a homogeneous market is a professional organization. A museum would serve a heterogeneous market.

Further Classification by Type of Mission — Internal Focus versus External Focus

Most NPOs have a mission focused on its external clients or on its internal clients. For example, those NPOs whose mission is to focus on internal clients are those concerned with serving members such as professional clubs, boy scouts/girl scouts, fraternities and sororities, churches, and others. Usually membership is restricted by such characteristics as profession, age, preferences, and other criteria.

Those NPOs whose focus is on serving clients outside of the organization are concerned with helping to solve some of society's problems. Examples would be charitable organizations, social welfare, legal services, and research societies, among others.

Further Classification by Use of Volunteer Employees and Money

One of the cost reduction strategies in the operations of an NPO is to use volunteer employees and officers of the non-profit organization. According to a recent Gallup poll, employee volunteerism is a $150 billion business and growing every day. The Gallup figure is the dollar value of time contributed.[6] Non-profit organizations may therefore be classified as those using a heavy dose of volunteer employees. For example, NPOs which use volunteers extensively would be a chamber of commerce, a church, or a civic organization.

Voluntary donations of money is a way to raise revenues for those NPOs which have a difficult time to break-even economically. Those NPOs which solicit voluntary contributions differentiate from those NPOs that have to raise revenues from governmental subsidies. Examples of volunteer NPOs would be the Salvation Army, cancer society, an educational athletic program, and museums.

Combined Classification Schema for Non-profit Organizations

If we combine the four criteria for describing various NPOs, we can depict the schema as shown in Figure 1.1. What is proposed here is a set of different kinds of NPOs and a set of commodity characteristics that differentiate non-profit organizations. Perhaps the scheme would suggest that any NPO providing a collective good/service would be a more effective and efficient one if it were government financed, while those whose goods/services are provided for individual consumption would be more effective and efficient if they were provided by private organizations, financed and subsidized by clients rather than government, and be considered tax paying organizations.

Further, the classification scheme might serve as a basis for generating a set of generic strategies for each type of non-profit organization. For example, a core strategy for a Salvation Army would be to match the individual services (food, lodging, job seeking) with a heterogeneous market of consumers (the underprivileged and homeless), using a heavy dose of volunteer donors of money and other resources to accomplish an externally-oriented mission.

A city fire department, on the other hand, would have to match a collective set of services with a homogeneous set of consumers (all live in the same city

Figure 1.1
Classification Schema for Non-profit Organizations

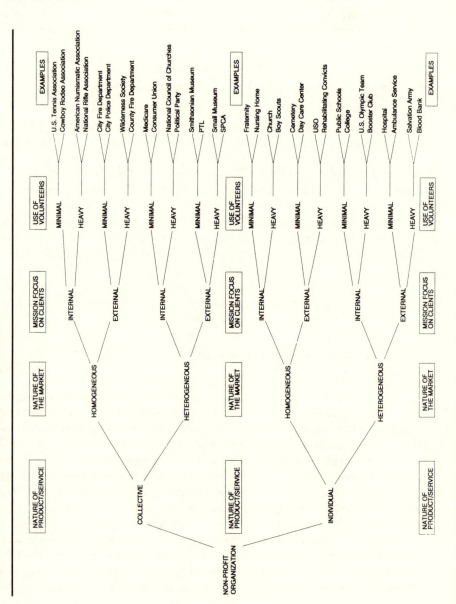

and have a similar need for fire protection), using tax money rather than financial donations and using very few volunteers.

The scheme suggests that not all non-profit organizations are the same. There are differences. These differences might suggest ways of managing them, based on different strategies.

THE ECONOMIC IMPACT OF NPOs

Within the non-profit sector, the federal, state, and local governments are estimated to employ 16 to 20 percent of the total labor force. Purchases by governments sustain another 8 to 10 percent of the labor force. In total, then, government accounts for 25 to 30 percent of the labor force in the United States.

The not-for-profit, non-tax-supported organizations employ 6 to 8 percent of the total labor force. Together, then, the governmental and non-profit sectors employ approximately one-third or more of the labor force.

Estimates have been made of the output of goods and services of NPOs. These estimates suggest that about one-fourth of the gross national product is attributable to non-profit organizations. Such a figure is closely correlated to the number of people employed by non-profit organizations.[7]

Further evidence of the impact of NPOs is suggested by the growth pattern in the number of NPOs. For example, during the 1967–1976 decade, the total number of NPOs, including those not required to file with the IRS, increased from 309,000 to 763,000, an increase of 147 percent. During the same decade, the number of private corporations increased by 37 percent, while the number of partnerships and single proprietorships increased by 24 percent.

In mentioning the size of the non-profit sector, one should be aware of the fact that the number of volunteer workers is not included in the labor force statistics. A poll taken by Gallup in 1981 found that adults volunteered an average of 102 hours per year. With the adult population being about two-thirds of the labor force, the 102 hours per adult is equivalent to nearly 11 billion hours of volunteer labor or, in person-hours, about 8 percent of the labor force. The number of volunteers per institution was found to be .95 per proprietary institution, 1.94 per governmental institution, and 3.10 per private non-profit institution.[8]

Waldemar A. Nielson, in his book *The Endangered Sector*, states that size is the least important measure of the impact of the not-for-profit sector, or the third sector, as it is called. More important, Nielson states, is what it does and what it represents. The direct functions that third-sector organizations try to perform are familiar ones. They teach, cure, engage in the search for new knowledge, entertain, preach, agitate for reform, and operate in the large sphere of life that does not center on power and authority or on the production and acquisition of material goods and money. Nielson believes that these organizations embody the countervalues and complementary beliefs to our competitive, capitalistic, materialistic, and egalitarian culture.[9]

SIMILARITIES AND DIFFERENCES IN PROFIT, GOVERNMENTAL, AND NON-PROFIT ORGANIZATIONS

There are probably more similarities than differences in managing the affairs of these three types of organizations. However, there are some obvious differences.

1. Non-profit organizations have no owners, unless one considers the general public as owners. As a result, no monetary dividends are paid. Further, the NPO has to rely on means of financing other than issuing stock.
2. Most NPOs have some volunteers who perform work not for pay. As a result, special types of motivations may be required for volunteers.
3. The customers of NPOs are not necessarily those people who pay for the services of the NPO; that is, the users or consumers of the NPO's services are sometimes not the same people who pay the prices of the services. For example, the clients of a Salvation Army unit are those who consume the food, lodging, and other services, but those who donate money and other resources are the ones who pay for the Salvation Army's services. As a result, the marketing of the NPO's services requires attention to differing target markets.
4. The community in which the NPO operates usually has to directly subsidize the activities of the NPO. As a result, fund raising becomes crucial to the organization.
5. The members of society in general are concerned about improving the quality of life for society. The NPO has this concept in mind as one of its basic objectives.

Other differences observed by the author, who with his students has analyzed at least 100 NPOs, are listed in Table 1.3. Throughout this book, some of the differences among non-profit, profit-making, and governmental organizations will be highlighted, based on the doctoral dissertation of William R. Stevens.[10]

Once the preceding preliminary information about non-profit organizations is known, managers of NPOs should examine the remaining chapters in this book which are concerned with administrative strategies (not tactics) for managing the affairs of a non-profit organization. Throughout the text a series of self-help guidelines is offered to help NPO administrators either make strategic decisions or evaluate the strengths and weaknesses of their NPO. These guidelines may be helpful in improving the effectiveness of the NPO in achieving its basic mission and related objectives.

Table 1.3
Differences in Managing Profit and Non-profit Organizations (Based on Field Experience)*

Variable	Non-Profit Organizations	Profit Organizations
Product/Services	Usually services	Products and services
Ownership	No legal owners	Private owners
Taxes	Tax exempt	Taxed
Mission	Improve quality of life	Usually profits
Image Objectives	Importance of image	Image not too important
Objectives	Difficult to measure	Fairly easy
Impact	1/4 of GNP	3/4 of GNP
	25-30% of labor force	Remainder
Philosophy of CEO	Social, cultural, political values dominate	Economic values dominate
Board of Directors	Voluntary	Financial interest
External Environment	Fairly stable	Fairly unstable
"Industry" Appraisal	Difficult to determine	Fairly easy
Competitive Appraisal	Some competition	Fairly competitive
Internal Appraisal	Weak marketing	Strong
	Weak financing	Strong
	Weak management	Strong
	Weak analyses of financial ratios	Strong
Objectives and Strategies	Weak service-market match strategy	Usually strong
	Weak market share, growth, and profit strategies	Strong
Internal Operations and Purchasing Function	Usually strong	Also strong
Internal Marketing Function	Market focus - weak	Strong
	Pricing - weak	Strong
	Promotion - weak	Strong
	Personnel - weak	Strong
Pricing Related to Products/Services	Pure public and quasi-public pure products and pricing are crucial	Private products and competitive pricing
Personnel	Volunteers used	Not used
Raising Capital	Fund raising	Not used
Accounting	Fund accounting AICPA 78-10	Not used Not used
Organization Structure	Variety of ways	By function or product
Who Pays for Services	Variety of sources-- clients, donors, government, grants	Paid for by customers

*Over the past 10 years, the author with the assistance of his students, both graduates and seniors, has made managerial analyses of numerous NPOs: religious groups, schools, cultural organizations, other instruction and training programs, health services, scientific research programs, business and professional organizations, mutual organizations, membership benefits organizations, sports clubs, youth groups, legal aid programs, and others.

SELECTION OF AN NPO FOR ANALYSIS
AND EVALUATION PURPOSES

As a possible self-help project, you may wish to analyze and evaluate a non-profit organization. What kinds can you choose from?

The IRS has developed a scheme of classes and subclasses for the major types of NPOs. In addition to the religious, educational, cultural, and other organizations listed in the chapter, there are many other kinds to choose from:

1. Health services and related programs: hospitals, auxiliary facilities, nursing homes, health clinics, rural medical facilities, blood banks, cooperative hospital service organizations, rescue and emergency services, nurses' register plans, community health planning groups, mental health care organizations, group medical practice associations, in-faculty group practice associations, hospital pharmacies, parking and food service providers, and others.

2. Scientific research programs: contract or sponsored scientific research for industry, scientific research for the government, and disease research, and others.

3. Business and professional organizations: chambers of commerce, real estate associations, boards of trade, business regulators, better business bureaus, professional associations, professional association auxiliaries, industry trade show and convention display sponsors, research and development groups, professional athletic leagues, municipal insurance underwriting services, assigned risk insurance programs, tourist bureaus, and others.

4. Farming and related organizations: farm bureaus, agricultural groups, horticultural groups, cooperative marketing and purchasing organizations, crop financing operations, dairy herd improvement associations, breeders associations, and others.

5. Mutual organizations: mutual ditch, irrigation, telephone, or electric companies or the like; credit unions; groups providing reserve funds or insurance for domestic building and loan associations; cooperative banks; mutual savings banks; mutual insurance companies; and others.

6. Employee or membership benefit organizations: fraternal beneficiary societies; groups devoted to improving working conditions; associations of municipal employees; associations of employees; member welfare associations; strike benefits groups; fringe benefits associations; unemployment, pension, or retirement benefits programs; vacation benefits groups; group legal services plans; and others.

7. Sports, athletic, recreational, and social organizations: country clubs, hobby clubs, dinner clubs, variety clubs, dog clubs, men's and women's clubs, hunting or fishing clubs, swimming or tennis clubs, other sports clubs, community centers, community recreational facilities, groups offering training in sports, travel tour groups, amateur athletic associations, fund-raising sports event organizers, and others.

8. Youth organizations: Boy Scouts, Girl Scouts, Boys Clubs, Little League, FFA, FHA, 4-H, Key Clubs, YMCA, YWCA, YMHA, camps, delinquency prevention programs, and others.

9. Conservation, environmental, and beautification organizations: groups organized to preserve natural resources, combat or prevent pollution, acquire land for preservation, promote soil or water conservation, and preserve scenic beauty; wildlife sanctuaries; garden clubs; and others.

10. Housing organizations: groups providing low-income housing, low- and moderate-income housing, housing for the aged, instruction and guidance on housing, and other housing-related services.

11. Inner-city or community organizations: homeowners associations concerned with area redevelopment or renewal or development, associations formed to combat community deterioration or attract new industry, industry retraining programs, community promotion groups, loan or grant programs for minority businesses, crime prevention groups, volunteer firefighters organizations and/or auxiliaries, community service organizations, and others.

12. Civil rights organizations: groups formed to defend human and civil rights, eliminate prejudice and discrimination (based on race, religion, sex, national origin, etc.), lessen neighborhood tensions, and so on.

13. Litigation and legal aid organizations: public interest litigation services, voter information and voter education programs, groups supporting or opposing or rating political candidates, groups providing facilities for political campaign activities, and others.

14. Advocacy organizations: groups concerned with firearms control, the selective service system, national defense policy, weapons systems, government spending, taxes or tax exemptions, separation of church and state, government aid to parochial schools, U.S. foreign policy, U.S. military involvement, pacifism and peace, the U.S. economic-political system, communism, right-to-work legislation, zoning or rezoning, highway or transportation systems, the rights of criminal defendants, capital punishment, stricter law enforcement, ecology, consumer protection, the medical care system, the welfare system, urban renewal, student busing to achieve racial balance, racial integration, the use of intoxicating beverages, the use of drugs or narcotics, the use of tobacco, the prohibition of erotica, sex education in public schools, population control, legalized abortion, and other issues.

15. Other activities directed to individuals: groups supplying money, goods, and services to the poor and gifts or grants to individuals; marriage counseling services; family planning services; credit counseling services; job counseling services; draft counseling services; referral services; rehabilitation programs for convicts, alcoholics, drug abusers, and compulsive gamblers; day care centers; programs providing services for the aged; and others.

16. Activities directed to other organizations: community chests; United Fund; booster clubs; groups providing gifts, grants or loans, non-financial services, or facilities to other organizations; and others.

17. Other purposes and activities: cemetery or burial services, perpetual care funds (for cemeteries and columbaria), emergency aid funds, groups testing products for public safety, consumer interest groups, veterans' programs, patriotic organizations, domestic organizations with activities outside the United States, title holding corporations, groups concerned with prevention of cruelty to animals,

achievement prizes or awards, erection or maintenance of public buildings, cafeteria or restaurant or snack bar, thrift shop, book or gift or supply store, advertising, loans or credit reporting, Indians (tribes, cultures, etc.), fund raising, and others.

Requirements

1. Select an NPO that you would like to analyze — hopefully one for which you are a manager.
2. Classify the NPO by the methods suggested in the chapter.
3. Get the following:
   3.1 Articles of organization, bylaws, and such
   3.2 Tax-exempt status
       3.2.1 Determination letter
       3.2.2 Initial filing of Form 1023
       3.2.3 Employer identification number
       3.2.4 Annual information returns, if required, on Form 990
       3.2.5 Other general information
4. Once you acquire the general information, you are ready to make more general as well as specific analyses suggested in the remaining chapters.

Notes

1. This section states:

Sec. 501 Exemption from tax on corporations, certain trusts, etc.
(a) Exemption from taxation. — An organization described in subsection (c) or (d) or section 401(a) shall be exempt from taxation under this subtitle unless such exemption is denied under section 502 or 503.
(b) . . .
(c) List of exempt organizations . . . .
    (1) . . .
    (2) . . .
    (3) Corporations, and any community chest, fund, or foundation, organized and operated exclusively for religious, charitable, scientific, testing for public safety, literary, or educational purposes, or to foster national or international amateur sports competition (but only if no part of its activities involve the provision of athletic facilities or equipment), or for the prevention of cruelty to children or animals, no part of the net earnings of which inures to the benefit of any private shareholder or individual, no substantial part of the activities of which is carrying on propaganda, or otherwise attempting, to influence legislation (except as otherwise provided in subsection (h)), and which does not participate in, or intervene in (including the publishing or distributing of statements), any political campaign on behalf of (or in opposition to) any candidate for public office.

2. Department of the Treasury, Internal Revenue Service, *Application for Recognition of Exemption Under Section 501(a)*, revised July 1981 (Washington, D.C.: Government Printing Office, 1981).

3. This draft is taken from Department of the Treasury, Internal Revenue Service, *Tax Exempt Status for Your Organization*, publication 557 (Washington, D.C.: Government Printing Office, January 1982), 582.

4. Bruce R. Hopkins, *The Law of Tax-Exempt Organizations* (New York: John Wiley, 1979), 5.

5. Joseph E. Stiglitz, *Economics of the Public Sector* (New York: Norton, 1986): 102–3.

6. "Value of Volunteerism Placed at $150 Billion," *Arkansas Gazette*, 2 September 1989, 36.

7. David L. Rados, *Marketing for Non-Profit Organizations* (Boston: Auburn House, 1981), 5.

8. Burton A. Weisbrod, "Assets and Employment in the Non-Profit Sector," *Public Finance Quarterly* 10, no. 4 (10 October 1982): 410–13.

9. Waldemar A. Nielson, *The Endangered Sector* (New York: Columbia University Press, 1979), 4.

10. William R. Stevens, "A Comparison of For-Profit and Not-for-Profit Organizations: Chief Executive Officers' And Officials' Perceptions" (Ph.D. diss., University of Arkansas, 1985).

2

The Nature of Management

Management involves the integration of internal organizational resources and functions with external environmental forces to accomplish objectives. The key word here is *integration*. Management requires the integration of operative and managerial functions and a host of resources, such as money, manpower, materials, and methods, to accomplish both organizational and personal objectives through an exchange of resources between the organization and the various external and internal resource contributors or stakeholders.

Management involves making decisions about the strategic direction and the resulting strategies of the organization after appraising both external and internal influences, assessing future trends and factors, and weighing alternative means to achieve the organization's mission and related objectives.

Once the strategic decisions are made, managers have to administer the operative functions and allocate resources through a variety of analytical decisions. Managers have to carry out decisions by providing leadership and a culture, by structuring jobs, by setting rewards and motivations, and by using power to achieve organizational and personal goals. Managers have to design organizational structures and administrative systems that affect strategy execution. Finally, managers have to evaluate and control functions and resources to make sure that the goals and objectives and the organizational mission are accomplished. In so doing, managers have to deal with several external environmental issues, such as changing societal values, governmental involvement, and competition.

What distinguishes management from other disciplines is its integrative nature. It is general in nature, not specialized, drawing on several disciplines to accomplish the mission and related objectives of the organization and its stakeholders. What are the implications of our definition of management?

LEVELS OF MANAGEMENT

First, this definition of management suggests that there are different levels of management — the top level, the middle level, and the bottom level. The top level makes decisions about the mission and related objectives and the strategies affecting their accomplishment. The middle level makes decisions that integrate the production, marketing, staffing, and financing functions of products and services in order to accomplish the mission. The bottom level makes supervisory decisions about employees who implement or carry out the fundamental decisions about producing and marketing the products/services of the organization.

In a very small organization, all of these levels will not have emerged because the manager is required to be the strategic, operative, and supervisory decision maker and implementer by himself/herself. However, as the organization grows, the manager will retain the strategic decisions and delegate the operative production and marketing functions to middle-level managers, who in turn will delegate the detailed functions to supervisory managers who deal with employees. See Figure 2.1 for an illustration of this concept of levels in relation to the definition of management.

Skills Vary by Level of Management

Managers at different levels deal with different types of problems and decisions. As a result, different skills are required of them, although all managers need the same combination of skills: (1) conceptual skills, (2) human skills, (3) technical skills, and (4) drive.

The *drive* is crucial to all managers. It involves the ability to push one's self toward accomplishing both organizational and personal objectives. Drive expresses itself both internally and externally. A manager with drive may be seen as having a "tiger in the tank" or as an "eager beaver." Sometimes drive is called persistence. Whatever its characteristics are, all successful managers have it.

Conceptual skills involve the ability to think both creatively and analytically about ideas and to apply them to specific situations facing the manager and the organization. These skills allow a manager to see relationships and to visualize the big picture — assessing the external environment and the internal strengths and weaknesses of the organization and understanding how they relate to the organizational mission and related objectives. Conceptual skills allow a manager to assess a situation and then decide on strategies and tactics to accomplish objectives.

Human skills come into play in getting things done with the help of people. They involve the ability to relate, communicate, motivate, lead, and get along with people. While they are important at all levels of an organization, they are more so at the bottom than at the top. They relate not only to employees at the bottom levels, but also to suppliers and customers at the middle levels and to community, government (and society at large), and other managers at the top levels.

Technical skills involve the ability to use knowledge, methods, technology, techniques, equipment, materials, and other non-human resources in per-

Figure 2.1
Organization Levels

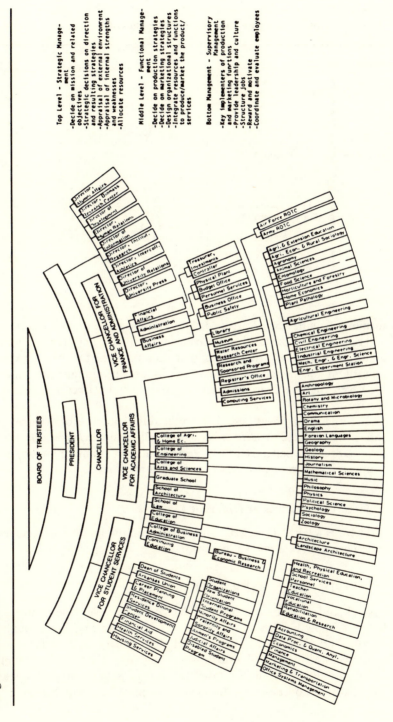

Top Level - Strategic Management
-Decide on mission and related objectives
-Strategic decisions on direction and resulting strategies
-Appraisal of external environment
-Appraisal of internal strengths and weaknesses
-Allocate resources

Middle Level - Functional Management
-Decide on production strategies
-Decide on marketing strategies
-Design organizational structures
-Integrate resources and functions to produce/market the product/services

Bottom Management - Supervisory Management
-Key implementers of production and marketing functions
-Provide leadership and culture
-Structure jobs
-Reward and motivate
-Coordinate and evaluate employees

BOARD OF TRUSTEES

PRESIDENT

CHANCELLOR

VICE CHANCELLOR FOR FINANCE AND ADMINISTRATION

VICE CHANCELLOR FOR ACADEMIC AFFAIRS

VICE CHANCELLOR FOR STUDENT SERVICES

Director, Alumni Affairs
Director, Biomass Research Center
Director of Development
Director, Human Relations
Director of Information
Director, Institut. Research
Director, Intercoll. Athletics
Director of University Relations
Director, University Press

Financial Affairs
Administration
Business Affairs

Treasurer, Investments
Controller
Physical Plant
Budget Office
Personnel Services
Business Office
Public Safety

Library
Museum
Water Resources Research Center
Research and Sponsored Programs
Registrar's Office
Admissions
Computing Services

College of Agri. & Home Ec.
College of Engineering
College of Arts and Sciences
Graduate School
School of Architecture
School of Law
College of Education
College of Business Administration
Continuing Education

Bureau - Business & Economic Research

Dean of Students
Arkansas Union
Career Planning & Placement
Residence Dining Services
Student Development Center
Financial Aid
Health Services
Housing Services

Student Organizations
New Student
International Student Programs
Minority Affairs
Fraternity and Sorority Affairs
Women's Programs
Judicial Affairs
Disabled Student Program

Air Force ROTC
Army ROTC

Agri. & Extension Education
Agri. Econ. & Rural Sociology
Agronomy
Animal Sciences
Entomology
Food Science
Horticulture and Forestry
Home Economics
Plant Pathology

Agricultural Engineering

Chemical Engineering
Civil Engineering
Electrical Engineering
Industrial Engineering
Mech. Engr. & Engr. Science
Engr. Experiment Station

Anthropology
Art
Botany and Microbiology
Chemistry
Communication
Drama
English
Foreign Languages
Geography
Geology
History
Journalism
Mathematical Sciences
Music
Philosophy
Physics
Political Science
Psychology
Sociology
Zoology

Architecture
Landscape Architecture

Health, Physical Education, and Recreation
School Services
Personnel
Teacher Education
Vocational Education
Rehabilitation
Education & Research

Accounting
Data Proc. & Quant. Anyl.
Economics
Finance
Management
Marketing & Transportation
Office Systems Management

Figure 2.2
Managerial Skills at Various Levels of Management

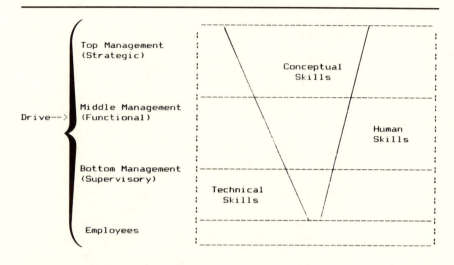

forming activities necessary to help accomplish the organization's mission and related organizational and personal objectives. They are more important at the lower levels of management than they are at the top. As a person moves upward in the hierarchy, technical skills usually diminish in importance. However, these skills are necessary to produce and market the organization's services.

The relationships of these skills to the different levels of management are shown in Figure 2.2. *Drive* is crucial at all levels, *technical skills* are more important at the supervisory level, *conceptual skills* are more important at the strategic level, and *human skills* are needed at all levels.

Time Perspectives at Different Levels

There is a fairly direct relationship between the level of management and time perspective, as shown in Figure 2.3.

WHAT DO MANAGERS DO?

Several studies have been made to determine what activities managers perform and how much time they devote to each activity. For example, S. J. Carroll and D. Gillen have reported that managerial function time (not operative function time) can be separated into a set of eight functions, called the PRINCESS functions (*P*lanning, *R*epresenting, *I*nvestigating, *N*egotiating, *C*oordinating, *E*valuating, *S*upervising, and *S*taffing). There

Figure 2.3
Time Perspectives and Levels of Management

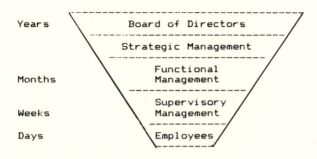

appears to be minimum time spent on these eight functional areas, but that managers in different jobs and at different levels had different time patterns. The results are summarized in Table 2.1.

Later studies found that two of the princess functions — notably representing and negotiating — had been dropped because they were not performed at the functional and supervisory levels. Rather, these two were performed at the strategic level.

Of course, people classified as managers to not spend 100 percent of their time on managerial functions. They spend a great deal of time on operative functions, such as operations, marketing, finance, and personnel.

In general, the things that managers do can be boiled down into two major activities: (1) making decisions and (2) executing or carrying out those decisions. For example, in making decisions, managers constantly seek information from whatever source — internal or external. They monitor the external and internal environments for bits of data to help them make decisions. These decisions made usually involve resource allocations and functions to be performed.

Once decisions have been made, managers are concerned about executing or carrying them out. They play the role of strategy/tactic implementer. The role of leader comes into play, as do those of spokesperson, figurehead, and liaison among the people (both inside and outside the organization) who provide resources or who perform functions to carry out the decisions. The role of a negotiator in both acquiring and allocating resources takes on significance. A conflict handler role becomes evident, and a disseminator of information role becomes crucial in coordinating various functions. When a manager executes, he/she has very little structure to aid in carrying out decisions. His/her attention is diverted many times during a day, flitting from one role to another, but always with the purpose of implementing decisions through people who provide resources or who perform various functions to implement decisions.

Table 2.1
Work Activities, Subjects of Work Activities, Types of Interpersonal Contacts, and Performance of Management Functions of Managers in One Organization

Work Activities	Proportion Of Time
Conversing with others	41%
Preparing and writing, letters, reports, etc.	19
Reading and reviewing reports, letters, etc	18
Operating equipment	05
Minor clerical (filing, sorting, etc)	05
Personal activities	05
Thinking and reflection	03
Walking and travel	02
Mathematical computation	01
Inspecting products, procedures, etc	01
	100%

Subject of Work Activities	
Materials and goods	28
Employees	22
Money and finances	19
Purchases and sales	11
Facilities and equipment	11
Methods and procedures	09
	100%

Types Of Interpersonal Contacts	
Subordinate (own departments)	21
Manager (another department)	11
Superior (own department)	05
Person outside the company	05
Other departments	04
Combination	03
Non-Manager	01
None	50
	100%

Management Functions	
Investigating	26
Coordinating	21
Planning	19
Supervising	12
Evaluating	09
Negotiating	07
Staffing	05
Representing	02
	101%

Source: Stephen Carroll and Dennis Gillen, "Are the Classical Management Functions Useful in Describing Managerial Work?" *Academy of Management Review* 12, no. 1 (1987): 38–51.

What Functions Do Managers Perform at Various Levels?

A *function* is the work that is performed to either make or carry out a decision. Typically the work of a manager involves decisions about *planning*, which is the work of determining in advance what the objectives are and how they will be accomplished. Information is the chief resource needed to make decisions about planning. More time is spent on planning at the strategic level than at the supervisory level.

Once a decision about planning is made, *resources* have to be acquired. Here decisions involve negotiating with resource providers — normally the employees, other managers, suppliers, creditors, the government, the community, customers, and people representing society at large. More time is spent acquiring resources at the middle level than at the top or bottom levels.

Once resources are acquired, a manager has to make decisions about *organizing* those resources — that is, prescribing formal relationships among people, resources, and functions and allocating resources to the people and functions so as to accomplish objectives.

Then he/she has to make decisions about *leading*, which involves influencing other people (both inside and outside the organization) to do what the manager wants them to do to accomplish the organization's objectives. More time is spent in leading at the bottom level than at the top level.

Next, usually some decisions have to be made about *coordinating* the efforts of people (both internal and external) by communicating with them so they do something at the right place, at the right time, in sufficient quantity, and with sufficient quality to accomplish the organization's objectives. Coordinating time is more important at the top level than at the bottom level.

Then decisions have to be made about a *control* system to make sure that objectives have been accomplished as they were planned — to keep the organization on track. Controlling time is practiced at the top level and even more at the middle level, rather than at the bottom level.

Another function normally performed at the top level is that of *representing* the organization at various events.

There may be other functions to be performed, but these are the major ones. Before they are performed, decisions have to be made concerning their execution. While they are being performed, they create certain roles that a manager has to fill. After they are performed, hopefully the organization will accomplish some of its objectives. But these functions and decisions are not performed in a vacuum. They concern the basic operative functions of an organization.

The Decisions Affecting the Operative Functions

Because each organization has a mission and related strategies, it has to have some means to implement the mission and strategies. As a result, certain operative functions have to be performed to carry out its mission. There is a fairly universal fit between the mission and the types of functions necessary to provide goods/services for an organization's customers/members/students/clients/parishioners or whatever they are called. Decisions have to be made by managers concerning the operative functions of production, marketing, finance, and personnel.

The creation of a service-market match strategy requires two matching fundamental and universal functions: (1) *producing* the products/services and (2) *marketing* the products/services. These two functions may be called the *value-added functions* because they add value for client satisfaction. Every operating entity needs to perform these two *line* or *core* functions around which all other functions revolve. Managers have to decide which of these two functions will be more important to carry out the organization's strategy and then allocate resources accordingly.

Another group of functions indirectly helps the line functions of producing and marketing. They are called *service functions* or *helper functions* because they help the line functions produce and market the products/services necessary to carry out the mission. They do not directly provide the value added for clients, but they do provide the resources to help carry out the line/core functions. Examples are the *finance* function which acquires money, the *personnel* function which acquires manpower, and the *office* and *accounting* functions which acquire information that managers use to make decisions. Once resources are acquired, managers allocate those provided by the service functions, such as money and manpower. Managers have to decide on the relative importance of the helper functions in carrying out the product-market match strategy in order to achieve the mission of the organization.

Staff functions are a special breed of functions which provide advice to the managers of both the line and the service functions to help them make better decisions. Examples are the *legal, public relations, tax*, and sometimes *personnel* and *finance* functions. The people hired to perform these functions give advice to the management, generally for decision-making purposes.

Now, if we combine the managerial functions and the operative functions into a matrix (see Fig. 2.4), we can show the relationships among them and create a possible method of evaluating how managerial decisions affect both the managerial and the operative functions.

MANAGERIAL DECISION MAKING

It is this author's contention that managers get paid for making decisions and for carrying them out. A manager executes or implements decisions by performing both managerial and operative functions. But what about the actual making of decisions? What is involved?

Decision making usually involves several steps. First is the identification of a problem that needs attention. That problem usually means that the organi-

Figure 2.4
A Matrix of Decisions About the Organizational Mission and the Related Product-Market Match Strategy Integrated into Various Functions

Managerial Functions	Production	Marketing	Finance	Personnel	Overall
Planning					
Acquiring					
Organizing					
Leading					
Coordinating					
Controlling					
Overall					

<------Operative Functions ------>

zation is not achieving certain objectives, such as the mission and related objectives of growth, profit, maintenance of market share, image, industry leadership, survival, improvement of the quality of life for society, and others that organizations pursue. Consequently, problem identification and related objective determination are two crucial steps in making decisions.

Determining the factors causing the problem is another step, followed by gathering information about the factors. These two steps should help generate decision alternatives in relation to the problem and objectives.

Once alternatives are generated, then the factors are evaluated against the alternatives, allowing a decision to be made by weighing the factors against the alternatives.

These are the crucial steps involved in making decisions. Managers may not follow them in the sequence suggested. In fact, they often do not, but they do consider them in making decisions. Sometimes they use hunches rather than gathering data about the factors. Sometimes they muddle through. At other times they follow a scientific method by experimenting first before making a final decision.

Some suggestions have been made to make sure that weighty decisions are carefully considered. Decisions usually involve a change in the organization, and change has been researched by organizational behavioralists. Based on their observations, various steps have been proposed to diagnose change.

1. Canvass alternative courses of action.
2. Survey the full range of both organizational and personal objectives to be fulfilled and the values implicated by the choice of alternatives.
3. Weigh the costs and risks of negative consequences that could flow from each alternative (use Murphy's Law).
4. Search for new information about factors relevant to evaluation of the alternatives.

5. Take account of new information even when the new information does not support the alternative initially preferred.
6. Re-examine the positive and negative consequences of all alternatives before making a final choice.
7. Make detailed plans for implementing the final choice.

Note the careful examination and re-examination of factors and alternatives. The reason is obvious: Decisions are not always correct. Incorrect decisions create costs, confusions, frustrations, and a whole host of dysfunctions among people and the organization. To make sure decisions are correct, careful analysis of the factors is suggested.

The Situational Approach to Major Decision Making

Major decisions may be made by using a situational approach. It provides the basic rationale underlying the decision-making processes which suggests that each decision made in an organizational setting is dependent on the variables inherent in that particular situation. This situational approach may be described by using an "if-then" analysis. Overly simplified, *if* the situational variables are "X," *then* the appropriate course of action is "Y."

The situational approach suggests that for any specific type of major decision or action (such as growth, share of market, survival, and others), a set of generic factors emerges, regardless of the type of organization or its environment. More specifically, there are common factors for major decisions that remain constant across organizational lines. Therefore, for any major decision made in an organization, there are some universal considerations that must be assessed in light of that organization's particular situation.

The situational approach uses what is called a *decision matrix*. Such a decision-making matrix provides an orderly and comprehensive approach to organizational decisionmaking, evaluation, and prescription. Guidelines are suggested for many key decisions concerning major organizational objectives and important functional areas.

Obviously a decision-making matrix could not be provided for every organizational decision. Additionally, not every factor relevant to all situations can be included in the matrix guidelines presented. Rather, the guidelines include the generic factors that theory suggests must be considered in the decision-making situation. In many cases, decision-making factors must be added, adapted to fit the particular situation, or both.

Generally, the steps involved in the matrix methodology for major decision making are as follows:

1. Properly identify the major decision and problem.
2. Review administrative theory factors concerning such problems or decisions.
3. Identify possible alternative solutions or actions.

4. Analyze the actual situation compared to the theoretical factors and alternatives.

5. Make the final decision based on an evaluation of the actual versus the theoretical.

6. Prescribe possible courses of action to implement the decision.

Such a decision-making methodology typically appears in the following matrix format:

```
                              Major Decision:

Theoretical
Situational   Alternatives    Actual Situation      Evalu-    Prescrip-
Factors___  ->Go_____No Go ->Compared to Theory ->ation   ->tion_____

#1
#2
#3
#4
#5
Overall Evaluation and Prescription:
```

The situational approach suggested here is not new. However, it is one that the author was forced to recognize when empirical research was performed on cases of actual organizations and on feasibility studies with his students. Ever since then, the author has used the situational approach in conducting management audits, in teaching cases (both live and textbook cases), and in research. But it was encouraging to find that other people had advocated the situational approach before the 1950s.

Ralph C. Davis stated in the late 1940s that executive leadership depended on the executive's ability to face the facts in a situation, interpret the facts properly in light of the situation's requirements, and follow the course of action the facts dictate.[1] Preceding him was Mary Parket Follett who in the 1930s suggested that the facts of a situation dictated what types of coordination were to be employed by a leader.[2] Preceding her was Harlow S. Person who, in writing about scientific management in the late 1920s, stated that situations may change, causing changes in leadership.[3]

The military establishment has followed the "estimate of the situation" as being a vital concept in determining the solution to a problem and the resulting actions to be taken. In fact, as far back as Karl Von Clausewitz in the early 1890s, writing on war, he stated that the situation dictated what actions should be taken based on generic factors facing a decision maker.[4]

An Example of the Situational Approach Using the Matrix Method

Perhaps an example of a major marketing decision facing a symphony orchestra may help to illustrate the situational approach using a matrix methodology. A symphony orchestra was considering ways to increase its ticket revenues after the managers and board of directors had made the strategic decision to grow. The marketing function had to integrate the growth strategy into its actions and was considering a general marketing strategy.

Its present marketing strategies were minimal at best. The symphony had no sales personnel to market the orchestra and related services. The prices were below the market for similar entertainment even though the symphony was in a monopoly position regarding other symphonies. However, there was a great deal of indirect competition in the area for the entertainment dollar. Although the quality of the symphony orchestra was considered high, relatively few people knew about it because the only promotion being done was to the present patrons by means of newsletters and to the public by means of free public radio announcements.

The symphony had no generally recognized place (except for a gymnasium) to play its concerts. Consequently, it moved its playing dates to surrounding cities whenever a suitable place could be found. Tickets were sold for cash only, although most of its wealthy patrons were excellent credit risks.

The managers of the symphony wanted to increase its revenues (maybe even maximize them) because the symphony was losing and had been losing money for some time, its deficit being made up by donations from various private sources.

The symphony was in the maturity stage of its life cycle. It had grown in previous years, but it had reached a plateau in ticket revenues for the past few years.

A plentiful supply of seats was available for most concerts except when a noted guest artist, like Beverly Sills, was also billed.

The preceding information was gathered from an analysis of the records and interviews with the managers and various board members. They wanted to make a small profit (not the maximum, but enough to keep afloat). They also wanted to grow by selling more season tickets. Also dominant in their philosophy was a desire to maintain their image by providing high-quality music for their clientele.

Considering the brief description of the situation facing the symphony, the key strategic marketing decision was whether to use an aggressive marketing strategy, a balanced one, or a minimal one.

Generic Theoretical Situational Factors

There are three general marketing strategies that an organization can adopt. The first is an *aggressive* strategy, characterized by generating a great deal of promotion, varying prices, changing the times and places at which the products/services are offered, differentiating the products/services from those of competing organizations, hiring creative salespersons to promote the products/services, spending lots of money on marketing activities, and so forth. The second general marketing strategy is a *minimal* one, characterized by doing very little promotion, pricing below market, offering services at traditional places and times, spending very little money on promotion and salespersons, and so forth. The third is a *balanced* marketing strategy, an in-between strategy that differs from an aggressive strategy and a minimal strategy only in degree.

These three strategies are appropriate alternatives for any organization. However, not every organization needs an aggressive strategy, nor does every organization need a balanced strategy or a minimal one. The situation facing each entity is obviously different, calling for an analysis of the factors that dictate which of the three alternative strategies is most suitable for each organization. But what factors suggest the appropriate general marketing strategy that an organization should pursue?

The first major factor is the nature of the market competition facing the organization. If it is in a monopoly position, with no direct competitors in its market area, then a minimal marketing strategy is suitable. However, if the organization is in an oligopoly market position, with a few competitors in its market area, then a balanced marketing strategy is called for. If there is a high degree of competition and several competing products/services in its market area, this would suggest an aggressive marketing strategy. Further, if there are many other forms of indirect competition, then the organization should pursue a balanced marketing strategy.

The second major factor is the quality of the products/services offered. If the organization has high-quality products/services, a minimal marketing strategy is called for, other factors being equal. If it is in a weak market position with low-quality products/services, a minimal marketing strategy should be pursued. If the products/services are of medium quality, this would suggest a balanced strategy.

A third major factor is the revenue strategies that the managers may desire to pursue. For example, if the managers want to maximize the organization's revenues from its products/services, then the organization should adopt an aggressive marketing strategy. If it wants to minimize revenues, then it should pursue a minimal strategy. However, if it wants to balance its revenues — not maximizing and not minimizing — then a balanced marketing strategy is called for.

A fourth factor is the stage in the life cycle of the product/service. For example, if it is in the development stage and needs to gain a foothold in the market, then the organization should follow an aggressive marketing strategy. If it is in the growth stage, then a balanced strategy would seem to be appropriate. If it is in the maturity stage, then a balanced marketing strategy should be employed. If it is in the decline stage, then a minimal marketing strategy becomes appropriate unless, of course, the organization wishes to get out of the decline stage by various other strategies.

The financial position of the organization is another factor affecting the decision as to whether to follow an aggressive, balanced, or minimal marketing strategy. If the organization is heavily in debt, then it would seem appropriate to engage in an aggressive marketing posture. If it is only moderately in debt, an aggressive strategy would also be appropriate. If it is not in debt, a minimal strategy should be followed, other factors being equal. If it is currently losing money, then an aggressive strategy should be pursued.

Another factor is the production capacity of the organization. If there is plenty of unused production capacity, there is justification for using an aggressive strategy to fill up the unused capacity. Empty capacity costs money and loses the potential revenue that the capacity was built for. On the other hand, where the capacity is filled, a minimal strategy may be used unless, of course, an administrator wants to make sure that full capacity is used. In that case, a balanced strategy would be most appropriate.

A final factor concerns the managerial philosophy regarding the objectives of the organization. For example, if the managers want to make a profit, a balanced marketing strategy would seem appropriate. If the managers want to improve the image of the organization, a balanced strategy would be useful. If the managers want to maintain the organization's share of the market, a balanced strategy would again seem to be appropriate. If the managers want the organization to grow, then an aggressive marketing strategy should be followed.

Further, if the managers really desire to provide a product/service for their clientele, then they should follow a balanced marketing strategy. Likewise, if an objective is to ensure some degree of survival and continuity, a balanced strategy would be an appropriate one to use.

These factors may be summarized and put into a decision model for an administrator to use in deciding which general marketing strategy his/her organization should use. The theory is presented along with the three alternatives. The administrator may assess the actual situation facing his/her organization and compare the actual situation to the theory. Then an evaluation can be made, allowing the strengths and weaknesses to be analyzed, by comparing actual to theory. Once the strengths and weaknesses are weighted for each factor, an overall evaluation can be completed, allowing the administrator to arrive at an overall decision — that is, whether to follow an aggressive, balanced, or minimal general marketing strategy.

The model is summarized in Table 2.2.

Comparison, Evaluation, and Prescription

Now, with the preceding information in hand and with knowledge about the theoretical situational factors, an analyst can use the matrix approach to arrive at a decision regarding what general marketing strategy the symphony should use. It is presently using a minimal strategy.

The symphony is in a monopoly position, suggesting a minimal strategy, which it is presently following. Such a factor would signify a strength for the symphony and indicate continued use of its minimal strategy. However, it also faces a great deal of indirect competition, suggesting a balanced strategy. But it is using a minimal strategy, which in this situation is a weakness. The prescription would be to follow a balanced strategy.

The quality of the symphony is considered to be high. As such, this factor is a strength, suggesting a minimal strategy, which it is presently using.

Management, however, desires to increase and perhaps to maximize its revenues, suggesting a balanced and perhaps an aggressive strategy. The organization is presently using a minimal one, suggesting a weakness. The prescription would be to use a balanced/aggressive strategy.

The symphony is in the maturity stage of its life cycle, suggesting a balanced marketing strategy. However, it is following a minimal strategy, making for a weakness and suggesting that a balanced strategy should be prescribed.

The financial position of the symphony is one of being in debt, suggesting an aggressive strategy. However, it is using a minimal one, making for a weakness. The prescription would be to use an aggressive strategy.

There is plenty of unused seating capacity for the symphony at its programs, suggesting an aggressive strategy. However, it is using a minimal one, suggesting a weakness. It should be following an aggressive strategy.

The managerial philosophy suggests that the symphony make a profit, improve its image, grow, and provide its patrons with satisfying music. These objectives suggest a balanced strategy, except for the growth objective which suggests an aggressive one. However, the symphony is using a minimal strategy. Weaknesses are shown, and the prescription is to use a balanced/aggressive strategy.

At this stage of the analysis, the individual factor evaluations and prescriptions would appear as follows:

Actual Situational Factors	Evaluation (After Comparing Actual vs. Theory)	Prescription
1. Monopoly position	strength	minimal strategy
Indirect competition	weakness	balanced
2. Quality of symphony	strength	minimal
3. Increase/maximize revenues	weakness	balanced/aggressive
4. Maturity stage of life cycle	weakness	balanced
5. In debt	weakness	aggressive
6. Unused capacity	weakness	aggressive
7. Profit objective	weakness	balanced
Image	weakness	balanced
Client service	weakness	balanced
Growth	weakness	aggressive
8. Others		

Table 2.2
Strategic Decision: What General Marketing Strategy to Follow?

Theoretical Situational Factors → affecting →	Alternatives			Describe and Compare Actual Situational Factors & Strategy Used	Evaluation Strength/ Weakness	Prescribe
	Aggressive Marketing Required	Balanced Marketing Required	Minimal Marketing Required			
1. Nature of Market Competition						
If the organization is in						
1.1 A monopoly position, then			X			
1.2 An oligopoly position, then		X				
1.3 A high degree of competition, then	X					
1.4 Indirect competition, then		X				
2. Quality of Products/Services						
If the products/services are						
2.1 High quality, then			X			
2.2 In between, then		X				
2.3 Low quality and weak position, then			X			
3. Revenue Strategies						
If the organization desires to						
3.1 Maximize revenues, then	X					
3.2 Balance revenues, then		X				
3.3 Minimize revenues, then			X			
4. Stages in Life Cycle						
If the organization is in the						
4.1 Development stage, then	X					
4.2 Growth stage, then		X				
4.3 Maturity stage, then		X				
4.4 Decline stage, then			X			

5. Financial Position

If the organization is
5.1 Heavily in debt, then   X
5.2 Moderately in debt, then   X
5.3 Not in debt, then   X
5.4 Currently losing money, then   X

6. Capacity of Facility

6.1 If there is unused capacity, then   X
6.2 If all the capacity is used, then
6.3 Unless all capacity has to be kept full; then   X

7. Philosophy of Management Regarding Objectives

If the organization wants to
7.1 make a profit, then   X
7.2 If to improve its image, then   X
7.3 If to maintain its share of the market, then X
7.4 If to grow, then   X
7.5 If to ensure continuity, then   X
7.6 If to provide client satisfaction, then   X

8. Other Factors

Overall Evaluation and Prescription:

Table 2.3
Strategic Decision: What General Marketing Strategy to Follow?

Theoretical Situational Factors ——→ affecting ——→	Alternatives			Compare and Describe Actual Situational Factors & Strategy Used	Evaluation Strength/Weakness	Prescribe
	Aggressive Marketing Required	Balanced Marketing Required	Minimal Marketing Required			
1. Nature of Market Competition						
If the organization is in						
1.1 A monopoly position, then			X	Monopoly position using a minimal strategy.	Strength	Minimal Strategy
1.2 An oligopoly position, then		X				
1.3 A high degree of competition, then	X					
1.4 Indirect competition, then		X		Indirect competition severe; minimal strategy used	Weakness	Balanced Strategy
2. Quality of Products/Services						
If the products/services are						
2.1 High quality, then			X	Quality considered high, minimal strategy used	Strength	Minimal
2.2 In-between, then		X				
2.3 Low quality and weak position, then			X			
3. Revenue Strategies						
If the organization desires to						
3.1 Maximize revenues, then	X			Management desires increased revenues; minimal strategy used	Weakness	Balanced/ Aggressive
3.2 Balance revenues, then		X				
3.3 Minimize revenues, then			X			
4. Stages in Life Cycle						
If the organization is in the						
4.1 Development stage, then	X					
4.2 Growth stage, then		X				
4.3 Maturity stage, then		X		Currently in maturity stage; minimal strategy used	Weakness	Balanced
4.4 Decline stage, then			X			

5. Financial Position

If the organization is					
5.1 Heavily in debt, then	X				
5.2 Moderately in debt, then	X		Currently losing money and in debt; minimal strategy used	Weakness	Aggressive
5.3 Not in debt, then		X			
5.4 Currently losing money, then	X				

6. Capacity of Facility

6.1 If there is unused capacity, then	X		Plenty of unused seating capacity; minimal strategy used	Weakness	Aggressive
6.2 If all the capacity is used, then		X			
6.3 Unless all capacity has to be kept full; then	X				

7. Philosophy of Management Regarding Objectives

7.1 If the organization wants to make a profit, then	X		Yes, profit desired along with image, client service; also growth desired; using minimal strategy	Weakness	Balanced
7.2 If to improve its image, then	X			Weakness	
7.3 If to maintain its share of the market, then		X		Weakness	Aggressive
7.4 If to grow, then	X			Weakness	
7.5 If to ensure continuity, then	X				
7.6 If to provide client satisfaction, then	X				

8. Other Factors

Overall Evaluation and Prescription: There is a fundamental weakness in using a minimal marketing strategy as suggested by nine weaknesses and two strengths. The actual situational factors suggest that the symphony should be using a balanced strategy with some tendency toward an aggressive one, even though the symphony is in a monopoly position with a high-quality service.

The overall evaluation of the situational factors would suggest a funda-mental weakness in following a minimal marketing strategy (nine weaknesses and two strengths). A possible prescription would be to follow a balanced strategy with some tendency toward an aggressive one. (Detailed recommen-dations could be made with further analyses of the marketing mix factors.)

Such an analysis as suggested is by no means perfect, but it can be used to make a general recommendation, based on a comparison of the symphony's actual situation to a set of generic theoretical situational factors. Weighting of individual factors could also be employed if the analyst wants to consider some factors as being more important than others.

This situational approach using a matrix method is the one being advo-cated. A completed analysis for the symphony is shown in an abbreviated format in Table 2.3.

Consequently, the situational approach, as modified by generic factors which theory suggests and put into a matrix format, serves as a focal point in making major decisions about administering the affairs of an organization. A combination of comparing theory to an actual situation, evaluating these comparisons, and allowing prescriptions to be made in light of these evalua-tions is the essence of the approach designed to achieve the mission and the related objectives and goals.

Mission and Related Objectives and Goals

An organization's reason for being is called its mission.

An *objective* is an end or purpose that is related to, and usually subsidiary to, the mission. Examples of objectives are promoting growth, maintaining mar-ket share, improving image, becoming a leader in the field, surviving, im-proving the quality of life, making a profit, and satisfying some of the needs of the organization's stakeholders.

A *goal* is a more specific objective, usually related to time and quantitatively measurable. An example would be to increase revenues this coming year by 10 percent. Objectives may be classified as (1) organizational objectives and/or (2) personal objectives of the stakeholders or resource contributors to the organization. There has to be a match, or fit, or congruence between organizational objectives and personal objectives if the organization wishes to prosper.

A hierarchy of mission and related objectives should also exist at different levels to help the managers accomplish them. A *hierarchy* is a ranking of such things as jobs, people, goals, and so forth. The mission, for example, is ranked at the top level as the most important purpose of an organization. An objec-tive is ranked next, followed by a goal. A hierarchy exists when the managerial levels are matched with appropriate objectives and goals. The mission, objec-tives, and goals are the reason for management's existence and provide the rationale for the integration of the functions and resources of an organi-zation.

Resources Used by Management

Resources are inputs that management uses to produce and distribute outputs. Management's job is to integrate these resources so as to attain objectives. *Stakeholders* are the resource contributors to an organization.

What are these resources, and what are the sources of them?

Resources	Sources of Inputs
	(Stakeholders)
1. Money, Operating	Clients/Donors
2. Money, Borrowed	Creditors, Long-Term
3. Manpower	Employees
4. Materials, Machinery	Suppliers
5. Place	Community
6. Protection	Government
7. Leadership	Management
8. Right to Do Business	Society/Government

These resources may be stated as the Ms of management — money, manpower, materials, machines, markets, minutes (time) — as well as place, information, and others.

THE EXTERNAL ENVIRONMENT OF MANAGEMENT

When managers work or function within the organization, the internal environment or culture prevails. However, managers also have to deal with the organization's external environment — those factors, forces, and events outside the organization that affect its mission, related objectives, and goals.

The interface or match of the organization and its resource contributors (stakeholders) is the immediate external environment facing the managers. This resource environment is of primary concern to supervisory managers who have to use the resources to produce and market a good/service for client satisfaction.

The interface or match between the organization and its industry is the next external environment facing managers. This industry environment is of importance to the middle or operative managers who are always affected by the competitors who make up the industry.

A third interface is the competitive environment facing the organization. Even though a not-for-profit organization may not face direct competition, it always faces indirect competition for its revenues and resources. Competition is a major variable that determines the strategy of an NPO.

The interface or match between the organization and its general economic and non-economic environment is of importance to the top or strategic managers. They have to periodically scan the economic environmental forces, factors, and events to determine the general strategies available to them. Such factors as the demand, supply of resources, competition, and state of the economy become crucial.

In addition, non-economic factors are important to managers. These include socio-cultural, politico-legal, ethico-religious, technological, physical, and aesthetic factors. Any of these may affect an organization — favorably, unfavorably, or not at all. They may provide threats, or they may provide opportunities. In either event, managers have to scan the external environment and match their strategies with it.

Integration of Resources, Functions, and Environment

Integration is a key concept of management. It involves the fitting together of resources, functions, and environment to reach the mission and related objectives. Integration is concerned with mixing and matching.

Mixing occurs when the right ingredients are mixed to achieve some goal or objective. For example, if managers want to sell a product or service, they have to mix the right product, with the right price, with the right sales personnel, at the right place, with the right promotion, and with credit. Such a combination is called the *marketing mix*. Then managers have to match the market mix with the target market to make a sale.

If an organization has several services, it has to achieve an optimal product mix among its stars, its cash cows, its problem children, and its dogs. When that service mix is correct, cash flows will occur in the proper sequence to help achieve objectives.

Matching or fitting or making resources and functions congruent is another aspect of integration. For example, a growth objective, as well as its related strategy, has to match a favorable external environment with favorable organizational resources before it can be formulated and implemented.

Mixing and matching of resources, functions, and environment are the parts of integration. Integration is closely associated with the function of *coordination* — bringing together functions at the right time and place and in the proper quantities and quality to achieve objectives. However, integration is a broader concept since it brings together into a whole the various internal resources and functions and the external environment to accomplish objectives — the essence of management.

SUMMARY

Management involves the integration of internal organizational resources and functions with external environmental forces to accomplish objectives. What distinguishes management from other disciplines is the integrative nature of its job. Management is general in nature, not specialized, drawing on several disciplines to accomplish the objectives of the organization and its stakeholders.

There are different levels of management. The top level makes decisions about the mission and related objectives and strategies affecting its accomplishment. The middle level makes decisions that integrate the production, marketing, personnel, and finance functions to produce and distribute goods and services in order to accomplish the mission. The bottom level makes supervisory decisions about employees in order to implement or carry out the strategic decisions.

At the different levels, various managerial skills are required. Drive is crucial at all levels. Conceptual skills are more important at the top level, while human skills and technical skills are more important at the lower levels. At the various levels, the time perspectives of managers differ. The board of directors and the chief executive officer are concerned with years, the functional managers with months, and the supervisory managers with weeks and days.

Two major activities confront managers: (1) making decisions and (2) executing or carrying out those decisions. In so doing, they fill various roles, perform varied activities, and are involved in managerial functions.

Managers make decisions affecting their work. They plan, acquire resources, organize the resources, lead people, coordinate their efforts, and set up control systems to help the organization and its resource contributors accomplish the organization's mission and related objectives.

Managers also make decisions about the operative work or functions — production, marketing, personnel, and finance — that have to be performed to accomplish the mission of the organization. The line/core functions are production and marketing. The service functions are personnel and finance and accounting. Staff act as advisors in this decision-making process. Decisions have to be made about the relative importance of the operative functions in order to allocate resources to them.

Managerial decision making consists of several steps: (1) identifying problems, (2) determining objectives, (3) determining situational factors, (4) generating alternatives, (5) evaluating the factors against the alternatives, and (6) making a decision by choosing a course of action from among the alternatives. Careful analysis of each of these steps is suggested, especially for major, weighty decisions. Mistakes are costly.

The situational approach, using a matrix methodology, is recommended for making major decisions. This approach suggests that for any major decision facing an organization, there is a set of generic factors that emerges. Knowledge of these factors is crucial for making major decisions. However, each organization faces different situations, thus requiring an analysis of the situational factors that affect each alternative generated. An example was given, using a set of seven generic factors and three alternatives. When each actual factor was analyzed and then compared and evaluated against the set of theoretical situational factors, a prescription emerged as to the proper alternative to be adopted.

The organizational mission and related objectives and goals have to be arranged in a hierarchy and made congruent with the personal objectives of the stakeholders. The resources that managers use to accomplish the mission and objectives are provided by these resource contributors or stakeholders of the organization.

Management has to match the factors, forces, and events in the four environments facing the organization — its immediate resource environment, its industry environment, its competitive environment, and the general economic and non-economic environment — to develop a strategy to accomplish the mission.

The integration of resources and functions in order to achieve objectives is accomplished by making and implementing decisions regarding the proper mix and match of various resources, functions, and the environment.

Self-Help Questions

The following are self-help questions for you to answer to see if you understand the nature of management. Apply your answers to your organization if you can.

1. Management has been defined in many ways:
   a. Management is getting things done through people.
   b. Management is the process of seeking desired outcomes by utilizing the available resources and influencing the human relationships of the organization.
   c. Management is the art and science of accomplishing organizational and personal objectives through people and other resources.
   d. Management is the function of executive leadership.
   Find three more definitions. Discuss what you think is a definition of management for your organization.

2. Who is involved in making decisions and performing functions at the top level of your organization? At the middle level? At the bottom level?

3. What is meant by drive? By conceptual skills? By human skills? By technical skills? Which do you think is most important to a manager? Apply your answer to your organization.

4. What is the relationship between time and the various levels of management? Does this relationship exist for your organization?

5. With what form of activities are managers involved? With what substance are these activities involved? To whom and with whom are the substance and form of contacts directed? What are the functions of managers? Why are they performed?

6. Do managers in your organization spend all of their time on managerial functions? With what other functions are they involved?

7. In general, what are the two functions that managers perform? Do they perform them differently at various levels of management? What about your organization?

8. What are operative functions? Are they fairly universal for any organization? What do you call your operative functions?

9. Draw a matrix of both operative and managerial functions for your organization. Use it to evaluate how well your organization is performing its functions. Put a grade (A, B, C, D) in each cell that reflects your subjective judgment as to how well the function is being performed. Based on each cell, describe the strengths and weaknesses of the organizational functions. For example, a grade of D in the financial planning cell would signify a weakness, whereas a grade of A in acquiring resources for production would signify a strength.

10. Describe the steps involved in managerial decision making. Does your organization follow them?

11. What is meant by situational decision making? What are theoretical situational factors? How are they used to match an actual situation with the theoretical situational factors? What is meant by evaluation and then prescription?

12. What is a mission? An objective? A goal? Describe the factors that differentiate the three in terms of specificity, focus, time, measurement, scope, and level of management. What about your organization?

13. Classify objectives. Give examples in your organization.

14. What is meant by a hierarchy of objectives? Give an example in your organization.

15. What resources are used by management? For what purpose? Who are stakeholders? Describe them for your organization.

16. Describe the four external environments facing your management. Relate them to levels of management.

17. What is meant by integration? By mixing? By matching? Of what?

18. What is management?

Notes

1. Ralph C. Davis, *The Fundamentals of Top Management* (New York: Harper, 1951).

2. Mary Parker Follett, *Dynamic Administration; The Collected Papers of Mary Parker Follett*, eds. Henry C. Metcalf and Lyndall Urwick (Bath, England: Management Publications Trust, Ltd., 1942).

3. Harlow S. Person, ed., *Scientific Management in American Industry* (New York and London: Harper, 1929).

4. Karl Von Clausewitz, *Principles of War*, trans. and ed. by Hans W. Gatzke, (Harrisburg, PA: The Military Service Publishing Co., 1943).

References

Allen, Louis A. "Managerial Planning: Back To Basics." *Management Review* 70, no. 4 (1981): 15–20.

Anderson, C. R. *Management: Skills, Functions, and Organizational Performance.* Dubuque, Iowa: William C. Brown, 1984.

Boyatzis, R. R. *The Competent Manager: A Model for Effective Performance.* New York: Wiley, 1982.

Bray, D. W., R. J. Campbell, and D. L. Grant. *Formative Years in Business: A Long Term AT&T Study of Managerial Lives.* New York: Wiley, 1974.

Carroll, S. J., and W. H. Taylor. "A Study of the Validity of a Self-Observational Central Signaling Method of Work Sampling." *Personnel Psychology* 21 (1968): 359ff.

————. "Validity of Estimates of Clerical Personnel of Job Time Proportions." *Journal of Applied Psychology* 53, no. 2 (1969): 164–65.

Carroll, Stephen J., and Dennis J. Gillen, "Are the Classical Management Functions Useful in Describing Managerial Work?" *Academy of Management Review* 12, no. 1 (1987): 38–51.

Fayol, Henri. *General and Industrial Management.* London: Pitman, 1949.

Gillen, D. J., and S. J. Carroll, "Relationship of Managerial Ability to Unit Effectiveness in More Organic Versus More Mechanistic Departments." *Journal of Management Studies* 22 (1985): 668–76.

Hay, Robert D. *Introduction to Business.* New York: Holt, Rinehart & Winston, 1968.

Katz, R. L. "Skills of an Effective Administrator." *Harvard Business Review* 52, no. 5 (1974): 90–102.

Kotter, J. P. "What Effective General Managers Really Do." *Harvard Business Review* 60, no. 6 (1982): 156–67.

Mahoney, T. A., T. H. Jerdee, and S. J. Carroll. "The Jobs of Management." *Industrial Relations* 4, no. 2 (1965): 97–110.

Mintzberg, H. A. "The Manager's Job: Folklore and Fact." *Harvard Business Review* 53, no. 4 (1975): 49–61.

Penfield, R. V. "Time Allocation Patterns and Effectiveness of Managers." *Personnel Psychology* 27, no. 2 (1974): 245–55.

Stagner, R. "Corporate Decision Making." *Journal of Applied Psychology* 53, no. 1 (1969): 1–13.

Stewart, R. "A Model for Understanding Managerial Jobs and Behavior." *Academy of Management Review* 7, no. 1 (1982): 7–13.

3

The Nature of Strategy

STRATEGY

George A. Steiner has suggested the following:

The word strategy moved into management literature from its military usage. Strategy was defined as an action taken by a manager to offset actual or potential actions of competitors (Chandler, 1962; Cannon, 1968; Ansoff, 1969; Cooper and Schendel, 1971; Christensen, Andrews, and Bower, 1973). Initially the principal focus was on the concept of strategy and the processes by which it was formulated and implemented. While there is no consensus in the field, many scholars today have broadened these concepts and view "Strategic Management" as including the process by which organizational missions, purposes, objectives, strategies, policies and action programs are formulated, evaluated, implemented and controlled so that desired organization ends are achieved.[1]

According to Steiner, the strategic process is made up of many elements.

One is establishing basic objectives and goals which management wishes to achieve in the future. In conjunction with goal setting is an examination of present trends of the enterprise, future environmental possibilities and their relationship to firm activities, and a variety of external and internal affairs that have a bearing upon both the goals sought and the manner in which the enterprise wishes to achieve them. Alternative courses of action are examined and the enterprise chooses those policies, plans, or strategies (the words are used interchangeably at this point) to achieve the objectives sought.[2]

Harvard historian Alfred P. Chandler defines strategy as "the determination of the basic long-term goals and objectives of an enterprise, and the adoption of courses of action and allocation of resources necessary for carrying out these goals."[3]

Another author and researcher, William F. Glueck, characterizes a strategy as follows:

A strategy is the means used to achieve the ends (objectives). A strategy is not just any plan, however. A strategy is a plan that is unified: it ties all the parts of the enterprise together. A strategy is comprehensive: it covers all major aspects of the enterprise. A strategy is integrated: all the parts of the plan are compatible with each other and fit together well.

A strategy is a unified, comprehensive, and integrated plan relating the strategic advantages of the firm to the challenges of the environment. It is designed to ensure that the basic objectives of the enterprise are achieved.

A strategy begins with a concept of how to use the resources of the firm most effectively in a changing environment.[4]

A 1974 survey of 111 corporate planners on what strategy means revealed that "a near-consensus view would be that it includes the determination and evaluation of alternative paths to an already established mission or objective and, eventually, choice of the alternative to be adopted."[5]

Steiner and John B. Miner note that strategy was originally developed from the Greek word *strategos,* meaning "general" or "the art of the general."

Specifically, strategy is the forging of company missions, setting objectives for the organization in light of external and internal forces, formulating specific policies and strategies to achieve objectives, and assuring their proper implementation so that the basic purposes and objectives of the organization will be achieved.[6]

James C. Collier comments in terms of the external environment.

First and foremost, strategy has to do principally with things external to the company rather than internal to it. It is generally because of the external environment and its everchanging nature that we are so concerned with strategy formulation. Were it not for these changing conditions, their impact upon the company and the presenting of opportunities to it, our strategy would be relatively simple and unchanging. And so strategy is directed primarily at change as opposed to efficiency of operations.[7]

Robert Mainer claims that strategy should always be stated "in terms of the relationships between the organization, its resources and capabilities, and its total environment, suppliers, technology, [and] government," as well as other related economic and noneconomic environmental variables.[8]

Dan E. Schendel and Charles W. Hofer studied the different definitions and concepts of strategy advocated by various leading experts in the field and developed a composite definition structured around four components — scope, which can be defined in terms of product-market matches and geographic territories; resource deployments and distinctive competences; competitive advantage; and synergy — and three organizational levels — corporate, business, and functional.[9] While this definition excludes goals and objectives, it recognizes that the achievement of objectives is the aim of strategy and that the combination of objectives, strategy, and policies forms a "grand design" or master strategy for the firm.

One of the oldest notions about strategy is that promulgated by William

H. Newman, James P. Logan, and Harvey Hegarty, who state that their concept of a strategy and policy is based on a model developed as a lineal descendant of a diagnostic approach for the strategic management of a firm. The model sets forth the relationships among environment → company → strategy → policy → organization → execution, with feedback loops.

According to Newman, Logan, and Hegarty strategy concentrates on basic directions, major thrusts, and overriding priorities. Strategy involves identifying the services to be offered, selecting the resource conversion technology, determining the major steps to accomplish objectives, and establishing criteria for measuring achievement. Strategy is a plan for adapting company action to its environment, which is continually changing. A strategy should be concerned with where a company should be headed in the future. All of these characteristics are determined by the top managers of a firm.[10]

From all these definitions, we may summarize some characteristics of a strategy. Strategy is the means to the ends of an organization. It requires careful monitoring and analysis of changes in the organization's external environment. Furthermore, it takes into account the relationship between the forces in the external environment and the internal resources of an organization. Strategy involves the determination of the long-term mission and the related objectives of the firm and ultimately prescribes the courses of action for gaining a competitive advantage. Finally, it results in a managerial allocation of resources to most effectively reach those objectives. A strategy is a series of integrated future activities that are designed to provide the direction, the means of creating value, and the product-market mix necessary to achieve the mission and/or objectives of an organization and that serve as criteria by which resources are allocated.

POLICY

Policy has been defined by academicians in various ways. However, a close look at the many definitions reveals that four elements are stated or implied in almost all of them: a principle, a recurring situation, a guide to thought and action, and a reference to the achievement of an objective. A synthesis of these four elements provides a definition of an organizational policy: A *policy* is a general statement of a principle or a group of related principles that serves as a guide to thought and action for a recurring situation and that facilitates the achievement of an objective.

Statement of a Principle

A principle is a statement of an administrator's philosophy that hopefully reflects a general or fundamental truth. It shows the reason for a policy or the rationale behind a policy. That principle or concept normally is a reflection of a person's philosophy or value system. As such, the administrator is putting his/her philosophy on the line when he/she adopts a policy for other people to follow.

General Guide to Thought and Action

A policy is a general (not a specific) guide to thought and action. It serves as a general outline of the path to be followed, sets the general limits of action, and establishes a standard for thought and action. A policy is broader than a rule, which is a specific guide to action. It is also more general than a procedure, which is a series of sequential steps to carry out a policy.

Recurring Situations

Policies are established to ensure uniformity and consistency of thought and action, which suggests in turn that policies are established as a result of strategic situations that are likely to recur. Examples of recurring situations are those involving marketing, production, finance, personnel, research, and other functional areas. Perhaps recurring situations can also be classified as those dealing with customers, creditors, community, government, owners, management, employees, suppliers, and society in general (not necessarily in that order).

Achievement of an Objective

The purpose of establishing a policy is to reach an objective — an organizational objective and/or a personal objective of the contributors of resources to an organization. A policy statement either sets forth or implies the objective or goal and then gives the general path or outline that is to be followed in order to achieve that objective or goal. Various policies may be used to achieve the organizational objectives of client service, growth, profit, survival, service to various contributors, quality of life, image, and others.

THE DIFFERENCE BETWEEN STRATEGY AND POLICY

Strategies are determined by (1) the CEO's perception of his/her philosophy; (2) the mission and objectives that he/she wishes to accomplish; (3) an appraisal of external environmental factors, forces, and events; and (4) an appraisal of the internal environment of the organization. Strategies are initial and tentative attempts by administrators to respond to conditions of uncertainty and change in the internal and external environments. Once the strategies have been formulated, integrated, and implemented and have been found to be working — that is, found to accomplish objectives — they then become policies. Strategies are designed for changing situations, whereas policies are designed for recurring situations. This is the fundamental difference.

Strategies are pervasive and general in nature, whereas policies are more specific and serve as guides to thought and action in specific situations. Policies, however, become guides to thought and action over time when a similar situation arises. For practical purposes in management, strategy and policy are often used interchangeably.

CLASSIFICATIONS OF STRATEGIES AND POLICIES

Several bases exist for classifying types of strategies and policies.

1. They may be classified by the organizational structure/hierarchy.
2. Strategies and policies may be classified on the basis of specific organizational functions.
3. They may logically be based on key organizational objectives.
4. The satisfaction of certain needs of various resource contributors could form the basis for classifying specific strategies and policies.

Other possible bases exist for policy and strategy classification — for example, generic strategies such as market focus, service enhancement, and cost reduction.

Hierarchical Strategies and Policies

Master strategies encompass an organization's complete strategic system, including the basic mission, purposes, objectives, and policies, as well as the resource allocation process. Glueck[11] and others refer to this same basic group of higher level strategies as "grand strategies."

Steiner[12] states that strategies designed for specific purposes, such as resource deployment, could be termed "program strategies." When major strategies take on detail, substrategies evolve, followed by tactics. At some point in the process of filtering detail, organizational levels become important bases for classifying strategies and policies.

Many authorities agree that the top-level or corporate-level strategic set is differentiated from the remaining levels. H. Igor Ansoff[13] calls this level an "enterprise strategy," which is, in effect, a collection of substrategies. Schendel and Hofer[14] maintain that organizations are multimission institutions with many businesses. They logically differentiate the corporate-level and the business-level strategies and policies which are all part of the overall strategic portfolio.

Organizations frequently consist of many separate, related and sometimes unrelated entities; that is, they are really "holding companies or holding organizations." For example, a university is really a collection of separate colleges which are made up of functional departments. Or a city government is really a corporate organization made up of several separate, related "businesses" (such as police, fire, sanitation, airport, sewage, courts, and others), which in turn are organized into functional areas.

Thus, it makes sense to classify strategies at the top of a hierarchy as corporate-level or enterprise-level strategies. The separate entities that make up the next level use business or organizational strategies, followed by the next level, which uses functional strategies. The top-level strategies (the corporate-level strategies) are concerned with the overall direction of the organization, the business-level strategies are concerned with different services provided for clients, and the functional-level strategies are concerned with the operative functions of operations/production, marketing, finance, personnel, and information systems. A possible fourth level might also be considered. However, this level is usually concerned with tactics — not strategy.

Functional Strategies and Policies

Functional strategies and policies are intended to integrate organizational objectives and strategies into a functional area, as well as to relate the policies of various functional areas with changes in the functional area environments. These are usually called administrative, operations/production, marketing, financial, and personnel strategies and/or policies.

Some authorities consider functional area strategies as part of the levels of strategy of the hierarchical strategic system discussed above. Arthur A. Thompson, Jr., and A. J. Strickland, for example, discuss four major levels of organizational strategy: (1) corporate strategy, (2) line of business (or just business) strategy, (3) functional area support strategy, and (4) operating-level strategy. They maintain that functional area support strategy

deals with how the key functional areas of the business should be managed and how the resources allocated to each functional area are to be made effective and efficient in their contribution to the accomplishment of the overall business strategy. Each of the activities within a single business, most especially the key activities, ought to be integrated and fit together to form a smoothly functioning and mutually reinforcing unit. Thus, functional area support strategies are major corollaries of the line of business strategy — they give it substance, completeness, and concrete meaning as applied to a specific function in the business (production, marketing, finance, R. & D., personnel). They indicate how each subactivity in the business is to be managed for the accomplishment of the strategy of the overall business unit.[15]

Thompson and Strickland provide the term *operating-level* strategies for the strategic guidelines that operating-level managers develop and use in managing their areas of responsibility.

In general, operating-level strategies deal with the nuts and bolts of how various activities of the functional area strategies will be carried out (pricing approaches, discounts, credit arrangements, inventory levels, amount of promotional activity, raw material purchasing, and the like). Thus, the differences between functional area strategy and operating-level strategy pertain to matters of role and scope in the overall business strategy and to the level of management where the respective strategic actions tend to be taken.[16]

Strategies and Policies Based on Organizational Objectives

Glueck defines organizational objectives as those ends that the organization seeks to achieve by its existence and operations. He further states that if the objectives are the ends, the strategies are the means to those ends. Therefore, the ends provide a logical framework for categorizing the strategies.

Objectives precede the strategic management process. This is so because it is difficult to formulate strategies if you do not know why the enterprise exists. After objectives are set, the strategic management process begins: analysis and diagnosis, choice, and implementation of the strategy.[17]

Thompson and Strickland point out the following:

As concerns the long-run, most organizations have need for:

1. Marketing objectives, to create a viable, sustainable customer base and market for its products/services;
2. Technology-innovation objectives, to keep products/services up-to-date and competitive (thereby avoiding obsolescence);
3. Profitability objectives, to cover the risks of economic activity, test the validity of the organization's contributions, and generate the financial capital requisite for preserving (and enhancing where desirable) the organization's productive capability;
4. Efficiency objectives, to remain cost competitive and to make judicious use of the economic resources entrusted by society to its care;
5. Resource supply objectives, to conserve whatever human, capital, and natural resources are needed for continuing to supply customers (society) with the organization's products/services; and
6. Social responsibility objectives, to keep a watchful eye on how well the organization performs in accord with societal expectations, and to take full responsibility for and justify the impact which its activities have on the environment at large.[18]

Organizational objectives and personal objectives of contributors may be classified as

1. Organizational objectives
   a. Service objectives
   b. Growth objectives

    c. Image objectives
    d. Survival objectives
    e. Quality of life objectives
2. Personal objectives of customers, creditors, community, government, donors, managers, employees, suppliers, society (and others if necessary).

It could be suggested that a set of specific strategies and policies follows the basic organizational objectives and that strategies, or the means to the ends, logically are formulated to carry out the specific objectives.

Strategies Based on Resource Contributors

Strategies exist for clients' needs and for the needs of employees, suppliers, creditors, and others, such as donors, the community, the government, and society in general.

Donald L. Bates and David L. Eldredge[19] parallel this analysis when they discuss organizational goal formulation in terms of a relationship that exists between the organization and the "larger society." In effect, goals must involve the claims of various groups. Hal Pickle and Frank Friedlander[20] list seven of these groups, including the organization's (1) owners, (2) customers, (3) suppliers, (4) employees, (5) creditors, (6) community, and (7) government.

Bates and Eldredge comment further on interest groups.

Each interest group represents a segment of society with which the organization must interact, and each interest group may present conflicting demands upon the organization which must be satisfied if it is to survive. When goal formulation is viewed in this manner, it becomes clear that an organization's management has only a limited amount of freedom to set the goals of the organization.[21]

Consequently, it would seem that strategies and policies may be classified around the contributors of resources to an organization — customers, creditors, community, government, donors, management, employees, suppliers, and society in general.

Generic Mission Strategies

A set of generic or universal strategies exists for any organization that is concerned with accomplishing its mission(s). If an organization desires to provide goods and services for the benefit of its clients, and in turn benefit the organization, then it has to pursue three generic strategies: (1) product/service enhancement strategies, (2) cost reduction strategies, and (3) market focus strategies. These three can be grouped into an overall product/service-market match strategy; that is, an organization has to provide a product/service that is properly focused to serve its markets if it wants to survive.

CHARACTERISTICS OF "GOOD" STRATEGIES

Strategy researchers have suggested that every organization has a strategy. Some are "good," and some are not. Those strategies that accomplish the organization's mission and related objectives do have some distinguishing characteristics.

Create a Competitive Advantage

Inherent in the organization's external environment is the factor of competition. Every organization has direct and indirect competitors. Consequently, a characteristic of an effective strategy is the concept of a competitive advantage. An organization that has a competitive edge over its competitors will be more likely to attract resource contributors or stakeholders to its cause than will an organization that does not have a competitive advantage. Other factors being equal, an organization that has a competitive edge will attract more and better clients, donors, employees, suppliers, and other resource contributors, all of whom will contribute to its success in accomplishing both the organizational and the personal objectives of the resource contributors.

Create Value

A good strategy is one that creates value for the resource contributors of an organization. This means that a strategy has to create product and/or service benefits that a client will consume. Or the strategy has to reduce the costs so that price decreases become possible. When the benefits exceed the costs, then the product/service has value that can be translated into a competitive advantage. Reducing costs and increasing product benefits (usually by product/service enhancement) are two ways to create value.

Any strategy (let's say a growth strategy of adding related services) likewise has to create increased value for the organization itself if that strategy is to be called a "good." The added benefits of growing by adding another service have to exceed the costs of administering the addition. If additional benefits are generated by the strategy, then the organization should see an increase in its revenues. If not, then the strategy is not a good one. Benefits have to exceed costs to create value.

Integrate Actions

An overall strategy for the organization has to have a series of integrated actions. It has to tie other functions and activities together into a unified whole. The various activities have to fit and have to match the overall strategy so that the competitive advantage will create a force or mass so unified that another competitor will not be able to find the cracks in the overall strategy.

Give a "Direction" for the Organization

Every NPO faces a strategic decision regarding the direction of the organization. There are three choices: (1) to move forward (grow), (2) to maintain its present position (stay the same), and (3) to cut back (reduce growth and expenses). Any core strategy should provide the basis for determining the direction of the organization. The direction usually is a result of the CEO's appraisal of the external environment and of the organization's mission and its related objectives, all of which are affected by the CEO's philosophy and his/her perception of these situational variables.

Create a Value Thrust to Accomplish a Mission

In addition to the direction, a core strategy has to provide some value that gives a thrust to the series of integrated plans that make up the strategy. There are, again, three thrusts: (1) product/service enhancement (improving the products or services via differentiating, innovating, or improving the quality, plus other activities), (2) market focus (segmenting the market or concentrating on a market, for example); and (3) cost reduction (reducing the costs of a product or service via production, marketing, financing, or personnel activities in addition to managerial decisions). These three thrusts are closely allied to strategies pursued to accomplish the mission of the organization by providing various products/services that create value to satisfy the needs of clients.

Create a Product/Service-Market Mix

Further, because most NPOs offer a variety of services, a strategy should suggest a proper mix of products/services to serve the needs of its markets. A rather simple mix of services and markets can be illustrated by the following four-cell matrix, consisting of old and new services and old and new markets:

```
                    Mix of Services and Markets

              ___Old Services_____New Services_____

     Old
   Markets



     New
   Markets

```

If an NPO wishes to grow — that is, to move forward in its direction — it can pursue the following mix of services and markets:

- Offer old services into a new market
- Offer new services into an old market
- Offer new services into a new market
- Differentiate an old product in an old market

Or if an NPO wishes to maintain its position, its best mix is to pursue its old markets with its old services.

Or if an NPO wishes to cut back, its best mix is to cut back any growth and reduce the expenses of its old services in its old markets.

Combine Direction, Value, Thrust, and Mix

If we were to combine some characteristics of strategy, we might wish to integrate the three into the following matrix:

Mission: To create services to meet the needs of clients. *Core strategy*: To match the services with the clients' needs. *Characteristics of the strategy*:

Direction	Mix of Products/Markets	Value Thrust
Move forward	Old services/new market	Market focus
	New services/old market	Service enhancement
	New services/new market	
	Differentiated old services/old market	
Maintain	Old services/old market	Cost reduction
Cut back	Old services/old market	Cost reduction

Provide Strategic Fit

A strategy has to fit or be congruent with at least four variables, as perceived by the CEO.

1. The philosophy of the CEO who has to carry it out
2. The external environmental factors, forces, and events
3. The objectives for which it is formulated
4. The internal resources and functions of the organization that implement it

These four variables, as perceived by the CEO, are the determinants of sound strategy, as shown in the "Red Cross" diagram that follows.

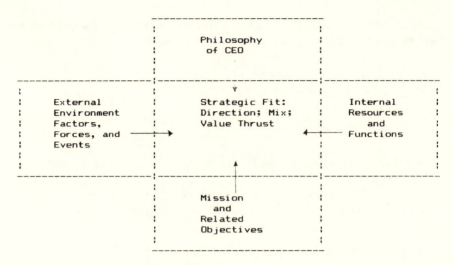

STRATEGY FORMULATION

Some sort of planning framework is necessary to administer the strategic affairs of an organization. Consequently, the author suggests an overall strategic model consisting of three stages: (1) overall organizational strategy formulation, (2) strategy integration into the functional areas, and (3) strategy implementation. The first — strategy formulation — is really a type of long-range planning. This type of planning includes a managerial philosophy that determines the mission and related objectives of an organization and a managerial assessment of the external and internal environment of an organization, all of which involve a managerial determination of strategies that help to plan for the long-run survival of the organization.

Managerial Philosophy

Organizational Mission: To Create Goods and Services to Satisfy
the Human Needs by a Product-Market Match Strategy

A non-profit organization exists to satisfy human needs by creating products and services that are consumed by the organization's potential clients. These clients are usually willing to exchange their resources for the goods and services produced and distributed by the non-profit organization. In exchange for creating and distributing goods and services for its clients, an organization must receive some sort of "profit" (revenues that exceed expenses), or else some sort of financial subsidy must take up the financial slack if expenses exceed revenues. But the key concept that provides the mission and that justifies the existence of an organization is the ability of the product/service to match the needs of the client. This concept is called the *product-market match strategy.* It provides the basic rationale for the administration of the affairs of a non-profit organization. One of the substrategies is to segment the market (market focus strategy).

Goods and Services Have Benefits and Costs

Goods and services created by a successful product-market match have two characteristics. The first is that the goods and services create client utilities, which are the abilities of goods or services to satisfy needs. When the utilities or benefits of the good or service are paid for by the clients or donors of an organization, they provide the revenues from which the expenses of providing those utilities are paid. The basic strategy is one of product/service enhancement.

The second characteristic is that the goods and services that are produced and distributed have some costs attached to them. These costs become the expenses of managing an organization. Hopefully, the revenues will exceed the expenses; if they do not, the organization will usually fail. Consequently, a cost reduction strategy has to be pursued.

Goods and Services Must Create Value

When people see that a good or service is worthwhile to them, they are willing to give up something in order to obtain it. In other words, the good or service becomes of value to them. Value is created when a person sees that the benefits associated with a good or service are greater than its costs. When the goods and services created by a non-profit organization are shown to have value — i.e., when the benefits are greater than the costs in the eyes of the clients and donors — then those goods or services create the mission of the organization.

The Organizational Mission Is Affected by Managerial Philosophy

The process of perceiving some need of potential clients and then creating a good or service to satisfy that need becomes one of the major tasks of a top executive of a non-profit organization. The perception and creation of the goods and services are dependent on the philosophy of the top executive whose personal values influence the production, distribution, and financing of those goods and services and the staffing for them.

The personal values that make up the individual philosophy of any top executive become the filters through which opportunities are seen to satisfy the needs of people, assessments are made of the internal and external environments, subjective objectives and strategic decisions are made from which policies and procedures are set, the strategies of the various operations are integrated, and the tone and climate of the implementation of strategies are set.

Several personal values make up a managerial philosophy. Technological values, for example, determine whether a manager will accept the use of computers in managing the organization or continue to use manual methods of information processing. Economic values will determine whether a manager is cost conscious or whether he/she spends money fairly easily. The political values of a manager will determine whether he/she is a conservative and does not desire rapid change or whether some degree of liberalism and desire for rapid change is present. Legal values will determine his/her respect for the law. In addition, the manager's social values will affect his/her notion of whether it is necessary to work long hours or just enough to get the job done. Cultural values will influence his/her decisions about race and sex, and ethical values will affect his/her evaluations of whether actions are right or wrong — say, in promotions or in dealing with potential clients. Religious values will affect opinions formed in dealing with other people, and aesthetic values will help to determine the beauty of the physical environment in which the organization operates. All these values — technological, economic, political, legal, social, cultural, religious, ethical, and aesthetic — are part of a managerial philosophy that influences the formulation, integration, and implementation of strategies to satisfy client needs by creating goods and services that reflect a successful product-market match.

Managerial Assessment of the External and Internal Environments

Once an executive has determined in his/her own mind that a need exists for possible goods and services, he/she should check out this subjective mission proposal by spending some time and money to make an environmental appraisal of the proposed goods and services and the need for them. Both internal and external appraisals should be conducted.

Internal Appraisal by Management

If the organization is already in existence, an internal management audit should be made. Its purpose is to identify the strengths and weaknesses of the present organization, particularly in terms of the managerial and operative functions and the resources necessary to produce and distribute the goods and services. If the strengths are evident, an obvious strategy is to capitalize on them. The weaknesses will show where changes need to be made or will constrain a proposed strategy. At least three appraisals should be made: functional, resource, and financial.

External Environmental Appraisals

A managerial appraisal of external environmental forces needs to be made to determine what effect the various uncontrollable external factors will have on the goods and services offered to clients. If those factors can be identified, the task of devising a strategy to design the goods and services to serve the clients is made much less risky. If the managers know what the future holds (and this is difficult to anticipate), the function of strategic planning will be much easier to accomplish.

Several uncontrollable external environmental factors need to be investigated. For example, economic factors may influence the decision to offer various goods and services to clients. Analyses are required of the general condition of the economy, demand, supply of resources, competition, and the like. These factors affect organizations when their survival depends on revenues exceeding expenses of producing and marketing goods and services.

Political environmental factors need to be checked. If a nonprofit is located in a traditional Democratic stronghold, it would be rather difficult to get much support for a conservative, free-enterprise-sponsored program fostered by Republican administrators. Or a politically conservative community would express a great deal of reluctance in supporting an urban project proposed by liberal politicians.

Social environmental factors sometimes have a significant impact on an organization's success. For example, a school was very successful in part because it was the only school in a suburban town. When population flight occurred and families moved from the suburbs into the metropolitan area, the school lost most of its students. What effect would this phenomenon, based on population flight, have on the success of other schools?

Legal environmental factors affect the operations of non-profit organizations. When the U.S. Congress passed the Civil Rights Act, the operations of all organizations were made subject to close scrutiny to determine whether discrimination existed in relation to male and female employees. Of course, many other laws that have legal implications for organizations have been passed.

Technological environmental factors are always affecting organizations. Various inventions, improvements, and innovations in equipment, machinery, and the like influence the tenor and operation of any organization's production and marketing efforts.

Physical environmental factors are playing a more influential role in the operation of organizations. Concerns with various forms of pollution – air, water, solid waste, land, and noise – are a constant challenge to the managers of organizations. Other factors such as climate also influence their operation.

Religious environmental factors have to be considered. For example, the role of church groups has a strong bearing on various services offered. Religious influences in communities play a strong role in the operation of various non-profit organizations' missions.

There may be other environmental factors over which most executives have very little control, but they have to be considered in administering an organization. Some may be very important and may cause changes to be made. Others may not. But a successful executive needs to make an appraisal of the non-controllable environmental factors that affect the organization, particularly when key strategic decisions are to be made.

At least four external environmental appraisals are suggested: (1) a resource availability appraisal, (2) an industry appraisal, (3) a competitive appraisal, and (4) a general external environmental appraisal of both economic and non-economic factors, forces, and events.

Making Assumptions About the Internal and External Environments

Once the mission and the appraisals have been made (using the internal or micro approach and the external or macro approach), the executive should state the assumptions implicitly made as part of his/her appraisals. For example, one assumption could be that the economy will stay the same. Another could be that the strengths of the organization will not change. Or there may be other assumptions that the executive makes. But he/she will be able to make better strategic decisions if he/she states the assumptions on which those decisions are to be based.

Managerial Determination of Strategies

The Organization's Mission and Related Objectives

With the goods and services proposed, the environmental analyses made, and the assumptions stated, the executive is ready to state the organization's mission and related objectives. There are usually several objectives that an organization wishes to accomplish. The organizational mission is to create products and services for its clients. The organization's reason for existence becomes its primary mission and determines the nature of the organization and related objectives.

Organizational objectives related to its mission might include the following:

1. To increase the organization's size (growth)
2. To maintain its continuity
3. To make a "profit"
4. To improve its image
5. To maintain its share of the market
6. To improve the position of its industry
7. To become a leader in its field
8. To serve the needs of its resource contributors
9. To improve the quality of life for society

The various objectives may be grouped into broader categories such as service objectives, survival objectives, growth objectives, image objectives, quality of life objectives, and others. But they should be known before the various forecasts are made and the strategies developed for the successful administration of a non-profit organization.

General Economic Forecasts

With the organizational objectives stated, the executive is faced with the necessity of making a general economic forecast in order to determine the economy's effects on the nature of the goods and services provided by the organization. An executive may purchase an economic forecasting model or make his/her own. Several universities and some private agencies prepare their own forecasts, which are made public from time to time. The point is that the general economy is a key uncontrollable factor which does affect the operation of a non-profit organization. For example, if the economy is on the decline, charitable contributions may decline.

"Industry" Forecasts

After seeing the effects on an organization of a general economic forecast, the executive should next investigate the "industry" forecast — that is, the forecast for the fields in which the organization operates. Such factors as the trend of the supply of resources, the trend for demand, the general outlook, competition, and so forth can provide guideposts for determining whether the industry is attractive, unattractive, or neutral. Such an appraisal helps in determining the strategic direction of an organization.

Target Market Focus

The target market focus strategy attempts to predict the specific markets in which the organization should distribute its goods and services; that is, it attempts to determine who would consume the services that the organization would create. An effort should be made to identify the specific people and their characteristics that make up the market the organization plans to serve. Demographic information should be analyzed as to who the people are, how many there are, where they are, why they would buy the goods and services, when they would use them, and what their psychographic interests, opinions, and activities are. Such information might allow the organization to segment its market and then differentiate its goods and services to serve those segmented markets.

Revenue and Expense Forecasts

With a target market delineated, an attempt should be made to determine a revenue forecast for the organization. This revenue forecast can later be matched against a forecast of the expenses of administering, producing, marketing, financing, and staffing the operation. Allocation of resources becomes crucial at this stage.

The preceding steps are associated with the formulation of overall organizational strategies. The next step is the integration of these overall organizational strategies into the operative functional areas of an organization and the allocation of resources into the functional areas in light of the strategies determined.

INTEGRATION OF OVERALL STRATEGIES INTO OPERATIVE FUNCTIONS

The mission and the resulting related strategies of the organization dictate the integration of the overall strategies into the operative functions of an organization: production/operations, marketing, finance, and personnel. For example, when the product-market strategy becomes an organizational strategy of a firm, then various substrategies to carry out this overall strategy have to be integrated into the operative functions. Moreover, certain more important key functional strategic decisions have to be integrated with the product-market match strategies.

Production Strategies

Various production strategies for the creation of the goods and services have to be decided on in light of the product-market match. Production objectives should flow from the overall organizational objectives: For example, should the organization's production function increase production volume, reduce costs, improve product/service quality, or improve production processes? If these become the objectives, what strategies should be considered? Key strategic decisions affecting the production function include whether to produce manually or by machine, what the production layout should be, and whether to produce for stock or for order. Other key decisions involve whether to make or buy the component parts of the product or service and how many suppliers to use. These are key strategic decisions for most organizations, and they depend on factors that are both externally and internally derived.

Marketing Strategies

Once the goods and services are created, how does the organization market them to its clients? Does it segment the market? What characteristics of the goods and services are to be differentiated? What price strategy is to be used? How does the organization promote its services? What channels of distribution are to be used? What types of sales personnel should it use? What types of financial strategies are to be used in selling the products and services — credit, trade-ins, installments? These key strategic decisions face each organization.

Financial Strategies

Where does the organization get the money to finance its operations — from operations, from donors, from borrowing, from volunteers? Does it have a financial budget — operations and capital budget — to help managers plan and evaluate? These and other financial strategies have to be decided in managing a successful organization.

Personnel Strategies

Manpower is a chief resource used in creating the goods and services of an organization. The success of a non-profit organization is sometimes directly attributable to the goods and services created by its personnel. Such strategies must be considered in relation to sources of personnel. What types are needed? What are their duties? By what methods does the organization pay them? How does it lead them? What about personnel evaluation? Should volunteers be used? These and other strategies have to be determined.

Functional Objectives

Each of the various functional strategies (production/operations, marketing, personnel, and finance) should have a set of detailed functional objectives which relate to the overall objectives of the organization. These functional objectives can be used for planning and evaluating purposes in managing each of the various functional areas. For example, marketing might state its objectives in terms of market share, units to be sold, cost of selling, growth in total revenues, and so forth. Personnel might use interview, selection, and absenteeism rates as specific functional objectives. The finance function might use a return on investment rate, inventory turnovers, and other financial ratios as specific functional objectives. Functional objectives, specified in quantitative terms if possible, are very useful in determining the degree of success achieved in managing a functional area of an organization and in creating and implementing various strategies.

IMPLEMENTATION OF STRATEGIES

Once strategies are formulated and integrated into the functional areas, there comes the third stage — strategy implementation. Normally, the executives of an organization have to determine strategies, as well as implement them, and certain universal managerial functions are necessary to implement strategies. A function such as short-term planning to implement strategies has to be performed. Resources have to be acquired to carry out the implementation. Various organizational structures have to be created to implement strategies. Leadership styles are needed to implement operations and changes in strategies. Coordination of thought and action is essential to implement strategies. Further, some type of evaluation has to be made to determine whether strategies have been successful and objectives have been accomplished. These are normally called the managerial functions necessary to implement strategies to accomplish objectives. They create an internal organizational culture which influences "how we do things around here."

Some activities are needed to see if the strategies work. If they do not, some sort of restrategizing or reevaluating becomes necessary. The whole process described may have to be evaluated again to see where errors existed and to make changes. But the framework suggested may be used to administer a non-profit organization.

CHANGES IN OVERALL STRATEGIES AND THEIR EFFECT ON THE ORGANIZATION

The three basic processes in strategic management are (1) strategy formulation, (2) integration of the strategies into the operative functional areas, (3) and then implementation by the performance of the managerial functions. These three processes are vitally related in terms of sequencing. When an executive formulates a change in a policy or strategy, then it becomes obvious that integration and implementation will also have to change. A glance at Figure 3.1 summarizes the processes involved in strategic formulation, integration, and implementation.

Self-Help Questions

Here are some more questions for you to answer to see if you understand the nature of strategy and the processes of strategy formulation, integration, and implementation. Apply your answers to your organization.

1. What is the origin of the word *strategy?* Relate your answer to your organization's management.
2. Distinguish between *strategy* and the *process* of *strategy.*
3. Discuss the means-end chain as applied to strategy. Apply it to your organization.
4. How would you define *strategy?*
5. How would you distinguish between a *strategy* and a *policy?*
6. Strategies may be classified in several ways. Discuss the following classifications:
   a. Hierarchical strategies
   b. Functional strategies
   c. Organizational objectives and related strategies
   d. Resource contributors and strategies
   e. Generic strategies
7. What are the three stages of the process of strategy? Discuss and apply them to your organization.
8. Strategy starts with the mission of the organization. Is this statement true or false? Discuss. Relate your answer to the product-market match strategy.
9. Who usually determines the mission and related objectives and their match with various strategies? What determinant is involved?

Figure 3.1
Strategic Planning Model

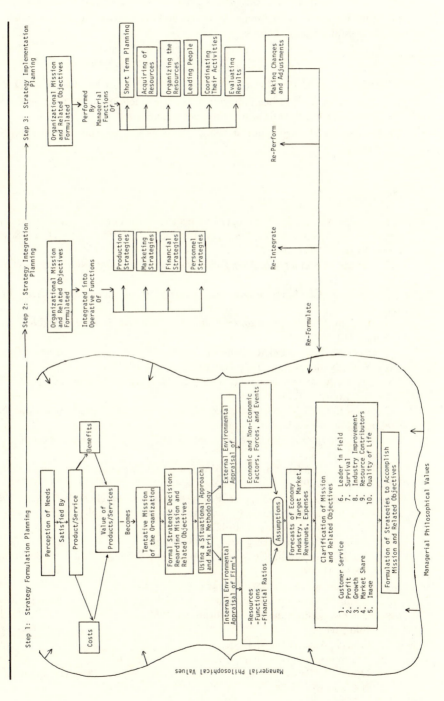

10. What is the role of the external environment in strategic process? Discuss.

11. What is the role of the internal resources and functions of the organization in the process of strategy? Discuss.

12. What are some objectives of your organization? Discuss.

13. Discuss various forecasts that are related to the process of strategy.

14. Once strategies have been formulated, what needs to be done next? Discuss.

15. Once strategies have been integrated into the functional areas, what needs to be done next? Relate your answers to your organization.

16. Discuss the characteristics of "good" strategies. Does your organization have them?

Notes

1. George A. Steiner, "Contingency Theories of Strategy and Strategic Management," in *Strategic Management*, eds. Dan E. Schendel and Charles W. Hofer (Boston: Little, Brown, 1979), 405.

2. George A. Steiner, ed., *Managerial Long Range Planning* (New York: McGraw-Hill, 1963), 11.

3. Alfred P. Chandler, *Strategy and Structure* (Cambridge, Mass.: MIT Press, 1962), 13.

4. William F. Glueck, *Business Policy and Strategic Management* (New York: McGraw-Hill, 1980), 9.

5. James K. Brown and Rochelle O'Connor, *Planning and the Corporate Director* (New York: National Industrial Conference Board, 1974), 11.

6. George A. Steiner and John B. Miner, *Management Strategy and Policy* (New York: Macmillan, 1977), 19.

7. James R. Collier, *Effective Long-Range Business Planning* (Englewood Cliffs, N.J.: Prentice-Hall, 1968), 101.

8. Robert Mainer, "The Case of the Stymied Strategist," *Harvard Business Review* 46 (June 1968): 40.

9. Dan E. Schendel and Charles W. Hofer, eds., *Strategic Management* (Boston: Little, Brown, 1979), 11.

10. William H. Newman, James P. Logan, and Harvey Hegarty, *Strategy, Policy, and Central Management*, 9th ed. (Cincinnati: Southwestern Publishing Co., 1985), 10.

11. Glueck, *Business Policy*, 121–42.

12. Steiner, *Managerial Long Range Planning*, 20.

13. Ansoff, Igor, "The Changing Shape of the Strategic Problem," in *Strategic Management*, 41–42.

14. Schendel and Hofer, *Strategic Management*, 13.

15. Arthur A. Thompson, Jr., and A. J. Strickland III, *Strategic Formulation and Implementation* (Dallas: Business Publications, 1980), 62.

16. Ibid., 64.

17. Glueck, *Business Policy*, 35.

18. Thompson and Strickland, *Strategic Formulation*, 64.

19. Donald L. Bates and David L. Eldredge, *Strategy and Policy* (Dubuque, Iowa: William C. Brown, 1980), 20.

20. Hal Pickle and Frank Friedlander, "Seven Societal Criteria of Organizational Success," *Personnel Psychology* 20, no. 2 (1967): 166.
21. Bates and Eldredge, *Strategy and Policy*, 20.

References

Ansoff, H. Igor. "The Changing Shape of the Strategic Problem." In *Strategic Management*, eds., Dan E. Schendel and Charles W. Hofer. Boston: Little, Brown, 1979, p. 30.
———. *Corporate Strategy.* New York: McGraw-Hill, 1965.
———. "Strategies for Diversification." *Harvard Business Review* 35, no. 5 (September/October 1957): 113–24.
Bates, Donald L., and David L. Eldredge. *Strategy and Policy.* Dubuque, Iowa: William C. Brown, 1980.
Brown, James K., and Rochelle O'Connor. *Planning and the Corporate Director.* New York: National Industrial Conference Board, 1974.
Busch, Edgar T. "Theory of Formal Organization and Its Acceptance by the Business Practitioner." Ph.D. diss., University of Arkansas, 1970.
Chandler, Alfred P. *Strategy and Structure.* Cambridge, Mass. MIT Press, 1962.
Collier, James R. *Effective Long-Range Business Planning.* Englewood Cliffs, N.J.: Prentice-Hall, 1968.
Cooper, Arnold C. "Strategic Management: New Ventures and Small Business." In *Strategic Management*, eds., Dan E. Schendel and Charles W. Hofer. Boston: Little, Brown, 1979, p. 316.
Glueck, William F. *Business Policy and Strategic Management.* New York: McGraw-Hill, 1980.
———. *Business Policy: Strategy Formation and Management Action.* 2d ed. New York: McGraw-Hill, 1976.
Guth, William D. "Corporate Growth Strategies in the 1980's." In *Business Policy and Strategic Management*, William F. Glueck. 3d ed. New York: McGraw-Hill, 1980.
Hofer, Charles W. "Toward a Contingency Theory of Business Strategy." *Academy of Management Journal* 18, no. 4 (December 1975): 784–810.
Kast, Fremont E., and James E. Rosenzweig. *Contingency Views of Organization and Management.* Chicago: Science Research Associates, 1973.
Lawrence, Paul R., and Jay W. Lorsch. *Organization and Environment: Managing Differentiation and Integration.* Cambridge, Mass.: Harvard University, Graduate School of Business Administration, 1967.
Mainer, Robert. "The Case of the Stymied Strategist." *Harvard Business Review* 46 (June 1968): 40.
Miller, Danny. "Towards a Contingency Theory of Strategy Formulation." *Academy of Management Proceedings* (August 1975): 64–66.
Newman, William H. "Strategy and Management Structure." *Academy of Management Proceedings* (August 1971): 88–93.
Pickle, Hal, and Frank Friedlander. "Seven Societal Criteria of Organizational Success." *Personnel Psychology* 20, no. 2 (1967): 165–78.

Schendel, Dan E., and Charles W. Hofer, eds. *Strategic Management.* Boston: Little, Brown, 1979.

Steiner, George A. "Contingency Theories of Strategy and Strategic Management." In *Strategic Management,* eds. Dan E. Schendel and Charles W. Hofer. Boston: Little, Brown, 1979, p. 405.

———, ed. *Managerial Long Range Planning.* New York: McGraw-Hill, 1963.

Steiner, George A., and John B. Miner. *Management Strategy and Policy.* New York: Macmillan, 1977.

Thompson, Arthur A., Jr., and A. J. Strickland III. *Strategy Formulation and Implementation.* Dallas: Business Publications, 1980.

Waters, Gail. "An Investigation of Specific Situational Factors Toward the Development of a Contingency Model of Strategic Growth." Ph.D. diss., University of Arkansas, 1981.

PART II
Determinants of Strategy Formulation

*T*he next five chapters present the determinants of strategy formulation: (1) the philosophy and characteristics of the NPO's chief executive officer and the management team; (2) the mission and related objectives of the NPO; (3) the CEO's perception of the external environmental factors, forces, and events; and (4) the CEO's perception of the internal environmental resources and functions of the NPO. There may be others, but these four usually determine the overall purpose and related strategies of the NPO. These four determinants provide the strategic fit of strategy formulation as shown below.

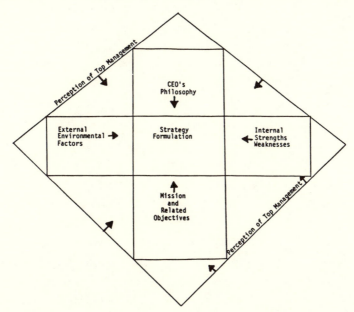

The fifth chapter deals with the NPO's board of directors and its role in strategy formulation, integration, and implementation.

4

The Chief Executive Officer and Team of Managers

The chief executive officer and his/her team of managers are the key determinant of the organization's mission and related objectives and the strategies that are pursued to accomplish them.

THE CEO AS A VISIONARY

The chief executive officer is the person with a vision of client needs that the organization can satisfy. His/her vision sets the stage for the type of organization that exists. The CEO needs to have some dream, some imagination, some revelation, some unusual discernment, some foresight, or some perception of a mission or task to be accomplished. That vision is translated into reality when a mission is stated. That vision can be formulated by having the CEO ask, "What type of product/service do we have now to satisfy the needs of our clients? What type should we have in the future? What should we be like five years from now?" The answers to these questions come from the vision of the CEO — from his/her perception of what needs people want to satisfy and what the organization has to do to satisfy these needs.

For example, the mayor, the city manager, and their city government team should have a vision for the future of their city before they can realize the city's economic potential. If they perceive that their city should strive to fulfill its potential for economic growth, they have to have a vision of a place that has amenities such as arts and cultural facilities, sports and recreational facilities, parks and other green spaces, historical places of significance, an unpolluted environment, restaurants, shopping, and city festivals, to name a few.

Their vision would suggest that they must have input from members of all the various groups that compose the community, not just from those currently in power. Their vision should see a better image of the city, as viewed by outsiders and residents themselves. Their vision should see active cooperation between the public and private economic sectors because each can benefit from the other's success. Their vision should see strategically planned long-term objectives and goals that relate to their perception of the mission of their city — to provide the necessary services to its citizenry to improve the quality of life for the community.

The CEO and the team should be willing to do what is necessary to see that their vision is carried out. The question is whether the CEO and his/her team are ready, willing, and able to formulate, integrate, and implement the organization's strategies.

PHILOSOPHICAL VALUES OF THE ADMINISTRATORS

The CEO's vision and those of the supporting team are influenced by the philosophical values of the NPO administrators. Their value systems or philosophies would consist of several types of value sets — of economic, technological, social, political, legal, religious, ethical, aesthetic, and other values derived primarily from the cultural environment of the administrators' backgrounds. Values are concepts that are considered desirable.

Values become the beliefs and attitudes that form an administrator's frame of reference and help determine the objectives and strategies that he/she will consider. All administrators have a set of values that affects their visions, and these visions influence their decisions and actions. Once these values are ingrained, they do not change except over a period of time.

Values are important because they determine the strategies and eventually the policies used to accomplish objectives. Values also affect the administrators' environmental appraisals of the non-profit organization and become the filters that administrators use to determine whether the external and internal environmental factors are favorable or unfavorable for the NPO. These values likewise become the filters that administrators unconsciously use to make difficult decisions. They set the tone for organizational strategy and implementation. They become, in short, a major variable in setting the objectives, determining the strategies to be used, and appraising both the external and the internal environments of an NPO. They help answer the question whether managers are ready and willing to carry out a strategy.

Values Influence Organizational Culture

An NPO's culture is derived from various tasks, problems, activities, and values that the administrators have. Culture consists of shared values, such as aggressiveness, defensiveness, conservatism, liberalism, and so forth, which set a pattern for an organization's activities and methods of behavior. That pattern is instilled in lower-level managers and employees and passed on by succeeding generations of people. The actions of administrators and other managers are the key factor in achieving a culture that determines whether the organization's major objectives and strategies can be achieved. A culture may be defined as "Here's how we do things around here."

The administrators' philosophy will determine the relative importance of operations, marketing, finance, and personnel within the organization. Managerial philosophies will determine what type of internal culture will exist. For example, a top-down system of management based on values of a directive leader will create a mechanistic culture. Or perhaps a participative leader with certain values will support a bottom-up system of management, which will create an organic culture. The relative importance of decisions regarding objectives, operative functions, and managerial systems results from the fact that they create a certain type of culture. These decisions are crucial and depend a great deal on the philosophical values of the CEO and the other administrators of an NPO.

Determining Administrators' Values, Beliefs, and Attitudes

Values or beliefs or attitudes (the terms are often used interchangeably) should be determined because they play a very important role in objective setting and strategy formulation. A value survey may be employed to determine those administrative values. For example, the following statements would measure whether an administrator's values are conservative, middle of the road, or liberal in nature in several categories.

Test Your Philosophical Beliefs
(Check what you believe in)

1. Economic Beliefs

Basic self-interest should govern the way an organization is run.	Self-interest plus the interests of resource contributors should govern.	Enlightened self-interest, plus the interests of re-source contributors, plus society-at-large interests should govern.
1 2	3 4 5	6 7
I am a profit maximizer.	I am a profit satisfier.	Profit is necessary, but so are other objectives.
1 2	3 4 5	6 7
What's good for me is good for my country.	What's good for my organization is good for our country.	What's good for society is good for our organization.
1 2	3 4 5	6 7
Money and wealth are most important to me.	Money is important but so are people.	People are more important than money.
1 2	3 4 5	6 7

Let the buyer beware.   Let's not cheat the   Let the seller
(Caveat Emptor)   customer.   beware.   (Caveat
                                                        Venditor)

     ----   ----   ----   ----   ----   ----   ----
      1   2   3   4   5   6   7

Labor is a commodity   Labor has certain rights   Employee dignity
to be bought and   which must be recognized. must be
sold   satisfied.

     ----   ----   ----   ----   ----   ----   ----
      1   2   3   4   5   6   7

Accountability of   Accountability of man-   Accountability of
management is to   agement is to the owners   management is to
owners.   _and_ customers, em-   the owners, con-
                             ployes, suppliers and   tributors, and
                             other contributors.   society at large.

     ----   ----   ----   ----   ----   ----   ----
      1   2   3   4   5   6   7

Free enterprise is the   Free enterprise occas-   Free enterprise--the
best thing the U. S.   ionally exploits the   system of profit and
has going for it.   many for the benefit   private property--
                             of the few.   many times exploits
                                                        the many for the
                                                        benefit of the few.

     ----   ----   ----   ----   ----   ----   ----
      1   2   3   4   5   6   7

Management has the   Labor and management   Labor should have a
right to decide organ-   have to get along with   voice in deciding
izational policies.   each other.   organizational
                                                        policy.

     ----   ----   ----   ----   ----   ----   ----
      1   2   3   4   5   6   7

A person should be   A person is worth a lot.   There should be a
allowed to make as   Let a person make a lot   cap on how much
large an income as   of money.   income a person
possible   makes.

     ----   ----   ----   ----   ----   ----   ----
      1   2   3   4   5   6   7

Labor gets what it's   Management and labor   Labor does not get
worth. The free market   should decide on how   its fair share of
dictates this.   much labor is worth.   what it produces.

     ----   ----   ----   ----   ----   ----   ----
      1   2   3   4   5   6   7

The right of labor to   The right of labor to   The right of labor
organize and bargain   organize and bargain   to organize and bar-
collectively should   should be regulated by   gain collectively
be free of govern-   law to protect business   should be guaran-
mental interference.   and the public.   teed to protect
                                                        labor unions.

     ----   ----   ----   ----   ----   ----   ----
      1   2   3   4   5   6   7

2. Political Beliefs

| That government is best which governs least. | Government is a necessary evil. | Organizations and government must co-operate to solve society's problems. |

```
  -----    -----        -----    -----    -----        -----    -----
    1        2            3        4        5            6        7
```

| Keep government out of individual and family life. | Let government programs exist only to the extent that individuals and families cannot support themselves. | Government must seek to provide each individual and family with adequate economic opportunity, through public programs if necessary. |

```
  -----    -----        -----    -----    -----        -----    -----
    1        2            3        4        5            6        7
```

| Public welfare programs are wrong; relief is a private affair. | Public welfare programs are best left to state and local governments. | Public welfare programs are needed and are best coordinated and carried on by the federal government. |

```
  -----    -----        -----    -----    -----        -----    -----
    1        2            3        4        5            6        7
```

| Housing and slum clearance problems are matters that are best handled by private property owners acting in their best interests. | Let state and local government handle housing and slum clearance. They are closest to the problem. | Housing and slum clearance are problems that need to be addressed with an expanded and . more extensive federal program. |

```
  -----    -----        -----    -----    -----        -----    -----
    1        2            3        4        5            6        7
```

3. Social-Cultural Beliefs

| Employee personal problems must be left at home. | We recognize that employees have needs beyond their economic needs. | We hire the whole person. |

```
  -----    -----        -----    -----    -----        -----    -----
    1        2            3        4        5            6        7
```

| I'm a rugged individualist and I'll manage the organization as I please. | I am an individualist, but I recognize the value of group participation. | Group participation is fundamental to our success. |

```
  -----    -----        -----    -----    -----        -----    -----
    1        2            3        4        5            6        7
```

| Minority groups are inferior. They must be treated accordingly. | Minority groups have their place in society but their place is inferior to mine. | Minority groups are people like you and I are. |

```
  -----    -----        -----    -----    -----        -----    -----
    1        2            3        4        5            6        7
```

| Thrift is an important virtue. Waste not, want not. | We must save, but at the same time spend to make money. | You can't take it with you. |

```
     1         2         3         4         5         6         7
```

| I believe in survival of the fittest. | Competition is important but so are people. | People are more important than being the best. |

```
     1         2         3         4         5         6         7
```

4. Legal Beliefs

| The law is sacred. Don't violate it. | It's all right to occasionally break the law. | It's all right to break the law if it's for a good cause. |

```
     1         2         3         4         5         6         7
```

| Don't evade the law even if you don't violate it. | It's okay to evade the law if you actually don't violate it. | Legal evasion is okay. Laws were meant to get around. |

```
     1         2         3         4         5         6         7
```

| Laws are made for the benefit of all. I respect the laws. | Laws are made for the benefit of small selfish groups, but I still respect it. | I cannot respect the law because they are made for the benefit of small selfish groups. |

```
     1         2         3         4         5         6         7
```

5. Religious Beliefs

| One who believes in God leads a satisfying life, regardless of time. | One who believes in God leads a more satisfying life in the long run. | I'm a religious skeptic. Religion does not add much to the quality of life. |

```
     1         2         3         4         5         6         7
```

| Without the church there would be a collapse in morality. | Church is okay. We need it as a social institution. | The church is okay for other people, not me. |

```
     1         2         3         4         5         6         7
```

| God will take care of you. | God helps those who help themselves. | God does not help anybody. |

```
     1         2         3         4         5         6         7
```

6. <u>Physical Evironmental Beliefs</u>

The natural environ-
ment controls one's
destiny.

One can manipulate
one's environment.

One must preserve
the environment.

```
 ----    ----    ----    ----    ----    ----    ----
  1       2       3       4       5       6       7
```

I believe in using
natural resources
because they are
available.

Conservationism requires
that natural resources
be put to their wisest
use.

Natural resources
must be locked up
in order to save
them for future
generations.

```
 ----    ----    ----    ----    ----    ----    ----
  1       2       3       4       5       6       7
```

7. <u>Technological Beliefs</u>

Technology is
very important.

Technology is important
but so are people.

People are more
important than
machines.

```
 ----    ----    ----    ----    ----    ----    ----
  1       2       3       4       5       6       7
```

Technology improves
the quality of life
for society.

Technology improves the
quality of life for some
but not for others.

Technology rarely
improves the qual-
ity of life for
society.

```
 ----    ----    ----    ----    ----    ----    ----
  1       2       3       4       5       6       7
```

8. <u>Aesthetic Beliefs</u>

Aesthetic values?
What are they?

Aesthetic values are
okay, but not for us.

We must preserve
our aesthetic
values and we'll
do our part.

```
 ----    ----    ----    ----    ----    ----    ----
  1       2       3       4       5       6       7
```

I am not an aesthetic
person.

Aesthetic are important
but not my main concern.

I am an aesthetic
person.

```
 ----    ----    ----    ----    ----    ----    ----
  1       2       3       4       5       6       7
```

These statements have been researched by the author to give an appraisal of the values and beliefs of administrators. The answers *1* and *2* would reflect conservative values. The answers *6* and *7* would reflect liberal values. The reader might wish to determine his/her values by answering the statements.

Profile of Philosophical Beliefs

Add your scores for each category of beliefs and divide the total by the number of items in each category. Fill in your score in the profile below.

	Conservative		Middle-of-Road		Liberal		

	Conservative		Middle-of-Road		Liberal		
1. Economic Beliefs	1	2	3	4	5	6	7
2. Political Beliefs	1	2	3	4	5	6	7
3. Socio-Cultural Beliefs	1	2	3	4	5	6	7
4. Legal Beliefs	1	2	3	4	5	6	7
5. Religious Beliefs	1	2	3	4	5	6	7
6. Physical Environmental Beliefs	1	2	3	4	5	6	7
7. Technological Beliefs	1	2	3	4	5	6	7
8. Aesthetic Beliefs	1	2	3	4	5	6	7

Connect each score with a heavy line. This line represents your profile of philosophical beliefs.

In addition to a subjective determination of values (as expressed by the survey), more objective "clues" may help to determine a managerial philosophy.

"Clues" to Managerial Philosophy

	Philosophy is Conservative	Philosophy is Middle-of-the-Road	Philosophy is Liberal
1.	Concern for Economic Values		
	a. Slow Growth —Compared to "Industry" Revenue Growth Less Than "Industry"	Steady Growth Compared to "Industry" Same As "Industry"	Fast Growth Compared to "Industry" Revenue Growth Greater Than "Industry"
	—Compared To Itself Change in 5-year revenues Less than 5%	Change in 5-year revenues 5-20%	Change in 5-year revenues More than 20%

b. Small amount of Leverage	Moderate Leverage	Highly Leveraged
No Long Term Debt	Moderate Lt Debt 0-35%	High Lt Debt More than 35%
-Total Debt ÷ Total Assets Less than 10%	10-60%	More than 60%
c. Costs Important Total Costs ÷ Revenues Going Down During 5 years	Cost Reducer Total Costs ÷ Revenues Staying Same During 5 years	Cost Not Important Total Costs ÷ Revenues Going Up During 5 years
d. Top-Down Style of Management Formal Planning System Structured Organization Centralized Decisions Tight Control	Mixed Style of Management Mixed Style of Management	Bottom-up Style of Management Informal Planning System Unstructured Organization Decentralized Decisions Loose Control
e. Little Innovation	Moderate Innovation	Great Deal of Innovation

2. Concern For Socio-Cultural Values

Low Concern For a. Employees $Fringe Benefits and Pensions ÷ Total Payroll 20% or less	Middle-of-Road 20-50%	High Concern for Employees $Fringe Benefits and Pensions ÷ Total Payroll 50% or more
b. Low Concern for Quality of Life for Society Charitable contributions as % of revenues None		High Concern for Quality of Life Charitable contributions as % of revenues 3/10 of 1%
c. Mechanistic Internal Organizational Culture -Vertical Communications Flow	Mixed Internal Culture	Organic Internal Organizational Culture -Vertical and Horizontal Communications Flow
-Low Commitment -Non-Participative Leadership Style -Opinions Ignored		-High Commitment -Participative Leadership Style -Opinions Welcome

3. Concern For Aesthetic (Beauty) Values

a. Spartan Facilities Depreciation Total ÷ No. of Employees Is Low		Plush Facilities Depreciation ÷ No. of Employees Is High

4. Concern for Legal-Ethical Values

High Concern Number of Lawsuits is Small		Low Concern Number of Lawsuits is Large

5. Concern for Political Values

Republican CEO and Team	Independent Mixed Team	Democrat CEO and Team

6. Concern for Religious Values

Catholic Orthodox Jewish Fundamentalist Beliefs	Presbyterian Methodist Mixed Beliefs	Universalist Unitarian Humanist Beliefs

OVERALL PHILOSOPHY (DISCUSS):

Profiling Philosophical Values of a CEO and Other Executives

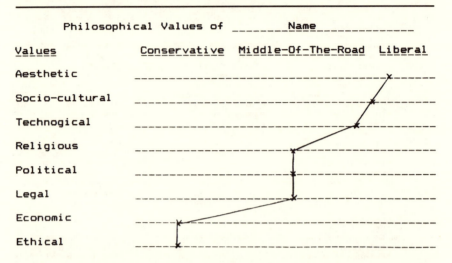

This set of values would indicate a CEO who is very much concerned with the physical appearance of high-quality services; who is concerned with treating suppliers and employees with integrity and honesty; who does not place too much emphasis on price, advertising, and competitors; and who has a middle-of-the-road philosophy regarding government, religion, and the legal system. He/she would not be a risk taker and would probably finance the organization by means other than debt. He/she would not value profitability too highly, but would place emphasis on client satisfaction.

The information for such a profile could come from surveys made by the chief executive officer. More objective information (as suggested) might also be used. Admittedly, such information would be sketchy, intuitive, soft, and difficult to quantify. However, it could be useful in determining the strategies of an organization because the philosophical values of the chief executive officer and the managerial team play a significant role in strategic decisions, particularly if no other information is available on which to base such decisions.

TOP MANAGEMENT TEAMS AND THEIR EXPERIENCE, EDUCATION, AND FUNCTIONAL EXPERTISE

Are managers able to carry out a strategy? Research has been conducted to determine which kinds of functional experience enable top managers to perform better.[1] In general, it has been found that when managers have marketing, sales, and product R&D expertise, as well as experience with those functions that deal with the vagaries of the external environment, an organization has a better chance of accomplishing its mission and related objectives. Those managers who concentrate on the input functions of operations/production, accounting, and the like do not perform as well as those who pursue the output functions do. Such research evidence supports our view that two of the biggest weaknesses of NPOs are the lack of marketing expertise and the lack of finance expertise at the top management level.

Further, top managers who have a broad college education perform better than those who have narrow educational training do. It follows that those managers who have a technical degree would perform better if they also had an MBA degree which stresses the operative and managerial functions of decision making and the execution of those decisions in areas that technical degrees do not emphasize. This principle is particularly true at the top level of an organization.

Managers who have managerial experience in at least two or three organizations have also been found to outperform those who do not have this characteristic.

Top management teams that demonstrate a preponderance of output functional experience (as opposed to input functional experience), employment in multiple organizations (as opposed to just one organization), and broader educational training (as opposed to technical training) will outperform those that do not, whether findings are based on criteria of inter- or intraindustry productivity.[2] Researchers believe the combination of these three factors creates an environment that encourages top managers to consider external forces, to adapt to different organizational cultures, and to evaluate subjective evidence.[3]

What does this research mean for the top management team of an NPO? It suggests that top management selection and development should be geared toward these three principles: (1) managers with external functional experience (marketing, sales, R&D, and perhaps finance) should be a part of the team, (2) managers with a broad educational background should be a part of the team, and (3) the team should consist of experienced personnel with managerial backgrounds in at least two organizations. It means that the leadership of the NPO should be able or have the capability to implement the strategies to accomplish the mission and related objectives.

STRATEGIC DECISION-MAKING PROCESSES

Top managers and their team members can pursue at least three strategic decision making processes: (1) dialetical inquiry, (2) devil's advocacy, and (3) consensus. Which is best?

Research has been going on for several years, but a recent study has concluded that both dialectical inquiry (DI) and devil's advocacy (DA) teams have yielded recommendations and assumptions of significantly higher quality than the average of those of the individuals on their respective teams, whereas consensus teams have not.[4] Moreover, the recommendations of DI teams and DA teams have significantly exceeded even those of the best individuals on the respective teams. There were no significant differences for consensus teams. Such findings would suggest that NPO managers and their teams follow a devil's advocacy and/or dialectical inquiry approach to strategic decision making.

The devil's advocacy approach develops a solid argument for a reasonable recommendation and then subjects that recommendation to an in-depth, formal critique. The devil's advocate attempts to show why the recommendation should not be adopted. Through repeated criticism and possible revision, the approach leads to mutual acceptance of the recommendation. Proponents of this decision-making approach believe that good recommendations and assumptions will survive the most forceful and effective criticism and will probably yield sound judgments.[5]

In the dialectical inquiry approach, two opposing recommendations, based on contrary assumptions, are developed from the same data. The two recommendations and their respective assumptions are subjected to an in-depth, critical evaluation through a debate between two groups. Following the debate, the two groups should settle on an acceptable decision. Each side is trying to win the debate, but in the end, hopefully, a more sound judgment will be made.[6]

In the consensus approach, each group member is given the opportunity to present his/her recommendations and the reasons therefore, stating the data in a clear, logical manner. Via discussion, questioning, and exchange of information and opinion, the group seeks a better recommendation than might be produced by a single person. It is not necessary that each person be completely satisfied with the decision — only that each can accept it.[7]

SUMMARY

Top-Management Evaluation

After reading this chapter, the CEO might consider evaluating the management of his/her NPO. You, as the CEO, are asked to do the following:

I. Determine the vision of the CEO.
   A. What is it?
      1. Give some evidence.
   B. Does your team of managers support the vision?
      1. Give some evidence.
II. Determine the philosophical values of the CEO.
   A. Take the value survey.
      1. Be honest in your answers.
      2. Plot the profile.
      3. Does it reflect your philosophy?

B. Give some objective clues as to your philosophy.
   1. Use the guidelines suggested.
   2. Give evidence.
C. Do the qualitative data support the objective data?
D. The philosophical data should help determine whether the top manager is ready and willing to formulate, integrate, and implement a strategy.

III. Do Step II for your team of managers.
  A. Do Step IIA.
  B. Do Step IIB.
  C. Do Step IIC.
  D. Do Step IID.

IV. Describe the education, previous experience, functional experience, age, interests, hobbies, and other characteristics of the CEO and the team of managers.
  A. Make a personal data sheet for each person.
  B. Evaluate, as best you can, the strengths and weaknesses of the top management team, including yourself. See the guidelines in Chapter 4.
    1. Make a matrix of characteristics for your top management team using the following model. Fill in the cells. Reach an evaluation of both the individual members and the team.

Characteristic	Team Member	Team Member	Team Member	Team Member	Team Overall Evaluation
Age					
Date Started Work					
Tenure in Current Job					
No. of Organizations Worked					
Total No. of Jobs					
No. Jobs Current Org.					
Graduation Date					
Graduation Date 2nd Degree					
Job Title					
Functional Experience					
Main Career Path					
Directorships					
University Degree					
2nd Degree					
Type of Degree					
Type of 2nd Degree					
Sex					
Marital Status					
Overall Evaluation of Each Member					

C. Are your managers able to formulate, integrate, and implement the strategies?

V. Describe the decision-making processes used by the management team.
  A. Devil's advocacy?
  B. Dialectical inquiry?
  C. Consensus?
  D. Determined by the CEO?
  E. What is your overall evaluation?

VI. What is your overall evaluation of the CEO and his/her team? Are they ready, willing, and able to formulate, integrate, and implement a strategy?

Notes

1. David Norburn and Sue Birley, "The Top Management Team and Corporate Performance," *Strategic Management Journal* 99 (1988): 222–37.
2. Ibid.
3. Ibid.
4. David M. Schweiger and William R. Sandberg, "The Utilization of Individual Capabilities in Group Approaches to Strategic Decision Making," *Strategic Management Journal* 100 (1989): 31–43.
5. Ibid., 34.
6. Ibid., 33.
7. Ibid., 34.

5

The Mission and Related Objectives

A mission is the purpose of an organization, the fundamental task that it sets out to accomplish. The mission is usually developed as a result of the NPO administrator's perception of an unsatisfied need. Such a need can usually be satisfied by the creation of a product/service designed to fill that need.

DETERMINING THE MISSION

This process of determining the fundamental mission of an NPO is very subjective, but it is a process that has to be performed. An NPO administrator usually enacts the environment of which he/she is a part. When a need is perceived, then that administrator thinks of a way to create a product and/or service to fill that need. Sometimes the need perception comes first; sometimes the product/service creation comes first. Both are necessary for the existence of a non-profit organization. The concept of need perception and creation of a product and/or service to satisfy that need is the basis for the fundamental mission of a non-profit organization — to create products/services to satisfy customer/client needs.

The products and services created to satisfy customer/client needs have three fundamental characteristics which each administrator has to subjectively evaluate before he/she can proceed. The first characteristic is that the product/service has costs attached to it. These costs have to be subjectively assessed and added up to determine the total cost of producing and selling the product/service. Usually included are labor costs, materials costs, and overhead costs, which collectively have to be assessed to determine whether the total cost exceeds the total revenue that might be generated through the sale of the product/service.

The second characteristic that has to be subjectively evaluated is the various utilities or benefits of the product/service. Do the utilities — that is, the form, place, time, possession, and service utilities of the product/service — provide enough total benefits to entice a potential client/donor to pay for the product/service?

If the total utilities or benefits of the product/service are greater than the costs of the product/service, according to the subjective evaluation of the administrator, then the product/service is assumed to have its third characteristic of value. The value of the product/service is usually expressed in the marketplace as a price that a person is willing to pay for the product/service.

A Transit System Example

Let us examine a situation in which a university vice-president became aware of a factor in the external environment that had become a sore spot with the faculty, students, townspeople, and staff—namely, student parking. He saw parking problems and traffic congestion on and near the campus because of the lack of parking spaces on the campus, which was being crowded in by the growth of the city. He became aware of increased parking violations, class tardiness, and unsafe conditions at pedestrian crosswalks. Overall, he perceived an atmosphere detrimental to the safety and convenience needs of students, faculty, staff, and townspeople. So he decided to propose an internal university transit system.

Benefits of a Transit System

He made a list of the tentative benefits or utilities of his proposed transit system. Such a system would

1. Eliminate excessive use of autos, taxis, motorcycles, and bikes on the campus — that is, help relieve traffic congestion.
2. Provide energy savings to students in the form of reduced gasoline consumption.
3. Increase the availability of campus parking spaces for faculty and off-campus students.
4. Decrease the number of parking tickets which become frustrating to students and faculty.
5. Reduce class tardiness by providing more parking spaces and reduced traffic congestion.
6. Reduce traffic accidents and improve safety for faculty and students on campus.
7. Be used by an estimated 3750 riders each day.

Costs of a Transit System

In addition, he made a list of the possible costs of the transit system:

1. The estimated yearly cost of a proposed transit system would be $252,000.

Salaries	$125,000
Fuel & supplies	22,000
Maintenance	50,000
Insurance	5,000
Depreciation on buses	50,000
Total	$252,000

2. Total cost of 240 days divided by an estimated ridership each day of 3,750 would equal a cost of $.28 per trip for each rider.

Value of the Transit System

He then estimated that the revenue for supporting the transit system could be generated by charging each student a $10 fee to be included in student tuition for each semester (14,000 students $\times$ $20 = $280,000, which he estimated would be sufficient to provide the revenue necessary for covering the expenditures). He perceived that the proposed benefits would outweigh the dollar costs and would create a valuable service for students and faculty.

His subjective proposal would have to be checked out in more detail, but if he found it to be feasible, he could state that the fundamental mission would be one of serving the transportation needs of students and faculty while on or near the campus.

Service-Market Match and Generic Strategies

A preliminary subjective evaluation of the transit service revealed that the benefits provided by the proposed service outweighed the costs associated with it. Thus, the service had value, and it became the mission of the organization to produce and sell the proposed service, hopefully at a profit or at least at a break-even point. However, the proposed service had to match the needs of the students if the organization was to be successful. Thus, the service-market match concept was created. Let's discuss the theory and strategies of a service-market match.

If clients have a set of needs that they perceive can be satisfied by a service that provides benefits greater than the cost given up, that service has value to the clients and they would be willing to pay cash to acquire the service. A two-way exchange relationship is immediately set up between the clients and the non-profit organization. When the clients pay for the services, revenue is generated for the organization which hopefully is sufficient to offset the costs of producing and selling the service. When the revenues are greater than the costs/expenses, profit is created which becomes a value to the organization. That profit generation, combined with client satisfaction, then becomes the mission of the organization. Both the clients and the organization have to perceive the value of producing and selling the services for the mission to exist. Creation of value for both then becomes the basic strategy of the organization.

How is value created for both the clients and the organization? A generic strategy that is pursued is called the *service-market match strategy.* In fact, this strategy has three substrategies that must be pursued. They are generic in nature in that they apply to any organization.

A closer look at the preceding theory reveals that value is created when the organization enhances the benefits of its services — that is, more benefits are perceived by the clients. Thus, the first substrategy is actually a set of strategies that may be called the service enhancement strategy. Examples would include offering innovative service, differentiating service, guaranteeing the service, making the service better, making the service more available in terms of time and place, promoting the service more, having better sales personnel, offering the service for credit and cash, and so on. The basic idea is to create more benefits for the clients — that is, to enhance the value of the service.

A second generic substrategy designed to create value is to reduce the costs of producing and selling the service and to pass the cost savings on to clients in the form of reduced prices. A cost reduction strategy makes the NPO more competitive and more profitable and also creates value for the clients. Costs might be reduced by various strategies that affect raw material costs, labor costs, and various overhead or capital costs, as well as other costs.

A third generic substrategy intended to create value is called a market focus strategy; that is, the NPO focuses in on a more specific target market. Rather than wasting resources appealing to everyone, the strategy would be to identify the needs of specific client groups, segment those needs, and design the service to satisfy those specific needs. Value is thus created by eliminating wasteful uses of resources for both the clients and the non-profit organization.

Let us review the theory of the service-market match strategy and its three related generic substrategies to create value.

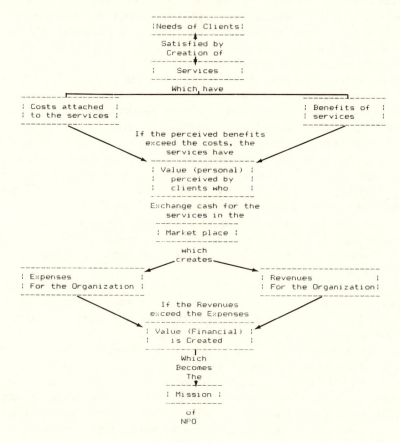

The service-market match strategy is supported by the three generic sub-strategies of (1) market focus, (2) cost reduction, and (3) service enhancement. All three are concerned with creating value for the clients and the organization. Two types of value are thus created: (1) value for the clients and (2) value for the non-profit organization.

Before going ahead with the creation of a service, a manager would be wise to see whether the service would indeed match the needs of potential clients. Or if a manager wanted to see whether strengths or weaknesses existed in the service's ability to match the needs of actual clients, he/she would be wise to analyze whether the clients' perceptions match his/her perceptions of the service.

If the service-market perceptions of both the clients and the managers were fairly well matched and if the organization was successful in generating revenue from the service sufficient to cover the expenses of producing and marketing the service, it would be a wise strategy to capitalize on the service. On the other hand, if there was a fairly wide gap between the clients' and the managers' perceptions of the service, then it would be a wise strategy to correct the deficiencies in the market match. The basic strategy would be to capitalize on the service's strengths and to correct the weaknesses, if any.

The Need for a Fund-Raising Strategy

Our theory is based on the assumption that sufficient revenues would be generated by the services of the NPO to offset the costs of creating the service. What strategy would be pursued if the costs exceeded the revenues?

A fund-raising strategy would have to be implemented to offset the excess costs of the NPO's services. Such fund raising is fairly common to many NPOs that offer services that do not generate sufficient revenues to offset their costs. (A discussion of the factors associated with fund raising is presented later.)

Feedback on the Service-Market Match

There is one way for an NPO to sustain superior performance: take exceptional care of its clients via superior service and superior quality. This basic strategy is not built on the exceptional genius of the leadership of the NPO, but on the attitude that client service should become an obsession with the NPO's personnel. For example, client courtesy means courtesy not only from the sales personnel but also from the accounting department, the purchasing department, and the engineering and operations people. Not only can these people provide superior service, but also they can create quality in every aspect of the NPO that is just a touch better than what is normally expected.

How can the NPO's leaders make sure that superior quality and client service prevail? The style of leadership that is often used is MBWA (managing by wandering around). That means to wander with clients and vendors and employees and whoever else is involved with providing client service, to be in close and continual contact with the NPO's clients, to get firsthand information on their attitudes about the services of the NPO, and to adapt. The importance of listening to clients is sometimes called *naive listening* — listening to end users, not intermediaries, and listening without preconceived notions about what to expect in order to get the real message about the clients' feelings.

MBWA involves three functions of leadership — listening, teaching, and facilitating — but it is not easy. The leader's ability to listen is exposed. The leader's honesty (or lack of it) is exposed. His/her ego is exposed, especially if naive listening is practiced. But MBWA is an excellent way to gain feedback about the NPO's service-market match strategy.

Another form of feedback or naive listening is for the leadership to volunteer to listen to clients who phone the NPO's toll-free 800 number with complaints (and occasionally praise) about the NPO's services. Virtually all NPOs who use this method say the same thing: The biggest share of new ideas comes from the users. Service innovation is an effective part of the service-market match strategy.

Some NPOs provide another form of client feedback regarding the services of the NPO through their suggestion and evaluation post cards which clients may fill out. While not as effective as personal or telephone contact, the suggestion and evaluation cards do gather information that is useful in providing superior quality for clients.

Quality issues are important to NPOs that are successful in gaining a competitive edge. Evidence from many NPOs speaks loud and clear: NPOs that find ways to differentiate their services on a quality basis tend to be winners.

Quality is not a technique, no matter how good, even though the best techniques — quality circles, statistical quality control — are of value. Quality can be obtained at all levels of the organization only by paying attention to it, living it, and spending time on it, no matter what the job. Quality comes from people who are committed and who care for it — that is, people who believe that something can be made better, that beauty is achievable, that perfection is something to strive for.

Those leaders who recognize that superior client service and superior quality are fundamental to a service-market match strategy are those who recognize that revenue enhancement is more important than cost reduction. Market dominance combined with lowest cost is nice if an NPO can achieve it, but quality and superior service come first. That is what wins clients and allows an NPO to reap the benefits of a successful service-market match strategy.

The Relationship of the NPO's Mission and the CEO's Philosophical Values

Managerial values influence the organization's objectives and related strategies, particularly when there are no clear-cut facts on which to base decisions. When this happens, administrators will fall back on their values or beliefs which will influence the strategic decisions and objectives they will formulate. There is a fairly direct relationship between administrators' values and the objectives and strategies of an organization.

The Red River City Hospital

A short case might best illustrate this relationship. The local Red River City Hospital was built with local community donations and has sought to meet the medical needs of the citizens of Red River. The board of directors consists of four members appointed by the municipal government and six members appointed from the six different churches in the community. The board has broad professional representation and seeks to be responsive to the community that it serves.

The hospital is a not-for-profit organization. Operating expenses are paid in full from fees charged to patients. Other funds restricted for the purchase of land, buildings, and equipment come from a local sales tax (one percent), gifts, and development foundation funds.

The hospital views its mission as filling unmet community health needs related to recurring minor surgery, with a competitive emphasis where other hospitals are perceived to be inefficient in those areas. The hospital presently has filed a certificate of need for surgery in the state. Presently, the hospital maintains excellent geriatric and physical rehabilitation facilities. The hospital does not want to become a regional medical center with expensive diagnostic equipment. Moderate growth in its targeted market areas is sufficient for the board of directors.

In analyzing the strengths and weaknesses of the hospital, the administrator felt that the hospital's strong community support, competent staff and physicians, and diversity were its strong points. When asked what he thought the hospital's weak points were, he stated: "The hospital needs to acquaint people with its wide range of services, the hospital needs to have surgical services available as soon as possible, and the hospital needs to shed its image as 'an old people's hospital.' "

He discussed the organizational mission and related objectives and gave his views about them. He ranked them in order of importance.

Evaluation of Red River City Hospital's Achievement of Organizational Mission and Related Objectives

Organizational Mission and Related Objectives	Administrator's Evaluation	
	Strong	Weak
1. Quality of life for society	x	
2. Patient satisfaction	x	
3. Survival	x	
4. Image improvement		x

```
Organizational                              Administrator's
Mission and Related                         Evaluation
Objectives_____                          Strong   Weak
```

	Organizational Mission and Related Objectives	Strong	Weak
5.	Industry improvement	x	
6.	Maintenance of market share		x
7.	Growth	x	
8.	Profit	x	
9.	Leader in the field		x
10.	Satisfying the needs of:		
a.	patients	x	
b.	creditors	x	
c.	community	x	
d.	government	x	
e.	board of directors	x	
f.	management	x	
g.	employees	x	
h.	suppliers	x	
i.	society in general	x	

He thought that the Red River City Hospital was a very strong organization. Of the three weaknesses, only one — that of having a relatively poor public image — affected the hospital significantly. Another — being a leader in the field — was not a major objective of the hospital administrator. It was generally thought that the image problem would take care of itself in time via word of mouth, newspaper coverage, and increased physician referral. Maintenance of market share was not a major objective either.

Overall, the administrator may be characterized as having a liberal philosophy with middle-of-the-road tendencies. On a scale of one to seven, with one representing most conservative and seven representing most liberal, he ranked in these categories as follows (see profile on next page):

Economic beliefs	5.2
Political beliefs	5.25
Socio-cultural beliefs	6.2
Legal beliefs	3.3
Religious beliefs	3.7
Physical environmental beliefs	6.0
Technological beliefs	6.0
Aesthetic beliefs	6.0

With the above profile in mind, it was not surprising that the administrator ranked "quality of life for society" and "patient satisfaction" as first and second in terms of important objectives for the hospital. Further, he ranked "profit" eighth in importance in a group of ten objectives. Profit is not as highly esteemed an objective to one with liberal tendencies. One with such liberal philosophical beliefs might be an asset for a service-oriented non-profit organization. In fact, during discussion of the profits which the hospital has enjoyed in the past several years and anticipates this year, the emphasis

Philosophical Beliefs of Red River City Hospital's Administrator

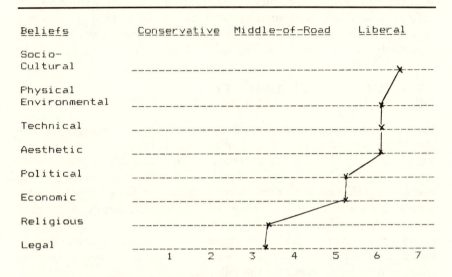

was on the reinvestment of profits in the hospital to reduce fees to patients or to improve benefits for the employees.

The administrator is people oriented and concerned with the welfare of his patients and employees. The hospital is service oriented for the community of Red River. The personal beliefs of the administrator and the objectives of the hospital blend very well. As evidence of this, his tenure as an administrator had exceeded that of the average hospital administrator, and his continued service as an administrator at the Red River City Hospital was envisioned for the future.

In summary, he ranked the objectives of the hospital in the following order of importance: quality of life for community, patient satisfaction, survival, image improvement, industry improvement, maintenance of market share, growth, profit, and leader in the field.

His personal philosophy meshes very well with Red River City Hospital's objectives and was largely responsible for the hospital's recent success. His liberal socio-cultural beliefs (6.2) support the hospital's goal of serving the community with good, low-cost medical service. His liberal technological beliefs (6.0) again support the hospital's objective of providing people-oriented, inexpensive, "low-tech" hospital care, leaving the "hi-tech," expensive services to other hospitals. His slightly liberal economic beliefs (5.2) — indicating he is economically pragmatic, but growth oriented — have probably been responsible for the hospital's recent growth and economic prosperity. His slightly conservative legal beliefs (3.3) — indicating adherence to the law — are probably a positive quality for a hospital administrator in view of the fact that the health industry is highly regulated.

All in all, his philosophical beliefs seem very conducive to successful management of a municipal hospital. Taking into account the administrator's beliefs and his desire to continue as administrator, the hospital's success and growth in the last few years, and the hospital's strong community support, it is probable that the hospital will prosper at least in the near future.

TYPES OF RELATED OBJECTIVES — ORGANIZATIONAL AND PERSONAL

Since non-profit organizations are the means of providing services for persons, there are two ways to classify objectives: (1) organizational objectives and (2) personal objectives of stakeholders who contribute resources to an organization. The NPO's organizational objectives are based on the concept that the organization is an entity separate and apart from the people who contribute resources to it in exchange for the resources that the entity provides for its contributors.

Organizational objectives are determined usually by the administrators but sometimes by the members of the non-profit organization. Some of the most common ones for an NPO are the following:

Mission: To produce and sell a service to satisfy clients.
Related Objectives:

1. Grow
2. Improve image
3. Maintain survival
4. Make a profit or at least break even
5. Maintain market share
6. Satisfy some of the needs of stakeholders, including
   a. Clients
   b. Community
   c. Creditors
   d. Government
   e. Donors (if they exist)
   f. Managers
   g. Employees
   h. Suppliers
   i. Society in general

It is important to note that each NPO has to decide what its actual organizational objectives *are* and what they *should be* and to decide the degree of emphasis to give to each one in relation to the others. And those decisions are usually influenced by the administrators' values or beliefs.

EVALUATION OF THE NPO'S ORGANIZATIONAL MISSION AND RELATED OBJECTIVES

Among the evaluations suggested in this book is one that evaluates how well the NPO is accomplishing its objectives. Some type of evaluation of the organizational mission and related objectives has to take place before strategies can be intelligently evaluated. The following discussion elaborates on how this evaluation may be accomplished.

Some type of descriptive evidence is needed to evaluate each NPO objective as to whether it has been or is being accomplished in a strong manner or a weak manner. An evaluation of an actual NPO should reveal some evidence of whether its objectives are being achieved. For example:

- If a church has as its mission the creation and marketing of its spiritual services to satisfy member needs, what type of evidence would suggest that the church is meeting this mission? Perhaps the best measure is the actual attendance at church services. How many loyal members does the church have? What percentage of members attend church services? The same questions could be raised about Sunday school services and other related services that the church provides. How many are repeat attenders?
- If a church has profit as an objective, various measures of profitability might be used, such as a profit return on total assets, profit return on church revenue, profits per employee, and profits per member.
- If growth is an objective, descriptive evidence might include percentages of member and revenue growth for the past five years, expressed in numbers of members or dollars of revenues (taking out inflation, if possible).
- If maintenance of market share is an objective, some statistical measure of market share would be appropriate evidence.
- If image is an objective, some type of image survey might be appropriate.
- If maintenance of survival is an objective, the best evidence would be the length of time that the church has been in operation.
- If improving the quality of life for society is an objective, some type of activity that demonstrates such would be appropriate evidence.
- If satisfying the needs of its resource contributors is an objective, then some evidence is needed to show how the church accomplishes this.

Once each objective is evaluated by descriptive evidence as being a strength or weakness, an overall evaluation may be made of the NPO's objectives, suggesting problem areas facing the NPO or strengths that the NPO may capitalize on. These areas would suggest strategies to be followed to either improve the accomplishment of weak objectives or maintain the accomplishment of strong objectives.

An Evaluation of an NPO's Mission and Related Objectives

The East Fork Baptist Church was concerned about the number of inactive members who had not participated in church activities. Consequently, the pastor requested that an evaluation be made of the church, the major one in a town of 1,600 residents. The following was the evaluation made by a management team of the church's mission and related objectives.

Evaluation of East Fork Baptist Church's Mission and Related Objectives

Mission	Importance	Descriptive Evidence	Evaluation
1. Producing church services to meet the needs of its members	xxx	462 members of whom 126 attended on the average; $87,000 total tithes and offerings during the year; members who participate are very much pleased with the church services (according to our survey) of pastor visitations, counseling, education, funerals, weddings, family programs, bus, music, and nursery; yet a sizeable majority does not participate in church activities.	Strength and Weakness

Related Objectives

Mission	Importance	Descriptive Evidence	Evaluation
2. Growing in size and operations	xx	Membership has grown from 219 ten years ago to 462 this year; value of property has increased from $45,000 to $595,000 in 10 years; total tithes and offerings have increased from $12,000 to $87,000 in 10 years.	Strength
3. Making a profit	x	A yearly profit is being made to cover operating expenses--just enough to break even, but not enough to repay long-term debt.	Strength and Weakness
4. Improving its image	x	A survey of participating members indicated an excellent image; image not known for non-participants.	Strength and Possible Weakness
5. Maintaining its share of the market	x	Total weekly average attendance of seven churches in East Fork is 410, of which the East Fork Baptist Church has 125, --30% of the market.	Strength

Mission	Importance	Descriptive Evidence	Evaluation
6. Maintaining its survival	x	Church has been in existence for 40 years, with several pastoral changes.	Strength
7. Improving the quality of life for society	xxx	The pastor asserts that the quality of life in East Fork has improved because of the church's opposition to alcohol, drugs, card playing, and gambling.	Strength?
8. Satisfying some of the needs of its			
a. Members	xxx	Participants are satisfied, non-participants are questionable.	Strength and Possible Weakness
b. Employees	xx	Volunteers are satisfied.	Strength
c. Management	xx	Pastor and church officers seem satisfied, but a high turnover of pastors exists.	Strength?
d. Suppliers	x	They are paid.	Strength
e. Creditors	x	Behind in their payments.	Weakness
f. Community	x	Community supports their efforts.	Strength
g. Government	x	No problems.	Strength
h. Society in general	x	Seems to be satisfactory.	Strength?

Overall Evaluation: The church's basic strengths in accomplishing its mission and related objectives are evident. However, there are some weaknesses, suggesting that some better strategies are needed in certain areas of member service and financial control.

Distinguishing Mission, Objectives, and Goals

A further refinement of organizational purposes is the concept of goals. Three words — mission, objectives, and goals — often are used interchangeably, but distinctions can be drawn among all three terms.

Dimensions	Mission	Objectives	Goals
1. Purpose and thrust	The fundamental reason for being; service-market match	Related to mission; open ended	Implementation of objectives
2. Time frame	Long term; usually not changed, but may be modified	Enduring; timeless; may be changed	Temporal; time-phased; intended to be superseded by subsequent goals

Dimensions	Mission	Objectives	Goals
3. Specificity	General; reflection of philosophy	Broad, deal with generalities	More specific; stated in terms of a particular result and time
4. Focus and scope	External; oriented to clients	External, related to outside resource suppliers; firm oriented	Internal; related to employees and managers; concerned with resource allocation
5. Measurement	General terms; may be stated in units/revenues	General; may be quantified, usually in relative terms	More specific; usually stated in absolute terms; quantified

The mission is usually a result of the executive's perception of a need and a possible service to fill that need. An objective is related to the mission in terms of profit, growth, image, service, and quality of life for the people whom the organization serves. Goals are used to implement the mission and related objectives.

SUMMARY

For the NPO you have selected to evaluate, please perform the following tasks:

    I. Write a brief history of your NPO.
   II. Describe the client needs to be satisfied and each of the related services to satisfy those needs.
     A. Describe the basic mission of the NPO.
       1. Get a copy of your mission.
     B. For each service/product, list
       1. Benefits
       2. Costs (labor, material, overhead)
       3. Values
     C. Determine whether the benefits are greater than the costs, or vice versa.
  III. Describe the mission and related objectives and their relative importance.
       1. Use the guidelines suggested.
       2. Interview your board members and team of managers.
       3. Compare answers.
       4. See Step VII for help.
  IV. Evaluate the accomplishment of your mission and related objectives.
       1. Use the guidelines suggested.
       2. Make sure of the accuracy of the descriptive evidence and the relative importance of the objectives.

V. Describe the feedback measures you use to sustain superior services.
  A. MBWA
  B. Toll-free telephone number
  C. Post card
  D. Others
VI. Describe the goals, objectives, and mission of your organization.
  A. Give examples of goals.
  B. Give examples of objectives.
VII. Fill in the blanks regarding the mission and related objectives and strategies.

Identification of Organizational Mission and Related Objectives and Purposes for _____

Which of the following do you perceive as your organizational mission, objectives, and purposes (not personal objectives)? (Yes/No/Don't Know) What relative importance do you attach to each (1 for very low importance to 7 for very high importance)?

	Yes/No/?	Importance (1–7)
A. Organizational Mission		
1. To produce goods/services with enhanced benefits	!--!--!--!	
2. At reduced costs	!--!--!--!	
3. To create value	!--!--!--!	
4. For client satisfaction and	!--!--!--!	
5. To break even in so doing	!--!--!--!	
B. Related General Objectives		
1. Growth		
To increase our size	!--!--!--!	
To maintain our size	!--!--!--!	
To reduce our size	!--!--!--!	
2. Profit		
To increase our profits	!--!--!--!	
To maintain our profits	!--!--!--!	
To reduce our profits	!--!--!--!	
To break even	!--!--!--!	
3. Share of Market		
To increase our market share	!--!--!--!	
To maintain our share	!--!--!--!	
To reduce our share	!--!--!--!	
4. Image		
To improve our image	!--!--!--!	
To maintain our image	!--!--!--!	
To change our image	!--!--!--!	
5. Leader in Our Field		
To be the leader	!--!--!--!	
To be one of the leaders	!--!--!--!	
To maintain our leadership	!--!--!--!	
To cut back our leadership position	!--!--!--!	
6. Survival		
To survive	!--!--!--!	
To die	!--!--!--!	

	Yes/No/?	Importance (1-7)

7. Our "Industry's" Position
        To improve its position
        To maintain its position
        To reduce its position
8. Quality of Life for Society
        To improve the QOL
        To maintain the QOL
        To reduce the QOL
9. Other Related Objectives
        (Please Identify)

C. Our Overall Purpose (Reason for Being):
    To Satisfy Some of the Needs of
    Resource Providers
        1.   Clients
        2.   Employees
        3.   Donors
        4.   Suppliers
        5.   Long-Term Creditors
        6.   Management
        7.   Community
        8.   Government
        9.   Competitors
        10. Society in General

Comments:

D. Please rank the following as to their relative importance.
        1.   Mission   No. 1 _____
        2.   Profit   2 _____
        3.   Growth   3 _____
        4.   Image   4 _____
        5.   Leader in Field   5 _____
        6.   Survival   6 _____
        7.   Industry's Position   7 _____
        8.   Quality of Life   8 _____

E. Please rank the following as to their relative importance.
        1.   Clients   No. 1 _____
        2.   Donors   2 _____
        3.   Employees   3 _____
        4.   Suppliers   4 _____
        5.   Management   5 _____
        6.   Creditors   6 _____
        7.   Government   7 _____
        8.   Community   8 _____
        9.   Competitors   9 _____
        10. Society   10 _____

Comment:

Name

Title

Organization

Strategies to Accomplish the Organizational Mission

I. Strategy direction for the organization: Which strategic direction do you perceive the organization to be pursuing?
   __A. To improve its position   (Build)   (Move ahead)
   __B. To maintain its position   (Hold)   (Stay the same)
   __C. To reduce its position   (Harvest)   (Cut back)
   __D. Other? _____
   Comment:

II. Describe the service-market mix pursued to accomplish the mission. Put each service that the NPO offers in the proper square.

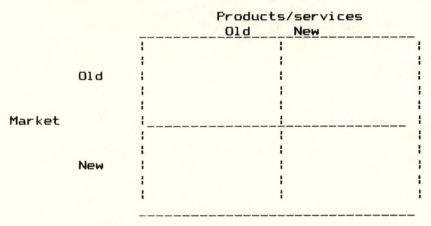

III. Strategies to create value: Which value strategies do you perceive the organization to be pursuing?
   A. Market focus strategy
      __ 1. Segmenting a specific target market
            (Market segmentation/niching)
      __ 2. Hitting that specific target market hard
            (Market concentration)
      __ 3. Pushing for no specific target market
            (Mass marketing)
   B. Enhancing the product/service by
      __ 1. Product innovation (Making new products/services)
      __ 2. Product differentiation (Making our products/services different
            from those of competitors)
      __ 3. Improving product quality
            (Adding product value)
   C. Reducing the costs of the product/service
      1. Production/operations costs
          __ a. Labor
          __ b. Material
          __ c. Capital
          __ d. Other

      2. Marketing costs
        __ a. Labor
        __ b. Material
        __ c. Capital
        __ d. Other
     __ 3. Personnel costs
     __ 4. Financial costs
     __ 5. Managerial costs
     __ 6. Other costs
IV. Do the strategies create value?
    A. For the clients?   Yes ____   No ____   Don't Know ____
    B. For the organization? Yes ____   No ____   Don't Know ____
 V. Do the strategies create a competitive advantage?
    A. Describe or give an example of the competitive advantages.

6

Administrator Appraisal of the NPO's External Environment

The fundamental mission and related objectives of a non-profit organization, usually determined by the top administrators, are accomplished by various strategies. What helps administrators formulate these strategies? One answer is an appraisal of those external and internal environmental factors that influence strategy formulation.

STRATEGY FORMULATION AND THE NPO'S EXTERNAL ENVIRONMENT

An NPO's immediate external environment consists of those people who contribute various resources to help achieve the NPO's organizational mission and related objectives. These people consist of the NPO's clients/customers, employees, suppliers, creditors, donors, government, community, and society at large. For example, the clients usually provide the revenues from which the NPO operates. The employees provide their talents, time, and loyalty. The suppliers provide the raw materials and equipment to produce the NPO's product/service. The creditors lend money to the NPO. The donors contribute the financial capital to start and underwrite the operation of the organization. Governmental units provide protection for the NPO. The community provides the physical environmental resources. Society at large gives the NPO the right to conduct its operations. In return for the provision of these resources, the NPO has the obligation to help satisfy some of the needs of these resource contributors.

The interface between the NPO and its immediate resource contributors establishes the external relationships that help to dictate NPO strategies. For example, if the donors do not donate enough money to the NPO, then obviously the NPO cannot grow and has to make do with what it has. If there are not enough voluntary employees, then some types of strategies have to be formulated to get them. If the community does not provide support for the NPO, then the NPO has to reconsider its primary mission and related objectives.

Beyond the immediate interface of its resource contributors is another external environment that dictates the NPO's strategies. This external environment is one over which the NPO has very little control. It consists of factors, forces, and events that influence the NPO positively, negatively, or sometimes not at all. The external environment may act as a threat, or it may act as an opportunity for the NPO. Enlightened administrators should make an appraisal, based on their perceptions, of the factors, forces, and events that either favor or do not favor the NPO. Some type of crude scanning of the external environment and an ensuing evaluation of these factors become necessary if a strategic decision is being formulated.

EXTERNAL ENVIRONMENTAL FACTORS AFFECTING STRATEGIES

Economic Environmental Factors

The major economic external environmental factors that influence an NPO's strategy are (1) the demand for the NPO's services, (2) the supply of resources available to produce the services, (3) the nature of the competition facing the NPO, and (4) the state of the economy.

The demand for the NPO's services is influenced by several factors: for example, the price of the services; the characteristics of the services; the characteristics of the target market; the promotion of the services; the availability of the services with regard to the right quantities, at the right place, at the right time, and with the right complements; the right personnel to sell the services; the proper financial arrangements to sell the services; and the product/service life cycle.

There are other determinants of demand. The price of the NPO's services is one. The price of substitute goods or services is another. Further, there is the price of complementary services. For example, the price of attending a collegiate football game is determined in part by the teams playing the game, the price of substitute entertainment, and the price of travel, lodging, food, and other complementary services related to getting to and from the game.

Another variable is the purchasing power of the clients, usually measured by per capita income or the income of the person purchasing the services. Obviously, the number of clients who purchase the services or potential clients who may purchase the services is another variable.

The tastes and preferences of the target market comprise another variable. Such factors as the nature of the services, who sells them, the advertising, the place, and the credit terms are all variables to be considered. In addition, the expectations of the clients affect demand. For example, if the clients expect a supply shortage or a price increase, they may purchase now rather than later.

If the demand for the NPO's services can be measured in units or dollars, and if the preceding demand factors can be quantified, then fairly sophisticated demand forecasts can be made. Furthermore, if the demand can be predicted, then other functional strategies of the NPO (operations, personnel, and finance) can be formulated and integrated into these functional areas.

The availability of resources to produce the services is another external economic factor that influences an NPO's strategies. The fact that raw materials, supplies, labor, money, land, management, and other resources that may be in short supply helps to determine strategies. The lack of any one of the fundamental resources may prevent an NPO from implementing a strategy. Usually, the availability of resources serves as a restraining factor in strategy formulation, integration, and implementation.

The competitive situation facing an NPO also influences its strategies. Competition for resources *and* for clients plays a key role in strategy formulation. An NPO in a monopoly situation (one seller) can use strategies not available to NPOs in a highly competitive situation or in an oligopoly situation (a few sellers). In addition, indirect competition in the form of substitute goods and services influences various strategies (notably price and promotion). An NPO facing a monopsony situation (one buyer) or an oligopsony situation (a few buyers) may have difficulty achieving its survival objective.

The state of the economy also influences strategy formulation. Usually, an NPO is affected positively or negatively by depressions, recessions, inflation, wartime, and peacetime. Each NPO is affected differently by the state of the economy. Among the quantitative tools by which the state of the economy is measured are the gross national product, consumer price index, industrial production index, and unemployment rate. These quantitative measures can be correlated to other demand and supply variables to estimate the growth or decline of the NPO's industry. They can also be used to estimate the NPO's revenues, from which cost estimates can be derived, using financial ratio analyses.

Other external economic variables may have an influence on an NPO and its industry. Successful strategy formulators have to perceive them for their NPO because each NPO faces unique external environmental threats and opportunities. Different variables create situations that differ for each NPO, thus forcing NPO administrators to scan the economic environment for the situational variables unique to them.

An external environmental matrix may be used to help make a strategic decision. Figure 6.1 is suggested as a guide for making such a matrix of external economic environment factors.

Socio-Cultural Environmental Factors

The socio-cultural environment plays a dominant role in client relations for most NPOs. The major social variables are population and its related demographics. Such factors as population growth/decline, age, sex, marital

Figure 6.1
Suggested Guide for Managerial Appraisal of External Economic Factors

---

                                          Strategic Decision
                                          Alternatives_____
                                          Favorable/Unfavorable/Not Sure
                                                    OR
    External Economic Factors   -------> Opportunity/Threat/Not Sure
    Affecting a Strategic Decision
                                                    OR
                                          Strength/Weakness/Not Sure

---

A. Demand For The NPO Services
    1. Price
        a. of the NPO's services
        b. of substitute services
        c. of complementary services
    2. Nature of target market
        a. number of actual clients
        b. number of potential clients
        c. income per actual client
        d. income per capita of potential clients
        e. increasing/decreasing/same/of
            clients/income/over time
    3. Taste and preferences of clients
        regarding the NPO services
        a. availability as to
            1) right place
            2) right time
            3) right quantities
            4) complements
        b. promotion/publicity/advertising
        c. personnel to sell services
        d. credit/cash terms
    4. Characteristics of services
        a. stage in life cycle
        b. seasonality
        c. other characteristics
    5. Expectations of clients
    6. Other factors

B. Availability of resources to produce the service
    1. Labor
    2. Capital
    3. Land
    4. Management
    5. Raw Materials
    6. Supplies
    7. Other resources

C. Competitive situation facing the NPO
    for clients and resources
    1. Monopoly
    2. Oligopoly
    3. Highly competitive
    4. Indirect competition with substitutes
    5. Monopsony
    6. Oligopsony
    7. Others

D. State of the economy
    1. Depression
    2. Recession
    3. Good times
    4. Peace time   Measured by GNP, Price
    5. War time   Index, Unemployment
    6. Inflation   Rates, other measures
    7. Interest rates
    8. Others

E. Other external economic factors

    Overall Evaluation and Possible Prescription:
    (Summarize your appraisal and reach a tentative strategic
    decision, based on economic factors)

status, job, and income level affect the types of clients and employees of the NPO and the community in which it operates.

Other social variables include the education level of society and the urbanization of society, along with crime levels, minority group statistics, and other societal variables with which many NPOs eventually are concerned.

Cultural factors are concerned with cultural trends affecting life styles of people and their mores, taboos, prejudices, attitudes, interests, and opinions. These are external environmental factors over which the NPO has very little control.

Political-Legal Environmental Factors

Various laws that are passed directly affect the affairs of most NPOs. The political party in power also affects the strategies of an NPO, whether positively, negatively, or sometimes not at all. For example, when there is a switch in political power, many governmental NPOs are directly affected as far as their financial support is concerned.

Other External Environmental Factors

The technological environment affects an NPO's production processes and its equipment. The introduction of computers, for example, affects the information system of an NPO.

The physical environment sometimes affects an NPO's strategies. Such factors as climate, terrain, and geography might affect location, types of services, and other strategies.

The aesthetic or beauty environment may affect strategies, depending on the nature of the NPO.

All of the external environmental factors that are beyond the control of the administrators of NPOs pose either a threat or an opportunity, are either favorable or unfavorable, or are a strength or a weakness for the NPO. The scanning of the environment by the chief administrators is a constant task, suggesting some type of management information system which they may rely on to analyze those factors affecting an NPO's survival, market share, image, and ability to serve its clientele with its services. If an NPO does not have its own scanning system, perhaps it might rely on other organizations that perform these scanning services.

Figure 6.2 is a guide to evaluating the non-economic external environmental factors of an NPO. It should be used as a supplement to the economic factor analysis suggested earlier.

Once the economic and non-economic external environmental appraisals have been made, administrators may wish to describe the total external environment by using the following descriptors.

External Environment Facing _____Name_____

Certain						Uncertain
-----	-----	-----	-----	-----	-----	-----

Friendly						Hostile
-----	-----	-----	-----	-----	-----	-----

Stable						Changing
-----	-----	-----	-----	-----	-----	-----

Predictable						Unpredictable
-----	-----	-----	-----	-----	-----	-----

Not Risky						Risky
-----	-----	-----	-----	-----	-----	-----

Uni-faceted						Multi-facted
-----	-----	-----	-----	-----	-----	-----

Restrictive						Non-restrictive
-----	-----	-----	-----	-----	-----	-----

Not stressful						Stressful
-----	-----	-----	-----	-----	-----	-----

Smooth						Volatile
-----	-----	-----	-----	-----	-----	-----

And A Final Conclusion

Favorable						Unfavorable
-----	-----	-----	-----	-----	-----	-----

Such an analysis of the external environment might prove helpful when a strategy is implemented in designing the organization culture, fostering the appropriate leadership style, and making other decisions where the external environment plays a significant role.

LIMITING FACTORS AND THE PHILOSOPHY OF THE ADMINISTRATORS

When making an appraisal of the external environment, several factors may be identified which may have different importance or weights attached to them. When the factor weights are not known (which is usually the case), the administrators' experience and/or philosophy usually determines the importance of those key factors that limit the accomplishment of an organizational objective.

If the administrators are very conservative, the key factors, according to their conservative beliefs, are the ones that serve as restraints to making the strategy work. On the other hand, if the administrators are very liberal in

Figure 6.2
Suggested Guide for Managerial Appraisal of External Non-economic Factors

```
                                            Strategic Decision
                                            Alternatives_____
                                            Favorable/Unfavorable
                                                  OR
External Non-Economic Factors   ------->    Opportunity/Threat
    Affecting a Strategic Decision
                                                  OR
                                            Strength/Weakness
--------------------------------------------------------------------
A.  Socio-cultural factors
    1.  Population and demographics
        of population
    2.  Socio-cultural factors
        a.  education
        b.  urbanization
        c.  crime
        d.  housing
        e.  minorities
        f.  others
    3.  Life-style trends
    4.  Mores, prejudices, attitudes
    5.  Others

B.  Politico-legal factors
    1.  Various laws
    2.  Political party in power
    3.  Rules and regulations
    4.  Others

C.  Physical environmental factors
    1.  Climate
    2.  Terrain
    3.  Geography
    4.  Others

D.  Technological factors
    1.  Innovations
    2.  Others

E.  Ethico-religious factors

F.  Aesthetic factors

G.  Other external environmental factors

Overall Evaluation:
(Summarize your appraisal and reach a tentative strategic
decision, based on the non-economic factors)
```

their beliefs, they usually do not have much concern for limiting factors. Administrators with a middle-of-the-road philosophy may want to find a way to get around the limiting factors or to live with the limiting factors. If the administrators (1) cannot live with the limiting factors or (2) cannot get around the limiting factors, then the chances for success are limited by those factors.

Most NPOs have factors that limit their effectiveness and efficiency in accomplishing their organizational mission and related objectives. Murphy's

Law (Anything that can go wrong, will!) suggests that when there are limiting factors, an NPO administrator will do well to recognize them and act accordingly.

In addition to the external environmental factors and the philosophies of the administrators, a strategy formulation is also affected by the special environmental factors of an NPO.

SPECIAL ENVIRONMENTAL APPRAISALS

The NPO's "Industry" and Its Competition

Since an NPO's "industry" may be subject to special factors that other industries may not be, and since an individual NPO usually is a part of an industry that may affect its future, a special appraisal of factors in the NPO's industry may be desirable. The term *industry* implies a number of organizations producing similar products. Since most NPOs are producing services as opposed to products, perhaps the term *industry* is not appropriate. The word *institution* might be used since most NPOs are members of an institution which might be defined as a group of organizations producing similar services. However, both the terms *industry* and *institution* will be used in this discussion.

Industry appraisal has been recognized by various authorities as a special determinant of strategy. Consequently, an industry appraisal seems appropriate in addition to a general external environmental appraisal of the threats and opportunities, strengths and weaknesses, or favorable and unfavorable factors affecting a strategic decision, particularly those involving market share, growth, and survival.

Most NPOs belong to an institutional association, usually national in scope. This association usually comprises the industry or national market of an NPO. A practical definition of an institutional industry is a group of NPOs producing products/services that are similar in nature and that are used to satisfy a common demand (having similar product-market matches). Usually the product-market matches of one NPO are substituted for those of every other NPO in the group; that is, the products/services of one NPO can be purchased by the people in the same market as a substitute for the products/services of a similar NPO. The usual strategy followed by an NPO is to differentiate its products/services from those of other NPOs in the same industry to create either actual or perceived differences in the minds of the people who comprise the market. For example, the church industry is composed of thousands of churches, each of which tries to differentiate its doctrines from other doctrines.

The definition of an NPO's market is extremely important for an NPO that has an objective of maintaining its market share and that has to formulate a strategy to accomplish this objective. Share of the market refers to the share (expressed in percentage terms) of overall industry revenues received by the NPO. Therefore, it is wise to make an appraisal of industry characteristics to determine those factors that allow an NPO to be successful in maintaining its market share or perhaps increasing its market share. The latter is a growth strategy, whereas the former is a maintenance of market share strategy.

"Industry" Appraisal or "Institutional" Appraisal

Industry attractiveness is what is being analyzed — that is, whether the industry has a high, medium, or low attractiveness. For example, a college is a part of the higher education industry. A local church is a part of the religion industry. Do these industries have a high attractiveness, or do they have a medium attractiveness? By attractiveness we mean the capability of attracting increased revenues, employees, and other resources so necessary to accomplish the NPO's mission. If the industry attractiveness is low, for example, it would be fairly difficult for an NPO to grow, unless, of course, it had a distinctive niche in that industry. The attractiveness variable is a key one in determining the direction of the organization — that is, whether to grow, to maintain its position, or to cut back.

An industry appraisal is composed of several factors.

1. The size of the market is a key factor in determining the growth potential for an NPO. Lack of a sizeable market would restrict opportunities for an NPO that desires to grow. If the size is large, this would suggest a highly attractive industry; if low, this would suggest a low attractiveness.

2. Market growth rate is important. If the market is growing, this would suggest a high attractiveness. Low market growth rate would suggest a low attractiveness.

3. Excess capacity in the industry would not be attractive.

4. Further, the fact that the industry produces commodity- or near-commodity-type products or services would make it unattractive.

5. A high degree of cyclicality in the market would also be an unattractive factor.

6. The stage of the industry's life cycle is a crucial factor for an institutional appraisal — that is, whether the institution is in the development stage, the growth stage, the mature stage, and/or the decline stage. The growth stage would suggest attractiveness, while the decline stage would suggest less attractiveness.

7. The pricing practices of the industry are important to an NPO. For example, profit margin becomes a key factor. If a price is sufficiently high to offset the production costs and break even, an NPO might enter the market. If the price is not high enough, then an NPO might leave the market.

8. The diversity of services of NPOs in the industry becomes a key factor in an institutional appraisal. The number of NPOs, services offered, size, institutional leaders, geographic location, and other characteristics of the NPOs are factors that have to be known. High diversity is attractive.

9. The competitive structure of the institutions is important. Are there many competitive NPOs in the industry? Or does oligopolistic competition exist? Is the

industry subject to indirect competition in the form of substitute goods and services? Too many diverse competitors in the industry make it very difficult to break even. Too much indirect competition also makes it very difficult to break even. Price competitiveness is very difficult to overcome. Ease of entry into the market is a key factor for an NPO considering entry into a market or for an NPO already in the market.

10. Institutional profitability is another key factor in an institutional appraisal. Why enter or stay in a market in which break-even is marginal?

11. The technology employed is another factor. Whether an NPO has the necessary technology would be a key in deciding whether to enter, to hold its position, or to divest. The possibility of technological change would be another factor.

12. Inflation vulnerability is another factor to be considered, along with other economic factors, such as whether the institution is recessionproof, depressionproof, or wartimeproof.

13. Threats of entry into the industry are considered unattractive because of increased competition. High capital requirements to enter and high "*switching*" *costs* for clients are considered highly attractive.

14. The ease with which suppliers can increase prices and clients can reduce prices would make an industry unattractive.

15. Then there is the power of the government. Government subsidies for organizations are considered attractive. However, a high number of regulations and very rigorous licensing would have low attractiveness.

16. High power among labor unions is considered unattractive.

17. High exit barriers also suggest unattractiveness.

18. Socio-cultural factors, such as demographics, life styles, education, housing, urbanization, and others, should be considered because they affect the demand for the institutional services. Any such factor that is changing would be considered unattractive.

19. Physical environmental factors, such as air, water, land, noise, and solid waste pollution, have to be considered in an institutional appraisal. These factors increase costs, affect the NPO's image, and determine the NPO's social responsibility.

Other institutional factors that affect an NPO's success in reaching its objectives might also be considered.

An NPO that is considering whether to stay in an industry, divest itself from an industry, or build its position should consider the preceding factors. They may be used as a guide for determining the attractiveness of an industry. See Figure 6.3.

A College Football Example

As an example, industry attractiveness can be evaluated in conjunction with a decision as to whether the University of Arkansas Razorback football team should stay in the Southwest Conference composed of nine collegiate teams

Figure 6.3
Analysis of Industry Attractiveness (From the View of an Established NPO)

Industry Factors ----->	Industry Attractiveness High	Medium	Low
1. Market Factors			
a. Size of market			
Large	x		
Small			x
b. Market growth			
Fast	x		
Slow			x
c. Life cycle of market			
Growth	x		
Maturity		x	
Decline			x
d. Excess capacity exists in this industry to serve the market			x
e. Industry consists of commodity/ near commodity products/services			x
f. Cyclicality of the market			
High			x
Low	x		
g. Diversity of the market exists			
High	x		
Low			x
2. Competition Factors			
a. Numerous/equally balanced competitors			x
b. Several diverse competitors			x
c. Dominant competitor exists			x
3. Threats of New Entrants into Market			
High			x
Low	x		
a. Capital requirements to enter			
High	x		
Low			x
b. "Switching" costs of clients			
High	x		
Low			x
4. Power of Suppliers to Increase Prices			
High			x
Low	x		
5. Power of Clients to Reduce Prices			
High			x
Low	x		
6. Power of Government			
a. Subsidies available			
High	x		
Low			x
b. Number of regulations			
High			x
Low	x		
c. Government financing available			
High	x		
Low			x
d. Licensing			
High			x
Low	x		

Figure 6.3 (continued)

Industry Factors ----->	Industry Attractiveness		
	High	Medium	Low
7. Power of Labor Unions			
High			x
Low	x		
8. Exit Barriers			
High			x
Low	x		
9. Substitute Products Available			
Many			x
Few	x		
10. Economic Vulnerability as to Inflation, Wartime, Recessions, Depressions			
High			x
Low	x		
11. Changes in Socio-Cultural Environment			
High			x
Low	x		
12. Changes in Technology Employed			
High			x
Low	x		
13. Changes in the Physical Environment			
High			x
Low	x		
14. Other Factors			

Overall Evaluation: (Reach a conclusion as whether the NPO's "industry" is attractive, unattractive, or moderately attractive.)

(eight in Texas and one in Arkansas) or whether it should consider joining the Big Eight. See Figure 6.4.

COMPETITIVE ENVIRONMENTAL APPRAISAL

The structure of competition from the seller's point of view is a key factor in making an appraisal of the NPO's competition. Generally, there are four degrees of competition: (1) highly directly competitive, with a great number of sellers in the industry; (2) directly competitive, but with a few sellers in the market, sometimes called oligopolistic competition; (3) no direct competition, with one seller in the market, called monopolistic competition; and (4) indirect competition in the form of substitute goods or services which may have severe to moderate effects on the NPO.

Where NPOs face a high degree of direct competition with a large number

Figure 6.4
Industry Appraisal for a College Football Team

Razorback Football Team
and its
"Industry" Factors Affecting ---> SWC "Industry" Attractiveness

	Low	Medium	High

1. Size of Market
    Size of fan attendance for
    about half of teams in the
    SWC is large. The other
    half is very marginal at best.
    Razorback fan attendance is
    consistently large compared
    to other college teams. The
    size of the total market could
    be larger.   x (Medium)

2. Market Growth
    Razorback fan attendance has sold
    out the stadia for several seasons--
    no more room for growth. About
    half of the other teams have
    reached stadium capacity. The
    other half has very little growth.
    Overall, the SWC has reached
    maturity in fan attendance, with
    some small growth occasionally
    and some yearly declines.   x (Medium)

3. Pricing Practices
    Prices for SWC football tickets are
    not competitive with other confer-
    ences, usually one to two dollars
    less than other major football
    conferences. Some pressure exists
    to raise ticket prices.   x (Medium)

4. Diversity of Market
    All competing teams are located in
    Texas, with the exception of the
    Arkansas Razorbacks. The state-
    supported teams in Texas draw very
    well, but privately-owned schools
    do not. In addition, there are
    several other football conferences
    in Texas. (Big Eight schools have a
    wider diversity covering a wider
    geographic area.)   x (Medium)

5. Competitive Structure
    The SWC is in essence an oligopoly
    of nine teams. The eight teams in
    Texas are highly competitive.
    However, ease of entry into the SWC
    is very difficult for other teams.   x ------> x (Low to High)

Figure 6.4 (continued)

	Low	Medium	High

6. Industry Profitability
   About half of the teams make a profit
   on football. The other half are
   marginal at best. Football profits
   serve as a cash generator for the
   subsidization of non-revenue sports.   x

7. Technology Employed
   The teams in the SWC employ the latest
   technology in college football, keeping
   up with teams of national caliber.   x

8. Inflation Vulnerability and Other
   Economic Factors
   Inflation plays a negative role in
   college football, affecting all colleges
   with increased costs and expenses. However, college football seems to be re-
   cession-proof. It probably would be
   affected negatively by a depression and/or
   wartime.   x

9. Socio-Cultural Changes
   Football fans are notoriously loyal, conservative, middle to upper class, from
   both agricultural and commercial backgrounds. No socio-cultural changes are
   evident.   x

10. Physical Environment
    Pollution is not deemed a problem. The
    SWC stadia are kept up well. No problems
    seem to exist with the physical environ-
    ment, except perhaps parking.   x

11. Legal Restrictions
    The SWC abides by all rules and
    regulations of the NCAA.   x

12. The power of government, and the
    power of suppliers, the power of
    labor unions, and the power of
    fans are not significant for
    collegiate football.

13. It would be difficult to exit
    from the SWC although it could
    be done.

14. Other factors.

	Low	Medium	High
Total	0	7	5

Overall Evaluation: The industry attractiveness of the SWC
football teams is medium to high.

of sellers, usually in fragmented industries (as opposed to concentrated industries), they have characteristics different from those of NPOs facing other forms of competition. They usually have a very small share of a national market. Why? Because the nature of their products/services prevents any concentration of a large share of a national market. For example, NPOs that sell such services as symphonies, football, or education find it difficult to concentrate a large market share in one place. These services cannot be stored. In addition, NPOs that have tailor-made products/services (as opposed to standardized products/services) usually cannot take advantage of economies of scale, and they remain relatively small in terms of a national market share. Personal service firms usually have a very small national market share, although they may command a large share of a local market. Specialty services have a small market which makes national concentrations difficult to accomplish.

Those NPOs that are numerous, highly fragmented, and relatively small make for fierce competition. Usually that means low prices with resulting low profit margins for established NPOs. The relative ease of entry is a negative factor in terms of a competitive appraisal. Price cutting and marginal profitability are also negative factors.

Oligopolies, on the other hand, have distinct differences. They are fairly easy to monitor in terms of competitive actions because they are so few in number. Oligopolies are usually capital intensive which makes entry into the market fairly difficult. When entry is difficult, competition is eased which makes for higher prices and resulting higher chances of breaking even.

Monopolies have the best of competitive worlds. Usually they do not have to worry about direct competition — they are given specific market territories with no competitors. Prices are usually set high enough to make a profit, and easy entry is normally not allowed. It is common to see NPO monopolies in local markets — for example, public schools, public hospitals, and governmental units.

What can an individual NPO in a competitive industry do about competition? The generally accepted strategy is to try to get a competitive edge over competitors and to push this competitive edge to either maintain or increase its market share. It would seem that a competitive advantage would offer a good general strategy for accomplishing the mission and related objectives of growth, survival, market share, image, and others.

Competitive advantage involves choosing those competitive factors by which "victories" over competitors are clearly achievable. Competitive advantage works well when resources are committed to those factors that are (1) sheltered from the changes in the external environment and (2) protected from competition. The strategy of competitive advantage was originally based on achieving high levels of internal operating efficiency — for example, by obtaining a cost advantage for the NPO's product/service — but it has become generally accepted that a competitive advantage could also be obtained by becoming more competitive in the marketplace. Competitive position, usually expressed in terms of market share, can frequently overwhelm internal operating efficiencies. Moreover, a strong competitive position makes relative success highly likely even if internal operating performance suffers in comparison with competition, but a weak competitive position and a weak internal operating position probably guarantee a lack of success.

What factors contribute to a competitive advantage? Generally, they are the marketing factors. A number of different factors may be used, both external and internal.

1. Competitive advantage can be accomplished by establishing services in areas that can be sheltered from the unknown consequences of environmental change and that can be protected within that area for some length of time.

2. A strategy that might be used to protect the competitive position of an NPO would involve a fully protected patent position. A 17-year advantage offers a great deal of competitive advantage.

3. Another protective strategy employs barriers of various kinds — for example, licensing agreements stressing a monopoly position and making market entry very difficult, public financing through a regulatory agency, and the like.

4. Early market entry by aggressive initiative and/or competitor inaction provides an extended period of time in which to achieve brand identification and client loyalty, together with a good distribution network. This early entry allows an NPO to achieve economies of scale in both operations and marketing.

5. The service leader that differentiates products/services in a certain class range or size range can also achieve a protected position. Of course, other competitors will do the same, but a temporary absence of service differentiation will help to protect an NPO's market share and client loyalty.

6. Pricing can be another factor for getting a competitive edge, particularly if the NPO also has a low-cost advantage. Non-profit hospitals usually have lower prices than do for-profit hospitals because they pay no taxes.

7. A low cost structure may result from economies of scale, experience, volume, the use of volunteer labor, the change from a process layout to a product layout, and other production strategies. A credit union's costs are usually lower than a bank's costs.

8. Channels of distribution might be another competitive factor that could give an NPO a competitive advantage. In addition, the actual locations from which the services are sold could provide a competitive advantage.

9. The use of an aggressive promotion strategy might be used to gain a competitive edge. Further, the use of creative sales personnel, coupled with support and service personnel, might be the competitive factor needed to gain competitive advantage.

10. Wise use of *credit*, rather than cash, is a financial strategy that might also be used to gain a competitive advantage.

11. Probably one of the major factors is concentration on a particular *market segment* rather than spreading one's self too thin in all markets.

Figure 6.5
Factors Involved in a Competitive Appraisal

```
Competitive Factors                            Competitive Position
                                               Of A NPO_____

                                               Weak   Average  Strong
------------------------------------------------
A.  External Factors
    1.  Market structure
        a.  High degree of direct
            competition
        b.  Oligopolistic
        c.  Monopolistic
        d.  Indirect competition with
            substitutes
    2.  Barriers (regulatory agency
        approval, special licensing,
        making ease of entry very
        difficult)
    3.  Patents

B.  Internal Factors
    1.  Product/service innovations
    2.  Product leader through
        differentiation
    3.  Pricing
    4.  Cost structure of production
    5.  Channels of distribution
    6.  Location
    7.  Promotion
    8.  Sales personnel
    9.  Credit/cash
   10.  Market segmentation
   11.  Others

Overall Competitive Appraisal of the NPO with Possible
Prescriptions:
```

What spells the difference between success and failure? The answer usually involves (1) an appraisal of the industry factors, (2) an appraisal of competitors' strengths and weaknesses, (3) an appraisal of the NPO's strengths and weaknesses, (4) a determination of who has a competitive advantage in which factors, (5) a determination of strategies to use to take advantage of competitive strengths and/or to overcome weaknesses (taking advantage of strengths is preferred), (6) integration of the strategy into operative functions, and (7) implementation of the strategy.

Guidelines for making an appraisal of the competitive position of an NPO are presented in Figure 6.5.

An example of the Razorbacks' competitive position is shown in Figure 6.6.

COMBINING THE INDUSTRY AND COMPETITIVE APPRAISALS

An NPO may develop multiple situations to compare the competitive and industry positions of its different services. These situations may be useful in

Figure 6.6
Razorback Competitive Appraisal

	Razorbacks Competitive Position in SWC Football		
Competitive Factors ---------------->	Low (Weak)	Medium ____	High (Strong)
A. External Factors			
1. The Razorbacks operate in a virtual monopoly position in the State of Arkansas. Other small colleges do compete, not to any great extent. However, competition is fierce in surrounding states for football players.	x		x <---> x
2. Razorback football does compete with other forms of entertainment. However, most of its home games are "sellouts" and have been for several years.		x	x
3. The SWC ruling body makes it very difficult for other teams to enter the market.			x
4. The make-up of the SWC consists of 8 Texas teams and 1 Arkansas team. The domination of Texas teams in the SWC does irritate the Razorbacks, especially on umpiring prejudices and travel to Texas.	x		
5. Patents are not applicable			
B. Internal Factors			
1. The Razorbacks are not known as innovators.	x		
2. The Razorbacks are traditional leaders in football in the SWC. However, Texas and Texas AM are the dominant leaders.		x	
3. There is a differentiating factor in football for the Razorbacks--strong fan loyalty and support.			x
4. Pricing for tickets does not offer the Razorbacks a competitive edge. Most SWC school prices for tickets are about the same.		x	
5. The Razorbacks do not have a cost advantage. In fact, higher travel costs to play Texas teams are a disadvantage. If the Razorbacks played in the Big Eight conference, travel costs would be relatively even for other Big Eight teams. At present, travel costs for Texas-based teams give them an advantage.	x		
6. Channels of distribution for tickets are direct to fans for all schools.		x	
7. Location of Razorback football is a distinct disadvantage compared to other schools. If the Razorbacks switched to the Big Eight, location would be an advantage.	x		
8. Promotion and free publicity are available to the Razorbacks. Other schools have the same.		x	

Figure 6.6 (continued)

```
Competitive Factors        ---------------->     Low    Medium   High
                                                 (Weak)  ____    (Strong)
------------------------------------------------
     9.  Sales personnel are not required to sell
         tickets since most home games are "sell-
         outs."  However, other SWC schools have
         difficulty in getting "sellouts."                            x
    10.  All tickets are sold for cash, the same
         for other SWC schools                            x
    11.  The market for tickets is the whole State
         of Arkansas, whereas the State of Texas
         has to split its market among 8 other SWC
         teams.                                                       x
    12.  It has been a tradition to play SWC teams.
         It would be fairly difficult to get out of
         the SWC and to get into the Big Eight,
         although the possibility does exist.      x
                                        Total      6       7          6

Overall Competitive Appraisal:

         The Razorbacks have a medium or average competitive
         position within the SWC.  There are several strong
         factors but also some weak and average factors.
```

deciding whether to invest, hold, divest, or build various service units under its control.

An NPO may use the preceding two appraisals (industry and competitive) to determine nine strategic situations. For example, the analysis in Figure 6.7 describes these strategic situations, suggests directions, and prescribes some strategic moves, based on the NPO's industry appraisal and its competitive appraisal.

In Figure 6.7, F, H, and I would suggest a growth direction or a move ahead. C, E, and G would suggest a maintenance direction. And A, B, and D would suggest a cutback direction. The value of this analysis is that it suggests the strategic direction of an NPO based on the industry's attractiveness and the NPO's competitive position.

Not only does such an analysis suggest various strategies for an NPO to use for its own services, but also it might be used to plot the NPO's competitors' positions. Gathering the data to make such an analysis might be a valuable contribution to an NPO that has been complacent about its competitors. The basic drawback is the qualitative data, usually assessed by various managers. Further, once a decision is made — for example, to divest a service — it becomes difficult to actually implement that decision.

If we were to analyze the industry attractiveness of the Southwestern Conference as "average" and the competitive position of the Razorbacks as "medium," we would suggest their basic strategy would be to "proceed with care." A wait-and-see strategy about joining the Big Eight or leaving the SWC would probably be the more appropriate, based on the analysis.

Figure 6.7
Combining the Industry and Competitive Appraisals

	Strategic Situation	Suggested Direction To Be Pursued	Prescribed Strategic Moves
A.	Low industry attractiveness and weak competitive position	Cut back	Disinvest; time your exit; minimize your losses; get out while you can
B.	Average industry attractiveness and weak competitive position	Cut back	Consider exiting; perhaps a phased withdrawal; maybe specialize; seek niches, if possible
C.	High industry attractiveness and weak competitive position	Maintain	Commit resources or get out; double your efforts or quit; major effort is required; seek niches; specialize
D.	Low industry attractiveness and medium competitive position	Cut back	Get in position to divest; prune services; minimize investment of resources
E.	Average industry attractiveness and medium competitive position	Maintain	Slow growth—same rate as the market; identify growth segments; specialize; invest resources selectively
F.	High industry attractiveness and medium competitive position	Grow	Try harder; increased effort is required; more resources are needed; segmentation; identify weaknesses and build on strengths
G.	Low industry attractiveness and strong competitive position	Maintain	Selected harvesting maybe; seek cash flow; maintain overall position; invest at maintenance levels
H.	Average industry attractiveness and strong competitive position	Grow	Identify growth segments; invest strongly in resources; maintain position elsewhere; green light to go
I.	High industry attractiveness and strong competitive position	Grow	Seek dominance; strong commitment for resources, both externally and internally; protect your position

These nine different situations may be useful in deciding the direction of the NPO, that is, whether to grow, maintain, or cut back (build, hold, divest). For example, situations, F, H, and I would suggest a growth direction or a move ahead. Situations C, E, and G would suggest a maintenance direction. And situations A, B, and D would suggest a cut back direction. The value of this analysis is that it suggests the direction and resulting strategic moves of an NPO, based on a careful appraisal of the NPO's industry attractiveness and its competitive position.

Similar analyses could be made for any service of an NPO that has made appraisals of both its industry and its competitive position.

SUMMARY

An Appraisal of the External Environment of a Non-Profit Organization

You are asked to make a *tentative* evaluation of the external environmental factors that positively or negatively affect your NPO. The word *tentative* is suggested because you may want to change your mind once you have performed further analyses.

   I. Use a matrix approach as suggested in this chapter.
- A. Use the guidelines.
- B. Back up each factor with facts in a sentence or paragraph showing the significance of each factor to the NPO.
- C. Make sure each factor is external — not internal.
- D. Determine the key factor(s).
- E. Summarize your analyses.

  II. Make an appraisal of the following environments in which your NPO operates:
- A. Economic environment
- B. Socio-cultural environment
- C. Political-legal environment
- D. Physical environment
- E. Ethical-religious environment
- F. Aesthetic environment
- G. Others, if appropriate

 III. Describe and evaluate the external environmental factors, and reach a general evaluation and/or prescription, if appropriate.

 IV. Prepare industry and competitive appraisals if the NPO is in a competitive position.
- A. Use the factors suggested in the chapter.
- B. Get industry data from the institutional association of which the NPO is a 'member.
- C. Determine the strategic direction of the NPO, using the analysis of industry attractiveness and competitive position.
  - 1. Situations F, H, and I suggest moving forward.
  - 2. Situations C, E, and G suggest maintaining your present position.
  - 3. Situations A, B, and D suggest cutting back.

7

Administrator Appraisal of the NPO's Internal Environment

There are at least four determinants of strategy: (1) the philosophy of the administrators, (2) the mission and related objectives they choose, (3) their appraisal of the external environment of the NPO, and (4) their appraisal of the internal environment of the NPO. This chapter is concerned with making an evaluation of the resources of the NPO, the functions that the NPO performs, and some productivity measures. The basic question to be answered is whether the NPO has the resources and the competence to formulate a strategy and to carry it out.

RESOURCE EVALUATION

Resource Reciprocity

The fundamental resources of an NPO have to be available for a strategy to be formulated, integrated, and implemented. What kinds of resources are needed, where they come from, and how they are acquired are questions that have to be addressed.

The underlying logic behind the acquisition of resources is basically moral or ethical in nature. A client, for example, knows that only by giving cash to an NPO can he/she acquire the scarce services he/she needs. Likewise, an NPO can survive only if it contributes services to a client in exchange for the client's contribution of cash. This reciprocity is an ethically neutral method by which the exchange between the NPO and the people who contribute to it increases the well-being of both parties. The reciprocity should help to satisfy some of the needs of both the NPO and the client. This neutral method means that an increase in the personal gain of the individual yields a gain to the organization as well. This net gain for each party is not achieved at the expense of each other.

There are two other methods of acquiring scarce resources. One is an ethically negative method by which a person or an NPO acquires resources by violence or fraud. The other method is ethically positive or altruistic in that resources are given or donated to either the person or the NPO without requiring anything in return. Acquiring resources by the altruistic method is fairly common to NPOs. However, the concept of reciprocity of resources given for resources received is preferable for most NPOs.

Resource Contributors

If an NPO has an organizational mission of producing and selling services to satisfy the needs of its clients, the NPO will require various resources to carry out that mission. Clients as a group contribute the money resources, translated into revenue, which serve as the most fundamental financial resource for the ultimate survival of an NPO. In return for their contributions, the NPO has an obligation to satisfy to some degree the personal needs or objectives of its clients by (1) providing sufficient quantities of services, (2) at the right price, (3) available at the right place and (4) at the right time, (5) with adequate information about the service, (6) with convenience in mind, (7) with a level of quality (8) that ensures dependability and (9) a safe service, (10) with proper complaint handling and (11) truthful information and (12) overall client service, plus (13) other characteristics that may be peculiar to the nature of the NPO and its relationship with its clients.

The reciprocity theory suggests that employees of an NPO are willing to exchange their time, effort, loyalty, and support for the attainment of certain employee resources. Some of the resources that most employees desire and that an NPO has an obligation to try to provide are as follows: (1) adequate wages, (2) acceptable working conditions and hours, (3) acceptable NPO policies, (4) good morale, (5) an opportunity to develop relationships with co-workers, (6) job security, (7) fringe benefits, (8) good management relations, (9) control over the job, (10) information about the NPO's activities, (11) job satisfaction, (12) recognition, (13) responsibilities, (14) a feeling of esteem, (15) two-way communications, (16) development and advancement, (17) a chance to make the most of one's talents, (18) being considered an individual without regard to race, creed, sex, or color, and (19) other resources that may be peculiar to a particular type of NPO.

Long-term creditors (bondholders, banks, and the like) contribute borrowed capital and in return would like to acquire (1) repayment of principal, (2) an acceptable rate of interest, (3) security on the money lent, (4) knowledge about the use of funds, and (5) other factors, depending on the nature of the NPO.

Suppliers of raw materials, equipment, and the like desire such things as (1) consideration of them as a dependable source of supply, (2) a fair price for materials, (3) promptness in making payments on orders, (4) an opportunity to sell at a reasonable profit, (5) adequate specifications and descriptions on orders, (6) an adequate lead time on orders, (7) prompt replies to inquiries, (8) adequate information about present and future activities, (9) an opportunity to present products to the NPO, (10) impartiality of treatment regarding competition, and (11) others.

Managers themselves wish to acquire resources in exchange for the leadership they contribute to the NPO. These include (1) an adequate salary, (2) fringe benefits, (3) good working conditions, (4) an opportunity to participate in organizational policy and administration, (5) an atmosphere for teamwork, (6) responsibility, (7) good relationships with peers, (8) an opportunity to learn, (9) a chance to create a good organizational image, (10) freedom in decision making, (11) recognition, (12) an opportunity for advancement, (13) an opportunity to achieve organizational objectives, (14) freedom to find new and better ways of performing a job, and (15) others.

Governmental units wish to obtain resources in their dealings with an NPO. Government provides protection in various forms for an NPO. In return, federal, state, and local governmental units would desire (1) conformity of NPO operations to legal requirements and (2) adequate information about the NPO's activities.

Communities wish to acquire certain resources in return for providing the environment in which the NPO operates. Such resources include the following: (1) community citizenship from the NPO, (2) civic-minded behavior by the NPO's management and employees, (3) information about the NPO's activities, (4) attractive facilities, (5) promotion of community improvement, (6) prevention of offensive residue from entering the community, and (7) others.

The acquisition of resources from these various resource contributors may be translated into a set of organizational resources which are vital to accomplishing the strategies necessary to achieve the NPO's mission and related objectives. How strong are these resources? Are there any weaknesses in them? How can an evaluation be made of them?

Balance Sheet Evaluation of Resources

One type of evaluation may be similar to a financial balance sheet. A list of resource strengths (assets) and a list of resource weaknesses (liabilities) may be appraised by the NPO administrator. For example, a balance sheet evaluation of the East Fork Baptist Church may be made as shown in Figure 7.1.

The evaluation in Figure 7.2 should serve as a checklist to help you determine the strengths and weaknesses of your organization in terms of its resources.

A REPORT CARD APPRAISAL OF MANAGEMENT OF OPERATIONS

In addition to a resource evaluation, an additional appraisal of the internal operative and managerial functions can be made, using an academic grading system to evaluate these functions.

Figure 7.1
East Fork Baptist Church Resource Strengths and Weaknesses

Resource Strengths (Assets)	Resource Weaknesses (Liabilities)
1. Recent additions and location of the Church Family Life Center help meet more member needs	1. Less than 10% of the members tithe
2. Active member participation in church operations helps to keep a preferred market position	2. Record keeping is questionable
3. Revenues and tithes are tax deductible to members, and church is not taxed	3. Operating costs are increasing
4. Every member has a vote-- democracy in church affairs	4. Mission activities are struggling
5. Members are willing to spend time and money on the new building	5. Sunday school has weak attendance in summer
6. Family Life Center helps to keep youths out of trouble	6. Bible studies are poorly attended
7. New members are constantly being baptized into the church	7. Financial resources to pay off debt are lacking
8. Baby sitting is well administered by rotating couples each week, providing a father-mother role	8. Not all church members participate in church affairs
9. Pot luck dinners each month promotes fellowship	
10. Revivals are held to motivate members	
11. The pastor is dedicated and is well liked by members	

Overall Evaluation: The Church's resources outweigh its weaknesses. However, there are enough weaknesses to prevent the Church from fully achieving its objectives.

Every NPO has to "produce" a service, "market" that service, "finance" that service, and "personnel" it (whatever names may be given to these operative functions). Further, every NPO has administrators who have to "plan," "acquire" resources, "organize" these resources, "lead" the people involved, "coordinate" their efforts, and "evaluate" how well the plans and objectives have been accomplished. These are the managerial functions that are applied to the operative functions. The two functions — operative and managerial — can be constructed into a matrix and a grade assigned to each cell in the matrix. Figure 7.3 is an example for the East Fork Baptist Church. Some type of crude appraisal for each matrix cell is needed, based on

Figure 7.2
Evaluation of Organizational Resources

Please check Yes or No in evaluating the resources of your organization. Please make comments, if you wish.

Products/Services   Yes   No

1) Are the products/services significantly different from those of competitors?   _____ ____

2) Is the quality of the products/services better than that of market competitors?   _____ ____

3) Is the quality of the products/services better than it was this time last year?   _____ ____

4) Are funds allocated to product/service development?   _____ ____

5) Has a new product/service been introduced in the past 3 years?   _____ ____

6) Is money spent to improve methods of making products/services?   _____ ____

7) Is the "product life cycle" a factor in your operation?   _____ ____

8) Do you have an advantage in the form of copyrights or patents?   _____ ____

9) Have you prevented any product/service safety suits from being filed against your organization?   _____ ____

10) Does your production process or layout include the latest changes?   _____ ____

11) Are you a low-cost producer?   _____ ____

12) Are subsidies sometimes necessary to provide your products/services?   _____ ____

13) Do you supply a written guarantee with your products/services?   _____ ____

14) Do you provide multiple lines of your products/services?   _____ ____

Comments:

Market Position

1) Do you have a preferred market position?   _____ ____

2) Do you have less than three major competitors?   _____ ____

3) Are funds allocated for market research?   _____ ____

4) Do you have a clearly defined market?   _____ ____

5) Have you divided your market into segments?   _____ ____

6) Is competition a critical factor in your pricing policy?   _____ ____

7) Do you have an advertising budget?   _____ ____

8) Are the products/services available at different times and places?   _____ ____

9) Can customers obtain any desired quantity of products/services?   _____ ____

Figure 7.2 (continued)

10)   Is training provided to sales personnel?   _____ ____

11)   Do you have a credit policy?   _____ ____

Comments:

<u>Management</u>

1)   Are sufficient managers available at different times
     and places?   _____ ____

2)   Are managers ready, willing, and able?   _____ ____

3)   Do managers generally agree with the mission and
     objectives of the organization?   _____ ____

4)   Does the organization have an executive development
     program?   _____ ____

5)   Does a variation of age and experience of managers
     exist at the top level?   _____ ____

6)   Is there a balance between outside and inside members
     on the board of directors?   _____ ____

7)   Do finance and audit committees exist on the board
     of directors?   _____ ____

8)   Does a good relationship exist between the chief
     executive and the board of directors?   _____ ____

9)   Does a possibility exist for conflict of interest
     among board members?   _____ ____

10) Is the board of directors an active agent in the
     management of the organization?   _____ ____

Comments:

<u>Employees</u>

1)   Are qualified employees readily available?   _____ ____

2)   Are wages and benefits normally acceptable?   _____ ____

3)   Do you have a plan to minimize layoffs?   _____ ____

4)   Do you have a safety or accident prevention program?   _____ ____

5)   Do you have a program designed to decrease
     absenteeism and turnover?   _____ ____

6)   Do you have a formal employee training program?   _____ ____

7)   Are your wages and benefits competitive with those of
     other organizations in the area?   _____ ____

8)   Are the employees oriented on the mission and
     objectives of the organization?   _____ ____

9)   Is an employee morale survey periodically performed?   _____ ____

10) Does the pay and benefits plan consider both merit
     and seniority?   _____ ____

Comments:

134

Figure 7.2 (continued)

<u>Money</u>

1) Does cash + securities + receivables amount to more than liabilities due within one year? _____ ____

2) Is the amount of your investment more than two-thirds of total assets? _____ ____

3) Does revenue consistently exceed expenses? _____ ____

4) Does total revenue exceed twice total assets? _____ ____

5) Does the ratio of revenue per employee equal or exceed that of the nearest competitor? _____ ____

6) Are most operating funds generated internally by the organization? _____ ____

7) Is the interest rate currently being paid equal to or lower than that paid by your nearest competitors? _____ ____

Comments:

<u>Materials</u>

1) Are raw materials readily available? _____ ____

2) Is quality of raw materials normally available at the right price? _____ ____

3) Is more than one source of raw materials available? _____ ____

4) Do you have a plan to prevent running out of raw materials? _____ ____

5) Do you have a plan to minimize over- and under-stocking of inventories? _____ ____

6) Is storage space designed for normal inventory levels? _____ ____

7) Does a system exist for protection against loss of inventory? _____ ____

Comments:

<u>Plant/Equipment</u>

1) Have the organization's facilities been brought up to date during the past 5 years? _____ ____

2) Is depreciation recorded for major items of equipment? _____ ____

3) Are the facilities adequately insured? _____ ____

4) Is there a physical security program for your facilities? _____ ____

5) Is there enough space for possible growth? _____ ____

Comments:

Figure 7.2 (continued)

<u>Relationship with Resource Contributors</u>   <u>Yes</u>   <u>No</u>

Do you have a good relationship with

  1)   Customers/Clients   _____   ____

  2)   Employees   _____   ____

  3)   Donors   _____   ____

  4)   Suppliers   _____   ____

  5)   Long-term creditors   _____   ____

  6)   Community   _____   ____

  7)   Government   _____   ____

  8)   Management   _____   ____

  9)   Society in general   _____   ____

 10)   Competitors   _____   ____

 11)   Others (please list)

Comments:

<u>Environmental Scanning System</u>

		Yes	No	
1.	Does the organization have an external environmental scanning system that gathers information that allows the organization to adapt to its external environment?			
2.	Does the scanning system use both written and personal sources of information?			
3.	Does the scanning system use both external and internal sources of information?			
4.	Does the scanning system make use of computers?			
5.	Does the scanning system allow the managers to perceive reduction in environmental uncertainty?			
6.	Does the external environmental scanning system gather information about the immediate resource providers: customers, competitors, employees, managers, donors, suppliers, creditors, government, community, society, and others?			
7.	Does the scanning system gather detailed information about the organization's industry?			
8.	Does the scanning system gather detailed information about your competitive position?			
9.	Does the scanning system gather detailed information about the general external environment, inclued the following:			
	a. economic environment demand			
	b. supply of resources			
	c. competition			
	d. state of the economy			
	e. other			
	f. socio-cultural environment			

Figure 7.2 (continued)

	Yes	No
g. political-legal environment		
h. technological environment		
i. ethical-religious environment		
j. physical environment		
k. aesthetic environment		

10. Does the organization have an adequate internal management information system regarding
    a. financial and accounting information
    b. marketing information
    c. operation/production information
    d. personnel information

Overall Evaluation	Needs Work	Strength	Weakness
1) Products/Services	_____	_____	____
2) Market Position	_____	_____	____
3) Management	_____	_____	____
4) Employees	_____	_____	____
5) Plant/Equipment	_____	_____	____
6) Money	_____	_____	____
7) Materials	_____	_____	____
8) Relationship with Resource Contributors	_____	_____	____
9) Environment Scanning System	_____	_____	____
10) Other resources	_____	_____	____

Comments:

Figure 7.3
Report Card Appraisal of East Fork Baptist Church's Performance of Its Managerial and Operative Functions

Managerial Functions	Operative Functions				
	Church Operations	Marketing	Finance	Personnel	Total
Planning	B	C	D	A	C+
Acquiring	B	A	B	A	B+
Organizing	B	B	B	B	B
Leading	C	C	C	C	C
Coordinating	C	C	D	B	C
Evaluating	C	D	D	C	C-
Total	B-	B-	C-	B	B-

evidence from an actual appraisal of an NPO. What type of evidence can be used? Figure 7.4 may be used as a guide.

Let us consider the managerial planning function for each of the operative functions. Operations planning is evident when an NPO has a operations schedule and perhaps some research and development. Marketing planning is evident when a revenue forecast is used in addition to market research. Financial planning is evident when both operating and capital budgets are prepared. Personnel planning is evident if the NPO has a manpower planning document and perhaps a training program. Overall planning can be a summary of all the operative planning. However, long-term planning should also be appraised, usually by the NPO administrators and board of directors.

The acquisition of resources for operations can be evidenced by the existence of an organizational purchasing agent and a raw materials inventory control program. Marketing acquisition can be evidenced by an increased number of clients and revenues. Financial acquisition is usually evidenced by dollar increases in loans and donations. Overall acquiring of resources could be a summary, plus the ability of the NPO to acquire resources in addition to raw materials, markets, money, and manpower. For example, executive talent, space, information, and equipment should also be appraised.

The managerial function of organizing can be evidenced by the existence of a personnel organization chart for each of the operative functions of operations, marketing, finance, and personnel and for the total organization. In addition, a physical layout chart of the operations function would be evidence of organization. The existence of job descriptions would be evidence of organization. An authority and responsibility manual would also be evidence.

The managerial function of leading can be shown by the leadership styles used in the organization's operative functions. Morale surveys are evidence, as are productivity ratios.

Coordination, especially between those who produce the products/services and those who market them, can be evidenced by the number and types of meetings that are held by the NPO. Coordination of thought among the various operative functions has to exist, and this existence can be shown by minutes of the various meetings. Written procedures for operations can be evidence of coordination of action among the operative functions.

The evaluation of operations can be evidenced by a quality control function, the number of rejects, the times the NPO is out of inventory, the unit costs of production, and other evaluative measures. The evaluation of marketing can be evidenced by the number of client/customer complaints, returned goods, and the like. Financial evaluation can be evidenced by the use of financial ratios, and personnel evaluation by the use of absenteeism, accident, and grievance ratios. All these evaluations should be evidenced by written reports with appropriate standards for each operative function.

Figure 7.4
Guidelines for Evaluating the Performance of Managerial and Operative Functions

---

                                                            (S)   (W)
                                                      Strength / Weakness
                                                         Unknown (Unk)

I. Mission and Related Objectives
    A. Marketing
        1. Does the marketing function have
            objectives?
        2. Do the objectives fit in with the
            overall mission and related
            strategies?
        3. Have the objectives been
            translated into specific goals?
        4. Have the goals been accomplished?

    Remarks:

    B. Production/Operations
        1. Does the production/operations
            function have objectives?
        2. Do the objectives fit in with the
            overall mission and related strategies?
        3. Have the objectives been translated
            into specific goals?
        4. Have the goals been accomplished?

    Remarks:

    C. Personnel
        1. Does the personnel function have
            objectives?
        2. Do the objectives fit in with the
            overall mission and related strategies?
        3. Have the objectives been translated
            into specific goals?
        4. Have the goals been accomplished?

    Remarks:

    D. Finance
        1. Does the finance function have
            objectives?
        2. Do the objectives fit in with the
            overall mission and related strategies?
        3. Have the objectives been translated
            into specific goals?
        4. Have the goals been accomplished?

    Remarks:

    E. Overall evaluation of functional objectives:

II. Planning Function
    A. Marketing
        1. Does the marketing function forecast revenues?
        2. Does a marketing plan exist?
        3. Are proper personnel involved in making the
            plan?
        4. Does the plan entail
            a. Perceiving new opportunities
            b. Perceiving new threats

Figure 7.4 (continued)

(S)   (W)
Strength / Weakness
Unknown (Unk)

    c. Improving market research
    d. Creating a marketing information system
    e. Widening the client base
    f. Achieving intensive market penetration
    g. Improving distribution channels
    h. Improving distribution/client
       relations
    i. Implementing a better pricing strategy
    j. Employing a dynamic sales staff
    k. Analyzing the target market
    l. Creating niches via segmentation
    m. Other (describe)

Remarks:

B. Production/Operations
    1. Does the production/operations function
       forecast input and output needs?
    2. Does a production/operations
       planning and control plan exist?
    3. Are proper personnel involved in
       making the plan?
    4. Does the plan entail
       a. Improving R&D
       b. Innovating
       c. Establishing pilot programs
       d. Carrying out team projects
       e. Providing top quality
       f. Creating superior products/
          services
       g. Emphasizing intangibles
       h. Creating uniqueness
       i. Differentiating
       j. Specializing
       k. Responding quickly
       l. Turning production/operations into
          a marketing weapon
       m. Utilizing distinctive production/operations
          methods
       n. Determining proper layout
       o. Producing for stock or on order
       p. Choosing the proper location for facilities
       q. Plotting an experience curve
       r. Other

Remarks:

C. Personnel
    1. Does the personnel function forecast
       personnel needs?
    2. Does a personnel plan exist?
    3. Are proper personnel involved in
       making the plan?
    4. Does the plan entail
       a. Incentive pay plans
       b. Training and development
       c. Pay schedules
       d. Fringe benefits
       e. Promotions
       f. Working conditions
       g. Other hygiene factors
       h. Union/employee relations

Remarks:

Figure 7.4 (continued)

(S)   (W)
Strength / Weakness
Unknown (Unk)

D. Finance
    1. Does the finance function forecast money needs?
    2. Does a financial budget exist?
    3. Are proper personnel involved in making the budget?
    4. Does the plan entail
       a. Cash flows
       b. Capital budget
       c. Insurance needs
       d. Proper accounting concepts
       e. Relations with financial institutions
       f. Others

Remarks:

E. Overall evaluation of functional planning:

III. Acquiring Resources
  A. Marketing
    1. Does the marketing function have a dynamic sales force?
    2. Are achievement quotas set?
    3. Have sales figures in terms of units and/or dollars been obtained?
    4. Have the dollars from sales been allocated properly?

Remarks:

  B. Production/Operations
    1. Does the production/operations function have a purchasing agent?
    2. Are specifications for materials and facilities available and followed?
    3. Have materials and facilities been obtained at the right time, at the right place, in sufficient quantities, and at the right price in light of proper quality?
    4. Have the materials and facilities been allocated properly?
  C. Personnel
    1. Does the organization have a personnel agent to acquire personnel?
    2. Are specifications and descriptions for jobs available and followed?
    3. Have personnel been obtained at the right time, place, quantity, quality, and price?
    4. Have personnel been allocated properly?

Remarks:

  D. Finance
    1. Does the organization have a financial officer to acquire money?
    2. Does a capital budget prescribe the amounts and types of capital to be obtained?
    3. Has capital been obtained at the right time, at the right place, and at the price, and in sufficient quantities?
    4. Has the capital been allocated properly?

Figure 7.4 (continued)

(S)   (W)
Strength / Weakness
Unknown (Unk)

Remarks:

E.   Overall evaluation of functional acquiring:

IV. Organizing
    A. Marketing
        1. Does everyone in marketing know who his/her boss is?
        2. Does everyone know the relationship of his/her job to other jobs?
        3. Does everyone know the relationship of his/her job to the mission and related strategies to accomplish the mission?
        4. Does the organization structure allow for
            a. Team projects
            b. Individual expertise
            c. "Two deep" leadership
            d. Simplified and reduced structure
            e. Minimal staff
            f. Deference to the line
            g. Vertical and horizontal communication
            h. Decentralization where appropriate
            i. Fast action
            j. Emphasis on the structure to implement strategy
            k. Other

Remarks:

    B. Production/Operations
        1. Does everyone in production/operations know who his/her boss is?
        2. Does everyone know the relationship of his/her job to other jobs?
        3. Does everyone know the relationship of his/her job to the mission and related strategies to accomplish the mission?
        4. Does the organization structure allow for
            a. Team projects
            b. Individual expertise
            c. "Two deep" leadership
            d. Simplified and reduced structure
            e. Minimal staff
            f. Deference to the line
            g. Vertical and horizontal communication
            h. Decentralization where appropriate
            i. Fast action
            j. Emphasis on the structure to implement strategy
            k. Other

Remarks:

    C. Personnel
        1. Does everyone in personnel know who his/her boss is?
        2. Does everyone know the relationship of his/her job to other jobs?
        3. Does everyone know the relationship of his/her job to the mission and related strategies to accomplish the mission?

Figure 7.4 (continued)

(S)   (W)
Strength / Weakness
Unknown (Unk)

4. Does the organization structure allow for
    a. Team projects
    b. Individual expertise
    c. "Two deep" leadership
    d. Simplified and reduced structure
    e. Minimal staff
    f. Deference to the line
    g. Vertical and horizontal communication
    h. Decentralization where appropriate
    i. Fast action
    j. Emphasis on the structure to implement
        strategy
    k. Other

Remarks:

D. Finance
    1. Does everyone in finance know who his/her
        boss is?
    2. Does everyone know the relationship of
        his/her job to other jobs?
    3. Does everyone know the relationship of
        his/her job to the mission and related
        strategies to accomplish the mission?
    4. Does the organization structure allow for
        a. Team projects
        b. Individual expertise
        c. "Two deep" leadership
        d. Simplified and reduced structure
        e. Minimal staff
        f. Deference to the line
        g. Vertical and horizontal communication
        h. Decentralization where appropriate
        i. Fast action
        j. Emphasis on the structure to implement
            strategy
        k. Others

Remarks:

E. Overall evaluation of functional organizing:

V. Leading
    A. Marketing
        1. Does the leadership of marketing have the
            proper expertise to achieve its goals?
        2. Is the type of leadership style proper for
            the situation facing the organization?
        3. Has the leadership been successful in
            achieving goals?
        4. Does the leadership involve
            a. Listening to people
            b. Trust of people
            c. Respect for people's dignity
            d. Vision
            e. Cheerleading
            f. Drive
            g. MBWA
            h. Support
            i. Participation
            j. Allowance for mistakes

143

Figure 7.4 (continued)

(S)   (W)
Strength / Weakness
Unknown (Unk)

    k.   Recognition
    l.   Management by example
    m.   Direction
    n.   Handling conflict
    o.   Unifying people
    p.   Proper rewards
    q.   Other

Remarks:

B.   Production/Operations
    1.   Does the leadership of production/operations have the proper expertise to achieve its goals?
    2.   Is the type of leadership style proper for the situation facing the organization?
    3.   Has the leadership been successful in achieving goals?
    4.   Does the leadership involve
        a.   Listening to people
        b.   Trust of people
        c.   Respect for people's dignity
        d.   Vision
        e.   Cheerleading
        f.   Drive
        g.   MBWA
        h.   Support
        i.   Participation
        j.   Allowance for mistakes
        k.   Recognition
        l.   Management by example
        m.   Direction
        n.   Handling conflict
        o.   Unifying people
        p.   Proper rewards
        q.   Other

Remarks:

C.   Personnel
    1.   Does the leadership of personnel have the proper expertise to achieve its goals?
    2.   Is the type of leadership style proper for the situation facing the organization?
    3.   Has the leadership been successful in achieving goals?
    4.   Does the leadership involve
        a.   Listening to people
        b.   Trust of people
        c.   Respect for people's dignity
        d.   Vision
        e.   Cheerleading
        f.   Drive
        g.   MBWA
        h.   Support
        i.   Participation
        j.   Allowance for mistakes
        k.   Recognition
        l.   Management by example
        m.   Direction
        n.   Handling conflict
        o.   Unifying people
        p.   Proper rewards
        q.   Other

Remarks:

Figure 7.4 (continued)

(S)   (W)
Strength / Weakness
Unknown (Unk)

D. Finance
   1. Does the leadership of finance have the proper expertise to achieve its goals?
   2. Is the type of leadership style proper for the situation facing the organization?
   3. Has the leadership been successful in achieving goals?
   4. Does the leadership involve
      a. Listening to people
      b. Trust of people
      c. Respect for people's dignity
      d. Vision
      e. Cheerleading
      f. Drive
      g. MBWA
      h. Support
      i. Participation
      j. Allowance for mistakes
      k. Recognition
      l. Management by example
      m. Direction
      n. Handling conflict
      o. Unifying people
      p. Proper rewards
      q. Other

Remarks:

E. Overall evaluation of functional leading:

VI. Coordinating
   A. Marketing
      1. Does marketing have periodic internal meetings to coordinate thought and action?
      2. Does marketing have policies to coordinate thought and action?
      3. Does marketing have procedures to coordinate action?
      4. Does marketing have external relations with customers and other resource contributors to coordinate thought and action, including
         a. Group meetings
         b. Information systems
         c. Task forces
         d. Liaison roles
         e. Matrix structures
         f. Boundary spanners
         g. Trade associations
         h. Environmental scanning
         i. Other

Remarks:

B. Production/Operations
   1. Does production/operations have periodic internal meetings to coordinate thought and action?
   2. Does production/operations have policies to coordinate thought and action?
   3. Does production/operations have procedures to coordinate action?
   4. Does production/operations have external relations with resource contributors to coordinate thought and action, including
      a. Group meetings
      b. Information systems

145

Figure 7.4 (continued)

(S)   (W)
Strength / Weakness
Unknown (Unk)

    c.   Task forces
    d.   Liaison roles
    e.   Matrix structures
    f.   Boundary spanners
    g.   Trade associations
    h.   Environmental scanning
    i.   Other

Remarks:

C. Personnel
    1.   Does personnel have periodic internal
        meetings to coordinate thought and action?
    2.   Does personnel have policies to coordinate
        thought and action?
    3.   Does personnel have procedures to coordinate
        action?
    4.   Does personnel have external relations with
        resource contributors to coordinate thought
        and action, including
        a.   Group meetings
        b.   Information systems
        c.   Task forces
        d.   Liaison roles
        e.   Matrix structures
        f.   Boundary spanners
        g.   Trade associations
        h.   Environmental scanning
        i.   Other

Remarks:

D. Finance
    1.   Does finance have periodic internal
        meetings to coordinate thought and action?
    2.   Does finance have policies to coordinate
        thought and action?
    3.   Does finance have procedures to coordinate
        action?
    4.   Does finance have external relations with
        resource contributors to coordinate thought
        and action, including
        a.   Group meetings
        b.   Information systems
        c.   Task forces
        d.   Liaison roles
        e.   Matrix structures
        f.   Boundary spanners
        g.   Trade associations
        h.   Environmental scanning
        i.   Other

Remarks:

Overall evaluation of functional coordinating:

VII. Evaluating
    A. Marketing
        1.   Does marketing have quantitative and
           qualitative standards for measuring
           goal achievement?
        2.   Does marketing have measuring devices
           to evaluate properly?
        3.   Does marketing make interpretations of
           actual versus standard?

Figure 7.4 (continued)

(S)   (W)
Strength / Weakness
Unknown (Unk)

4. Does marketing take actions
   (positive and corrective) based on
   evaluations, recognizing
   a. Measuring what's important
   b. Murphy's Law
   c. People make mistakes
   d. Other

Remarks:

B. Production/Operations
   1. Does production/operations have
      quantitative and qualitative standards
      for measuring goal achievement?
   2. Does production/operations have measuring
      devices to evaluate properly?
   3. Does production/operations make
      interpretations of actual versus standard?
   4. Does production/operations take actions
      (positive and corrective) based on
      evaluations, recognizing
      a. Measuring what's important
      b. Murphy's Law
      c. People make mistakes
      d. Other

Remarks:

C. Personnel
   1. Does personnel have quantitative and
      qualitative standards for measuring
      goal achievement?
   2. Does personnel have measuring devices
      to evaluate properly?
   3. Does personnel make interpretations of
      actual versus standard?
   4. Does personnel take actions (positive
      and corrective) based on evaluations,
      recognizing
      a. Measuring what's important
      b. Murphy's Law
      c. People make mistakes
      d. Other

Remarks:

D. Finance
   1. Does finance have quantitative and
      qualitative standards for measuring
      goal achievement?
   2. Does finance have measuring devices
      (accounting) to evaluate properly?
   3. Does finance make interpretations of
      actual versus standard?
   4. Does finance take actions (positive
      and corrective) based on evaluations,
      recognizing
      a. Measuring what's important
      b. Murphy's Law
      c. People make mistakes
      d. Other

Remarks:

Overall evaluation of functional evaluating:

Figure 7.4 (continued)

VIII. Other management/operating functions that may be
       evaluated
       A. Negotiating   D. Public relations
       B. Representing   E. Others peculiar to the
       C. Legal   organization

IX. Overall evaluation
     A. Fill in the blanks of the matrix below
         with a letter grade (A, B, C, D) or with
         a number (4, 3, 2, 1).
     B. Does the grade* (subjectively determined)
         reflect management's ability to implement
         the organization's overall strategy?
     C. Does the grade* reflect what the
         organization does best? Least well?

NOTE: The "operative" functions may have to be renamed to
       adapt to the particular organization. However, every
       organization has to produce, to market, to staff, and
       to finance if it wants to create value for the
       organization and its stakeholders.

*Grades or Numbers
        A or 4 Excellent, superior
        B or 3 Good, above average
        C or 2 Average
        D or 1 Poor, below average

Postscript: Several evaluators are better than one.

                    Report Card Appraisal of Managerial and
                            Operative Functions

Organization:

Evaluated By:

Fill in the blanks with a grade (A,B,C,D) or with a number (4,3,2,1).

Managerial Functions	Operative Functions				Overall
	Marketing	Production/ Operations	Personnel	Finance	
I Objectives					
II Planning					
III Acquiring					
IV Organizing					
V Leading					
VI Coordinating					
VII Evaluating					
VIII Others					
IX Overall					

Comment: 1. Does management have any distinctive competencies?
          2. Does management have the ability to execute a
              strategic decision?
          3. Does the analysis of functional activities describe
              part of the organizational culture?

A grade can be subjectively assigned to each cell in the matrix, whether A+ or A−, a number, a letter grade, or some other means to indicate strengths and weaknesses in terms of how well the administrators of the NPO are managing the operative functions that exist in the NPO. These grades can be weighted and added, both horizontally and vertically, to give an overall appraisal of the NPO's strengths and weaknesses. Admittedly, this type of appraisal is fairly subjective. But it can be very useful to the administrators in appraising the internal environment of an NPO.

There is a key question to be asked when formulating and implementing a strategic decision: Is management *able* to implement a strategic decision? The analysis in Figure 7.4 is proposed to help determine the competencies of the NPO's management.

PRODUCTIVITY EVALUATIONS

A third type of NPO evaluation is one based on productivity ratios; that is, the NPO's inputs and outputs are measured by relating them to various criteria. For example,

- A college could use the cost per student credit hour as a measure of productivity, especially if this cost is compared over time and with the costs of similar institutions. Another criterion could be revenue generated per credit hour. Another might be cost per student or cost per faculty member.
- A church might use the number of people attending church divided by total church membership, cost per church member, or revenue per church member.
- A school bus program might want to use the cost per student transported, cost per mile, or maintenance cost per mile.
- An Economic Opportunity Agency (EOA) elderly nutrition program might want to use the cost per meal served or cost per person served, food cost per meal, labor cost per meal, or overhead cost per meal and then compare these productivity ratios over time and with those of other food establishments.
- A symphony might want to determine its cost per concert versus revenue per concert.
- A police department might want to calculate its cost per citizen served, cost per officer, or cost per square mile served. It might also want to know the number of crimes committed per 1,000 people or the number of cases closed divided by the number of cases reported.
- A prison might wish to know the number of inmates released divided by the number of repeaters who are returned to prison.
- A credit union might want to know the dollars of bad loans written off as uncollectible divided by the total dollars of loans made, cost of making a loan, revenue generated per loan, total revenues per employee, or total costs per employee.
- A hospital might wish to know the cost per patient-day or the total deaths divided by the number of patients admitted.

As an example, let us take a look at the case of a local school bus system which made the following analysis.

PRODUCTIVITY ANALYSIS OF OUR SCHOOL BUS SYSTEM

The school districts compared are Fayetteville, Springdale, Bentonville, Russellville, Siloam Springs, and Mountain Home. Of the six school districts, Springdale, Bentonville, and Siloam Springs were chosen as representative of school bus systems in the area ranging from somewhat larger (Springdale with 46 buses) to smaller (Bentonville with 30 buses and Siloam Springs with 19 buses) than Fayetteville's 37-bus system. Russellville was chosen for its unique tax situation (Arkansas Power and Light's Nuclear One reactor is in the Russellville School District), and Mountain Home was chosen as a comparable-sized school district in another area of the state having physical geography similar to that of the Fayetteville School District.

State aid is allocated to the school districts using a formula based on the average number of students transported daily. For schools of similar size, the percentage of total annual cost covered by state aid is identical — both Fayetteville and Springdale received state aid totaling 58 percent of total cost. The smaller schools had more of their funding provided by state aid. Russellville is an exception in that only 15 percent of its total cost is covered by state aid; this is the result of the large local tax revenues it receives from Nuclear One.

The most revealing cost area in terms of significance to the Fayetteville School District is mechanics' salaries as a percentage of total costs. In this area, Fayetteville's 11 percent figure exceeds the other five schools' average of 6.4 percent. This strongly indicates the possibility of some inefficiency in this area. A recommendation to reduce the annual outlay for mechanics' salaries might be justified. However, this figure may be the result of other factors not included in the data analyzed, such as the methods of reporting costs by the various school districts or the quality of service provided.

Overall, the above analysis indicates that the Fayetteville school bus system is well managed and compares well to other school bus systems both in the area and in the state. This is particularly evident when one notes that Fayetteville's annual cost per child of $90.39 is the lowest of the six schools analyzed.

The following cost figures are provided to facilitate analysis of the school bus service on a per-unit basis.

```
Fleet

    Cost of maintenance and operations of fleet        $191,534.23
    Cost per bus ($191,534.23 ÷ 47 buses)                4,705.20
    Cost per bus per day ($4,705.20 ÷ 175 days)             26.88
    Cost per mile ($191,534.23 ÷ 398,703 miles)              .48
```

Route Buses

Average miles each bus is driven on routes per day:
State average - 49.7 miles
Fayetteville - 55.2 miles
Average miles each bus is driven on routes per day:
State average - 8,946 miles
Fayetteville - 9,945 miles
Gallons of fuel used by each bus per route per day:
State average - 2,080 gallons
Fayetteville - 2,356 gallons

Route Buses

```
Total maintenance and operations               $175,999.52
Cost per bus per year ($175,999.52 ÷ 37 rt. buses)   4,756.74
Cost per bus per day ($4,756.74 ÷ 175 days)            27.20
Cost per bus per route run ($27.20 ÷ 2 runs)          13.60
Cost per mile ($175,999.52) ÷ 360,035 rt. mi.)          .49
Cost per day ($175,999.52 ÷ 175)                    1,005.71
Cost per day per student ($1,005.71 ÷ 3,871 studs.)     .26
```

Activity Buses

```
Miles traveled .....................................   30,745 mi.
#1   8,030 - 26%
#2   1,474 -  5%
#3   6,405 - 21%
#4  14,836 - 48%
    30,745
```

```
Maintenance and operation cost .....................  $6,410.44*
#1   $2,624.45   41%
#2      296.24    5%
#3    1,426.03   22%
#4    2,063.72   32%
     $6,410.44
```

```
Cost per mile (average) ............................         .21
```

*This does not include driver's salary.

According to information provided by the state department of education, buses driven on daily routes average 49.7 miles across the state, while Fayetteville's buses are driven an average of 55.2 miles. Buses driven on daily routes average 8,946 miles per year across the state, while Fayetteville's buses average 9,945 miles. Also, each bus in the state used an average of 2,080 gallons of fuel per route per year, whereas each Fayetteville bus used an average of 2,356 gallons.

These computations reveal that Fayetteville buses are driven farther each day on their routes and are driven more miles in a year. However, when compared to other schools in the state, Fayetteville's cost per child transported is lower, and its cost per bus is comparable to the cost per bus of other schools. This information indicates that the Fayetteville school bus system is operating efficiently and economically as compared to other school bus systems in the state.

Each NPO has various inputs and various outputs that can be compared to different criteria to determine effectiveness and efficiency. These productivity measures can be used to compare the NPO to similar NPOs. Furthermore, these productivity ratios can be compared over time to see if they are increasing, decreasing, staying the same, or experiencing seasonal variations. Productivity measures are excellent means of determining the strengths and weaknesses of a not-for-profit organization.

SUMMARY

Prepare a tentative evaluation of the strengths and weaknesses of your NPO's internal operations.

Your Appraisal of the Internal Environment

1. Make a balance sheet evaluation of the resources of the NPO.
    a. List the strengths (assets).
    b. List the weaknesses (liabilities).
    c. Reach a conclusion.
    d. Back up each resource strength or weakness with facts, in a sentence or paragraph.
    e. Use the guidelines suggested.
    f. Summarize your evaluation and/or prescribe, if appropriate.
    g. Remember that your evaluation is tentative. You may wish to add, delete, or change as your management audit continues!
2. Make a report card evaluation of both the operative and the managerial functions of the NPO.
    a. Use the guidelines suggested.
    b. Back up each cell with facts, usually facts supported in the balance sheet approach.
    c. Determine the operative functions. They may be called by different names.
    d. Assign a grade, based on your best judgment.
    e. Summarize and prescribe, if appropriate.
3. Select a series of productivity ratios for your NPO.
    a. Each NPO is unique in terms of its inputs and outputs.
    b. Compare the ratios over time.
    c. Compare the ratios with those of similar NPOs.
    d. Summarize and prescribe, if appropriate.
4. Determine your overall appraisal of the internal environment of your NPO.
    a. Strong?
    b. Weak?
    c. Mixed?

8

The Board of Directors

Members of a board of directors have different motivations for joining a board, but there is and should be one thing that binds them together — the mission of the NPO. The philosophical values of the board members may be directed toward the mission, but the degree of commitment to the mission may vary considerably among board members. Some may spend 100 hours a month on board affairs, some may spend 10 to 15 hours a month, and others may spend 2 to 4 hours a month at the board meeting. The degree of commitment will obviously affect the accomplishment of the NPO's mission.

There are many similarities between the boards of directors of profit and not-for-profit organizations. However, there are also some differences. For example, the reward system for directors of an NPO is non-monetary in nature, while board members of a for-profit organization are usually rewarded in both monetary and non-monetary ways.

The board of an NPO is relatively large, while that of a profit organization is relatively small — for example, 30 plus members for an NPO versus 10 to 15 for a profit organization. In addition, some NPOs have directors, honorary directors, advisory directors, and contributory directors. Given the large size, the differing value systems of individual board members tend to offset each other, allowing the CEO to dictate the strategies for the NPO.

Members of NPO boards are fund raisers and sometimes fund contributors, while members of profit boards represent the owners who supply the initial equity capital and then wait for their representative board members to generate additional capital. Further, some NPO board members also act as volunteer employees of the NPO, while such an activity is very rare among profit organizations.

The use of inside directors for an NPO is minimal, while it may be significant for a profit organization. The meeting attendance of NPO directors is 50–60 percent, while it is about 90 percent for a profit organization. The amount of directors' time given for an NPO is highly variable, while it is generally consistent for a private organization. The experience of board members for an NPO is highly variable, while it is substantial for a profit organization. The planning horizon for an NPO is relatively short, while it is longer for a profit organization. Regardless of the differences, the board members should exhibit commitment, dedication, and involvement and participate in the mission if the NPO is to accomplish it.

THE ROLE OF THE BOARD OF DIRECTORS

The legal responsibilities and philosophical values of board members suggest that they perform as long-range strategy makers. Their role means that they determine the organizational mission and related objectives. To do so requires that they make a continuous assessment of both the external and the internal environments of the organization, as perceived by them. Obviously, their values will be instrumental in these assessments.

In addition to their role as strategy makers, the board members should be the protectors of the various resource contributors to the organization. These contributors include the clients/customers, the capital providers, the money lenders, the managers, the employees (both permanent and volunteer), the suppliers, the government, the community, and society at large.

Further, the board members should be the evaluators of the accomplishment of the organizational mission and related objectives. If possible, the mission and objectives should be evaluated in quantitative terms or, if that is not possible, in qualitative terms so that they may be measured over a period of time and against other comparable organizations.

Board members should be the coordinators of thought about the mission and related strategies and the final approvers of them. That is the board members' responsibility, and they should be held accountable for them.

Board members may perform other duties, such as acquiring the CEO and other executives. They may also acquire key resources for the organization's survival. Further, they may dispose of the assets and other resources. In addition, board members are responsible for the performance of the operative functions, which they may delegate to other people.

THE SCOPE OF THE BOARD OF DIRECTORS

The organization may want to consider the composition of the board of directors. One decision involves whether to have an outside board, an inside board, or a balanced board.

Outside board members usually have a degree of independence that insiders do not possess. They also have relatively objective, impartial views about the organization that the insiders normally do not have. However, outside board members lack the detailed knowledge about the organization's strengths and weaknesses that the insiders have.

A balanced board takes advantage of the strengths of both outside and inside boards. The insiders can represent operations, marketing, finance, personnel, and other functional areas. The outsiders can represent clients, money contributors, money lenders, employees, suppliers, the community, special interest groups, and society at large.

The meetings of the board involve some decisions. Usually a quorum has to be present for a meeting to be official. How often should the board meet? The general answer is based on size. The bigger the organization, the more often the board should meet. The board of a relatively small organization usually meets annually, with special meetings as necessary, while that of a medium-sized organization usually meets quarterly, with special meetings as necessary. The board of a large-sized organization meets monthly, with occasional special meetings.

Committees of the board present another decision. Most boards have an executive committee, which is usually composed of three to five members. A chairman is elected by the full board, usually for a one-year term, renewable at the pleasure of the board. This executive committee meets fairly often, at least monthly, and is usually the strategy-making committee, being delegated most of the powers of the full board.

Functional committees are often created to determine policies of the organization. Such are the personnel, marketing, finance, and operations committees. Most organizations also have an audit committee. Special ad hoc committees are also created to study special problems which arise.

PROBLEMS FACING A BOARD

Selection of board members can be a problem. Board members who agree with the CEO and other board members all the time or who are compatible with everyone may not be the best ones for the organization. Compatibility makes meetings very pleasant, but it does not guarantee usefulness. Board members should be selected who can add knowledge in a culture of productive controversy. If they cannot, the organization lacks independent thinking and a probing inquiry into affairs affecting the organization.

It is at board meetings where the decision process, mentioned earlier, becomes important. A culture of productive controversy would suggest that the devil's advocacy and the dialectical inquiry processes of decision making would play a key role. Consensus management would not be as effective because many board members would "go along" with a decision, regardless of their feelings. When the CEO proposes, the board disposes, hopefully using the devil's advocacy and the dialectical inquiry processes.

Conflicts of interest may occur, especially among outside directors and the organization. The outside board members, especially the lawyers, accountants, bankers, and consultants, have potential conflicts of interest when they represent their companies in dealing with the organization. Questions may be raised as to whose side they are on. Theirs or the organization? Are they trying to sell their services to the organization? Someone else might have a better deal. When conflicts of interest occur, the outside board members may not be objective in giving advice.

In addition, board members can be held financially liable, especially if the organization fails and particularly if there is gross negligence on the part of board members.

Another problem is that of delegation of functions to the CEO. Theory holds that objectives, functions, authority, responsibility, and accountability rest with the board. Since the board cannot perform all functions, it has to delegate certain functions to the CEO to execute. A decision has to be made as to whether to keep certain functions at the board level or whether to delegate them to the CEO. What factors govern this decision?

- If the board perceives its function as coordinator of thought for the whole organization, then it should not delegate this function to the CEO.
- On the other hand, if the board perceives the function of its top executive to be coordinator of action, then it should delegate this function to the CEO.
- If the board perceives its function to be strategy formulator for the whole organization, then it should not delegate this function to the CEO.
- If the board perceives the function of its top executive as tactician, then it should delegate tactical functions to the CEO.
- If the board perceives its function as policy maker for the whole organization and for parts of the organization, then it should not delegate this function.
- If the board perceives the function of its top executive as executor of board policies, then it should delegate this function to the CEO.
- If the board has confidence in its top executive's expertise, judgment, attitudes, and other personal factors, then it should delegate whatever is appropriate to its CEO. If not, then it should not delegate.
- If the board and its top executive are involved in the beginning stages of the learning curve for any key aspect of the organization, then the board should not delegate until it has experience.
- If certain functions are legally and exclusively reserved for the board, then it should not delegate them to the CEO.

There may be other factors to be considered in this delegation decision, but the preceding ones are summarized as guidelines in Figure 8.1.

EVALUATING THE BOARD'S EFFECTIVENESS

If the board does a reasonable job of formulating strategies, then it also should do a reasonable job of implementing the strategies to accomplish the mission and related objectives. Some sort of feedback, either self-imposed or from outside sources, should be given to the board on how well it is performing. With such information the board can evaluate actual performance to see if its duties are effective.

Figure 8.1
Decision: To Delegate Functions of the Board of Directors to the CEO or Not?

		Alternatives	
Theoretical Situational Factors	Affecting	Delegate	Do Not Delegate
1.	If the Board perceives its function as a coordinator of thought for the whole organization, then		X
2.	If the Board perceives the function of its top manager as a coordinator of action, then	X	
3.	If the Board perceives its function as a strategy formulator for the whole organization, then		X
4.	If the Board perceives the function of its top manager as a tactician, then	X	
5.	If the Board perceives its function as a policy maker for the whole organization and for parts of the organization, then		X
6.	If the Board perceives the function of its top manager as an executor of Board policies, then	X	
7.	If the Board has confidence in its top manager's expertise, judgment, attitudes, and other person factors, then	X	
	7.1 If not, then		X
8.	If both the Board and the top manager are involved in the beginning stages of the learning curve for key aspects of the organization, then		X
9.	If certain functions are legally and exclusively reserved for the Board, then		X
10.	Other factors		

OVERALL EVALUATION AND POSSIBLE PRESCRIPTIONS:

Figure 8.2
Evaluation of Board Effectiveness*

Theoretical Situational Factors -------->Strength	Evaluation Strength But Needs Work	Uncertain	Weakness

I. Organization and Governance of the Organization's Board of Directors
A. Board Organization
1. The formal structure of the organization is clearly outlined in the bylaws specifying lines of authority and patterns of relationships.
2. The mission of the organization is clearly defined in the bylaws.
3. Bylaws provide clear duties for officers of the board.
4. Bylaws specify procedures for election of board members and officers, tenure of members and appointment of committees.
5. The board has an executive committee to handle matters which may come up between meetings and to which it may delegate certain decision-making responsibility.
6. The board has working committees such as finance, operations, personnel, marketing and resource development, through which work is channeled.
7. Committee assignments and responsibilities are in writing and copies are supplied to all.
8. Committee assignments are reviewed and evaluated periodically.
9. The board president supervises standing committee chairpersons, providing advice, support evaluation of progress in work assignments and feedback as needed.
10. There are no conflicts of interest among board members of other organizations which might have business with the organization.
11. Board members are aware of their financial liability in governing the affairs of the organization.

158

Figure 8.2 (continued)

Theoretical Situational Factors ------->Strength	Evaluation	Strength But Needs Work	Uncer- tain	Weak- ness
B. Recruitment, Selection, and Development of Board Members				
1. The organization has a written statement of qualifications for board members, along with duties and responsibilities.				
2. Organizational bylaws specify attendance re- quirements, provide for filling of vacancies and specify staggered terms for members to ensure a balance of both ex- perience and new ideas.				
3. Membership to the board is determined by criteria which include:				
a. Expertise in resource development, program and/or evaluation, finance, personnel or marketing;				
b. Ability to represent the organization with one or more resource groups that affect organization opera- tions;				
c. Ability to provide input to the organ- ization on issues which affect accomp- lishment of opera- tions;				
d. Demonstrated interest in the work of the organization and commitment to its goals;				
e. Willingness to carry out assignments within some area of special talent and competency;				
f. Willingness to attend board and committee meetings.				
4. The nominating committee so- licits nominations to the board from among staff, board, clientele and other active organization participants.				
5. The organization has an established orientation process for new board members as well as ongoing board training program for all members.				

Figure 8.2 (continued)

Theoretical Situational Factors --------->Strength	Evaluation Strength But Needs Work	Uncer-tain	Weak-ness
6. There is a balance of inside and outside board members, if appropriate.			
7. The organization has outlined a process for key leadership training which will ensure proper experience and commit-ment by potential future officers and committee chairpersons.			
8. The organization has a board member manual, which is re-vised periodically, which it provides to all board members.			
9. The bigger the organization, the larger the size of the board and vice versa.			
C. Board Meetings			
1. Board meetings are scheduled with a quorum present on a basis and with sufficient frequency to ensure board control and direction of the organization.			
2. Board materials, including agenda and study documents, are mailed to members in sufficient time for review in advance of board meetings.			
3. Board meetings deal primarily with strategic decisions and/or policy determination, review of plans, making board authorizations and evaluating the work of the organization.			
4. Routine matters which require official action, but little discussion are handled with dispatch. Time is not wasted.			
5. Minutes of board and com-mittee meetings are written and circulated to the members.			
6. Regular reports of committee work are made to the board.			
7. Board members have a good record of attendance at regularly scheduled board and committee meetings.			
8. Board meetings are pleasant, but they are conducted in a culture of productive controversy.			
9. Board members are given well-defined areas of responsi-bility.			
10. Board members provide the direction for the organiza-tion with the assistance of the CEO. Board members are not merely rubber stamps.			

160

Figure 8.2 (continued)

Theoretical Situational Factors -------->Strength	Evaluation Strength But Needs Work	Uncer-tain	Weak-ness
D. Decision-Making and Approval of Strategies and Policies			
1. The organization has sufficient policies, procedures and standards to guide it in its decision-making process.			
2. The organization has set up rules which determine the procedures for presenting business to the board for action.			
3. The CEO assures that the board has all the relevant facts for policy decisions but does not make the decisions.			
4. The board debates and decides issues, while the board chairperson facilitates the discussion and decision-making.			
5. Strategic decisions are most often made proactively for the purposes of attaining some new goal, establishing new directions or setting new or improved standards of performance.			
6. Policy decisions are seldom required as a reaction to some problem situation.			
7. The board serves as a coordinator of thought from all of its member inputs, both external and internal members.			
E. Evaluation			
1. The organization conducts periodic internal evaluations involving the board, which include:			
a. Evaluation of the board itself;			
b. Evaluation of the effectiveness of organizational administration;			
c. Evaluation of programs, including their determination, planning for implementation and results.			
2. The organization has predetermined standards of performance by which to measure its effectiveness.			

161

Figure 8.2 (continued)

Theoretical Situational Factors -------->	Strength	Evaluation Strength But Needs Work	Uncer- tain	Weak- ness
3. The board regularly monitors administrative and program activities to determine progress toward meeting objectives.				
4. The organization maintains appropriate statistics and financial information needed for evaluation.				
5. Statistical information maintained by the organization for each program is sufficient to answer both the planning needs of the organization and the reporting requests of funding sources.				
6. Products and/or services are directed to those clients most in need of services and are accessible to the client population to whom they are directed.				
7. Unit costs are appropriate for the service and clientele.				
F. Resource Contributors				
1. The organization has a system for obtaining input from individuals and groups affected by its planning of services, its methods of service delivery, and its service results.				
2. Individual board members and/or staff members participate actively as representatives of resource contributors to the organization.				
3. The organization maintains regular communications with resource contributors affecting its operation.				
4. The organization has an effective program for communicating its accomplishments to the broad community.				
G. Relations with the CEO				
1. The roles and responsibilities of board members and organizational staff are clearly delineated.				

162

Figure 8.2 (continued)

Theoretical Situational Factors ------->Strength	Evaluation Strength But Needs Work	Uncertain	Weakness
2. Board and staff (primarily the chief executive officer) have input into formulation of policy.			
3. The board assumes sole responsibility for policy determination and strategic decisions.			
4. The executive director executes policy through organization staff, service, and line personnel.			
5. The executive director is responsible for the internal administration of the organization.			
6. Board and staff are viewed as working cooperatively as a team, and each is recognized by the other as having a distinct and important role to play in the organization.			
7. The board has a procedure for conducting the performance review of the executive director.			
8. The board selects the CEO and other executives as necessary.			
H. Key Resource Development of Personnel and Finances			
1. The organization has written personnel policies, job descriptions and a job classification plan which are periodically reviewed and revised as needed.			
2. Personnel policies spell out procedures for handling both employee grievances and disciplinary procedures.			
3. Personnel policies include a performance review system.			
4. A wage and salary administration plan is designed to retain as well as attract competent staff.			
5. A finance, or fundraising committee of the board is charged with the responsibility of recommending and implementing a financial resource de-			

Figure 8.2 (continued)

Theoretical Situational Factors --------->Strength	Evaluation Strength But Needs Work	Uncertain	Weakness
velopment plan which is approved by the board and ensures that the organization has adequate financial resources to meet its objectives.			
6. The organization has a financial-planning component which provides for securing alternative funding when time-limited funding resources expire; or, provides for an orderly phaseout of services for which funds are no longer available.			
7. The organization has a diverse funding base which lessens disruption of services caused by withdrawal of funds from any one source.			
8. The organization is innovative in generating new sources of funds.			
9. A finance committee of the board is designated to oversee all finances, including meeting all legal financial requirements and adherence to fiscal policies, and reports to the board regularly on financial matters.			
10. The finance committee assists staff in developing the annual budget and regularly monitors expenditures and revenues.			
11. The board approves the annual budget and reviews regular financial reports of the operating budget and capital funds, if any.			
12. Financial reports are prepared for each major operating division of the organization and are used as management tools to guide the total organization.			

Figure 8.2 (continued)

Theoretical Situational Factors -------->Strength	Evaluation Strength But Needs Work	Uncer-tain	Weak-ness
13. The organization con-forms with generally accepted accounting principles.			
14. The organization has an annual audit which conforms with require-ments stipulated by the American Institute of Certified Public Accountants.			
15. The board takes responsibility to ensure that the organization maintains a fiscally solvent financial condition, including disposition of assets and any profits.			

Overall Evaluation and Possible Prescriptions.

*Adapted and modified from Peter P. Schoderbek, *The Board and Its Responsibilities* (New York: Kellogg Foundation and United Way, 1979).

The evaluation of board effectiveness in Figure 8.2 is a useful tool if each of the board members and the CEO personally fill out the evaluation to determine the board's strengths and weaknesses.

SUMMARY

The role of the board suggests that the members be committed to the mission of the NPO. The board members should be the strategy makers who determine how the mission will be accomplished. In addition, the board members should be the evaluators of the mission, the coordinators of thought about other objectives, and the performers of such other functions as acquiring resources and disposing of assets.

Board effectiveness depends on the organization and governance of the board, recruitment and selection of board members, timely meetings of the board, development of strategies and objectives, decision making and approval of strategies and policies, evaluation of operations, resource contributors, relations with the CEO, and development of key personnel and financial resources. An evaluation instrument is included for board members to fill out to determine their effectiveness.

An Audit of the Board

1. Determine, if possible, the commitment for each board member.
   a. How many hours does each spend on the NPO?
   b. Don't offend board members by asking this delicate question.
2. Determine attendance at board meetings.
3. Evaluate the following:
   a. Board's reward system
   b. Size of the board
   c. Inside vs. outside board members
   d. Meetings of the board
   e. Committees of the board
   f. Selection of board members
   g. Possible conflicts of interest
   h. Financial liability of members
   i. Delegation of functions to CEO
4. Have each board member fill out the instrument to evaluate board effectiveness.
   a. Record each member's check marks on a master sheet.
   b. Evaluate strengths and weaknesses.
   c. Make prescriptions.

9

Service-Market Match Strategies to Accomplish the NPO's Mission

PRIMACY OF THE CLIENT SERVICE MISSION

The organizational mission of any non-profit organization is to provide service to its clients, no matter what they are called—clients, members, students, patients, or regular customers. Service to those people who have a need and who consume the services provided is the number one purpose. Any non-profit organization that does not provide its services to its clients in a manner that satisfies some of their needs is one that is doomed to failure. The client service mission is primary, the very foundation on which the existence and success of any non-profit organization are built. It is the *sine qua non* for successful administration of a church, an educational institution, a political entity, a service organization such as a Kiwanis club, a non-profit professional organization, a hospital, or any other form of non-profit organization.

SERVICE-MARKET MATCH STRATEGIES: SERVICE ENHANCEMENT AND MARKET FOCUS

The means by which the primacy of the client service mission is accomplished is the match of the products/services offered by the non-profit organization with its clientele. As discussed previously, there are three fundamental strategies designed to create value for the NPO: (1) a service enhancement strategy, (2) a market focus strategy and (3) a cost reduction strategy. In this chapter we are going to discuss in detail the analyses of two of these strategies. One question needs to be asked: What service enhancement strategies should be used to focus on the needs of the clients in order to accomplish the primacy of the client service mission?

Service Description and Classification

Before an administrator attempts to answer that question, it becomes necessary to describe the nature of the services that the non-profit organization attempts to provide. Once that description is made, then the service may be classified by several criteria, most notably the following:

I. By Client
    A. Consumer Services
        1. Shopping
        2. Convenience
        3. Impulse
        4. Specialty
    B. Industrial Services
        1. Land
        2. Buildings
        3. Machinery and Equipment
        4. Raw Materials
        5. Component Parts
        6. Supplies
II. By Service Characteristics
    A. Necessity/Luxury
    B. Durable/Non-durable
    C. High Value/Low Value
    D. Technical/Non-technical
    E. Perishable/Non-perishable
    F. Seasonal/Non-seasonal
    G. Elasticity/Inelasticity/Unitary
    H. Standardized/Tailor-Made
    I. Many Other Characteristics (see below)
III. By Costs of Services
    A. Labor Intensive
    B. Capital Intensive
    C. Material Intensive
IV. By Competitive Position in the Market
    A. Highly Directly Competitive
    B. Indirectly Competitive with Substitute Services
    C. Monopoly Position
    D. Oligopoly Position
    E. Ease of Entry into the Market
V. Other Possible Classifications
    A. Stage in Product/Service Life Cycle
    B. Star, Cash Cow, Problem Child, Dog

Product Characteristics and Resulting Strategies

The reason for describing and classifying the characteristics of the services offered is to determine the types of substrategies to be used in providing the primacy of the client service mission. For example, whether a service is highly competitive or in a monopoly market position would be a most instrumental factor in determining whether a pricing strategy should be used to price the service below, at, or above the market. Perhaps the consumer or industrial type of service would be a most influential factor in deciding what type of promotion strategy is to be used in selecting a message and the media to be used. Whether a service is a necessity or luxury or of high value or low value might be a determining factor in developing a strategy related to what type of sales personnel to employ, what type of pricing strategy to employ, or what type of promotion strategy to employ. Whether a service is characterized as shopping, convenience, impulse, or specialty might be a factor in determining the location strategy. Each of the classifications is necessary for determining the various production, marketing, finance, and personnel strategies that a non-profit organization might employ in providing services for client satisfaction.

Competitive Advantage for the NPO

The NPO's services are also described and classified for competitive purposes. If competition is a key external factor facing an NPO (and it usually is), then a comparative analysis of the NPO's services needs to be made relative to the chief competitor of the NPO. Even if there is no direct competitor, there is usually an indirect competitor of the NPO. This key question must be answered: How do the competitor's services stack up against ours? Once that information is known, differentiation strategies can be pursued to gain a competitive advantage. Selection of a chief competitor is mandatory in this type of evaluation.

Caution should be used in classifying the services offered. Each particular service offered by a non-profit organization should be separately classified, rather than classifying groups of services. It may be that the varied services offered by a hospital, for example, are not alike. Are laboratory services the same as nursing services? Are operating room services the same as dietary services? Obviously not. Each separate service has distinct characteristics that may be important enough to differentiate the various substrategies to be used in administering the non-profit organization.

In a city government various services are performed that are different enough to be classified separately. For example, are the services of a fire department different from those of a welfare agency? Yes, they are. Consequently, the management of a fire department may use various service strategies that are different from those of a welfare agency. The point to be made is this: Each service offered to a group of clients usually is the major factor that dictates the varying production, marketing, financial, and personnel strategies that a manager uses to administer the affairs of the non-profit organization or any part of the organization. That is why careful analysis and understanding of the service characteristics are fundamental to accomplishing the NPO's mission of providing client service.

Focusing on the Needs of the Target Market for a Service-Market Match

Before service-market match strategies can be formulated intelligently, it becomes necessary to define the needs of the primary people for whom the non-profit organization exists — the clients. Most clients would prefer that the services be available in sufficient quantities at the right time and place to satisfy their needs. Obviously the service has to be designed in the right form in order to satisfy their needs — for example, hospital services, governmental services, educational services, or whatever other services must be provided to meet their needs. The quality of the service is important for client satisfaction. The price of the service is important. Adequate information has to be provided about the service to help the clients make informed decisions about the service. Complementary services may also be required. These fundamental needs are the ones that a service has to satisfy.

An effective administrator of a non-profit organization has to focus on the characteristics of the clients if service-market match strategies are to be wisely formulated. Such factors as who the clients are and where they are located become important. In addition, some information about how many clients there are is essential. Other characteristics are very useful in determining that segment of the market that the non-profit organization wishes to serve. For example, when do clients use the services? What are their consumption habits, cultural background, marital status, age, income bracket, and other personal characteristics? Some type of demographic research or experience becomes vital in determining the needs and characteristics of that segment of the market that the administrator selects as the one for which the services are offered. A market focus strategy of defining the target market becomes a vital step in designing a market-service match strategy which is so necessary for the formulation of all the strategies needed in administering the affairs of a non-profit organization.

In addition to demographic information, an administrator may wish to research the psychographics of the target market. Knowledge of the cultural life styles of the target market is essential in order to formulate strategies to reach that market. The psychographics of clients — that is, their activities, interests, and opinions (AIO) — might be very helpful in designing, pricing, and promoting products/services and in determining the types of personnel and financial strategies to use in marketing the products/services of the NPO.

An administrator may evaluate the strengths and weaknesses of the market target focus by using the following analysis:

Strategy: To Focus on the Target Market for Possible Market Segmentation

	Evaluate As To Strength/ Weakness/ Don't Know	Is There A Competitive Advantage Relative To Your Chief Competitor? Yes/No/ Same/ Don't Know	This Factor Needs More Attention
Market Target Segmentation			
1. Does the non-profit organization know the following characteristics of its market:			
1.1 Who they are			
1.2 How many there are			
1.3 Where they are			
1.4 When they come			
1.5 What they prefer			
1.6 Other demographic characteristics			
2. Does the NPO know the psychographic infor- mation:			
2.1 Activities			
2.2 Interests			
2.3 Opinions			

Overall Evaluation and Prescription:

ENHANCEMENT STRATEGIES

General Service Enhancement Strategies

If a non-profit organization is in a competitive market position, it usually becomes a wise strategy to differentiate its services from those of its competitors. The reasoning is that when a service is differentiated, there is a reasonable chance that a potential client will prefer to consume that service rather than that of the competitor. And if the non-profit organization relies heavily on money from clients to finance its operations, a service differentiation strategy becomes necessary to attract clients who will exchange their financial contributions for the services provided.

Another general service enhancement strategy is to imitate the service strategies of other similar non-profit organizations, particularly if the general service strategy satisfies client needs. Rather than becoming a leader in services provided, most non-profit organizations prefer to copy the services of other similar organizations. A service imitation strategy is a most likely one for many non-profit organizations.

A service innovation strategy is another possible general enhancement strategy to be used, particularly by those organizations that strive to become leaders in their field. If a non-profit organization has plenty of financial resources, it may be able to afford to use a service innovation strategy to satisfy the needs of its clients by creating new services.

If a non-profit organization wants to satisfy its clients, another general service enhancement strategy is to give its clients the opportunity to receive replacement services if the present services are unsatisfactory to the client. A replacement products/services strategy is a sound one if service enhancement is desired.

Another possible general enhancement strategy is that of providing guaranteed services for clients. If the nature of the service allows the organization to guarantee its services or return the client's money, then a guarantee is a sound strategy.

A non-profit organization may evaluate its general service enhancement strategies by analyzing the strengths and weaknesses of each enhancement strategy in relation to the primacy of the customer service mission and relative to its chief competitor.

Strategy: To Use General Service Enhancement Strategies to Match Client Needs

---

	Evaluate As To Strength/ Weakness/ Don't Know	Is There A Competitive Advantage Relative To Your Chief Competitor? Yes/No/ Same/ Don't Know	This Factor Needs More Attention
1. General Service Enhancement Strategies			
1.1 Differentiation of services			
1.2 Imitation of services			
1.3 Innovation of services			
1.4 Service replacement, if not satisfied			
1.5 Guaranteed services			
1.6 Other general service enhancement strategies			
Overall Evaluation:			

Enhancement Strategies Regarding the Form of the Services

If client needs are well analyzed (and this is no easy task), then it would seem to be a sound strategy to design the form of the services to enhance them. The size and shape of the services might be a crucial factor in satisfying client needs. The question of uniformity of services has to be considered. Should the service be standardized, or should it be tailor-made for each client? The safety of the service has to be considered to protect clients' health and prevent possible lawsuits against the organization. How the service is to be packaged and presented to the client might be a determinant in satisfying the clients' needs. Are the materials used in the design of the service the right ones? Are the materials available when the client wants them, in the right variety, of the proper quality, at the right price, and at the right time and place? How about the workmanship involved in providing the services? Do the services require skilled or unskilled employees, professional or nonprofessional training? These and other aspects of the service have to be considered if the form of the service is to be created and enhanced with client service in mind.

An evaluation of the strengths and weaknesses of the form of services enhancement can be carried out by the following analysis:

Strategy: To Use Enhancement of the Form of Services to Match Client Needs

		Evaluate As To Strength/ Weakness/ Don't Know	Is There A Competitive Advantage Relative To Your Chief Competitor? Yes/No/ Same/ Don't Know	This Factor Needs More Attention
2.	Form of Services Enhancement Strategies			
	2.1 Size and shape			
	2.2 Uniformity			
	2.21 Standardized			
	2.22 Tailor-made			
	2.3 Safety			
	2.4 Packaging			
	2.5 Materials Used			
	2.51 Quantity			
	2.52 Variety			
	2.53 Quality			
	2.54 Price			
	2.55 Place			
	2.56 Time			
	2.6 Workmanship			
	2.61 Skilled/unskilled			
	2.62 Professional/non-professional			
	2.7 Others			

Overall Evaluation:

Enhancement Through the Quality of the Services

The nature of client needs will also determine the quality desired in the services offered. Several criteria may be used in designing the strategies regarding the quality of services. Dependability of the services is a chief one. When the client desires the service, will it be there all the time, and will it be reliable? Adaptability of the service is another. Can the service be used for a variety of purposes and for a variety of people? Quality workmanship is another. Since most non-profit organizations' services are composed largely of labor, does the workmanship represent a professional, skilled effort? Quality materials and equipment are another criterion. Are the materials of high quality, and is the equipment of the highest quality necessary to do the job required? The opposites of high-quality services will usually detract from the services offered and cause the organization to fail in its mission. Those opposites are lack of dependability, lack of adaptability, sloppy workmanship, and poor-quality materials and equipment.

An evaluation of the quality strategies of the services offered may also be made:

Strategy: To Provide Quality Services to Clients

	Evaluate As To Strength/ Weakness/ Don't Know	Is There A Competitive Advantage Relative To Your Chief Competitor? Yes/No/ Same/ Don't Know	This Factor Needs More Attention
3. Quality of Service Strategies			
3.1 Dependability			
3.2 Adaptability			
3.3 Workmanship			
3.4 Materials			
3.5 Equipment			
Overall Evaluation:			

Availability of the Service

Clients usually desire that services be available in sufficient quantities, at the right place, and at the right time. If the services offered by a non-profit organization require complementary services, then perhaps those complementary services should also be available. And most clients prefer a variety of services from which to choose.

A strategy of providing sufficient quantities of the products and/or services at the right time and place would necessitate carrying a sufficient inventory of products/services so that the NPO will not run out when and if there is a significant run on the products and services by the clients. That strategy would also require sufficient working capital to carry an adequate inventory.

Keep in mind, however, that most NPOs do not carry inventories of products. Rather, they should carry enough people to provide the services required by their clients.

A strategy of carrying complementary products/services, as well as carrying a variety of lines, would also necessitate carrying a large inventory. Such a strategy would require working capital in sufficient amounts to finance the labor, materials, and overhead costs associated with inventories of the products/services offered to the client.

An evaluation of the availability of the non-profit organization's services may be made by using the following analysis:

Strategy: To Enhance the Service by Having Services Available

	Evaluate As To Strength/ Weakness/ Don't Know	Is There A Competitive Advantage Relative To Your Chief Competitor? Yes/No/ Same/ Don't Know	This Factor Needs More Attention
4. Availability Strategies			
4.1 Sufficient quantities			
4.2 At right place			
4.3 At right time			
4.4 Variety of services			
4.5 Complementary services			
Overall Evaluation:			

Financial (Pecuniary) Strategies

If the non-profit organization wishes to offer high-value services, then it might consider credit and perhaps trade-in and installment plans. Further, if credit is offered, then collection procedures become important.

An evaluation of the financial services strategies might be made by the following analysis:

Strategy: To Provide Financial Services to Enhance Client Value

```
                                      Is There A
                                      Competitive
                                      Advantage
                                      Relative To
                          Evaluate    Your Chief    This
                          As To       Competitor?   Factor
                          Strength/   Yes/No/       Needs
                          Weakness/   Same/         More
                          Don't Know  Don't Know    Attention
5.   Financial Strategies

     5.1   Cash only
     5.2   Credit
     5.3   Trade-ins
     5.4   Installment plans
     5.5   Collection
           procedures
     5.6   Others

     Overall Evaluation:
```

Services Information Strategy

If the potential clients are unaware of the services of a non-profit organization, there has to be some type of strategy for making information available to the clients. Most people would like to have information about the services so that intelligent decisions can be made whether to consume the services offered. Two fundamental strategies have to be considered: (1) what the message about the services is to be and (2) what types of media should be used to convey the message. These two decisions usually depend on the type of services offered, the nature of the clients/customers, and the stage of service life cycle.

The non-profit organization's information strategy may also be evaluated as to its strengths and weaknesses:

Strategy: To Make Clients Aware of Services Offered

```
                                      Is There A
                                      Competitive
                                      Advantage
                                      Relative To
                          Evaluate    Your Chief    This
                          As To       Competitor?   Factor
                          Strength/   Yes/No/       Needs
                          Weakness/   Same/         More
                          Don't Know  Don't Know    Attention
6.   Services Information
     Strategy

     6.1   Message theme
     6.2   Media used
     6.3   Others

     Overall Evaluation:
```

Pricing Strategy of Services Offered

If the services of a non-profit organization are offered to the consuming clients on a non-voluntary basis, then a pricing strategy has to be employed. The price is expressed in various terms, depending on the nature of the non-profit organization — for example, dues for professional service organizations, contributions for museums, offerings for churches, taxes for governmental units, student fees and tuition for educational institutions, prices for hospital services, and the like. Since no non-profit organization can survive without collecting some "price" for its services, it becomes necessary to devise some price strategy for the services offered. Three alternative pricing strategies are normally used: (1) pricing below the market price, (2) pricing at the market price, and (3) pricing above the market price. The market price can usually be determined by observing what competitors are charging for similar products/services or by observing what the prices of substitute products/services are.

Several factors affect the pricing strategy, including the quality of the services, the type of clients, the market structure, the service life cycle, and others, depending on the revenue objectives of the non-profit organization. For example, if a service is elastic in demand, the number of units sold will increase when the price is decreased, thereby causing a change in revenue. If a service is inelastic in demand, the number of units sold will not change when the price is increased, thereby causing an increase in revenue. If a service is unitary in demand, the number of units sold will change when the price is increased, but the revenue will stay the same. Pricing strategy, moreover, usually depends a great deal on the nature of the services offered as a key factor in determining whether to price below, at, or above the market.

The pricing strategy of the services offered may also be evaluated as to its strengths and weaknesses:

Strategy: To Price the Service to Match Client and NPO Needs

	Evaluate As To Strength/ Weakness/ Don't Know	Is There A Competitive Advantage Relative To Your Chief Competitor? Yes/No/ Same/ Don't Know	This Factor Needs More Attention
7. Pricing Strategies of Services			
7.1 Below the market price			
7.2 At the market			
7.3 Above the market			
7.4 Other			
Overall Evaluation:			

Sales Personnel Strategies

Since most services of an NPO are made and sold at the same time (a characteristic of a service is that it is usually produced and consumed at the same time), the proper personnel must be available to "sell" the service to the clients/customers. A conscious strategy should be developed as to whether an order getter (creative salesperson), an order taker (service salesperson), or an order helper (supportive salesperson) is needed. Usually the key factors in deciding this type of sales personnel strategy are the type of service, the type of client, and the stage in the life cycle.

However, some type of evaluation will ensure that the NPO has the right kind of sales personnel to enhance the services offered.

Strategy: To Enhance the Services Offered with Appropriate Sales Personnel

	Evaluate As To Strength/ Weakness/ Don't Know	Is There A Competitive Advantage Relative To Your Chief Competitor? Yes/No/ Same/ Don't Know	This Factor Needs More Attention
8. Sales Personnel Strategies			
8.1 Order getters			
8.2 Order takers			
8.3 Order helpers			
8.4 Combinations			
8.5 Others			
Overall Evaluation:			

Place Strategies

Those NPOs that have a high degree of competition, such as churches, colleges, service clubs, and the like, are often confronted with a place decision — that is, where to locate the NPO. Such factors as proximity to the target market, rent, parking, physical environment, channels of distribution, and others will play a role in such a strategic decision.

Some type of evaluation of the place is needed because it may become a key factor in enhancing the NPO's services.

Strategy: To Choose an Appropriate Location for the NPO

```
                                     Is There A
                                     Competitive
                                     Advantage
                                     Relative To
                          Evaluate   Your Chief   This
                          As To      Competitor?  Factor
                          Strength/  Yes/No/      Needs
                          Weakness/  Same/        More
                          Don't Know Don't Know   Attention
9.  Place Strategies

    9.1  Near the market
    9.2  Rent, if needed
    9.3  Parking
    9.4  Physical environment
    9.5  Distribution channels
         9.51  Direct
         9.52  Indirect
    9.6  Others

    Overall Evaluation:
```

AN INTERNAL EVALUATION OF SERVICE-MARKET MATCH STRATEGIES

Evaluating an NPO's service-market match strategy is an important internal analysis that should be employed by NPO administrators. This analysis pulls together those variables by explicitly asking the administrators about their perceptions of (1) the service attributes and classifications, (2) the target market profile, and (3) the service-market strategies. This analysis forces administrators to make specific comparisons between the NPO and its competitors in terms of the variables shown in the analysis below.

The service-market match is an internal evaluation and is not intended to be an external analysis which can be done by professional market researchers. But when administrators do not see strengths related to the variables, there are bound to be problem areas that need attention.

The analysis should be used intermittently to ensure that "gaps" do not develop between what the competitors have and what the NPO provides. Those gaps would suggest that the fundamental mission of client service is not being accomplished as well as possible.

When the analysis is finished and the overall evaluation is related to revenues, units sold, number of clients, complaints, and other measures, the service-market match strategy can be intelligently evaluated as to what the NPO's strengths and weaknesses are in relation to its fundamental mission and related strategies.

The analysis in Figure 9.1 is designed so that the administrators fill in the blanks (where appropriate), describe the variable (if possible), and compare

Figure 9.1
Product/Service-Market Match Strategies

TO ACCOMPLISH THE MISSION OF -----------------------
                                (NPO)
SEPARATE EVALUATION OF -----------------------------
                        (EACH PRODUCT/SERVICE)

Describe Variables and Evaluate the Perceptions of Management Strength/Weakness/Unknown	Is There Any Competitive Advantage Relative to Chief Competition? Yes/No	Prescription

I. Target Market Focus
    Analysis
    A. General characteristics
        1. Who are they?
        2. How many are there?
        3. Where are they?
        4. When do they consume?
        5. What quantity do
            they comsume?
        6. Demographics
            a. Age
            b. Occupation
            c. Sex
            d. Marital status
            e. Income
            f. Urban/rural
            g. Education
            h. Race
            i. Nationality
            j. Expenditure pattern
            k. Others

If the demographics and general characteristics for the actual and
potential markets can be identified and grouped, the chances of
formulating and implementing a market segmentation strategy are much
greater than if the demographics are not known.

    B. Psychographics (life styles)
        1. Activities--examples:
            Likes to create,
            imitates others,
            likes mobility,
            likes to shop,
            likes to cook,
            does housework,
            spends rather than saves,
            explores to seek knowledge,
            collects and preserves things,
            organizes and builds,
            acquires possessions,
            defends one's ideas,
            exhibits leadership,
            seeks entertainment.
        2. Interests--examples:
            Pleasure, social approval,
            power, prestige, adventure,
            conformity, affection,
            convenience, variety,
            opposite sex, order, economy,
            privacy, newness, curiosity,
            avoidance of failures.

180

Figure 9.1 (continued)

<table>
<tr><td>Describe
Variables
and Evaluate
the Percep-
tions of
<u>Management</u>
Strength/
Weakness/
Unknown</td><td>Is There
Any Competi-
tive Advantage
Relative to
Chief
<u>Competition?</u>
Yes/No</td><td>Pre-
scrip-
<u>tion</u></td></tr>
</table>

     3. Opinions--examples:
         Politics, economics, religion,
         race, marriage and family,
         work vs. leisure, brands,
         loyalty, prejudices.

Psychographics become important in highly competitive situations. They
help to design a product/service that is very beneficial in promoting,
pricing, placing, staffing, and financing the product/service.

    C. Market focus strategy being pursued:
       Which one(s)?
       1. Segmenting a specific market
          (Segmentation, niching)
       2. Hitting that specific market
          hard
          (Market concentration)
       3. Pushing for no specific market
          (Mass marketing)
       4. Others
    D. Overall Evaluation of Target Market Focus:

II. Product/Service Perceptions
    A. General description
       1. Attributes
       2. Major uses
       3. Others
    B. Classification scheme
       1. Convenience
       2. Shopping
       3. Specialty
       4. Impulse
       5. Consumer
       6. Industrial
       7. Other
    C. Characteristics
       1. Necessity/luxury
       2. Durable/non-durable
       3. High value/low value
       4. Technical/non-technical
       5. Perishable/non-perishable
       6. Seasonal/nonseasonal
       7. Cyclical/non-cyclical
       8. Standardized/tailor-made
       9. Stable/fad
     10. Postponable/non-postponable
     11. Complementary/non-complementary
     12. Stage of product/service life
         cycle
         a. development
         b. growth
         c. maturity
         d. decline
     13. Competitive position (describe)
     14. Cost intensive
         a. labor
         b. capital
         c. material

Figure 9.1 (continued)

Describe Variables and Evaluate the Perceptions of Management Strength/ Weakness/ Unknown	Is There Any Competitive Advantage Relative to Chief Competition? Yes/No	Prescription

```
          15.  High quality/low quality
          16.  Reliable/unreliable
          17.  Programmable/non-programmable
          18.  Trade-in value high/low
          19.  Franchised/non-franchised
          20.  Fast/slow
          21.  Personal/impersonal
          22.  Ease of maintenance (describe)
          23.  Skill required (describe)
          24.  Compatible/non-compatible
          25.  Risky/non-risky
          26.  Other characteristics

III.  Product/Service Enhancement
      Strategies (Increase Benefits
      to Customers)
      A.  Product/service benefits
          1.  Design and form
              a.  size and shape
              b.  uniformity
              c.  safety
              d.  packaging
              e.  materials used
              f.  workmanship
          2.  Differentiation
          3.  Innovation
          4.  Improved quality
              a.  dependability
              b.  adaptability
              c.  workmanship
              d.  materials
              e.  equipment
          5.  Imitation
          6.  Variety
          7.  Guarantees
          8.  Service replacement
          9.  Other benefits
      B.  Availability strategies
          1.  Right time
          2.  Right place
          3.  Right quantities
          4.  Right complements
          5.  Others
      C.  Place strategies
          1.  Distribution channels
              a.  direct
              b.  indirect
          2.  Site selection
              a.  parking
              b.  environment
              c.  near market
              d.  rent, if needed
```

Figure 9.1 (continued)

	Describe Variables and Evaluate the Perceptions of Management Strength/ Weakness/ Unknown	Is There Any Competitive Advantage Relative to Chief Competition? Yes/No	Prescription

D. Price strategies
   1. At market
   2. Above market
   3. Below market
   4. Based on cost
   5. What market will bear
   6. Others
E. Information strategies
   1. Message contents
   2. Media
   3. Inform/persuade/remind
   4. Others
F. Sales personnel strategies
   1. Order takers
   2. Order getters
   3. Order helpers
   4. Combinations
   5. Others
G. Financial (pecuniary) strategies
   1. Cash
   2. Layaway
   3. Credit
   4. Installment
   5. Trade-ins
   6. Collection methods

These strategies should enhance the product/service offered by the NPO.
Do they? Any weaknesses? Any competitive advantages?

IV. Actual "Costs" of
     Products/Services
     (From view of clients)
   A. Price
   B. Hassles
   C. Time wasted
   D. Delays
   E. More work required
   F. Risk of failure
   G. Too much space required
   H. Lack of maintenance
   I. Poor service
   J. Other "costs"

Are these costs so great that a potential or actual client will not buy or
will be forced to switch to another NPO?

V. Enhancement Strategies to
    Reduce Client "Costs"
   A. Reduce prices
   B. Reduce costs
      1. Delivery
      2. Installation
      3. Financing

Figure 9.1 (continued)

Describe Variables and Evaluate the Perceptions of Management Strength/ Weakness/ Unknown	Is There Any Competitive Advantage Relative to Chief Competition? Yes/No	Prescription

C. Reduce rate of usage
D. Reduce direct costs of
   using product/service
   1. Labor
   2. Fuel
   3. Maintenance
   4. Required space
E. Reduce indirect costs
   of using product/service
F. Reduce costs unconnected
   with product/service
G. Reduce cost of product/
   service failure and
   expected failure
H. Other strategies
   1. Faster time to process
   2. Less downtime
   3. Less monitoring
   4. Less inspection
   5. More rapid set-up time
   6. Reduced risk of damage
   7. Higher trade-in value
   8. Compatible
   9. Others

Will the benefits (enhancements) outweigh the "costs" so that clients will
use the products/services? Can a competitive advantage be achieved?

   Overall Evaluation (From Client's View) of Product-Market Match:

VI. Revenue Enhancement
    for the NPO
    A. Is price high enough to
       offset costs?
    B. Are quantities sold enough?
    C. Others

VII. Cost Reduction Strategies
     of an NPO
     A. General production cost
        reduction strategies
        1. Specialize to make one
           product/service
        2. Vertically integrate backwards
        3. Long production runs
        4. Take advantage of experience
           curve
        5. Research and development of
           processes
        6. Mechanization/automation/robotization
        7. Concurrent product-process development
        8. Computerization
        9. Others

Figure 9.1 (continued)

	Describe Variables and Evaluate the Perceptions of Management Strength/ Weakness/ Unknown	Is There Any Competitive Advantage Relative to Chief Competition? Yes/No	Prescription

B. Capital costs—reducing overhead
   1. Layout efficiencies
   2. Produce for stock or on order
   3. Avoid financial leverage
   4. Others
C. Labor costs
   1. Use of quality circles
   2. Reduction of labor force
   3. Avoid unionization
   4. Time and motion studies
   5. Suggestion systems
   6. Employee participation
   7. Incentive systems
D. Raw materials costs
   1. Use quantity purchasing
   2. Make or buy decision
   3. Just-in-time inventory
   4. Use a part — make a part
   5. Others
E. Managerial costs
   1. Centralize decisions
   2. Eliminate physical barriers between management and employees
   3. Avoid confrontation with employees
   4. "Open" communication
   5. Others

VIII. Does the NPO Make a Small Profit or Break Even?

IX. Is Financial Value Created for the NPO By Having Enough Revenue to Exceed the Costs?

Overall Evaluation (from NPO's View) of the Service-Market Match:

Evidence of a service-market match strategy to accomplish the mission:

	This Year	Last Year	Two Years Ago	Three Years Ago	Four Years Ago
$ Sales Revenue					
# Units Sold					
# Complaints					
$ Returned Goods					
# Repeat Customers					
% Market					
# Lawsuits					
% Revenue Growth					

   Other performance measures compared with industry and chief competitors

185

their performance with that of their chief competitors (if possible). This type of analysis is crucial if the NPO wants to design strategies to accomplish its mission.

SUMMARY

An Internal Evaluation of the Service-Market Match of Your Non-Profit Organization

How well does your NPO achieve its basic mission with its service-match strategies? Some types of analyses are suggested below.

    I. Describe and classify each of the NPO's services in detail.
    II. Describe and classify each of the chief competitor's services.
    III. Identify the focus of the target market for each of the services of the NPO, if possible.
        A. Make sure that all the target markets are considered.
        B. Use the guidelines suggested.
        C. Evaluate the target market and make possible prescriptions based on
            1. Demographics.
            2. Psychographics.
    IV. Do the same for the NPO's chief competitor, if possible.
    V. Describe and evaluate the match strategies, using an internal management evaluation.
        A. Use the suggested guidelines.
        B. Fill in the blanks as best you can.
        C. Reach conclusions regarding the NPO's match strategies.
    VI. Do the same for the NPO's chief competition, if possible.
    VII. Evaluate the product/service-market match and make prescriptions.
    VIII. You might want to compare your evaluations with those of your clients. See Chapter 10.

10

An External Client Evaluation of Strategies to Accomplish the NPO's Mission

There are at least two fundamental ways to evaluate an organization's service-market match strategies: (1) an internal evaluation (audit) by the managers themselves and (2) an external evaluation (audit) by the clients for whom the strategies are formulated. An evaluation of the strengths and weaknesses of the various service enhancement strategies designed to satisfy client needs has been presented in the previous chapter. This type of evaluation by the managers of a non-profit organization is an example of an internal evaluation or audit of those strategies designed to satisfy client needs. However, another type of external evaluation might be more valuable than the internal audit.

USING SEMANTIC DIFFERENTIAL

Perhaps a more effective way to audit the organization's service strategies is to have the actual clients of the NPO evaluate the services rendered to them. The methodology of this form of external audit is to have either an outside firm or the NPO itself make a client audit of the services offered to the clients. The auditors should select a random sample of clients of sufficient size and ask them to evaluate the services, including the quality, availability, price, personnel, and other strategies that the NPO's management has formulated. An effective instrument to use in an external audit is called a *semantic differential*, which is, perhaps, the best way to evaluate any concept. A series of bipolar adjectives are selected and arranged in such a manner as to have the client evaluate the various characteristics of the services that he/she consumes. Examples of a modified semantic differential are provided below.

Instructions

The purpose of this study is to measure the meanings of certain concepts by having you evaluate them against a series of descriptive scales. Please make your evaluations on the basis of what these concepts mean to you. You are to rate the concept on each of the scales in order.

Here is how you are to use these scales: If you feel that the concept is very closely related to one end of the scale, you should place your check mark as follows:

```
good    _x_ ___ ___ ___ ___ ___ ___  bad
```

OR

```
good    ___ ___ ___ _:__ ___ ___ _x_  bad
```

If you feel that the concept is quite closely (but not extremely closely) related to one end of the scale, you should place your check mark as follows:

```
strong___ _x_ ___ ___ ___ ___ ___  weak
```

OR

```
strong___ ___ ___ ___ ___ _x_ ___  weak
```

If the concept seems only slightly related to one side as opposed to the other side (but is not really neutral), then you should check as follows:

```
active___ ___ _x_ ___ ___ ___ ___  passive
```

OR

```
active___ ___ ___ ___ _x_ ___ ___  passive
```

The direction toward which you check, of course, depends on which of the two ends of the scale seems most characteristic of the concept you're evaluating. If you consider the concept to be neutral on the scale, if you feel both sides of the scale are equally associated with the concept, or if the scale is completely irrelevant or unrelated to the concept, then you should place your check mark in the middle space:

```
safe    ___ ___ ___ _x_ ___ ___ ___  dangerous
```

(Type of Service/Product) of (Name of NPO)

Good	___	___	___	___	___	___	___	Bad
Necessity	___	___	___	___	___	___	___	Luxury
Low Quality	___	___	___	___	___	___	___	High Quality
High Value	___	___	___	___	___	___	___	Low Value
Tailor Made	___	___	___	___	___	___	___	Standardized
Non-Technical	___	___	___	___	___	___	___	Technical

Non-Seasonal	___	___	___	___	___	___	___	Seasonal
Perishable	___	___	___	___	___	___	___	Non-Perishable
Durable	___	___	___	___	___	___	___	Non-Durable
Differentiated from Competitors	___	___	___	___	___	___	___	Not Differeniated from Competitors
Innovative	___	___	___	___	___	___	___	Not Innovative
Imitation of Others	___	___	___	___	___	___	___	Not Imitation of Others
Guaranteed	___	___	___	___	___	___	___	Not Guaranteed
Safe	___	___	___	___	___	___	___	Harmful
Well Packaged	___	___	___	___	___	___	___	Not Well Packaged
Professional	___	___	___	___	___	___	___	Not Professional
Well Designed	___	___	___	___	___	___	___	Not Well Designed
Dependable	___	___	___	___	___	___	___	Not Dependable
Adaptable	___	___	___	___	___	___	___	Not Adaptable
Dirty	___	___	___	___	___	___	___	Clean
Variety	___	___	___	___	___	___	___	No Variety
Competitive	___	___	___	___	___	___	___	Not Competitive
Reliable	___	___	___	___	___	___	___	Not Reliable
Valuable	___	___	___	___	___	___	___	Worthless
Rich	___	___	___	___	___	___	___	Poor

Availability of (Type of Service/Product)

Available	___	___	___	___	___	___	___	Not Available
Available at Right Time	___	___	___	___	___	___	___	Not Available at Right Time
At Right Place	___	___	___	___	___	___	___	Not at Right Place
Available In Sufficient Quantities	___	___	___	___	___	___	___	Not Available In Sufficient Quantities

Price of (Type of Service/Product

High	___	___	___	___	___	___	___	Low
Fair	___	___	___	___	___	___	___	Unfair
Good	___	___	___	___	___	___	___	Bad
Above Market	___	___	___	___	___	___	___	Below Market
Honest	___	___	___	___	___	___	___	Dishonest

Location of (Type of Service/Product

Convenient ___ ___ ___ ___ ___ ___ ___ Not Convenient

Good ___ ___ ___ ___ ___ ___ ___ Bad

Parking ___ ___ ___ ___ ___ ___ ___ No Parking

Easy Access ___ ___ ___ ___ ___ ___ ___ Difficult Access

Good Environment ___ ___ ___ ___ ___ ___ ___ Poor Environment

Pleasant ___ ___ ___ ___ ___ ___ ___ Unpleasant

Promotion of (Type of Service/Product)

Bad ___ ___ ___ ___ ___ ___ ___ Good

Tasty ___ ___ ___ ___ ___ ___ ___ Distasteful

Well Known ___ ___ ___ ___ ___ ___ ___ Not Well Known

Good Image ___ ___ ___ ___ ___ ___ ___ Poor Image

Honest ___ ___ ___ ___ ___ ___ ___ Dishonest

Weak ___ ___ ___ ___ ___ ___ ___ Strong

Active ___ ___ ___ ___ ___ ___ ___ Passive

Personnel of (Type of Service/Product)

Bad ___ ___ ___ ___ ___ ___ ___ Good

Active ___ ___ ___ ___ ___ ___ ___ Passive

Dishonest ___ ___ ___ ___ ___ ___ ___ Honest

Weak ___ ___ ___ ___ ___ ___ ___ Strong

Clean ___ ___ ___ ___ ___ ___ ___ Dirty

Pleasant ___ ___ ___ ___ ___ ___ ___ Unpleasant

Financing The (Type of Service/Product)

Cash Only ___ ___ ___ ___ ___ ___ ___ Other Than Cash

Credit Allowed ___ ___ ___ ___ ___ ___ ___ No Credit

Installments ___ ___ ___ ___ ___ ___ ___ No Installments

Trade-Ins ___ ___ ___ ___ ___ ___ ___ No Trade-Ins

Good ___ ___ ___ ___ ___ ___ ___ Bad

Facilities/Equipment

Good ___ ___ ___ ___ ___ ___ ___ Bad

Dirty ___ ___ ___ ___ ___ ___ ___ Clean

Ugly ___ ___ ___ ___ ___ ___ ___ Beautiful

Large ___ ___ ___ ___ ___ ___ ___ Small

Dark ___ ___ ___ ___ ___ ___ ___ Bright

Fragrant ___ ___ ___ ___ ___ ___ ___ Foul

```
Demographic Information:

      Sex
      Marital Status
      Educational Level
      Job
      Income Level
      Others

Psychographic Information:
      Activities
      Interests
      Opinions
```

AN EXAMPLE OF EXTERNAL EVALUATION USING A SEMANTIC DIFFERENTIAL

The sanitation department of a city government decided to have its clients and its managers evaluate the services offered by the department. The department offered twice-a-week collection of trash and garbage (Monday and Thursday or Tuesday and Friday with no Wednesday collection). The price was a flat $3.00 a month (for two cans) compared to a price of $3.50 in a neighboring city. Two city employees worked on each of the ten collection trucks and personally collected the garbage from tin cans provided by each customer. A high degree of personalized service was provided by the non-uniformed employees in that the two men usually picked up the trash and garbage at the back door of each residence. Curb collection was not practiced. The big trucks were fairly clean and noisy when driven, and sometimes trash was spilled when the wind blew. The department did not collect big items, such as refrigerators, tires, stoves, or tree limbs — only small trash and garbage that fit in cans. Complaints were occasionally made by clients (usually one or two a day). The managers were convinced that the city's sanitation services were extraordinary compared to those of comparable-sized cities.

The city had approximately 10,000 clients of which a random sample of 1,000 was surveyed by having them fill out a modified semantic differential which measured (1) the quality of the service, (2) the collection schedule, (3) the price of the service, (4) the employees who collected the garbage and trash, and (5) the collection trucks and equipment. In effect, the clients evaluated the various service strategies of the sanitation department — more specifically, the quality, the availability, the form, the personnel, the price, and other service strategies that the sanitation department offered to its clients.

The results of the 1,000 residential client surveys can best be shown in the following chart which graphically portrays in profile form the clients' perceptions of the service strategies compared to the same perceptions of the managers.

As can be seen, the chart consists of groups of bipolar adjectives which are arranged with 1 as "good" and 7 as "bad." Most of the bipolar adjectives are evaluative in nature; that is, they evaluate the different service strategies as to

Chart 10.1
Comparison of Residential Customers' Perceptions and Management's Perceptions of Customer Satisfaction With Services of the Sanitation Department

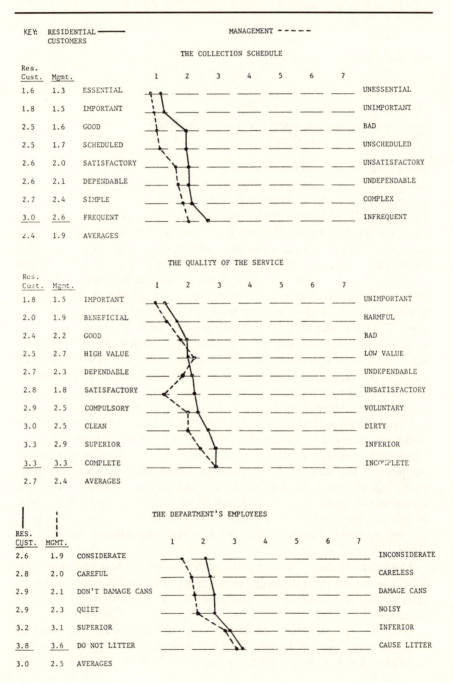

KEY: RESIDENTIAL ————   MANAGEMENT - - - - -
       CUSTOMERS

THE COLLECTION SCHEDULE

Res. Cust.	Mgmt.						
1.6	1.3	ESSENTIAL					UNESSENTIAL
1.8	1.5	IMPORTANT					UNIMPORTANT
2.5	1.6	GOOD					BAD
2.5	1.7	SCHEDULED					UNSCHEDULED
2.6	2.0	SATISFACTORY					UNSATISFACTORY
2.6	2.1	DEPENDABLE					UNDEPENDABLE
2.7	2.4	SIMPLE					COMPLEX
3.0	2.6	FREQUENT					INFREQUENT
2.4	1.9	AVERAGES					

THE QUALITY OF THE SERVICE

Res. Cust.	Mgmt.						
1.8	1.5	IMPORTANT					UNIMPORTANT
2.0	1.9	BENEFICIAL					HARMFUL
2.4	2.2	GOOD					BAD
2.5	2.7	HIGH VALUE					LOW VALUE
2.7	2.3	DEPENDABLE					UNDEPENDABLE
2.8	1.8	SATISFACTORY					UNSATISFACTORY
2.9	2.5	COMPULSORY					VOLUNTARY
3.0	2.5	CLEAN					DIRTY
3.3	2.9	SUPERIOR					INFERIOR
3.3	3.3	COMPLETE					INCOMPLETE
2.7	2.4	AVERAGES					

THE DEPARTMENT'S EMPLOYEES

RES. CUST.	MGMT.						
2.6	1.9	CONSIDERATE					INCONSIDERATE
2.8	2.0	CAREFUL					CARELESS
2.9	2.1	DON'T DAMAGE CANS					DAMAGE CANS
2.9	2.3	QUIET					NOISY
3.2	3.1	SUPERIOR					INFERIOR
3.8	3.6	DO NOT LITTER					CAUSE LITTER
3.0	2.5	AVERAGES					

192

Chart 10.1 (continued)

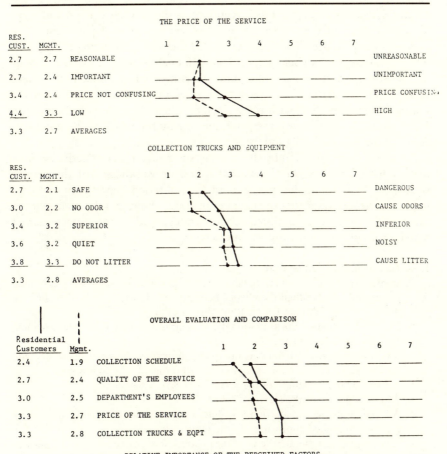

THE PRICE OF THE SERVICE

RES. CUST.	MGMT.		1	2	3	4	5	6	7	
2.7	2.7	REASONABLE								UNREASONABLE
2.7	2.4	IMPORTANT								UNIMPORTANT
3.4	2.4	PRICE NOT CONFUSING								PRICE CONFUSING
4.4	3.3	LOW								HIGH
3.3	2.7	AVERAGES								

COLLECTION TRUCKS AND EQUIPMENT

RES. CUST.	MGMT.		1	2	3	4	5	6	7	
2.7	2.1	SAFE								DANGEROUS
3.0	2.2	NO ODOR								CAUSE ODORS
3.4	3.2	SUPERIOR								INFERIOR
3.6	3.2	QUIET								NOISY
3.8	3.3	DO NOT LITTER								CAUSE LITTER
3.3	2.8	AVERAGES								

OVERALL EVALUATION AND COMPARISON

Residential Customers	Mgmt.		1	2	3	4	5	6	7
2.4	1.9	COLLECTION SCHEDULE							
2.7	2.4	QUALITY OF THE SERVICE							
3.0	2.5	DEPARTMENT'S EMPLOYEES							
3.3	2.7	PRICE OF THE SERVICE							
3.3	2.8	COLLECTION TRUCKS & EQPT							

RELATIVE IMPORTANCE OF THE PERCEIVED FACTORS
TO THE CUSTOMERS AND TO MANAGEMENT OF THE DEPARTMENT OF SANITATION

	PERCENTAGES	
	RESIDENTIAL	MANAGEMENT
QUALITY OF THE SERVICE	21.6	20.9
DEPARTMENT's EMPLOYEES	20.4	20.2
COLLECTION SCHEDULE	19.9	21.4
COLLECTION TRUCKS & EQPT.	19.2	19.2
PRICE OF THE SERVICE	18.9	18.3
	100.0	100.0

OVERALL EVALUATION WEIGHTED AS TO
RELATIVE IMPORTANCE TO CUSTOMERS AND TO MANAGEMENT

	RESIDENTIAL	MANAGEMENT
OVERALL WEIGHTED AVERAGE	2.93	2.63
OVERALL GRADE	B	A-

whether they are good or bad, beneficial or harmful, of high value or low value, and so forth. Since the actual clients' responses are scored and plotted on the charts, they become the perceptions of the services offered and serve as an evaluation of the service strategies of the sanitation department.

As can be seen, the clients have evaluated the services as being fairly good. The overall degree of client satisfaction with quality, price, collection schedule, personnel, and trucks and equipment is reasonably good. If the client perceptions are ranked according to degrees of goodness, the clients are reasonably satisfied first with the collection schedule, then with the quality, followed by the employees, the price, and finally the trucks and equipment. All of them are on the "good" side.

A comparable evaluation by the managers portrays a very effective service-market match analysis of the strengths and/or weaknesses of the service strategies. As a result, the managers of the sanitation department can capitalize on the strengths that the client evaluations show, and the management can also devise new or modified service strategies when the service-market match evaluations depict any weaknesses.

1. What conclusions can be drawn?
   a. In practically every evaluation, the managers' perceptions of the services offered are more favorable than the clients' perceptions. Managers think that they are doing a better job than clients think they are doing.
   b. Despite the "gaps," the sanitation department is doing a good job in providing the services to its clients.
   c. The major "gaps" (defined as one-point differences between managers' and clients' perceptions of the sanitation services) include the following:
      1. Satisfactory "quality" of the services — 1.8 vs. 2.8
      2. Low "price" of the service — 3.3 vs. 4.4
   d. All five strategies — collection schedule, quality, employee, price, and equipment — are ranked approximately the same in importance.
   e. The major strengths are the schedule of collections (twice a week), the personalized services of employees, and the quality of the service.
   f. The major weaknesses (and these are not too major) are
      1. Possible littering
      2. "High" price
2. What prescribed actions might the managers consider?
   a. Make the clients aware of the comparatively low price of the service (a comparison of prices in neighboring cities might be published in the local newspapers).
   b. Make a concerted and *visible* effort to have the employees pick up litter.
   c. Keep pushing the twice-a-week, personalized, backdoor service.

Such an analysis, using the semantic differential as the basic instrument for comparing the clients' perceptions of the services against those of the managers, hopefully would provide some of the information necessary to make a service-market match analysis, a beneficial method of measuring how well the NPO is accomplishing its basic mission.

USING OBJECTIVE DATA TO MEASURE EFFECTIVENESS

The data which the clients of the NPO give are subjective and subject to bias. Consequently, some types of objective, quantifiable information are needed to back up the soft subjective data. Some objective measures, compared over time, should be used, such as the following:

	This Year	Last Year	2 Yrs Ago	3 Yrs Ago	4 Yrs Ago	5 Yrs Ago
Revenues in $						
# Units Sold/Consumed						
% Revenue Growth						
# Clients						
# Complaints						
# Repeat Clients						
% Market						
# Lawsuits						
Other Info						

These types of objective data are needed to determine if the product-market match is being accomplished.

SUMMARY

An External Evaluation by Clients

You are asked to make an external evaluation of your clients' perceptions of your NPO's strategies. This analysis is optional; that is, you don't have to make it. But if you do, you will have feedback which might be very valuable if you want to improve your chances of accomplishing your NPO's mission.

I. Design a semantic differential for your clients.
   A. Make a trial run first.
   B. Iron out the bugs.
   C. Get professional help, if you desire.
II. Once satisfied,
   A. Use a random sample of clients (10 percent will do).
   B. Tabulate client responses.
   C. Tabulate your responses.
      1. Get other members of your management team to respond.
   D. Make a chart showing clients' perceptions.
   E. Make a chart showing your perceptions.
   F. Reach a conclusion.
III. Get objective data (as suggested).
IV. Evaluate and prescribe.

11

Maintenance of Market Share, Growth, and Profit Strategies

Some non-profit organizations are located in highly populated areas and are often faced with direct competition from other non-profit organizations and with other forms of indirect competition. Consequently, maintaining a share of the market for their non-profit services becomes a major objective for those organizations that are not in monopoly positions with regard to their competitive market position. Those non-profit organizations that have a great deal of competition are churches, colleges, service clubs (such as the Kiwanis, Lions, and Jaycees), and credit unions. Other types of NPOs are not in a competitive position because the administrators do not want competition. For example, public schools are assigned district "franchised" territories where no other public schools are allowed. The same rationale is used for other governmental agencies, such as fire departments, police departments, welfare agencies, and so forth, which are assigned exclusive territorial franchises. However, many NPOs are competing with others for a share of the market, whether the administrators are willing to admit it or not; examples include hospitals (public and private) and credit unions (organizational versus banks). When NPOs are highly directly competitive (e.g., church vs. church) or when public and private organizations compete (e.g., public hospital vs. private hospital), then the strategies to maintain market share (or perhaps even to increase market share) become very important to the NPO.

STRATEGIES TO MAINTAIN MARKET SHARE

Various service strategies which have been discussed may be employed in relation to the stages of a service life cycle. These include product, price, promotion, place, personnel, pecuniary, and target market segmentation strategies. Most products and services have a distinct life cycle with various stages, usually four: (1) development stage, (2) growth stage, (3) maturity stage, and (4) decline stage. Over time, these stages exist for most services, although it may be very difficult to determine exactly how long each stage exists and what stage a service is in. However, the concept of a life cycle does provide an opportunity for non-profit administrators to integrate the service strategies with the stages of the service life cycle.

Integration of Service Strategies and the Life Cycle

Stage 1: Development of a New Service

The development stage is characterized by a distinct lack of demand for the service, followed by slowly developing demand accompanied by a gradual rise in revenue or use of the services; a high financial risk; a need to work out the bugs in the service; and possible failures, high costs and expenses, and frustrations. Possible strategies to be used are as follows:

1.1 *Form of services strategies* — Take the initiative in designing the form of the service to fit client needs. Emphasize the packaging, safety, and degree of uniformity (standardization) in the service. Probably imitation of similar services would be appropriate, although innovation in the form of a new service might be advantageous. A liberal replacement of goods and services strategy might be appropriate to make sure clients are satisfied with a new service, which is likely to have faults and weaknesses.

1.2 *Quality of services strategies* — Adequate quality, meaning not too high, but stressing good-quality materials and good workmanship, should be pushed in the beginning. A "professional" setting is necessary.

1.3 *Price of services strategies* — If prices are charged, they should be high or above the market prices to ensure continuity of the service, which might have an uncertain future. (Prices may be lowered later.) If one wishes to enter the market quickly, a below-market price might be suitable.

1.4 *Information strategies* — Use a pioneering approach; that is, "try the service" with location, times, and general information. The best media might be newspapers, phone books, handbills, radio, and maybe TV.

1.5 *Availability strategies* — Institute the service in places and times where there is a high concentration of people. Have enough employees on hand to ensure adequate quantities of the services at the right place and time.

1.6 *Personnel strategies* — Use creative sales personnel backed up by missionary-type sales personnel. Use volunteer personnel, if possible.

1.7 *Pecuniary strategies* — Be willing to lose money during the development stage. Have plenty of liquid financial reserves. Use high prices and low costs for a high margin, if possible.

1.8 *Target market strategy* — Try to define the clients during this stage in order to find out who they are, how many exist, when they come, where they are, and what characteristics they possess.

For example, if a new credit union were established for an organization, the administrators would be wise to take the initiative to institute both the money-lending function and the money-acquiring function, stressing similar service characteristics of other credit unions and of banks. Perhaps a liberal lending strategy might be employed at first. Adequate quality of services would be pushed, but quality should not be too high (some higher quality services need to be saved for later when competition gets fierce). A professional setting for conducting business would be appropriate.

Prices for loans would be high at first, appealing to those who could pay them. They could be lowered at a later time to meet competitors' prices.

A general pioneering promotion strategy should be used, stressing the new service and using an informative approach in the normal media that employees see and hear. No high-powered salesmanship is to be suggested.

The credit union needs to be located in a place that many employees pass on their way to and from work, and it should have enough money on hand to lend. The credit union should be open in the early morning and after work, plus during the day.

The administrators must be willing to lose money at first, or at best perhaps break even. They need to have plenty of financial reserves available and should try not to operate on a shoestring. They also must identify the types of employees who use the credit union.

Stage 2: Growth of a Service

The next stage in the life cycle, the growth stage, is characterized by a rapid increase in revenues or use of the non-profit services. Other competing organizations might enter the market. There would be lots of copying or imitating of the services. There would be testing of different prices and perhaps places. The organization would operate at full capacity, and the need for additional facilities is very likely. Proposed strategies would be as follows:

2.1 *Form of services strategies* — Use a form of service differentiation, perhaps a functional or design improvement. Keep up with competitors, but differentiate in some way or another. Upgrade packaging and safety. Keep a liberal returned goods/services policy.

2.2 *Quality of services strategies* — Upgrade the quality, if possible, by getting better-quality materials, equipment, and workmanship. Keep the "professional" approach.

2.3 *Price of services strategy* — Reduce prices a little, but still keep them higher than market price, if possible.

2.4 *Information strategies* — Use a non-price competitive information strategy. Stress the differentiation strategy — perhaps some degree of "brand" differentiation. All available client media should be used. Keep a low-key approach, stressing quality.

2.5 *Availability strategies* — Open new places and new times for distribution of the services. Keep up with the increased demand.

2.6 *Personnel strategies* — Use creative sales personnel, backed up by supportive-type salespeople. More volunteers will probably be needed.

2.7 *Pecuniary strategies* — The organization should make a small profit or maybe break even. Keep plenty of financial reserves for growth.

2.8 *Target market strategy* — Client characteristics should now be identified and segmented, which should help produce, sell, finance, and staff the service.

Once our credit union gets on its feet, a growth in lending and saving will probably occur. When that happens, the administrators should adopt the following strategies to maintain their share of the market — that is, not to lose their clients.

They should differentiate their services from the competing services of the local banks by offering fast, personalized service and additional services. They should also keep the differentiation in front of all the employees, upgrading the quality.

Interest rates might be lowered for borrowers and upped for money suppliers. (Competition is getting strong.)

Stress should be placed on the differentiated services in the CU's advertising, suggesting the use of the CU rather than the bank.

If necessary, they should open a branch, asking for the employees' suggestions as to hours of operation.

The credit union should use order getters, but keep some order takers. Administrators also need to see about getting volunteers for auditing, serving on the board of directors, bringing in new members, and carrying out other tasks.

The CU should have sufficient finances to make loans and probably will make a little profit.

By this time, the administrators should have a pretty good fix on the characteristics of both the borrowers and the lenders of funds.

Stage 3: Maturity of a Service

The maturity stage is characterized by a high degree of market saturation and a steady decline in per capita consumption or use of the service, although there may be an overall increase in the use of the service. There would start to be overcapacity in service facilities, and there would be some difficulty in determining whether the maturity stage is happening over a long time period or a short time period. Service strategies may be suggested as follows:

3.1 *Form of services strategies* — Make a more significant attempt to differentiate the service, perhaps by adding complementary services, special deals, and the like. Try to design a service tailor-made for clients. Design the services for special market segments.

3.2 *Quality of services strategy* — Add higher-quality ingredients to finely tune the service.

3.3 *Price of services strategy* — Use competitive at-the-market price.

3.4 *Information strategies* — Use the differentiating characteristics of the service as message themes. Price might also be used. Media that communicate directly with clients should also be used.

3.5 *Availability strategy* — Try to hold places and times when the services are offered.

3.6 *Personnel strategy* — Use service sales personnel (neither order getters nor missionary types).

3.7 *Pecuniary strategies* — Be prepared for occasional financial losses. Use break-even analyses to determine possible strategies.

3.8 *Target market strategy* — Look for special markets.

Chances are very great that most organizations are in the maturity stage of life cycle since most churches, educational institutions, service organizations, hospitals, city governments, and the like have been in existence for many years. However, some non-profit organizations may be found in the development and growth stages, and the preceding service strategies are very appropriate for their managers to use.

If a church plotted its membership in terms of quantity and found that it was in the maturity stage, then the church administrators would be wise to follow these strategies.

Differentiation of church services from competing church services would be essential, perhaps by adding related church activities, special church services at different times and places, different sermons for different classes of members, different ministers, and so forth. A higher quality of services would be necessary to differentiate them from those of competitors.

The members would be encouraged to increase their pledges and be prepared for financial losses.

A finely tuned information strategy, such as mailing bulletins to individual members or perhaps going on TV or radio with sermons for shut-ins, would be essential. Maybe direct phone calls reminding members of church activities would be appropriate.

The church should try to hold on to the time and place where the church is located. It should not try to expand.

Plenty of quality volunteers will be needed to help administer the various services offered and to promote the church.

The church needs to look for special markets for members and adapt to the target membership.

The use of the preceding strategies should help the church to maintain its membership and not lose them to competitors.

Stage 4: Decline of a Service

The decline stage is usually seen as one in which revenues and/or use of the services is tapering off. There is constant overcapacity in facilities.

Failures of non-profit organizations are common during this stage. The preferred service strategies are as follows:

4.1 *Form of services strategies* — Possible mergers should be considered. In addition, special effort should be made to extend the life of the service (service life extensions) by means of (a) more frequent usage, (b) varied usage, (c) new users, and (d) new uses.

4.2 *Quality of services strategies* — Continue high quality, if possible. Adapt quality to specialized clients.

4.3 *Price of services strategies* — Price below the market. Use discounts, if possible.

4.4 *Information strategies* — Stress special deals, special discounts, and special promotions. Tailor the media to special customers.

4.5 *Availability strategy* — Cut back on places and times.

4.6 *Personnel strategy* — Use order takers.

4.7 *Pecuniary strategies* — Take the financial losses. "Beg" for financial resources from all possible sources. Consider liquidating the particular service.

4.8 *Target market strategies* — Identify hard-core clients by name, and adapt the services to them. Try to find new markets.

The big problem in the decline stage is extending the life of the service by the various service strategies of more use, varied use, new uses, and new users.

Suppose a social fraternity is faced with a declining market (as many of them are). Suggested strategies might include the following:

A possible merger might be considered. If not feasible, then the fraternity administrators should try to find more frequent usage (like using it in the summertime), more varied usage, new users (foreign students), and new uses. These would be difficult to implement. But high quality would be a must in every activity.

A below-the-market price strategy might be employed, using a discount if the whole academic year is paid for in advance.

The fraternity might have to cut back on the expense of a big house and consider renting a smaller facility.

Financial losses would necessitate begging for contributions from alumni.

If all else fails, then the fraternity should consider liquidating. Why compound a losing situation?

Evaluation of Maintenance of Market Share Strategies

The administrators of non-profit organizations may wish to evaluate each service against the following service strategies related to the life cycle:

Maintenance of Market Share Strategies

```
                                       INTERNAL
                                       STRENGTH/  RELATIVE    NEEDS
                                       WEAKNESS   TO CHIEF    MORE
                                       UNKNOWN    COMPETITOR  ATTENTION
```

1. Target Market Strategy

    1.1 Development stage--find out
         1.11 Who the clients are
         1.12 How many there are
         1.13 Where they are
         1.14 When they consume
         1.15 Special characteristics
    1.2 Growth stage--market is segmented
         in general
    1.3 Maturity stage--specialized market
         segmentation
    1.4 Decline stage--find out actual
         names of users

2. Form and Quality of Services Strategy

    2.1 Development--use
         adequate design and quality
    2.2 Growth--differentiate the
         service
    2.3 Maturity--a more finely tuned
         differentiation
    2.4 Decline--mergers or possible life
         extensions

3. Price of Services Strategy

    3.1 Development--high price
    3.2 Growth--lower price, still
         above the market
    3.3 Maturity--at the market
    3.4 Decline--below the market

4. Information Strategy

    4.1 Development--"try the service"
    4.2 Growth--stress differentiation
    4.3 Maturity--stress finer differentiation
    4.4 Decline--special deals

5. Availability Strategy

    5.1 Development--put at places and
         times where there is a high
         concentration of people
    5.2 Growth--open new places and times
    5.3 Maturity--hold outlets
    5.4 Decline--cut back

6. Personnel Strategy

    6.1 Development--creative sales
         personnel and missionaries
    6.2 Growth--creative and supportive
    6.3 Maturity--order takers
    6.4 Decline--order takers

```
                                         INTERNAL
                                         STRENGTH/  RELATIVE     NEEDS
                                         WEAKNESS   TO CHIEF     MORE
                                         UNKNOWN    COMPETITOR   ATTENTION

7.   Pecuniary Strategy

     7.1   Development--willing to lose money
     7.2   Growth--some profits/break even
     7.3   Maturity--occasional losses
     7.4   Decline--try to absorb losses


     Overall Evaluation and Possible Prescription:
```

THE GROWTH OBJECTIVE AND
RELATED STRATEGIES

Most NPOs have an objective of growing—either implicitly or explicitly expressed by the CEO of the NPO. Although a common objective, growth is not desired by all NPOs. However, most NPOs do have this objective in mind. For this reason, growth strategies have to be developed based on the appraisal of the organization's two environments—external and internal—and on the philosophy of the management.

If an NPO wishes to grow, it has to sell more of its services to obtain greater revenues. From this increased revenue, other NPO objectives may be achieved. But more service revenue is the fundamental way to grow. Increased revenues affect other measures of growth, such as increases in assets, number of employees, share of market, and so forth. However, these growth measures can be improved only through the increased revenues from the sale of services (unless, of course, additional subsidies can be obtained).

Types of Growth Strategy

There are four growth strategies that an NPO may want to consider in creating additional revenues from its services. The first, called *horizontal growth strategy*, is the sale of more quantities of its original services to its clients or potential clients. For example, if a university wishes to grow by increasing its student attendance, it may do so by setting up more campuses in various locations throughout its target market area. That is, another campus is usually added to attract students and is usually depicted in a horizontal fashion on the personnel organization chart, as shown below.

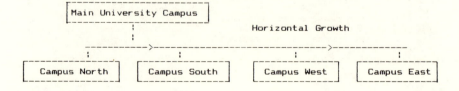

As each new campus is added, the university's student attendance and resulting tuition revenues would increase.

Another form of growth is called *circular growth* — adding related products and services to the original line of services. A third type of growth is called *lateral growth* or *conglomerate growth* — adding unrelated services to the NPO's original line. The fourth type is called *vertical growth* — adding organizational units that contribute to producing and selling a service from the raw material to the ultimate consumer. Each of these four growth strategies — horizontal, circular, lateral, and vertical — deserves special executive attention by any NPO wishing to grow.

Horizontal Growth Strategies

Horizontal growth faces practically every NPO during its life cycle. Selling more of the same services may be accomplished by several substrategies. If the NPO managers perceive a fast-growing market area in the environment, then horizontal growth may be tried. Or if a new market target area can be carved out by segmenting a market, horizontal growth can be tried. Or if an NPO can find more and better uses by differentiating its services, it may expand its market horizontally in this fashion. Or if an NPO can find a high-profit-margin market rather than a low-profit-margin market, it might wish to differentiate its services.

For example, suppose a collegiate athletic program wishes to grow by having greater attendance at its sporting events, thereby creating more revenues. It might use a variety of substrategies to grow. It could add women's sports, hopefully creating more attendees. It could play its home games in larger market areas, appealing to more fans. It could increase the scheduled number of games. It could add preseason exhibition games and postseason games. It could schedule games at night and/or on the weekend when more fans are available. All these substrategies would hopefully increase fan attendance and thereby increase its revenues.

A symphony orchestra might want to differentiate its concerts by presenting country-western, pop, light opera, swing, and other forms of music rather than classical opera. By differentiating its product line, it might appeal to more concert goers, thus creating additional revenues.

A credit union might wish to limit its small loans that lose money for a credit union to emergency-type loans and switch to larger-volume loans that pay for themselves and hopefully create revenues to pay for the money-losing loans.

Each of these examples is an attempt by the NPO to try to grow horizontally — that is, to sell more of the same services by using various substrategies to appeal to specific market targets, by appealing to high-profit-margin markets, by changing its services to appeal to different markets, by differentiating its services, or by using other horizontal growth strategies.

Circular Growth Strategies

Adding related products and services to the NPO's original line of services is known as circular growth. In the process of doing so, the NPO's strategy is to generate additional revenue to achieve its growth objective. For example, a collegiate athletic department has football as its major "product line" to generate revenues. But the athletic director also added basketball to create additional revenues. Further, he/she might add hockey, baseball, track, swimming, tennis, and other sports to create a "circle" of related sports:

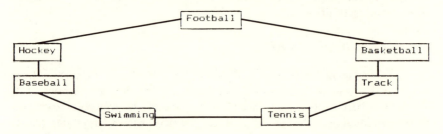

Most city governments provide a circle of related services to meet the needs of the citizenry; for example, they include police and fire departments for protection needs; sanitation, sewage, and health departments for health and safety needs; and various departments for welfare needs. Every time a city adds a related service, it hopefully will create revenues to offset the expenses of that related service.

A church, in addition to its church services, might add Sunday school classes, choirs, baby-sitting services, and a variety of other church-related services to form a circle of related services.

Hopefully, every time a related service is added to the original line, there will be a synergistic effect on both services; that is, each service will benefit from the existence of the other.

Vertical Growth Strategies

Another form of growth is vertical growth—that is, expanding to take on production and marketing functions that move the services from the basic raw material source to producing and marketing it to the ultimate client/consumer. For example, an agricultural cooperative organized as an NPO might look like the diagram shown.

This cooperative venture might start as a farmers' purchasing cooperative. Its first step in vertical growth would be to start an actual farm production cooperative. Then it would add a soils cooperative. These steps are known as backward vertical growth and are concerned with production efficiencies to produce more farm products and thus generate more revenues for its members. Then the cooperative would move forward by selling its products to

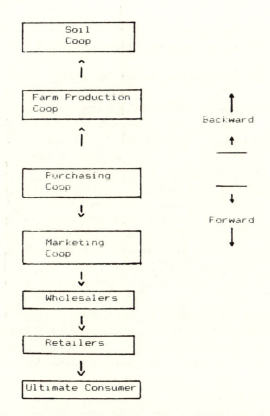

wholesalers, retailers, and the ultimate consumers. The forward functions are concerned with marketing efficiencies to sell more products.

Of course, if the NPO produces more products/services, it usually has to engage in horizontal growth strategies to sell more of the same products by finding new markets, expanding its old markets, differentiating its products, and the like.

Another example of vertical growth is a professional football team, organized as an NPO. The team starts out recruiting its players from colleges, which in turn recruit their athletes from high schools, which in turn get their players from junior high schools. This is a form of vertical supply of athletes. In fact, professional baseball started a backward movement, with Branch Rickey as the chief architect, to grow its own players by forming a minor league system.

A regional symphony might wish to establish a formal relationship with local colleges to recruit its musicians and perhaps with local high schools to recruit its talent, which they in turn get from junior high schools.

Normally, backward vertical growth is performed to ensure a continued source of raw material for the NPO. Once the production is increased, then the forward vertical growth will take place to market its increased production.

Lateral (Conglomerate) Growth Strategies

In order to accomplish its growth objective, an NPO might wish to add unrelated products/services to its original line. When it does so, it adds revenues to its original revenues. Although not very common for NPOs, lateral growth strategies could be employed if the NPO wanted to add a conglomeration of products/services under its corporate umbrella. As one can imagine, such lateral growth strategies would be very risky because it would be virtually impossible for the CEO of an NPO to keep track of and gain expertise in a variety of unrelated product lines.

The federal government and state governments are probably the closest examples of a conglomerate of products/services, which consists of a variety of unrelated services. The word *lateral* comes from the varied unrelated services offered by the government that spread out laterally on an organization chart. Since they cannot be administered effectively by a CEO, they are usually treated as separate entities governed by a commission or other entity, although they report to a central governing body.

The CEO of an NPO can evaluate growth strategies by using the summary guidelines to determine the strengths/weaknesses of the growth strategies in creating revenues to accomplish the growth objective.

Growth Objective Strategies

Strategies to Increase Revenues ------------>	Strength/ Weakness	Don't Know	Evaluation Needs Investigation
A. Horizontal Growth Strategy			
1. Take advantage of fast growth market			
2. Enter new market target area			
3. Differentiate service			
4. Sell high profit margin services			
5. Others (selling more of same services)			
B. Circular Growth			
1. Add related services to original line			
2. Synergism created			
C. Vertical Growth			
1. Add services from raw materials to ultimate consumer			
2. Backwards-production effectiveness			

```
                                          Evaluation
Strategies to                Strength/  Don't  Needs
Increase Revenues ----------> Weakness   Know   Investigation

      3.   Forward-marketing
           effectiveness
D.   Lateral Growth
      1.   Add unrelated
           products/services to
           original line
Overall Evaluation and Possible Prescription:
```

PROFIT OBJECTIVE AND RELATED STRATEGIES

To be non-profit, an organization must be set up to provide products/services not for the profit of the organizers, and no part of any net earnings can be distributed to its members, trustees, officers, or other private persons. However, there is nothing to prevent an NPO from making a profit for its own benefit.

Once obtained, profits (the excess of revenues over expenses) serve a major purpose which benefits an NPO without distributing these profits to the "owners" or organizers of the NPO entity. Profits serve as a major source of internal financing for the operations of the NPO. With profits, there is not too much need to look to external sources of financing – that is, to go begging for donations or to borrow money. Profits thus serve as a major means of financing the NPO. However, if a large growth program is being considered, profits alone might not be large enough to finance the growth. In such a situation, donations and borrowing might be appropriate.

A series of profits can serve as a financial cushion for the NPO. When mistakes are made, when inflation hits hard, when times are bad, or when the NPO loses money, the retained profits can offset these adversities.

When profits are made and kept, the NPO can improve its programs and services for the benefit of its clients/customers. It can increase its overall mission and thus contribute to the quality of life for society. For these reasons, a profit objective is a realistic one for most NPOs.

Most NPO administrators will admit, perhaps under stress, that making a profit is an objective for the NPO, although not the major one. Realizing a profit depends on increasing NPO revenues or reducing NPO expenses or a combination of both. But the NPO's revenue is the major source of its profit. Without sufficient revenues to cover the expenses of producing, marketing, and financing its services, there will be no profit to serve as a source of financing, as a financial cushion, or as a means of improving the quality of life.

There are various strategies that an NPO's managers might wish to pursue in making a reasonable profit: (1) balancing profits, (2) increasing revenues, (3) reducing expenses, (4) seeking a target profit, (5) breaking even, and (6) others.

Balancing profits with other NPO objectives is a conscious strategy that NPOs actually use. Examples include balancing the NPO's image with its profits and balancing its profits with employee wages, which would involve a tradeoff among the NPO, its clients, and its employees. Since most top executives of NPOs deal with a variety of contributors of resources to the organization, it would follow that they balance each contributor's resources against a possible profit for the organization. The importance of each (clients, creditors, community, government, managers, employees, suppliers, and society in general) and its relationship to a possible profit objective would probably depend on the philosophy of the top executives.

Increasing an NPO's revenues is a fairly common profit strategy. Increasing revenues, but not necessarily maximizing revenues, involves selling more of the NPO's products/services. Thus, all forms of growth strategies — horizontal, circular, vertical, and lateral — would be examples of increasing an NPO's revenues.

Reducing expenses is another form of profit strategy. When an NPO tries to economize by cutting costs, it usually considers a strategy to reduce expenses in order to increase its profits or at least to maintain its profits.

Seeking a target profit is sometimes a conscious profit strategy that an NPO might use. For example, seeking a 10 percent rate of return on its assets is a target profit strategy that a hospital might use. Sometimes an NPO may want to set a hurdle rate in adding new assets; that is, before any asset is acquired, it must earn a minimum of 5 percent return on revenues within three years.

Break-even profit is sometimes used as a conscious strategy. For example, when an NPO introduces a new product/service, that new product/service is expected to break even in the first year or two; that is, the revenues must cover both the variable and the fixed expenses. The use of a break-even formula can be useful in these situations to determine how much revenue is needed to break even:

$$\text{Breakeven} = \frac{\text{Fixed Expenses}}{1 - \frac{\text{Variable Expenses}}{\text{Revenues}}}$$

The gross margin [1 − (Variable expenses/Revenues)] must cover the fixed expenses of a proposed venture to determine the revenue needed to break even. (Other formulas to determine units or dollars might also be used.)

Most NPOs use a variety of profit strategies. Although profit is not an important objective of most NPOs, the professional NPO executive usually recognizes and uses varied strategies in various situations to at least make a profit or break even so that he/she is not forced to beg for donations.

The following guidelines might be used to evaluate various profit strategies that are used (and that might be used) by an executive of an NPO.

Profit Objective and Strategies

	Evaluation		
Situational	Strength/	Don't	Needs
Profit Strategies	Weakness	Know	Work

A. Balancing Profits (Tradeoffs)
B. Increasing Revenues
C. Reducing Expenses
D. Target Profit
E. Break-even Profit
F. Combination
G. Others

Overall Evaluation and Possible Prescription:

SUMMARY

Let's continue with your evaluation.

Market Share, Growth, and Profit Strategies

  I. Maintenance of Market Share
     A. Determine the stage of the NPO life cycle.
        1. Get past records for ten years or more, and plot units or dollars on a graph.
        2. Determine as best you can the stage of the life cycle.
     B. Determine the present strategies being pursued.
     C. Are they compatible with the stage? See the guidelines.
     D. Plot market share statistics.
     E. Evaluate and prescribe.
 II. Growth
     A. Determine possible growth strategies. See the guidelines.
        1. Horizontal
        2. Circular
        3. Vertical
        4. Conglomerate or lateral
     B. Plot growth statistics on a graph.
     C. Evaluate and prescribe.
III. Profit
     A. Determine profit strategies being pursued. See the guidelines.
        1. Balancing
        2. Increasing revenues
        3. Reducing expenses
        4. Others
     B. Plot profit statistics on a graph.
     C. Evaluate and prescribe.

12

Image, Survival, Quality of Life, and Other Strategies

Several other objectives relate to the overall mission of NPO—namely, image, continuity, quality of life, and others.

IMAGE IMPROVEMENT

Most NPOs hope to improve their image. In fact, image is usually more important to NPOs than it is to profit organizations. If a non-profit organization has a good image, then it has an ability to attract support from its donors, clients, members, and the community. The most fundamental strategies for image improvement are implemented when administrators realize that the services provided by the NPO have to be excellent if they are to be recognized by outsiders and by similar NPOs. If image improvement is a major objective, the chief strategy to be followed is to produce and market the services or products of the NPO for its clientele or members in a superior fashion.

Further, it is necessary to instill a positive attitude toward the NPO in the minds of the managers, employees, administrators, and members. Hopefully, this positive attitude is transmitted to all those associated with the staff—for example, the press and officials at community, state, and national levels.

An NPO is more likely to be recognized if its services and activities are televised or broadcast on the radio. Television is the chief way to improve the NPO's image, provided that its services are better than those of competitors.

An NPO hoping to improve its image must have good press relations. It is wise for the NPO to treat the press as an ally, not an enemy. Bad relations with the press could prove detrimental to the NPO's image.

When appearing before the public, the employees, members, and administrators should be well dressed. These people's appearance affects the overall image which influences the amount of support that outsiders are willing to give the NPO.

The NPO's image is likely to improve if its employees hold offices in professional and community organizations. The members of the professional organizations recognize this participation. Often they transfer their support to the NPO, represented by its civic-minded employees and administrators.

To improve its image an NPO might support other community projects. If the NPO participates in a desirable community building project, the community chest, the heart fund, or any other worthwhile cause, the NPO can improve its image and gain citizen support.

Another strategy is to stress beauty in the location and surroundings of the NPO. A beautiful setting could inspire good will toward an NPO.

There may be other strategies that a unique NPO could pursue to improve and maintain its image, but the ones mentioned could be evaluated by the administrator.

Objective: To Improve the NPO's Image

Strategies --------->	Strength/ Weakness	Don't Know	Needs Work
1. Excellent services/products			
2. Positive attitude of its managers, employees, members			
3. Television and radio coverage			
4. Press relations			
5. Image surveys			
6. Well-groomed employees, members, administrators			
7. Holding offices in professional organizations			
8. Support for community projects			
9. Stress beauty in its surroundings			
10. Others			

(column group header: **Evaluation**)

Overall Evaluation and Possible Prescriptions:

CONTINUITY OF THE NPO

Those NPOs at risk of losing their continuity are usually in that position because they are not breaking even or making a profit. Consequently, a major strategy for maintaining survival is to have sufficient revenues to offset the expenses of creating NPO services to satisfy the needs of their clientele. If those revenues are not sufficient, the NPO has to be subsidized in some way. NPOs usually have a better chance of getting subsidies than do profit organizations because people know that profit making is not a major objective of NPOs. But making a profit or at least breaking even is fundamental to the continuity of an NPO.

Another strategy is to keep substantial funds in reserve to cover emergencies due to financial losses. Because NPOs do not prosper every year, such reserves would help to ensure survival of the NPO during bad years. It is further advisable to distribute reserve funds among several financial institutions to ensure against losing the entire amount should one institution suffer a reverse.

Another strategy is to have several sources of supply for the materials and resources necessary for the management of the NPO, such as employee talent, money, equipment, space, and information. If one source dries up, then another is available; that is, try to avoid "putting all your eggs in one basket."

Likewise, it is advisable to have a variety of services or products available for client/member need satisfaction. If one service is not successful, perhaps another could be promoted to carry the NPO. Such a strategy would help to ensure survival of the NPO because if a certain service has several bad years, another can carry on during slack periods.

Providing for survival and continuity should be the goal of an executive development program. Reliance on one manager or one chief executive officer jeopardizes the continuity of the NPO. Consequently, a well-managed executive development program will develop its managers/executives using a variety of training methods, such as switching managers around so that they can learn several skills. Another strategy is to devise training programs that develop assistant managers into head managers or managers into chief executive officers. One mark of a successful NPO is the number of assistants who later become successful managers/executives of other institutions.

Obeying the laws and regulations of various governmental units is another way to ensure continuity. If the NPO violates the laws of government, it may be hauled into court, and if found guilty, it may eventually be put out of business. Likewise, ethical behavior is one way to ensure some degree of continuity; if people cannot trust an NPO to act fairly, honestly, and with integrity, there is very little reason to have dealings with that NPO.

The NPO must adapt to changes in the environment to maintain continuity. The reason is obvious: The only sure thing is constant change. If an NPO does not adapt to changes, the changing environment will leave it behind to die. If there are no forward-looking plans for an NPO, it is likely that the NPO will survive only by chance.

To help maintain survival, NPOs should have insurance programs for their major assets — both human and physical. A major fire or other disaster could wipe out an NPO. It is a wise strategy to maintain a substantial insurance program.

Having a preferred market position helps to ensure continuity of the NPO. A market share large enough to receive sufficient revenues is necessary for survival. An NPO has a preferred market position when it is part of a large market or when it has secured a monopoly position with regard to competitors. If an NPO has no direct competition for client/member revenues, chances are excellent for the NPO's continuity.

Finally, engaging in some sort of research and development, although fairly expensive for most NPOs, is one way to assure some degree of continuity. The R&D strategy can be used in relation to the services, employees, production, and marketing processes and to other areas. Hopefully, innovations will occur that may provide some assurance of continuity.

The following is a list of possible strategies used to maintain continuity. They may be evaluated by an NPO administrator.

Objective: To Maintain Continuity for the NPO

```
                                            Evaluation
                                   Strength/   Don't   Needs
     Strategies         --------->  Weakness    Know    Work

1.   Breaking even or making a profit
2.   Keeping large financial reserves
     for emergencies
3.   Insurance program for major
     assets
4.   Several sources of supply for
     important resources
5.   Variety of services/products
6.   Obey laws of government
7.   Having ethical behavior
8.   Adapting to environmental
     changes
9.   Preferred market position
10.  Research and development
11.  Executive development
     program
12.  Others

Overall Evaluation and Possible Prescriptions:
```

IMPROVING THE QUALITY OF LIFE FOR SOCIETY

Currently, the country is demanding that organizations try to improve the quality of life for society. Such an objective suggests that organizations be concerned with strategies dealing with pollution, minority groups, consumerism, urban problems, public recreation, and cooperation with government. An NPO can do its part, just like any other organization, to improve the quality of life.

A pollution strategy involves cooperation with local governmental units regarding solid waste, noise, air, water, and land pollution. It is imperative that an NPO not harm the physical environment in any way by any form of pollution.

Support for public recreation, for arts and cultural activities, and for medical, transportation, and other types of public programs is a natural strategy for NPOs since these types of activities are usually reserved for non-profit organizations. All of these functions are associated with an improved quality of life.

NPOs should support minority groups' desires and wants because of the basic human need of fairness to each other. Since minority groups have not been able, because of human prejudice, to reap the fruits of life to the same extent as whites have, special emphasis should be placed on strategies regarding assistance to minority groups if the NPO wants to improve the quality of life for society.

A strategy to cope with urban problems is fundamental for NPOs located in big cities. For example, NPOs could help to raise money for urban renewal projects, assist in youth programs during the summer months, help to transport people to and from events, and provide security for people who work in big cities where urban crime exists.

It is wise for NPOs to cooperate with the government, thereby helping to improve the quality of life. Since government is supposed to represent the citizens of society, it is a wise strategy to work with, rather than against, those people who are in government service. For example, working with HEW officials will help to resolve the issue of sex discrimination. It is wise to work with governmental officials regarding taxes, rules, regulations, and a host of legal problems. Together, government and NPOs can work toward a common objective — to improve the quality of life for society.

The consumerism movement is also designed to improve the quality of life. In support of this movement, NPOs must practice good ethics in dealing with their clients/members. This includes using honest promotion, handling complaints objectively, and holding events in safe places with adequate safety precautions. Since the clients/members provide much of the revenue for an NPO, they should be treated in a manner that the NPO administrator would like to be treated.

In summary, an NPO administrator may wish to evaluate the strengths and weaknesses of the strategies that improve the quality of life for society.

Objective: To Improve the Quality of Life for Society

Strategies ------>	Evaluation Strength/ Weakness	Don't Know	Needs Work
1. Not polluting the environment			
a. Solid waste			
b. Air			
c. Water			
d. Noise			
e. Land			
2. Support for public			
a. Recreation			
b. Arts and culture			

```
                                   Evaluation
                          Strength/  Don't    Needs
         Strategies    --------->   Weakness   Know     Work

         c.  Mass transportation
         d.  Medical facilities
         e.  Others
     3.  Support for minority groups
         a.  Race
         b.  Religion
         c.  Sex
         d.  Others
     4.  Support for urban problems
     5.  Deliberate cooperation with
           government
     6.  Support of consumerism
         a.  Truthful promotion
         b.  Complaints
         c.  Safety
         d.  Others
     7.  Other strategies

     Overall Evaluation and Possible Prescriptions:
```

OTHER POSSIBLE OBJECTIVES OF NPOS

Being a leader in its field may be an objective of an NPO. If so, the organization should be an innovator, developing new ideas other NPOs will follow. Being "first" in developing new concepts is a sign of being a leader which other NPOs will emulate.

Carving out fields for possible leadership is a necessary strategy. It is probably better to select those fields in which an NPO is strong rather than those in which an NPO is weak. Building on strengths rather than weaknesses makes sense if an NPO is to lead a certain field.

Once a field is decided on, some sort of research and development program must be initiated to produce innovative and successful techniques. Innovative thinking is fundamental to the R&D so vital to NPOs that aspire to leadership in various fields.

Objective: To Be a Leader in Its Field

```
                                   Evaluation
                          Strength/  Don't    Needs
         Strategies   --------->    Weakness   Know     Work

     1.  Being "first" in an activity
     2.  Carving out fields in which to
           be a leader
     3.  Research and development of
           an activity

     Overall Evaluation and Possible Prescriptions:
```

Most NPO administrators recognize that their programs will prosper if the position of their "industry" is improved. Various strategies may be used to improve an NPO's industry in general.

Joining professional and trade organizations that improve the industry is probably the favorite strategy of most NPO administrators.

Sometimes an NPO will sponsor special events that promote its industry.

Further, an NPO might wish to participate in special events that promote its industry.

Objective: To Improve the Position of the Industry

```
                                              Evaluation
                                   Strength/    Don't      Needs
        Strategies   ---------->   Weakness     Know       Work

1.  Joining professional and
    trade organizations
2.  Sponsoring industry
    events
3.  Participating in industry
    events
4.  Others

Overall Evaluation and Possible Prescriptions:
```

SIMILARITIES AND DIFFERENCES REGARDING OBJECTIVES

William R. Stevens surveyed 90 CEOs of profit organizations, 108 CEOs of not-for-profit organizations, and 73 CEOs of public administration organizations regarding various objectives of their respective organizations.[1] The CEOs were randomly selected from organizations all over the United States.

Profit

One of the statements Stevens asked the CEOs to respond to was

The major aim here is profit/surplus: SD   D   N   A   SA

Each CEO had to choose one of the five responses: strongly disagree, disagree, neutral/not applicable, agree, and strongly agree. Each response corresponded to a fixed number (e.g., SD = 1, N = 3, and SA = 5) and the results for this statement, expressed in means or averages, were as follows:

For-Profit	Not-for-Profit	Public
CEO Responses	**CEO Responses**	**CEO Responses**
4.11	1.68	3.01

There is a major difference among the three types of organizations in terms of whether profit is an objective. Such a finding would be expected.

Growth

Another statement presented was

Growth is an essential requirement for this organization's existence. SD D N A SA

The results, expressed in averages, showed the following:

For-Profit	Not-for-Profit	Public
3.99	3.47	3.41

There is not too much difference among the three, but growth is more important for the profit organization than it is for the not-for-profit and public organizations.

Market Share

Another statement presented was

Market share is an important objective. SD D N A SA

The results were

For-Profit	Not-for-Profit	Public
4.01	2.85	3.41

There is a major difference between the profit and the not-for-profit organizations and between the public and the not-for-profit organizations. The market share objective is especially important for profit organizations that are faced with a high degree of direct competition.

Image

Another statement which Stevens asked the CEOs of the profit, not-for-profit, and public organizations to respond to was concerned with image.

Image of the firm is an important objective. SD D N A SA

The results, expressed in averages, were as follows:

For-Profit	Not-for-Profit	Public
4.08	4.40	4.17

Again, there is not much difference. All three agree on the importance of image, with the not-for-profit CEOs perceiving it as more important than the profit and public organization CEOs do.

Survival

The statement presented was

One of the primary aims is survival. SD   D   N   A   SA

The results were

For-Profit	Not-for-Profit	Public
2.66	2.75	2.93

There is not much difference among the three. Since all types of organizations were in existence, survival is not considered that important.

Improving the Quality of Life

Another statement presented was

Improving the quality of life is an important objective.
SD   D   N   A   SA

The results were as follows:

For-Profit	Not-for-Profit	Public
3.66	4.25	3.74

All three types of CEOs consider quality of life to be an important objective, with the not-for-profit organizations considering it more important than the profit and public organizations do.

Client Service

Another statement presented was

Managers here possess a high degree of responsibility to serve the consumer. SD   D   N   A   SA

The results were as follows:

For-Profit	Not-for-Profit	Public
4.14	4.02	3.65

All three recognize the client-service mission, with the profit and not-for-profit organizations' responses being higher than those of the public organizations.

In summary, Stevens found some similarities and some differences in objectives as perceived by the CEOs of profit, not-for-profit, and public organizations.

SUMMARY

Other important objectives of NPOs are to (1) improve its image, (2) maintain continuity, and (3) improve the quality of life for society. Other possible objectives are to be a leader in its field and to improve the position of its industry.

Various strategies have been suggested to achieve those objectives. An evaluation checklist has been provided for the NPO administrator to determine the strengths and weaknesses of the NPO programs in light of the objectives and strategies suggested in the chapter.

Evaluation of Image, Survival, Quality of Life, and Other Strategies

   I. Image Improvement — Do you consider image an important objective for your NPO?
     A. If so, gather evidence to show whether the various strategies regarding image support or do not support the image.
     B. Be specific as to evidence; compare it to the guidelines.
     C. Are there any lawsuits against the NPO?
     D. Make an image survey.
       1. Use a semantic differential (see the suggested bipolar adjectives on the next page)
       2. Make a random sample of the general public.
       3. Graph the results.
       4. Evaluate and prescribe.
     E. Evaluate and prescribe.
  II. Continuity (Survival) — Is this objective important for your NPO?
     A. If so, gather evidence to support your evaluation.
     B. Be specific; compare it to the guidelines in the chapter.
     C. Show profit figures for the last five years.
     D. Are there any lawsuits against the NPO?
     E. The NPO experienced any unforeseen emergencies?
     F. Evaluate and prescribe.
 III. Improving the quality of life — Is this objective important?
     A. If so, gather evidence to support your evaluation.
     B. Be specific; compare with the guidelines.
     C. Evaluate and prescribe.
 IV. Leader in Its Field (if Appropriate)
     A. Evaluate and prescribe.

V. Improve the Position of the NPO's Industry (if Appropriate)
    A. Evaluate and prescribe.
VI. Summarize All Your Analyses About the NPO's Objectives.

Name of Non-Profit Organization

NAME OF NON-PROFIT ORGANIZATION

Good	---	---	---	---	---	---	---	Bad
Necessity	---	---	---	---	---	---	---	Luxury
High Value	---	---	---	---	---	---	---	Low Value
Rich	---	---	---	---	---	---	---	Poor
Reliable	---	---	---	---	---	---	---	Unreliable
High Quality	---	---	---	---	---	---	---	Low Quality
Clean	---	---	---	---	---	---	---	Dirty
Competitive	---	---	---	---	---	---	---	Not Competitive
Low Cost	---	---	---	---	---	---	---	High Cost
Safe	---	---	---	---	---	---	---	Harmful
Innovative	---	---	---	---	---	---	---	Not Innovative
Dependable	---	---	---	---	---	---	---	Not Dependable
Honest	---	---	---	---	---	---	---	Dishonest
Good Image	---	---	---	---	---	---	---	Poor Image
Strong	---	---	---	---	---	---	---	Weak
Active	---	---	---	---	---	---	---	Passive
Large	---	---	---	---	---	---	---	Small
Known	---	---	---	---	---	---	---	Unknown
Friendly	---	---	---	---	---	---	---	Unfriendly

Note: Add or delete bipolar adjectives as appropriate
      to measure the NPO's image.

Note

1. William R. Stevens, "A Comparison of For-Profit and Not-For-Profit Organizations: Chief Executive Officers' and Officials' Perceptions" (Ph.D. diss., University of Arkansas, 1985).

PART III
Strategy Integration into Organizational Functions

Once the overall core strategies — for example, direction, product-market mix, and creation of value strategies — have been formulated, these strategies have to be integrated into the universal organizational functions of production/operations, marketing, personnel, finance, and accounting.

Certain key functional strategic decisions have to be made in order to integrate the functional areas with the overall core strategies. The chapters that follow describe some of these decisions and suggest theoretical factors that an administrator has to consider in the situations facing an NPO.

13

Production/Operations Strategies to Accomplish NPO Objectives

Since the primary mission of an NPO is to produce and market a service to satisfy client needs, some type of production or operations function has to be performed to "produce" that service. This function is typically called by many names in different types of NPOs, but its major objective is to produce the services offered for the clients. Without the function of production, there are no services to be marketed, financed, accounted for, or managed. Most NPOs are relatively strong in the production/operations function.

If a service has some utility to satisfy a need of a client, it has certain benefits for which a client is usually willing to pay. The utility or benefit can be turned into value if the benefit is greater than the cost incurred to produce the service. For example, if a student is attending college (an NPO), he/she has certain needs to be satisfied — namely, the acquisition of knowledge and skills to help him/her in future life. Knowledge and skills are services that have benefits (or utility) for the student for which he/she is willing to pay tuition. Knowledge is "produced" by the professor who performs research based on years of experience, education, and training. The creation of knowledge and the organization of that knowledge into a course syllabus are functions of production. After he/she has created and organized the knowledge and skills, the professor shares them with his/her students.

OBJECTIVES OF THE PRODUCTION/OPERATIONS FUNCTION

The production/operations function has to be integrated into the overall strategy of the NPO. The words *production* and *operations* are used interchangeably. In an NPO, the word *operations* seems more appropriate. As a result, the operations objectives have to be formulated to fit into the overall NPO objectives. The operations manager has to perceive these objectives which serve as the targets or goals of the operations function. If the goals are known, it is much easier to formulate strategies to accomplish them.

Some of the more common operational objectives/goals are suggested in

Figure 13.1
Operational Objectives/Goals and Strategies

1. Which of the following do you as an operations manager of a NPO recognize as your organization's "actual" operational objectives/goals? (Yes/No)
2. What relative emphases are presently associated with each objective/goal? (7 for very great emphasis to 1 for very low emphasis)
3. Which of the following "should be" the operations objectives/goals? What emphasis "should be" placed on each? (7 for very great and 1 for very low)

	"Actual"		"Should Be"	
	Yes|No:	Relative Emphasis 7 to 1	Yes|No:	Relative Emphasis 7 to 1
	|Yes|No:	|7|6|5|4|3|2|1|	|Yes|No:	|7|6|5|4|3|2|1|

I. Operational Objectives/ Goals and Strategies
A. Producing services for client satisfaction
B. Reducing production costs
C. Producing more services
D. Improving quality of services
E. Improving our operational processes
F. Operating on time
G. Differentiating our services
H. Innovating services
I. Imitating services
J. Improving safety in services
K. Reducing pollution
L. Others

Figure 13.1. This analysis asks the operations manager to identify the "actual" objectives/goals and to place some degree of emphasis on them. Further, the operations manager is asked to identify the "should be" objectives/goals and to place some degree of emphasis on them. If there is a difference between the "actual" and the "should be," then a strategic gap is created for which strategic decisions have to be made.

These objectives also serve as crude standards to determine whether they have been accomplished after a period of time. When the objectives have become quantified, they may also serve as measures for a management-by-objectives (MBO) program.

AN ANALYSIS OF THE OPERATIVE STEPS

A fundamental analysis for the operations function is to determine the operative steps necessary to produce the service. Several tools are available to help analyze these steps. One of these, a workflow analysis, is illustrated in Figure 13.2.

Developed by industrial engineers, the workflow analysis is based on the observation of various steps in the production process and the creation of a series of symbols (a sort of shorthand) to depict the varied tasks performed in creating a service. For example, a large circle could symbolize an operation. A triangle might be a symbol for storage or file. A diamond might indicate an inspection or review step. A big D might signify a decision point. An arrow might signify transportation or perhaps a communication step, with the arrow signifying the direction of the communication.

Once the overall steps have been diagrammed, they might be amplified in sentence or word form so that a layman might understand (1) the steps involved, (2) who performs the steps and what other people are involved, (3) the time it takes to perform a step, (4) the supplies needed, (5) the equipment and facilities needed, (6) the direct expenses involved, and (7) other information necessary, depending on the type of NPO – for example, the confidentiality of information passed between client and employee, or perhaps the distance (in feet or other measurements) between steps in the workflow.

The crude workflow analysis suggested can be used to identify (1) efficiencies in operations (or inefficiencies), (2) the types of people to be recruited and trained by the personnel department, (3) the types of supplies, materials, and equipment to be acquired by the purchasing agent, (4) the expenses to be budgeted by the finance department, and (5) other decisions – for example, an organization chart, a layout chart, a production process, and a plant location. A workflow analysis is crucial if an NPO wants to accomplish efficiency in its operations. An efficient NPO can hopefully make a small profit or perhaps break even or perhaps minimize or reduce its expenses.

Figure 13.2
Credit Union Workflow Analysis for Making a Loan

	Who?	Time	Supplies	Equipment & Facilities	Direct Expense	Other
1. Potential borrower contacts, via phone or personally, one of three people, about possible loan. If loan is possible, borrower is told to come to credit union office.	Potential borrower ↑ manager, asst. manager, loan officer	5 minutes per applicant		Telephone Desk Chairs		Confidential Info
2. Preliminary screening of borrower is made to determine amount of loan, purpose, collateral, and so forth	Manager/assistant ↑ potential borrower	10 minutes				Confidential Info
3. Borrower seeks information about amount, payments, collateral, and so forth	Borrower ↑ manager, asst., loan officer	5 minutes		Separate room		Confidential Info
4. Borrower decides whether to borrow/not borrow	Borrower					
5. Borrower fills out application, helped by manager	Borrower	15 minutes	Loan form	Pencils Desk/chair		
6. Application inspected for accuracy, completeness, and so forth Key information Collateral Years Employed Character Income Debt Ratio Credit Rating Co-Maker, if applicable	Manager/Asst. Mgr ↑ borrower	3 minutes				

Positive

Negative

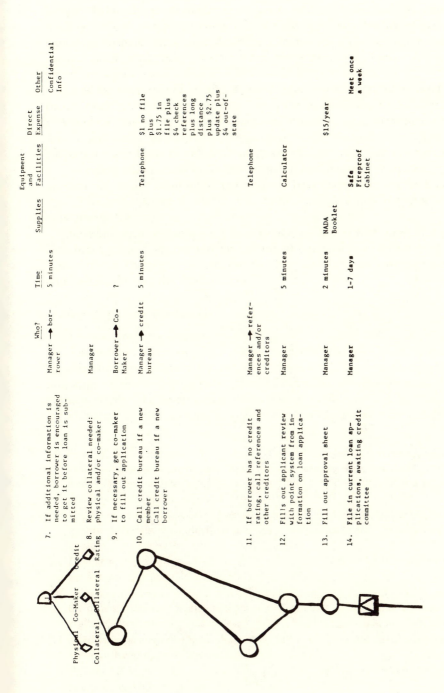

	Who?	Time	Supplies	Equipment and Facilities	Direct Expense	Other
7. If additional information is needed, borrower is encouraged to get it before loan is submitted	Manager → borrower	5 minutes				Confidential Info
8. Review collateral needed: physical and/or co-maker	Manager					
9. If necessary, get co-maker to fill out application	Borrower → Co-Maker	?				
10. Call credit bureau if a new member / Call credit bureau if a new borrower	Manager → credit bureau	5 minutes		Telephone	$1 no file plus $1.75 in file plus $4 check references plus long distance plus $2.75 update plus $4 out-of-state	
11. If borrower has no credit rating, call references and other creditors	Manager → references and/or creditors			Telephone		
12. Fills out applicant review with point system from information on loan application	Manager	5 minutes		Calculator		
13. Fill out approval sheet	Manager	2 minutes	NADA Booklet		$15/year	
14. File in current loan applications, awaiting credit committee	Manager	1-7 days		Safe Fireproof Cabinet		Meet once a week

Physical Co-Maker Credit

Collateral Collateral Rating

Figure 13.2 (continued)

	Who?	Time	Supplies	Equipment and Facilities	Expense	Other
15. Initial screening of loan applications for Years Employed Collateral Use of Money Character Credit History Debt Ratio Types of Outside Income No. of Dependents Other Loans Other Information	Credit Committee Chairman	10 minutes	Minutes of meeting form	Separate room		Confidential Info
16. Sorts out applications into A. Most likely approved B. Should talk about C. Negatives	Credit Committee Chairman					
17. Selects first priority loan applications and then second and then third	Chairman, Credit Committee					
18. Reads aloud approval sheet with selected items from loan application	Chairman → other Committee Members					
19. Reviews point scale	Committee					
20. Review detailed items more closely as point score gets lower	Committee					
21. Discuss each loan	Committee	1 hour a meeting				
22. Vote either yes/no	Committee					Confidential Info

Priority A
Priority B
Priority C
Priority D

	Who?	Time	Supplies	Equipment and Facilities	Expense	Other
23. If no, applicant has three alternatives A. Meet revised conditions for the loan B. Reapply C. Drop the request	Applicant					
24. Applicant is told orally of refusal	Manager → Loan Applicant	2 minutes		Telephone		
25. Applicant is told in writing of reasons for refusal	Manager → Loan Applicant	2 minutes	Refusal form	Typewriter		
26. If applicant meets new conditions, loan approved by loan officer	Loan Officer → Loan Applicant					
27. Loan application is filed for two years	Manager	1 minute		File Cabinet Fireproof		
28. Applicant is notified of loan approval	Applicant → Manager					
29. Type up loan papers A. Note agreement or promissory note B. Truth in lending C. Security agreement or mortgage agreement C.1 Notice of recision D. If auto loan, D.1 Insurance forms D.2 Title D.3 Current registration D.4 Title I form E. Payroll deduction	Manager	15-20 minutes 1 hr/mo	Typewriter note form T-I-L form security form Insurance Payroll deduction Voucher			

233

Figure 13.2 (continued)

	Who?	Time	Supplies	Equipment and Facilities	Direct Expense	Other
30. Applicant brings documents to Credit Union office	Applicant→Manager	?				
31. Applicant signs papers	Manager→Applicant	10 minutes		Pens		
32. Writes check and delivers to applicant	Manager→Applicant		Check			
33. File two copies of security agreement to "perfect" security at A. Courthouse B. Motor Vehicle Division-LR	Manager→Govt. Agency	2 minutes	Envelopes Stamps			
34. Notarize security agreements	Manager					
35. Draw check for payment	Manager		Check			
36. Mail to agency--check and agreement	Manager→Govt. Agency					
37. File complete loan documents				File Cabinet		

Overall Evaluation: Favorable
or
Possible Suggestions: None

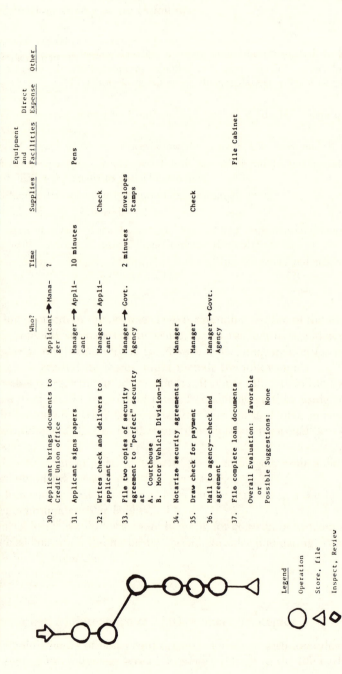

Legend

Operation ◯

Store, file ◁

Inspect, Review ◇

Decision ⬠

Communication ↑

STRUCTURED OR UNSTRUCTURED TASKS IN OPERATIONS

The workflow analysis serves as one means of determining whether the production tasks are structured or unstructured. The structured/unstructured characteristics are used as variables in determining at least two further analyses: (1) the leadership style and (2) the approach to be used by employees in dealing with clients in a personal-service NPO.

If the various operational steps are to be analyzed as to whether they are structured or unstructured, several factors must be investigated. For example,

- If there are detailed descriptions of models, pictures, blueprints, and so forth available to produce a service, then such would suggest a structured task.
- Another factor would be the availability of a person who has the expertise to tell whether a service is finished. Such a factor would also suggest that the task is a structured one.
- If there is an SOP (Standard Operating Procedure) that details the steps in production, such a factor would suggest a structured task.
- If certain ways are better for performing a step than others are, this would also suggest a structured task.
- If it is obvious when the correct service has been produced or when the service is finished, such a factor would suggest a structured task.
- If there are generally agreed upon standards that the service has to meet, this factor would suggest a structured task.
- If the standard is measurable on a quantitative basis, this would again suggest a structured task.
- If timeliness is an important factor in operations, this would suggest a structured task.
- Further, if the service is standardized or franchised (as opposed to tailor-made), such a factor would suggest a structured task.
- If the steps can be performed in such a way as to determine whether they can be improved, such a factor would suggest a structured task.

All these factors taken collectively would suggest a structured task, while the opposites of these factors would suggest an unstructured task.

The structure of a task is an important variable in further analyses of leadership, the internal organizational culture, and ways of dealing with clients in a service NPO.

Now let us take a look at some operational concepts of NPOs producing products and those producing services.

PRODUCTION AS A SYSTEM FOR CREATING PRODUCTS

Production may be defined as any process designed to transform a set of input resources into a set of output resources. Figure 13.3 illustrates this concept.

Figure 13.3

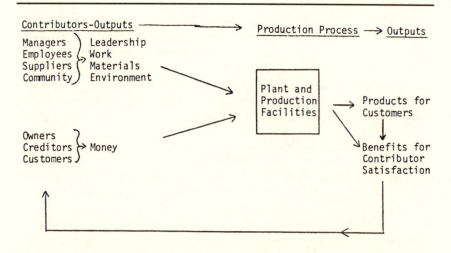

The production system can be very complicated. Many kinds of resources can be put in; a variety of outputs can emerge; the various production processes may be varied. But the idea of a system as the transformation of a set of input resources so that they yield a specified set of output products is the basic concept applied to an NPO that is engaged in creating products as opposed to services.

OPERATIONS AS A SYSTEM FOR CREATING SERVICES

A NPO that produces services is a little different from one that produces products. For example, one way to increase productivity in a manufacturing organization is to introduce a new type of transformation process, such as labor-substitution technology which results in increased output per man-hour of labor. This type of potential productivity gain is often difficult to attain in an NPO that produces services because of its high degree of labor intensiveness and/or lack of machine intensiveness.

A better understanding of increased productivity of service-type NPOs can be achieved by analyzing the components of the production system, particularly if the NPO has direct personal transactions with the client and the employee, as is often the case with NPOs engaged in counseling, consulting, education, nursing, credit union services, and the like.

One of the basic differences of a service NPO is the personal interface between the producer and the consumer of the services. The production function and the consumption function normally occur at the same time. This difference is vital when the client has a direct input in the production process. For example, a client has to give information to a credit union employee before a loan can be made. A case worker has to get information from a client before problems can be solved. A patient has to give information to a doctor or nurse before a diagnosis can be made. Usually the client's input is information, which is the raw material that has to be transformed by the NPO employee into the output services desired. Consequently, the clients do contribute directly to the satisfaction of their needs in transactions with the NPO's service employees.

This direct contact between client and employee is in direct contrast to a manufacturer of products which can control the amounts to be made, the time to make them, the length of the production run, the direct costs of production, and other variables. Because clients of a service NPO usually have unique problems that cannot easily be standardized, it is difficult to regulate the amounts of services for clients, the times to offer the services, how long the services will take, and the costs of creating the services. However, one source of potential increase in productivity is the client relationship. If there can be a high degree of cooperation between the client and the NPO employee, labor costs can be reduced, transaction time can be reduced, and hopefully the client can be satisfied.

The systems concept of an NPO that produces client services has to be a bit different from the systems concept of one that produces products. See Figure 13.4.

Figure 13.4

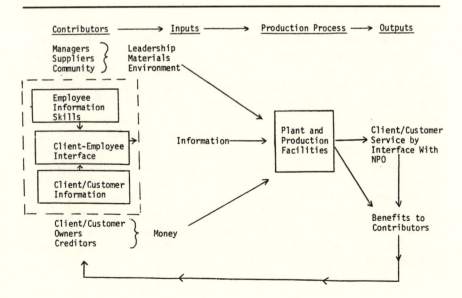

Improving Productivity in Service NPOs

Since the interface between the client and the employee is unique to a personal-service NPO, one suggestion would be to make the workflow relatively predictable, if possible. When services have relatively structured workflows, efficiency can be obtained by eliminating as much direct contact with the client as possible. By limiting these contacts, the NPO employees can do their tasks without too much interruption. Examples would include a sanitation department picking up garbage, a symphony practicing by itself before playing for its audience, and a credit union mechanizing a loan application. However, when services are not structured, it might be wise to schedule appointments for the client and the employees, as is done in the education, medical, legal, and counseling professions.

Measurement of the output is another problem in a service NPO. The services are not tangible, separable, storable, ownable, and transferable as in the case of producing products. A service is a bundle of outputs consisting of quantity, quality, time, expense, environment, place, and other variables. However, these can be measured by asking the client/customer to fill out a semantic differential, as suggested earlier.

The input of the client is probably the best place to start to improve productivity. If clients participate in the initial and subsequent information transactions and become involved in their goal achievement, their sense of responsibility will increase. They will feel partially committed to seeing how their needs will be satisfied if they participate with the NPO employee. In the final analysis, it is the patient who produces his/her health, the student who does the learning, and the client who solves his/her problems. Of course, the doctor, the teacher, and the consultant are also producers, but the client, by participating, increases his/her own satisfaction with the services rendered.

The teamwork of client and employee is also dependent on the client's perception of the employee's credibility in dealing with problems. When the client perceives that the NPO employee can and has met client needs, credibility is generated in the client's mind. The greater the NPO service employee's perceived credibility, the more satisfying the client will see the resulting services.

The teamwork can also be affected by the personality traits of the participants. If the personalities of the two are compatible, chances are better for improved productivity. The more closely matched the personality traits between the NPO service employee and the client are, the better the teamwork is, and the more productive they will be. (In such situations where the client/employee workflow is highly unstructured, there is less chance of realistically setting goals for the NPO service employee.)

Guideline for improving the productivity of the personal-service production function are suggested as follows:

Personal Service Productivity

Factors --------------->	Strength	Evaluation Weakness	Don't Know	Needs Work

A. When the workflow process
    is fairly structured
    1. Eliminate, as much as
        possible, direct con-
        tact with the client
    2. Perform other pro-
        ductivity measures

B. When the workflow process
    is not structured and is
    subject to peculiar prob-
    lems of the client
    1. Schedule appointment
        times for the client
    2. Encourage client par-
        ticipation in the
        information-gathering
        process
    3. Try to get the client
        to perceive employee
        credibility by various
        means
    4. Try to match person-
        ality traits of client
        and employee

C. Recognize that MBO is difficult
    to achieve where there is a
    high degree of workflow un-
    predictability because of
    measurement difficulties

D. Others

Overall Evaluation and Possible Prescription:

SUMMARY

In order to evaluate the production/operations function of the NPO you have selected, you are asked to get the cooperation of the "production" manager in order to make the analyses listed below:

1. Find out the "actual" and "should be" production objectives by interviewing the "production" manager to get his/her perceptions of the goals/targets/objectives and strategies. Use the chart suggested in this chapter.
   a. Get the "actual" and "should be" objectives and strategies.
   b. Get their relative importance from the "production" manager.
   c. Determine if there are any gaps between the "actual" and the "should be."
   d. Use the analysis as the standards for objective accomplishment (after you have made a complete analysis).
2. Make an overall workflow analysis, as suggested in the chapter.
   a. Use appropriate symbols.
   b. Amplify the symbols with words.

    c. Make sure you include the other information as to who, when, equipment, cost, supplies, and so forth.

3. If the NPO is a personal-service one, make the analysis suggested in the chapter to possibly improve productivity.

4. Complete your evaluations, and make possible prescriptions for each of your analyses.

    a. Use the guidelines suggested in the chapter.

    b. Add any others you prefer.

14

Operations and Purchasing Strategies Related to Other Objectives

THE OPERATIONS FUNCTION

Cost Reduction

Since cost reduction is a major strategy of most NPOs, the operations function is heavily involved in reducing the costs of its activities. Cost reduction strategies become a major focus for the manager of the operations function.

Probably the most convincing evidence of cost reduction strategies has come from data published by the Boston Consulting Group (BCG).[1] Their basic assumption states that costs appear to go down for value added by operations by about 20 to 30 percent every time total product experience doubles for the industry as a whole, as well as for individual producers. BCG ascribes this phenomenon to the well-known learning curve, which is based on labor costs and labor hours to produce a product. They then modify the learning curve by adding all the other costs, including development, distribution, capital, and overhead as well as labor and materials, and calling the resulting cost curve an experience curve. This concept can be illustrated graphically by a linear scale and by a double log scale, as shown in Figure 14.1.

Why do the costs go down? One reason is the actual learning that operative employees experience. Another is the improvement in production methods. Better scheduling and more efficient work organization play a part. Improved tools and machinery also can reduce costs. Technological improvements periodically provide cost breakthroughs.

As an example, lower costs usually are eventually translated into lower prices in order to meet competition, either for growth purposes or for maintenance of market share purposes. A price experience curve is the end result; that is, with increases in cumulative volume, the prices are correspondingly lowered.

In spite of the cost reduction, it is very difficult to use cost data for

Figure 14.1

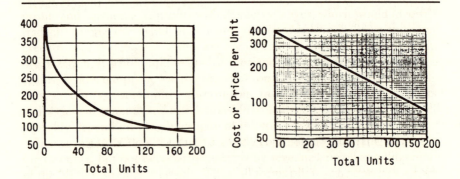

comparative purposes. Internal cost data are closely guarded secrets for most NPOs. Accounting practices with regard to depreciation, cost allocations, and capitalization are not comparable from NPO to NPO. Costs also do not go down in neat, smooth curves, but usually in a series of discrete steps depending on several factors.

However, if an NPO's costs can go down, such a strategy can be very beneficial to the NPO, providing that its revenues remain high. In addition, other objectives might possibly be achieved — that is, increased revenues due to possible lower prices, maintenance of market share with competitors, and perhaps a better image for the NPO.

Cost Cutting Strategies

What types of strategies can an NPO pursue if it wants to reduce costs? One is to have lengthy production runs in order to spread out the high initial set-up costs. The strategy is to minimize the effect of high overhead costs by allocating the total overhead costs among each unit of production in a lengthy run, thus reducing the unit cost.

Another associated strategy is to improve uniformity. If the products/services are uniform, rather than tailor-made, such a strategy would allocate the lower total indirect overhead costs associated with uniformly made products/services and result in a lower cost per unit.

The use of time and motion studies, advocated by the earlier scientific managers such as Frederick W. Taylor and his associates, can significantly reduce costs of the operational processes between labor and the machines used in producing the products and/or services of an NPO. Time and motion studies can be particularly effective and efficient if the standards derived are jointly participated in by both managers and employees. Unilateral time and motion studies instigated solely by managers, without consulting with employees, can be self-defeating. However, if the NPO is labor intensive, time and motion might be an appropriate strategy.

The substitution of machinery for manpower is a basic strategy that an NPO can use to reduce costs. Called by different names, such as mechanization, automation, and robotics, the basic idea is to reduce labor costs and to substitute capital costs of depreciation, maintenance, interest, and utilities for the labor costs.

Other cost reduction strategies might also be appropriate; for example,

1. Specialize to produce one service (and get good at it).
2. Vertically integrate backward to reduce material costs.
3. Computerize to reduce labor costs.
4. Use quality circles to reduce all types of costs.
5. Eliminate physical barriers between managers and employees.

Related Objectives and Operational Strategies

Maintenance of Market Share

Maintenance of market share suggests various operational strategies which have to be integrated into the maintenance of market share objective. For example, taking advantage of the experience curve to reduce unit costs so that unit prices can be reduced is a very effective operations strategy if the NPO wants to maintain its competitive position by using price as a competitive weapon.

Differentiating the service is another strategy that may be used as a competitive weapon. When the service is to be differentiated from that of competitors, the operations function, along with the marketing function, has to decide what type of differentiation is to be used — that is, color, design, form, variety, quality, or other possible differentiating features.

Service quality improvement is perhaps a key strategy to use if maintenance of market share is desired. The basic strategy is to use very high quality when the service is offered in a highly competitive market and is at the maturity stage of the life cycle. Medium quality is desirable during the growth stage when competition is not quite so keen. And lower quality is suggested during the development stage when competition is not a major variable in maintenance of market share. The basic relationship holds: The greater the degree of competitive pressure is, the higher the service quality has to be to equal or surpass competitors' services and to ensure that market share is maintained.

Extension of the service's life is another strategy used to maintain market share. Operations has to find a way to produce characteristics in the service that cause the service's life to be lengthened. Finding new uses for the service might be one way to do this. Adding features to the original service might be another. Extension of a service's life is fairly difficult to accomplish, especially if the service is in the decline stage when the demand has diminished.

Image

There are some strategies that operations can consider if the NPO wants to improve its image. Improving the quality of its services is one. Another is to design beauty into the NPO's facilities. A third is not to pollute its external environment.

Leader in the Field

Generally, for an NPO to be a leader in its field, its operations function has to engage in (1) service innovation, (2) operational process innovation, or (3) some combination. Further, the managerial philosophy must include a commitment to being the best in its field by actually devoting resources to innovation.

Survival

A variety of services must be produced if the NPO wants to survive. Reliance on only one service is very risky in an extremely competitive environment. Some CEOs believe that innovation is necessary for survival; that is, the NPO has to be a leader in innovation, or it has to adapt and follow the leader in order to survive.

Quality of Life

The design of safety into the NPO's services is a key strategy if the NPO wants to improve the quality of life for society. When the people of a society perceive that safety of services is critical, an NPO has to consider the negative repercussions of not improving the safety of its services — usually lower revenues, loss of profits, loss of image, and a poorer quality of life for the society that uses the NPO's services.

Another service strategy is to make repairs on faulty services and hopefully to offer a guarantee of their quality.

The avoidance of polluting the environment is another key strategy if the NPO wants to improve the quality of life for society. When the operations process causes air, water, land, noise, or solid waste pollution, then it is not contributing to the quality of life for members of society. A thought for the operations man that may guide him is that he is a man first and an operations man second. He has to live in the environment like everyone else and be willing not to condone the pollution of the environment as a result of operations processes. The priority is man first and operations second.

THE PURCHASING FUNCTION

The purchasing function in a modern NPO may be described as the procurement of raw materials, equipment, supplies, and services to aid in the production of goods or services for the clients of the organization. In material-intensive NPOs, the job of purchasing agent becomes very important because key decisions about purchasing can make a significant difference in the break-even point for the organization. The relationship of the purchasing function with the suppliers of materials becomes very important. Just what is the nature of the reciprocal relationship between the two? What makes for a good relationship?

Do suppliers contribute the following to the NPO: (1) the needed supplies, materials, services, and equipment, (2) at a fair price, (3) at the right time, (4) at the right place, (5) in the right quality, (6) with safety designed in the materials, (7) with proper service, (8) with truthful information, and (9) with any other characteristics needed? If so, there is a chance to have good relations with the NPO's suppliers.

Does the NPO contribute the following to its suppliers: (1) payment on time, (2) adequate lead time, (3) clear specifications, (4) fair treatment regarding its suppliers, (5) an equal opportunity for suppliers to present their wares, (6) at a reasonable price for the supplier to make a profit, (7) truthful and adequate information, (8) a chance to grow with the NPO, and (9) other necessary factors? If so, there is a chance to have good relations with the NPO's suppliers.

Is there an equitable exchange between the NPO and its suppliers? If so, good supplier relationships can occur which are so fundamental to the success of an NPO, particularly if the NPO's products/services are material intensive; that is, a major portion of its costs consists of raw materials. A guideline for determining the reciprocal exchange of contributions between the NPO and its suppliers is shown in Figure 14.2.

Purchasing Strategies

If the NPO administrators are to produce products/services to satisfy client/customer needs, then they should buy supplies that appeal to their clients, rather than buying those that the administrators prefer. If the clients are not satisfied, they will not contribute the revenues so vital to the NPO's success.

If the NPO is to break even, there are two major strategies to follow: (1) minimize the expenses of purchasing and (2) determine whether to make or buy.

Minimizing Purchasing Expenses

The minimizing strategy involves keeping an adequate inventory to satisfy the operations needs of the NPO, rather than ordering haphazardly.

- If growth is an NPO's objective, a forecast of the supplies and equipment needed to grow is essential. From a revenue forecast, NPO administrators can make a fairly accurate projection of the equipment and supplies needed for operations.
- If improved image is an objective, a common strategy is to buy only first-class

Figure 14.2
**Strategy: To Have An Exchange of Contributions Between
the NPO and Its Suppliers**

Theoretical Situational   Evaluation
Factors   Strength Weakness Don't Know Needs Work

A. Do the suppliers
    contribute the
    following to the NPO:
    1. Needed supplies and
        equipment in proper
        quantities
    2. At a fair price
    3. At the right time
    4. At the right place
    5. With the right quality
    6. With safety in mind
    7. With truthful
        information
    8. With proper service,
        if necessary
    9. Others

OVERALL EVALUATION OF SUPPLIERS:

B. Does the NPO contribute
    the following to its
    suppliers:
    1. Payment on time for the
        supplies furnished
    2. Equal opportunity for
        competitors to present
        supplies
    3. Adequate lead time
    4. Clear specifications
    5. Fair treatment with
        regard to competitors
    6. Reasonable price to
        make a profit
    7. Truthful and adequate
        information
    8. Chance to grow with
        the NPO's program
    9. Others

OVERALL EVALUATION OF THE NPO:

C. Is there an equitable
    exchange of contributions
    between
    1. The NPO and its suppliers?
    2. Who has the edge over
        whom?

OVERALL EVALUATION OF THE EXCHANGE AND POSSIBLE PRESCRIPTION:

materials and equipment which have to be made known to its employees and its clients/customers.

• If continuity of the NPO is desired, two basic strategies may be necessary: (1) having a sufficient supply of materials on hand so that the NPO never runs out of the materials necessary for its operations and (2) having more than one source of materials.

• If the NPO wants to improve the quality of life for society, the NPO's purchasing function could (1) buy materials from minority organizations whenever possible and (2) buy art and cultural objects to support people in the arts.

In summary form, the NPO administrators may evaluate the purchasing strategies used by analyzing the guidelines presented in Figure 14.3.

Deciding to Make or Buy

A major strategic decision which purchasing usually influences is known as a make or buy decision. This decision stems from an operational decision

Figure 14.3
Purchasing Strategies To Accomplish the NPO's Objectives

```
Theoretical Situational                       Evaluation
Factors_____     Strength  Weakness  Don't Know  Needs Work

A.  Service for its clients
    1.  Buy what the
        clients want rather
        than what the ad-
        ministrators want
    2.  Others

B.  Breaking even/making
    a profit
    1.  Minimize purchase
        costs
    2.  Decide whether to
        make or buy
    3.  Others

C.  Growth
    1.  Forecast needed
        supplies
    2.  Others

D.  Image
    1.  Buy first-class
        materials and
        equipment
    2.  "Reveal" them
    3.  Others

E.  Continuity
    1.  Have sufficient
        inventories on hand
    2.  Have more than
        one source
    3.  Others

F.  Quality of life for
    society
    1.  Buy from minority
        organizations
    2.  Buy art and cultural
        objects
    3.  Others

G.  Others

Overall Evaluation and Possible Prescriptions:
```

(particularly in relation to growth strategies) as to whether it would be cheaper to make various parts or to buy them from an outside supplier. This make or buy decision, however, can be expanded to a variety of decisions involving marketing, finance, operations, and personnel.

The make or buy decision can essentially be looked at as an internal or external source of supply decision—that is, whether the NPO can use its internal expertise, or whether it should use external expertise to acquire a needed resource. For example, the following decisions could be looked on as make or buy decisions: (1) whether to make a part or whether to buy it, (2) whether to hire a staff lawyer or to retain the services of an outside lawyer, (3) whether to buy a computer or rent computer time, (4) whether to train nurses or to use the services of a university nursing school, and (5) whether to hire sales personnel or to use the services of outsiders. Key to these various decisions are the situational factors facing the NPO. For example,

- If a large volume of resources is required, then it would be better to make them because of possible economies of scale.
- If the source of supply for the resources desired is strong, then it is better to buy because that source usually has expertise that the NPO does not possess. If the source of supply is weak, then the NPO should consider making its own. The strength of the source of supply is a key factor in making this type of decision.
- If coordination with the outside source of supply is difficult to achieve, then it would be wise to have the NPO make its resources.
- If the supplier is unwilling to furnish special services necessary for production, marketing, finance, or personnel, then it would be a better choice for the NPO to make the resources.
- Certain managerial factors must be considered in an internal-external source of supply decision. For example,
  - If the NPO's managers want to simplify their managerial tasks, then it is wiser to buy rather than make those resources.
  - If the managers want to focus their attention on things more important than the substance of the decision, then they should consider buying the resources.
  - However, if the managers are ready, willing, and capable of making the resource, then it would be wiser to make, other factors being equal.
- Flexibility is an important factor in a make or buy decision. If production, purchasing, and financing flexibility is desired within the organization (that is, if these functions do not wish to be tied down), then it behooves the NPO to buy the resources.
- If technological competence (usually in the form of qualified personnel) is not available to the NPO, then it is wise to buy these resources.
- Another factor involves the NPO's personnel. If there are large numbers of personnel problems and if the wages of personnel are too high to compete with other organizations, then it might be wise to use independent contractors who can perform the same jobs as the NPO's personnel.
- Further, if the NPO wants to reduce its financial investment, then a buy decision is

Figure 14.4
Strategic Decision: Make Or Buy

Theoretical Situational Factors__	Alternatives Make Buy	Evaluation Describe Actual Situation Factors	Strength/ Weakness

Prescription

A. Product-market match factors
   1. If a large volume of production is required, then   X

B. Purchasing factors
   1. If the source of supply is strong, then   ⠀⠀X
      If weak, then   X
   2. If coordination with outside sources of supply is difficult, then   X
   3. If the supplier is not willing to furnish special service, then   X

C. Managerial factors
   1. If management wants to simplify its managerial tasks, then   ⠀⠀X
   2. If management wants to focus its attention on more important things, then   ⠀⠀X
   3. If management is capable of making, then   X

D. Production factors
   1. If production, purchasing, and financial flexibility is desired, then   ⠀⠀X

E. Personnel factors
   1. If technological competence is not available, then   ⠀⠀X
   2. If wages are too high, if there are many personnel problems, and if independent contractors can do the job, then   ⠀⠀X

F. Financial factors
   1. If the firm wants to reduce its financial investment, then   ⠀⠀X

G. Others

Overall Evaluation and Possible Prescription:

best because making usually requires a large financial investment which the NPO might not be capable of acquiring.

These situational factors have been formalized into a guideline for making the decision whether to make or buy (see Figure 14.4).

Providing Storage and Maintenance

Adequate storage space has to be available for several reasons:

1. There should be room to organize supplies and equipment, permitting the use of older supplies first (FIFO). Unused supplies deteriorate and lose their effectiveness.
2. There has to be sufficient space for the handling equipment that moves initial and subsequent orders in and out of a storage area.
3. Employees must be able to move around comfortably in the storage area so that they can take inventory accurately.
4. Space is needed to mark and identify individual equipment.
5. Space is needed for the repair and maintenance of costly equipment.

Figure 14.5
Storage and Maintenance of Equipment and Supplies

```
Theoretical
Situational                                       Evaluation
Factors___                          Strength  Weakness  Don't Know  Needs Work

A.  Is adequate storage
    space available to
    1.  Permit use of older
        supplies
    2.  Prevent physical
        deterioration
    3.  Allow proper
        handling equipment
    4.  Allow for peculiar
        storage require-
        ments
    5.  Meet other space
        requirements

B.  Is adequate space available
    to
    1.  Allow issue and
        receipt upon
        signature
    2.  Identify and mark
        properly
    3.  Repair and maintain
        equipment
    4.  Take accurate
        inventory
    5.  Carry out other
        functions

Overall Evaluation and Possible Prescriptions:
```

If adequate space is not available, supplies and equipment will not be under proper care. Supplies could be lost, be stolen, or deteriorate. If these happen, the NPO will not be able to accomplish some of its objectives — client service, break-even, growth, image, and survival. See Figure 14.5 for an evaluation of storage and maintenance.

Using Inventory Control Methods

One of the easiest ways to lose money, to frustrate operations personnel, to run out of inventory, and to create a poor image is by not having a control system for the various inventories that an NPO may carry. Fundamental to good inventory control is the task of taking an inventory. If inventories are taken, it is easy to keep track of losses, gains, and usage.

Records have to be kept to maintain a good inventory control system. Usually an individual sheet for each piece of equipment is necessary. This sheet should have a record of the beginning inventory, the receipts, the issues, and the ending inventory. It is also wise to record the losses and reorder points, as well as the purchase orders. Such records, meticulously kept, serve as a protection against loss, theft, running outs, and rush orders.

Figure 14.6
Inventory Control

```
Theoretical
Situational                                    Evaluation
Factors__                      Strength  Weakness  Don't Know  Needs Work

A.  Does the NPO have an
    inventory control
    system for
    1.   Equipment
    2.   Supplies
    3.   Other

B.  Are inventories taken
    regularly for
    1.   Equipment
    2.   Supplies
    3.   Other

C.  Are adequate records
    kept showing
    1.   Beginning inventory
    2.   Receipts
    3.   Issues
    4.   Ending inventory
    5.   Purchase orders
    6.   Reorder points
    7.   Losses/gains
    8.   Other

D.  Do supplies and equipment
    have
    1.   A security system
    2.   Identification
    3.   Other

Overall Evaluation and Possible Prescriptions:
```

Also needed is some type of security system to prevent theft of the supplies and equipment. Marking equipment for identification purposes is necessary. Items subject to theft should be stored in a locked place. (Employee theft is a huge problem in our society!) See Figure 14.6 for guidelines for inventory control.

SUMMARY

Operations and Purchasing Strategies

I. How important are cost reduction strategies for the operations function? If they are important, do you pursue any of the following? (Describe).
   A. Have lengthy production runs
   B. Make uniform, standardized services
   C. Conduct time and motion studies
   D. Substitute machinery for manpower
   E. Specialize to produce one service
   F. Vertically integrate backward
   G. Computerize
   H. Use quality circles
   I. Eliminate physical barriers between managers and employees
   J. Others
II. What operational strategies are pursued to accomplish other NPO objectives? (Describe).
   A. Maintenance of market share
       1. Use experience curve
       2. Differentiate the services
       3. Improve quality
       4. Extend the life of the service
       5. Others
   B. Image
       1. Improve quality
       2. Design beauty into facilities
       3. Do not pollute
       4. Others
   C. Leader in the field
       1. Innovate in terms of services
       2. Innovate in terms of operational processes
       3. Others
   D. Survival
       1. Offer a variety of services
       2. Innovate
       3. Adapt to the environment
       4. Others
   E. Quality of life
       1. Design safety into services
       2. Guarantee quality

3. Do not pollute
4. Others

III. Is there an exchange of contributions between the NPO and its suppliers?
   A. Fill in the blanks in the guidelines suggested.
   B. Evaluate the strengths and weaknesses.
   C. Any prescriptions?

IV. What purchasing strategies are pursued to accomplish the NPO's mission and related objectives?
   A. Fill in the blanks in the suggested guidelines.
   B. Make an evaluation.
   C. Any prescriptions?

V. Is a make or buy decision required?
   A. Are there any situations in which the NPO has to decide whether to use an internal or an external source of supply? If so,
   B. Fill in the blanks in the guidelines suggested.
   C. Evaluate.
   D. Prescribe.

VI. Is the storage and maintenance function a strength or a weakness?
   A. Fill in the blanks in the suggested guidelines.
   B. Evaluate.
   C. Prescribe.

VII. Is an inventory control system needed?
   A. Fill in the blanks.
   B. Evaluate.
   C. Prescribe.

VIII. Make an overall evaluation of the operations function strategies.

	Strength/ Weakness	Needs Work	Don't Know
I. Operations Strategies			
A. Objectives			
B. Work flow			
C. Productivity analysis			
D. Cost reduction			
E. Relations with suppliers			
F. Purchasing			
G. Make or buy			
H. Storage			
I. Inventory			
J. Others			

Overall Evaluation and Prescriptions:

Note

1. Bruce D. Henderson, *On Corporate Strategy* (Cambridge, MA: ABT Books, 1979).

15

Marketing Strategies

Modern non-profit organizations are evolving from a production (operations) emphasis to a marketing emphasis. Heretofore, most NPOs had been heavily involved in producing the services that they provide for their clients. Not too much emphasis had been placed on marketing those services. However, a gradual change is taking place as competition increases among NPOs to sell the services that they provide.

THE MARKETING CONCEPT

The gradual evolution from a production orientation to a marketing orientation has been caused in part by the adoption of the marketing concept in our society. The marketing concept suggests that organizations that produce a product or service should focus their efforts on satisfying the needs of their clients, hopefully to realize a profit or at least to break even. This concept rests on two basic ideas. Foremost is the idea that all planning, strategies, policies, and operating procedures should be oriented toward the needs and wants of the clients. The second basic idea of the marketing concept is that obtaining revenues from the sales of the products/services is a major objective of the organization. These two bases of the marketing concept are tied together to suggest that by providing what the clients want, the NPO can achieve revenues sufficient to at least break even and perhaps make a small profit, thus ensuring survival without having to beg for donations from donors.

The marketing concept essentially means that the client is king. An application of this concept suggests that NPOs should strive to satisfy client needs — that is, to provide the market side of the service-market match strategies. Such a market orientation provides the basic framework for administering the affairs of an NPO that is fundamentally different from the production of service side of the service-market match strategies. Both the service and the market, however, should be emphasized if the NPO truly wants to satisfy the needs and wants of its clients.

If NPO administrators want to integrate marketing into their strategies and then to implement marketing strategies, they should have an understanding of the marketing function. The following definitions of marketing suggest the importance of that function to any organization with a product/service to sell:

- The human activity directed at satisfying needs and wants through exchange processes[1]
- A total system of interacting activities designed to plan, price, promote, and distribute want-satisfying products and services[2]
- As traditionally viewed, the function of finding customers[3]
- The performance of activities that direct the flow of goods and services from producer to user in order to satisfy customers and accomplish the organization's objectives[4]

Either explicit or implicit in all these current definitions of marketing is the concept of exchange, which requires the following conditions:

1. There must be at least two parties.
2. Each party must have a product or service that may be of value to the other.
3. Each party must be capable of communication and delivery.
4. Each party is free to accept or reject the offer.[5]

The exchange process calls for offering a product and/or service of value to someone in exchange for value. By providing this product/service, most NPOs acquire some consideration (usually money) from their clients. This consideration is normally more valued than that which is given up, explaining the motivation underlying the exchange. As a result, both parties have increased their value in the exchange.

Marketing, therefore, is an exchange process that requires an NPO administrator to know who the potential or actual buyers of the NPO's services are, how to research and understand the needs and wants of those buyers, how to design a valued product or service to meet those needs, how to effectively promote it, how to attach a price to the value, how to present it in a good place and under timely circumstances, how to organize and manage the marketing personnel who facilitate the exchange, and finally how to finance the exchange. Marketing lies at the heart of the service-market match strategies intended to achieve the client service mission of the non-profit organization.

THE EXCHANGE STRATEGY BETWEEN THE NPO AND ITS CLIENTS

The exchange process, implicit in the marketing function, suggests that the NPO's responsibility is to provide adequate quantities of the NPO's services in the right place. (The operations or production function creates the form utility.) In addition to quantities and place, the marketing function is responsible for creating time utility for the services. All three of these utilities, or benefits, are known as availability strategies. Further, the marketing function has to create possession utility, normally by the passage of title, through adequate price, information, and service utilities.

Having created these utilities for the clients, the NPO expects certain benefits in return. Clients are to exchange cash, payment on time, and a certain degree of loyalty for the NPO's services. If there is an equitable exchange between the NPO and its clients, chances are good that this reciprocity will result in revenues sufficient for the NPO to pay its expenses. But there has to be an equitable exchange (see Figure 15.1).

Figure 15.1
Strategy: To Ensure an Equitable Exchange Between the NPO and Its Clients

```
                                        Strength/            Needs
Factors --------- Affecting --------- Weakness  Unknown    Work

1.   Does the NPO provide the right
     benefits to its clients at the
          1.1   At the right place?
          1.2   At the right time?
          1.3   With the right service?
          1.4   In the right quantities?
          1.5   At the right price?
          1.6   With adequate information?
          1.7   With exchange of possession?
          1.8   Others?

2.   Do the clients/donors of the NPO
     provide benefits of
          2.1   Adequate cash?
          2.2   Payment on time?
          2.3   Loyalty?
          2.4   Others?

3.   Is there an equitable exchange
     between the NPO and its
     clients/donors?
          3.1   Yes
          3.2   No
          3.3   Don't know

4.   If not, who holds the upper hand?
          4.1   NPO
          4.2   Clients/donors
          4.3   Don't know

Overall Evaluation and Possible Prescription:
```

INTEGRATION OF OVERALL NPO OBJECTIVES
AND STRATEGIES WITH MARKETING

The NPO mission and related objectives suggest certain overall strategies that have to be pursued. Several of these strategies involve the marketing function. For example, if client satisfaction is the basic mission of the NPO, then it follows that marketing has to have certain of its strategies integrated into the overall objectives.

The important marketing strategies that must be integrated into the NPO's overall mission are the following:

1. Full identification of the target market in order to segment the market.
2. A combination of marketing strategies that suggests a marketing mix strategy to serve the target market.
   a. Service strategy — designing the service to match the target market's needs.
   b. Promotion strategy — using a message and media strategy to communicate with the target market.
   c. Price strategy — analyzing several factors that suggest whether to price above, at, or below the market.
   d. Place strategy — analyzing factors to determine where and when (availability strategy) to place the services in light of the target market.
   e. Personnel strategy — acquiring the appropriate sales personnel to service the target market.
   f. Pecuniary strategy — financing the sales between the NPO and its target market.

The preceding are marketing strategies that the manager of marketing has to integrate with the NPO's strategies to accomplish its basic mission and overall related objectives.

• If image is an important NPO objective, then marketing can use its promotion expertise to enhance the NPO's image through institutional advertising — that is, by promoting the NPO itself, in addition to promoting its services.
• If profit or break-even is an objective of the NPO, then marketing can use its expertise to create sufficient revenues to offset expenses. But the creation of revenues depends on the target market segmentation and the marketing mix strategy.
• If growth in sales revenues is an objective of an NPO, then marketing again has to pursue an aggressive strategy in relation to the marketing mix of product, place, price, promotion, personnel, and pecuniary factors in order to sell more of its services.
• If maintenance of market share is an objective of an NPO, then the marketing function has to adapt its market mix strategies to the proper stage of the product/service life cycle.
• If survival is one of the NPO's objectives, then marketing has to create a preferred market position by means of its marketing mix factors. It has to create a monopoly,

an oligopoly, or some niche in the market where it has a preferred market position with its clients.

• If quality of life is an NPO objective, then marketing has to support the overall strategies of the NPO with regard to pollution, consumerism, discrimination, government cooperation, and the like.

But before the NPO uses its resources to market its services, it should consider three general (rather than specific) alternative marketing strategies.

FACTORS AFFECTING A GENERAL MARKETING STRATEGY

There are three general marketing strategies that a non-profit organization may adopt. The first is an aggressive one, characterized by a great deal of promotion, price variations, changing times and places for services to be offered, service that is differentiated from the services of competing organizations, creative salespeople who promote the services, large expenditures on marketing activities, and so forth. The second general marketing strategy is a minimal one, characterized by very little promotion, no price changes, services offered at traditional places and times, small expenditures on promotion and salespeople, and so forth. The third is a balanced marketing strategy, an in-between strategy that differs from an aggressive strategy and a minimal strategy only in degree.

These three strategies are appropriate alternatives for any non-profit organization. However, not every NPO needs an aggressive strategy, nor does every NPO need a balanced strategy or a minimal one. The situation facing each NPO is obviously different, calling for an analysis of the factors that dictate which of the three alternative strategies is most suitable for each NPO. But what factors suggest the appropriate general marketing strategy that a non-profit organization should pursue?

The first major factor is the nature of the market competition facing the NPO. If the NPO is in a monopoly position, with no direct competitors in its market area, then a minimal marketing strategy is suitable. However, if the NPO is in an oligopoly market position, with competitors in its market area, then a balanced marketing strategy is called for. If there is a high degree of competition and several competing services in the NPO's market area, these would suggest an aggressive marketing strategy. Further, if there are many other forms of indirect competition, then an NPO should pursue a balanced marketing strategy.

The quality of the services that the NPO offers is the second major factor. If the NPO has high-quality products/services, a minimal marketing strategy is called for, other factors being equal.

A third major factor is the revenue strategies that the NPO may desire to pursue. For example, if the NPO wants to maximize its revenues from its services, then it should use an aggressive marketing strategy. If it wants to minimize its revenues, then it should pursue a minimal strategy. However, if it wants to balance its revenues — neither maximizing nor minimizing — then a balanced marketing strategy is called for.

The fourth factor is the timing or stage in the life cycle of the service offered by the NPO. For example, if the NPO's service is in the development stage and needs to gain a foothold in the market, then it should follow an aggressive marketing strategy. If it is in the growth stage, then a balanced strategy would seem to be appropriate. If it is in the maturity stage, then a balanced marketing strategy should be employed. If it is in the decline stage, then a minimal marketing strategy becomes appropriate, unless, of course, the NPO wishes to get out of the decline stage by using various other strategies.

The financial position of the NPO is another factor affecting the strategic decision of whether to follow an aggressive, balanced, or minimal marketing strategy. If the NPO is heavily in debt, then it would seem appropriate to engage in an aggressive marketing posture. If only moderately in debt, then an aggressive strategy would also be appropriate. If not in debt, a minimal strategy should be followed, other factors being equal. If the NPO is currently losing money, then an aggressive strategy should be pursued.

Another factor is the production capacity of the non-profit organization. If there is plenty of unused production capacity, there is justification for using an aggressive strategy to fill up the unused capacity. Empty capacity costs money and loses the potential revenue that the capacity was built for. On the other hand, where the capacity is filled, a minimal strategy may be used, unless, of course, an administrator wants to make sure that full capacity is used. In that case, a balanced strategy would be most appropriate.

A final factor concerns the managerial philosophy regarding the objectives of the NPO. For example, if the managers want to make a profit, to improve the image of the NPO, or to maintain its share of the market, a balanced strategy would seem to be appropriate. On the other hand, if the managers want the NPO to grow, then an aggressive marketing strategy should be followed.

Further, if the managers really desire to provide a service for their clientele, then they should follow a balanced marketing strategy. Likewise, if an objective is to ensure some degree of NPO survival and continuity, a balanced strategy would be appropriate.

These factors may be summarized and put into a strategic decision model for a non-profit administrator to use in deciding which general marketing strategy his/her NPO should adopt. The theory is presented along with the three alternatives. The CEO may assess the actual situation facing his/her NPO and compare it with theoretical situational factors. Then an evaluation can be made, analyzing the strengths and weaknesses by comparing actual to

Figure 15.2
Strategic Decision: What General Marketing Strategy To Follow

Theoretical Situational Factors → affecting →	Alternatives			Describe the Actual Situation and Compare Theory → to Actual	Evaluation Strengths/ → Weaknesses	→ Prescription
	Aggressive Marketing Required	Balanced Marketing Required	Minimal Marketing Required			
1. Nature of Market Competition						
If the NPO is in						
1.1 A monopoly position, then			X			
1.2 An oligopoly position, then		X				
1.3 A high degree of competition, then	X					
1.4 Indirect competition, then		X				
2. Quality of Products/Services						
If the products/services are						
2.1 High quality, then			X			
2.2 In-between, then		X				
2.3 Low quality, then	X					
3. Revenue Strategies						
If the NPO desires to						
3.1 Maximize revenues, then	X					
3.2 Balance revenues, then		X				
3.3 Minimize revenues, then			X			
4. Stages in Life Cycle						
If the NPO is in the						
4.1 Development stage, then	X					
4.2 Growth stage, then		X				
4.3 Maturity stage, then		X				
4.4 Decline stage, then			X			

Figure 15.2 (continued)

| | Alternatives | | | | | |
Theoretical Situational Factors → affecting →	Aggressive Marketing Required	Balanced Marketing Required	Minimal Marketing Required	Describe the Actual Situation and Compare With Theory →	Evaluation Strengths/Weaknesses →	Prescription
5. Financial Position						
If the NPO is						
5.1 Heavily in debt, then	X					
5.2 Moderately in debt, then	X					
5.3 Not in debt, then		X				
5.4 Currently losing money, then	X					
6. Capacity of Facility						
6.1 If there is unused capacity, then	X					
6.2 If all the capacity is used, then			X			
6.3 Unless, all capacity has to be kept full, then		X				
7. Philosophy of Management Regarding NPO Objectives						
7.1 If the NPO wants to make a profit, then		X				
7.2 If to improve its image, then		X				
7.3 If to maintain its share of the market, then		X				
7.4 If to grow, then	X					
7.5 If to insure continuity		X				
7.6 If to provide clientele satisfaction, then		X				

Overall Evaluation and Prescription:

theory. Once the strengths and weaknesses are weighted for each factor, an overall evaluation can be completed, allowing an overall decision to be made — that is, whether to follow an aggressive, balanced, or minimal general marketing strategy. This model is summarized in Figure 15.2.

TARGET MARKET IDENTIFICATION AND SEGMENTATION

Most NPOs are production oriented and do not concern themselves with target market identification and segmentation. A marketing-oriented NPO administrator, however, practices target marketing. Such a strategy is very helpful in accomplishing the NPO's organizational objectives in a fairly efficient manner.

The rationale for target market identification and segmentation is profit motivated. Rather than assuming that there is a large mass market available for the NPO's services (the typical production-oriented approach), the marketing-oriented NPO considers the market to consist of homogeneous, perhaps smaller markets that may be appealed to without wasting a lot of time, money, and energy. A target market may be segmented from a larger population with several advantages resulting in lower expenses. For example, why spend advertising money on a large population when only a few people benefit from it? Why design a service for everyone when only a few people use it? Why spend a great deal of time and money to train order getters when order takers are the type to use? Why sell on credit when cash is less expensive? Why spend money to open new outlets when there is not enough market to justify the costs? If there is a better way to save money in marketing, why not use it? Fortunately, market target identification and segmentation can save money and thereby reduce expenses so the NPO can make a profit or at least to not waste money needlessly. The market segmentation strategy is based on the concept that it is more profitable to zero in on a market, rather than appealing to a mass market.

Good marketing consists of at least two important strategies: (1) selecting a market target and (2) developing a market mix to appeal to the market target. These two strategies are intertwined, but a common approach suggests that the market target analysis comes first.

Market segmentation is an attempt to classify clients into a homogeneous group so that the service-market mix factors (product/service, price, place, promotion, personnel, and pecuniary factors) can be efficiently planned for and implemented. The strategy consists of answering (and perhaps researching) several questions about the actual and potential markets.

1. Step One — General Questions
   1.1 Who are the clients?
   1.2 Where are they?

1.3 How many are there?
1.4 When do they consume?
1.5 How much quantity do they consume?
2. Step Two — More Specific Questions
   2.1 What are the demographics of the target market?
3. Step Three — More Sophisticated Questions
   3.1 Why do they consume?
   3.2 What are the psychographics of the target market?
4. Step Four — In light of the answers, plan the
   4.1 Design ⎤
   4.2 Price   ⎥
   4.3 Promotion ⎬ of the NPO's services
   4.4 Place   ⎥
   4.5 Personnel ⎥
   4.6 Pecuniary ⎦

Step One — General Questions About the Market

Who are the clients of an NPO? This question should be answered first. More specifically, who decides to make use of the NPO's services, and who uses the services? For example, a hospital's clients are the patients who use and pay for the services, but the decision makers who puts the patients into the hospital are usually the patients' doctors. Both the user and the decision maker should be identified. Many times they are one and the same, but sometimes they are different.

Where are the clients? For most NPOs they are within a certain mile radius of the NPO, either locally or regionally. A political or economic subdivision might be used to identify the market — for example, a city, county, state, region, SMSA (Standard Metropolitan Statistical Area) urban area, rural area, and so forth. It becomes advantageous to know the whereabouts of the actual market as well as the potential market.

How many clients are there? The actual number and the potential number should be determined. If volume of service is crucial to the NPO's survival, some notion of actual versus potential numbers in the market area is crucial.

When do clients consume? Seasonality becomes a factor in the marketing strategy. In addition, the time of the month or day may be a key factor in determining the place and time at which to offer the NPO's services.

How much quantity do clients consume? Do they consume only one or several at one time? Some notion of the quantity becomes essential in producing the number desired and in marketing at the right time, at the right place, and in sufficient quantities to satisfy client needs.

The first step in market identification and segmentation is to answer the who, where, how many, when, and how much questions for the actual and potential markets.

Step Two — More Specific Questions About the Market

Demographic characteristics of the actual market become very helpful in segregating homogeneous markets. This information can be gathered from secondary sources, primarily from census data. Such factors as the following should be identified:

Sex	Race
Age	Nationality
Education	Households
Marital Status	Urban/Rural
Occupation	Population
Income	Expenditure Patterns

If the demographics for the actual market can be identified and grouped, the chances that a market segmentation strategy will be implemented are much greater than if demographics are not known.

Step Three — More Sophisticated Questions About The Market

If the NPO is in a highly competitive market situation, knowledge about the life styles of the clients becomes very important in segmenting the market. A more sophisticated knowledge of psychographics (the activities, interests, and opinions of the market) will be very helpful in making promotion, design, price, place, sales personnel, and financing decisions about the NPO's services.

The following psychographic information would be very helpful in segmenting a market:

Activities of the Client

Likes to create	Explores to seek knowledge
Imitates others	Collects and preserves things
Likes mobility	Organizes and builds
Likes to shop	Acquires possessions and things
Likes to cook, do housework	Defends and justifies one's ideas
Spends money rather than saving	Becomes a leader
Seeks entertainment	

Interests

Pleasure	Power
Social approval	Prestige
Conformity	Adventure
Affection	Convenience

Variety	Opposite sex
Comfort	Order
Economy	Privacy
Newness	Avoidance of failure
Freedom	Curiosity

Opinions

Race	Marriage and family
Politics	Work vs. leisure
Economics	Brand/store loyalty
Religion	Prejudices

Step Four — Planning the NPO's Services

These activities, interests, and opinions could be determined by utilizing a research instrument built around a modified semantic differential or a Likert-scale questionnaire or by having the client circle activities, interests, and opinions on a list provided.

If the information is available to answer general questions and to determine the demographics and psychographics of the actual and potential markets, then a series of market mix strategies can be planned and implemented. However, if the information is not available, the NPO administrators perhaps would be acting on hunch, superstition, and seat-of-the-pants-type information in making marketing strategic decisions involved in

1. The target market identification and segmentation
2. The marketing mix strategies of
    2.1 Product/service design
    2.2 Price
    2.3 Promotion
    2.4 Place
    2.5 Personnel
    2.6 Pecuniary

DIFFERENCES IN USERS AND DONORS OF AN NPO'S SERVICES

A peculiar problem for some NPOs is that sometimes the users of the NPO's services are not the same persons who pay for the services. For example, the users of the Salvation Army's services of food, clothing, lodging, and so on are people in need who do not have money to pay for the services they consume. The donors of money to the Salvation Army are the ones who are paying the price for the services, while the people in need are the ones using them.

When the donors who pay the prices and the users who consume the services are different, the NPO is faced with two markets. Consequently, separate analyses need to be made for both target markets — the donors and the users.

When an NPO has to be subsidized for its services offered, there are, in reality, two markets that need to be segmented and identified. Consequently, target markets for both have to be analyzed to see whether the needs of both the donor and the user are being satisfied.

SUMMARY

One of the fundamental weaknesses of most NPOs is their lack of marketing expertise. Consequently, an understanding of the nature of marketing is essential.

One of the fundamentals of marketing is the exchange process that goes on between the client who consumes the services and the NPO that produces the services. An equitable exchange has to exist if both the NPO and the client want to satisfy their needs.

A crucial decision that has to be made is whether the NPO should pursue an aggressive, balanced, or minimal marketing strategy. The factors that influence that decision are the nature of the competition, quality of services, revenue strategies, stage in life cycle, financial position, capacity of facility, and philosophy of managers regarding objectives.

A fundamental analysis has to be made of the target market to identify and segment it. Both demographic and psychographic variables must be investigated for actual users and for donors who pay for the services.

Evaluating the Marketing Function

1. Make an analysis of the equality of the exchange between the NPO and its clients.
   a. Consider both the users and donors.
   b. Use the guidelines suggested.
   c. Back up the factors with facts.
   d. Evaluate and prescribe.
2. Make an analysis of the general marketing strategy for the NPO.
   a. Use the guidelines suggested.
   b. Back up the factors with facts.
   c. Evaluate and prescribe.
3. Make an analysis of the target market.
   a. Consider both the users and the donors.
   b. Design an instrument to determine the demographics of the target market.
   c. Design an instrument to determine the psychographics of the target market.
   d. Gather data by interviews.
   e. Evaluate and prescribe.

Notes

1. Philip Kotler, *Marketing Management: Analysis, Planning, and Control* (Englewood Cliffs, N.J.: Prentice-Hall, 1976), 5.
2. William J. Stanton, *Fundamentals of Marketing* (New York: McGraw-Hill, 1971), 5.
3. Kotler, *Marketing Management*, 4.
4. Jerome McCarthy, *Basic Marketing* (Homewood, Ill.: Richard D. Irwin, 1975), 8.
5. See Kotler, *Marketing Management*, 60.

16

Market Mix Strategies — Service, Price, and Promotion

SERVICE STRATEGIES

From a marketing point of view, a service may be considered to be the sum of both the physiological and the psychological-sociological satisfactions given to clients to fill their needs and wants. For example, a participant in an intramural sports activity satisfies needs related to physical conditioning and physical health, but the services offered may also satisfy his/her needs for prestige, social approval, and socialization with others. The NPO's services should meet the needs and wants of clients as far as the physical aspects are concerned and as far as the packaging of the service is concerned. Likewise, the branding of the service and the related atmosphere when and where the service is consumed should be considered with client needs in mind — both the physiological and the psycho-social needs.

Service Differentiation in Competitive Environments

When an NPO is in a competitive environment (such as an oligopoly situation, a highly directly competitive situation, or a highly indirectly competitive situation with substitutes), a strategy that is often very effective is product/service differentiation. An organization that applies this concept should seek some differential advantage over its competitors by making its services different from those of its competitors. To differentiate means to have models, sizes, qualities, colors, packaging, branding, and atmosphere that differ from those of competing NPOs and non-NPOs.

Designing the Services

The operations/production function of an NPO is responsible for creating the physical form of the service. However, the marketing function, through some type of market research, usually can better specify the forms that will satisfy client needs than the typical production function can. Of major concern in the design of the NPO's services is the physical form, involving the size, shape, color, weight, and other variables affecting the physical characteristics. As stated before, the physical aspects should be considered along with the psycho-social aspects of the services, such as packaging and branding.

Packaging the Service

The service's "package" must provide the client with protection, convenience, sales appeal, information, and low price, if possible. If an NPO is offering products, most will require protection of some sort from damage caused by handling, breakage, shrinkage, spoilage, pilferage, and so forth. The materials and design should, therefore, protect the product.

A package can also be designed to provide convenience in handling—for example, by providing handles, closing and opening places, special shapes for storage, and other factors desirable for client convenience.

In addition, sales appeal can be enhanced by using good design, color, and copy on the package to attract and inform clients as to the weights, uses, and instructions for use of the product.

Creating Atmosphere for the Service

Since most NPOs have services to offer, more so than products, the distinctive factor of atmosphere must be considered. For example, a symphony orchestra certainly should not be offering its services in a barn. The atmosphere of a symphony should be conducive to the services offered—high-quality sound reproduction, a physical environment of plushness and quiet, well-dressed musicians, and so forth. Likewise, hospital services should be offered in a clean, well-lighted, colorful environment, not in a dirty, dingy, colorless environment. The atmosphere where and when NPO services are consumed should be considered to be a strategy, consistent with the nature of the service.

Branding the Service

Product branding and service branding are very helpful marketing strategies, particularly in competitive situations where product differentiation becomes a key strategy. Branding has evolved to meet both the NPO's needs and the client's needs.

A branded product/service usually is associated with high quality. As a result, clients can usually rely on buying high quality and can gain assurance that what they buy will be the same every time. In addition, a branded product/service normally meets some status needs for clients.

Branding is important to an NPO's marketing strategy because it encourages repeat buying if the quality remains high. Branding develops a preferred market position for an NPO, particularly in highly competitive situations. Branding may also improve and maintain an image for the NPO. As a result of these benefits, a wise marketing strategy may be to incur the costs of branding to take advantage of both the client's needs and the NPO's revenue needs.

A suggested guideline is presented to evaluate the product/service strategies from a marketing perspective (see Figure 16.1).

Benefits and Costs of Public Services Provided by NPOs

A service strategy problem unique to some NPOs is that of providing pure public and quasi–pure public services, as opposed to private services.

Figure 16.1
Strategic Guidelines for Marketing Services/Products

```
                                        Evaluation
Theoretical Situational                 Strength/   Not      Needs
Factors    ---------------------->      Weakness    Known    Work

   1.   Service/Product
        Differentiation Strategy
          1.1  Necessary?
          1.2  How differentiated?

   2.   Design of Service/Product's
        Physical Form
          2.1  Size
          2.2  Shape
          2.3  Color
          2.4  Weight
          2.5  Others

   3.   Packaging the Service/Product
          3.1  Protection
          3.2  Convenience in handling
          3.3  Sales appeal

   4.   Atmosphere in Consumption of
        Service/Product
          4.1  Conducive to service or
               product
          4.2  Consistent with
               service/product
          4.3  Others

   5.   Branding of Service/Product
          5.1  Consistent with quality
          5.2  Helps repeat buying
          5.3  Achieves preferred
               market position
          5.4  Maintains image

   6.   Other Strategies

Overall Evaluation and Possible Prescription:
```

A pure public service is available to everyone in a given area, and no one can be excluded from using it for non-payment. Examples are police and fire protection, streets, and a sewage system for a community and national defense for a nation. Pure public services are those that are used collectively and that cannot be packaged and distributed exclusively to a single person.

Many public services, however, are not pure public ones. These are called quasi-public services in that they have some characteristics of pure public ones, but also some characteristics of private ones. For example, a quasi-public service is available to anyone who wishes to use it, but a user may be required to pay a direct fee to do so. This distinction of direct payment makes it a quasi-public service. Examples would be a public transit system, higher education, some parks, and toll roads.

The differences between pure public services and quasi-public services may be highlighted by showing the differences between the two in terms of such characteristics as availability, fees, externalities, excludabilities, price sensitivities, and collection costs. These differences, summarized in Figure 16.2, suggest a closer analysis of the characteristics in the paragraphs to follow.

Externalities of Public Services

Let's take a look at the externalities. When a public service is produced and consumed, a direct internal relationship between the producer and the consumer is cemented by the incurring of costs and the receiving of benefits by both producer and consumer. The exchange of costs and benefits is consid-

Figure 16.2
Differences Between Pure Public and Quasi-Public Services

Characteristics	Pure Public Service	Quasi-Public Service
1. Availability to anyone for use	yes	generally, but not always
2. Direct fee required for use	no	yes
3. Externalities	high	lower
4. Excludability of some persons	cannot	can
5. Price sensitivity	relatively inelastic	relatively elastic
6. Collection costs	high and difficult to administer	not too high and relatively easy to administer
7. Divisibility of the product/service	no	yes

ered an internal one. When the costs and benefits of the internal exchange spill over to affect people who are not directly involved in the exchange — that is, where the people are external to the exchange — then these costs and benefits are labeled *externalities*. The external costs and benefits may be fairly high and significant in the case of pure public services, but not as significant in the case of quasi-public services.

To determine the externalities of a public service, several subjective analyses should be made of the internal benefits and costs of the producers and users and of the non-users. Take, for example, a university transit system that consists of several buses and drivers and that provides a "free" bus service for students living on and off campus. This service could be subjectively analyzed as to internal and external benefits and costs as follows:

From Student Rider's Perspective

Internal Benefits

1. Free ride to-from-on campus

2. Savings of wear and tear on personal auto
3. Savings on gas prices
4. No hassle of finding a convenient parking place and/or getting a parking ticket
5. Savings from possibility of not having to purchase an auto

Internal Costs

1. Sacrificing the comfort of a personal auto
2. Long waiting time for bus

3. Long walking distance to bus line
4. Possible overcrowding on bus

5. Possible stench from fumes of engine

From Student Non-Rider's Perspective

External Benefits

1. More convenient parking spaces available for parking autos?

External Costs

1. Having to wait behind buses while loading and unloading

From University's (Producer's) Perspective

Internal Benefits

1. Reduces traffic congestion

2. Reduces pollution?

3. Fewer traffic tickets required with fewer police required
4. Fewer accidents possible?

External Costs

1. More maintenance required on streets from heavier buses
2. Possibility exists to have to wait behind slow bus

From this fairly subjective analysis, one might conclude that there are not many externalities associated with the student transit system, suggesting that the transit system is a quasi-public service.

When the costs of a quasi-public service are paid for through a direct fee paid by a user, the benefits to the user are fairly direct and internalized. As a result, the externalities are usually less significant than are those of a pure public service where the external benefits are significant to a large number of people who may use the service. The external benefits from a sewage system involve the protection of the health and safety of the citizens of a community, which is probably more significant than are the taxes paid for its construction and usage. The externalities of a transit system are usually less significant than are those of police and fire protection. However, the significance of the external benefits and costs is often left to the political value processes of a community, state, or nation.

In the absence of significant externalities, there is not much justification for public support of the service; that is, the private market will hopefully provide the service.

Other Characteristics of Public Services

Most quasi-public services have a feature that allows some persons to be excluded from using them, whereas pure public services do not exclude anyone from using them. For example, a transit system can set up a collection box and require payment of a fare before a person can use the system. A public park can be fenced in and require payment of a fee before a person can enter. A gate can be built on a road to exclude certain persons from using the road, thus making it a toll road. Pure public services, on the other hand, cannot exclude persons from their use. It would be very difficult to exclude persons from national defense, from police and fire protection, and from other public services.

Free ridership occurs when a person enjoys the benefits of a quasi-public service without paying for those benefits. For example, suppose a student bus system is paid for by student fees, thus allowing any student to use the bus. However, if a townsperson gets on the bus at one end of the line and rides it to the other end of the line each day to get back and forth to work, without paying a fee, that person would be getting a "free ride" — that is, using the bus without paying for the ride.

When the quantity demanded and used changes significantly as a result of an increase or decrease in price, the service is said to be elastic or price sensitive. Most quasi-public services have a higher price sensitivity than do pure public services which are usually paid for indirectly through general taxes or other forms of indirect subsidies. For example, a bus system's use is rather price sensitive as compared to a public road's use. If a bus system raises its direct user fees, the number of riders will probably fall. If, however, taxes are raised, the number of people using a public road will not be significantly affected.

Another characteristic of pure public services is that they are not divisible into separate units. As a result, how are they to be paid for and by whom? Indivisible services usually have high collection costs attached to them in that intricate tax systems have to be created and administered to collect the taxes or other forms of indirect subsidies to finance the pure public service. These collection costs are relatively high and difficult to collect. On the other hand, quasi-pure services usually are divisible into units that can be priced fairly and paid for directly by the users. As a result, the collection costs are not too high and are relatively easy to collect.

PRICING STRATEGIES

The various characteristics of pure and quasi-pure services can be used to determine a pricing system.

Public and Quasi-Public Services

One of the first strategies that has to be addressed is whether to implement a direct-user-fee pricing system or some other indirect pricing system, notably through public taxes which everyone pays or through indirect subsidies collected by various governmental units and then paid to the NPO.

Therefore, one strategic decision facing an NPO administrator is the selection of a pricing system. What situational factors should be considered?

- The first factor is the degree of externalities of the NPO's services. If the services benefit the clients/members directly and if the externalities are not significant for society as a whole, then it would be wise to use a direct-user-fee pricing system. On the other hand, if the externalities are significantly great for the general public, then it would be wise to have the general public pay for the NPO's services through a taxing system of some sort.

- If some persons can be excluded from consuming or using the NPO's services, then it follows that a direct-user-fee pricing system should be used. However, if free ridership is fairly common, then an indirect pricing system has to be used.

- If the NPO's services are available for anyone to use, then an indirect pricing system through some form of taxation of the general public should be used.

- If there is a high degree of price sensitivity for the NPO's services, then it would be wise to have a direct-user-fee system. If, however, the price for the NPO's services is relatively inelastic, then an indirect pricing system should be used.

- If the collection costs are not too high and are relatively easy to administer, then a direct-user-fee pricing system is recommended. However, if the collection costs are high and are difficult to administer, then an indirect pricing system should be used.

Figure 16.3
Strategic Decision: Whether To Use a Direct-User-Fee Price

Theoretical Situational Factors →	Alternatives		Describe Actual System & Factors →	Evaluate As to Strength/ Weakness →	Prescribe
	Direct User Fee	Indirect System			
1. Direct Benefits and Externalities					
1.1 If the NPO's services benefit the clients directly and if the externalities are not significant for the general public as a whole, then use	X				
1.2 If the NPO's services create externalities which are significant to the general public, then use		X			
2. Excludabilities and Free Riders					
2.1 If persons can be excluded from using the NPO's services, then use	X				
2.2 If persons cannot be excluded and if free riders are commonplace, then use		X			
3. Collection Costs					
3.1 If collection costs are relatively low and if they are relatively easy to administer, then use	X				

3.2 If they are relatively high and difficult to administer, then use   X

3.3 If the NPO's services are divisible, then use   X

3.4 If the NPO's services are not divisible, then use   X

4. Price Sensitivity

4.1 If the NPO's services are relatively price sensitive, then use   X

4.2 If the NPO's services are relatively price insensitive, then use   X

5. Tax System

5.1 If a tax system based on direct use of the NPO's services cannot be employed, then use   X

6. Other Factors

Overall Evaluation and Possible Prescription:

Each of the preceding factors has to be evaluated and weighed subjectively to determine which pricing system should be used. Many times a combination of both systems will be suggested. For example, a symphony orchestra may use a direct user fee and also gain revenues from public support either through taxes or through a voluntary subsidy from the United Fund or a similar public agency because of the high degree of externalities involved for the general public through the services provided by the symphony.

A guideline for this strategic pricing decision is suggested in Figure 16.3.

Non-Public Services

Since pricing is such a vital decision in terms of the revenues of an NPO, it is wise for NPO administrators to consider the various factors affecting a pricing strategy for those services that are not public services.

There are three alternative pricing strategies for an existing service: (1) pricing above the market price, (2) pricing at the market price, and (3) pricing below the market price. For each service that the NPO markets, there should be a separate analysis of the situational factors that influence an administrative pricing strategy decision.

The first factor to be considered is the nature of the competitive situation facing the NPO. For example, if the NPO is in a highly competitive situation, then it would be a wise strategy to price *at* the market. Likewise, if the NPO is in a situation where there is severe indirect competition with substitute goods/services, then a wise strategy would be to price *at* the market price of the indirect substitutes. If the NPO is in an oligopoly market situation, then it would be wise to price *at* the market. However, if the NPO is in a monopoly position, then it might price *above* the market for any substitute goods or services if it wants to maximize its revenues.

A second factor is the quality of the services offered by the NPO. If the quality is high, then the NPO could price above the market, especially if the competitor's quality is average or poor. People will generally pay a higher price for quality if the quality is perceived as high.

A third factor is the high-quality promotion of a high-quality service. If the promotion quality is high and if the service quality is high, then the NPO can price above the market. Likewise, if the sales personnel are of high quality and if they give high-quality service to the NPO's clients, then the NPO can price above the market.

However, all three factors — service, promotion, and sales personnel — have to be of high quality and have to be consistent with each other in order for the NPO to price above the market. In addition, considerable evidence has to be available to back up the "high" degree of quality. If there is any doubt about the high quality, then the price should be at or below the market.

Another factor is the degree of client loyalty. If the NPO has a large number of repeat buyers of their services and if their buyers consistently support the NPO, then there is a high degree of client loyalty which would suggest that the NPO could price above the market.

If the NPO wants rapid penetration into the market, then it might be a wise strategy to price below the market, particularly if other service-market match factors are equal to those of their competitors.

A rather important factor is the personal philosophy of the administrators. For example, if the administrators desire to minimize revenues and do not want to grow, do not want to make a profit, or do not believe in maximizing revenues, chances are good that they will price below the market. There may be other philosophical beliefs that dictate an at-the-market strategy or an above-the-market strategy.

Other factors may dictate the NPO's pricing strategy, but the ones discussed are the major variables influencing whether to price at, below, or above the market.

An administrator may wish to use the pricing guidelines suggested to evaluate and to prescribe the NPO's pricing strategies, based on the situational factors facing his/her NPO (see Figure 16.4).

PROMOTION STRATEGIES

Once an NPO's services and price strategies have been integrated into the overall organizational strategies, there remains the task of promoting the NPO's services. Promotion basically involves communication about the characteristics of the services from the NPO to the clients/donors. As such, at least three (and perhaps more) strategies face the administrators — the content of the promotions, the types of messages, and the selection of media.

Content of the Promotion

The content of the promotion usually involves the characteristics and benefits of the NPO's services. (At this point, the reader is asked to review Chapter 4 which involves an analysis of the benefits and costs to arrive at the value of the NPO's services.) Each of the benefits may serve as the content of the messages to be conveyed to the clients/donors.

The content of the messages should be analyzed to see whether they appeal to the client's sense of sight, sound, action, smell, feel, and so forth. This analysis would be very helpful in determining the media to be used in promoting the services. For example, if a parks and tourism department wanted to promote the natural beauty and recreation activities of its area, then the content of the message would probably dictate a medium such as television that would take advantage of sight, sound, and action.

If the marketing function wants to play a significant role in promoting a good image for the NPO, in generating revenues for the NPO, or in promoting growth for the NPO, then it has to follow a sound message content

Figure 16.4
Administrative Pricing Strategy Guidelines

Theoretical Situational Factors ⟶ Affecting ⟶ [Price columns] ⟶ Describe Actual Price & Situation Factors ⟶ Evaluation ⟶ Prescription

Evaluation: Strength / Weakness

Theoretical Situational Factors	Price Below Market	Price At The Market	Price Above Market
1. If the competitive situation facing the NPO is:			
a. Monopoly			X
b. Oligopoly		X	
c. Highly Competitive		X	
d. Indirect competition with substitutes		X	
2. If there is a high quality product/ service and			X
3. High quality promotion and			X
4. High quality sales personnel and service			X
5. If there is a high degree of customer/ client loyalty			X
6. If the services are in various stages in product life cycle:			
a. Introduction			X
b. Growth			X
c. Maturity		X	
d. Decline	X		
7. If the NPO desires a rapid penetration of the market	X		
8. Personal philosophy of Management (depends)			
9. Other factors			

Overall Evaluation and Prescription:

strategy. For example, if the promotion is aimed at building credibility with the general public, then the content of the messages has to have several characteristics. Truthfulness is at the heart of credibility. To be convincing, the content of the messages has to be based on truth, not falsehood. If the public finds a misstatement in a promotion, then it is likely to suspect the remaining content. The content has to be factual, honest, and correct.

Another characteristic is sincerity, that priceless ingredient which indicates whether a person believes in what he/she is doing. Sincerity keeps the confidence of other people.

Another content variable is the use of a positive approach in the promotions. It is wise to avoid negative comments. Further, emphasizing what can be done or what is being done is much better promotion than emphasizing what is not being done. However, it is not wise to mislead by being too positive. If negative factors are being discussed, it is wise to sandwich them in between two positive comments.

Good promotion suggests that a person should not lose his/her cool. Showing anger and flying off the handle are costly forms of promotion because they lose friends, cause antagonism, and cost money, time, and effort. Associated with these negative messages are scolding, demanding, condemning, preaching, and bragging. Any messages suggesting these characteristics are likely to cause problems for NPO administrators.

Use of personal interest in promotions is a good approach. Referring to human beings, using informal language, and just being one's self are good tactics to follow if human interest is expected.

The preceding suggestions about the content of messages may be used, along with others, in successfully promoting services of the NPO by communicating with its clients/donors. A guideline is presented which may be helpful to NPO administrators (see Figure 16.5).

Type of Message — Persuasive, Informative, and/or Reminder

In addition to the message content, the type of message needs to be considered — that is, whether the message is to be persuasive, informative, and/or reminder message. The situational factors facing an NPO will usually dictate which type would be most appropriate for promoting the NPO's services.

A major situational factor, an external one, is the competitive position of the NPO. If the NPO is in a monopoly position with no direct competitors in its market area, then an informative message would be all that is needed. If it is in an oligopoly position, then a persuasive type is needed to get clients to buy its services. If there is a very high degree of competition, a persuasive type of message is needed. If there is severe indirect competition with substitute services, then a persuasive type is recommended. If the indirect competition is only moderate, then an informative and/or reminder type is needed.

Figure 16.5
Strategy: To Analyze the Content of Promotion Messages

```
Theoretical                                    Evaluation
Situational     ---------------->    Strength/      Not      Needs
Factors                              Weakness       Known    Work
```

1. Are the benefits of the NPO's
   services emphasized?

2. Has the content of the message
   been analyzed as appealing to
   2.1 Sight
   2.2 Sound
   2.3 Action
   2.4 Smell
   2.5 Feel
   2.6 Others

3. Does the content of the
   messages have credibility?
   3.1 Is it truthful?
   3.2 Is it factual?
   3.3 Is it honest?
   3.4 Is it correct?
   3.5 Others

4. Is the content sincere?

5. Is the content positive?
   5.1 Does it avoid negatives?
   5.2 Are negatives
        sandwiched?
   5.3 Others

6. Is the content "courteous"?
   Does it avoid
   6.1 Being angry?
   6.2 Condemning?
   6.3 Bragging?
   6.4 Scolding?
   6.5 Preaching?
   6.6 Demanding?
   6.7 Others

7. Is the content interesting?
   7.1 About people?
   7.2 Informal?
   7.3 Others

8. Others

Overall Evaluation and Possible Prescription:

The nature of the target market also dictates the message type. If there is a high degree of client loyalty, then all that is needed is a reminder message.

Another external factor is the stage of the NPO's service life cycle. If the individual service is in the development stage, then an informative message is needed. If it is in the growth stage, then persuasive and reminder messages are needed. If it is in the maturity stage, then persuasive and reminder messages are necessary. However, if the service is in the decline stage and if nothing can be done about that, a reminder message is all that is needed.

A major internal factor to be considered is the degree of quality of the NPO's service. If the quality is high, then only an informative message is needed. On the other hand, if the quality is low or average and if additional revenues are desired, then a persuasive message is required.

The production capacity of the NPO is another internal situational factor. If there is a great deal of unused capacity that carries a large amount of fixed expenses, then it is wise for the NPO to consider a persuasive message strategy. If the NPO is operating at full capacity, then an informative message is relevant.

The financial position of the NPO is another factor. If the organization is in debt, then it behooves the NPO to use a persuasive message strategy. If it is consistently losing money on its operations, then a persuasive message should be considered.

A managerial factor, based on the philosophical values and objectives desired by the managers, is the degree of potential client behavior desired. For example, if only an awareness of the services is desired, then an informative and/or reminder message is needed. If client familiarity with the services is desired, then an informative message is recommended. If the managers want the clients to understand the services, then an informative message is needed. However, if the managers want to get the clients to act by buying the services of the NPO, then a persuasive message is needed.

The revenue strategy desired by the NPO managers is another factor. If the managers desire to maximize revenues, then a persuasive message is needed. On the other hand, if they want to minimize revenues, then informative and reminder messages are the only types needed. If the managers want to increase revenues, then a persuasive message is needed, other factors being equal.

Finally, the organizational objectives desired by the managers will play a role in the type of message to be used. If the managers desire to make a profit, even though small, a persuasive message is needed. If the NPO wants to grow, then a persuasive message is needed. If maintenance of market share is desired, both persuasive and informative messages are needed. If customer service is desired, then informative and reminder messages are needed. Likewise, if the managers desire to improve the NPO's image and ensure its survival, both informative and reminder messages are needed.

There may be situational factors other than the ones mentioned, but those

Figure 16.6
Strategic Decision: Type of Message Strategy To Sell NPO Products/Services

Theoretical Situational Factors	Type of Message to Use			Describe Actual Situation Factors & Message Used →	Evaluate Strengths/Weaknesses →	Pre-scrip-tion →
	Persuade	Inform	Remind			
External Factors						
A. Competitive Position of the NPO						
1. Monopoly		X				
2. Oligopoly	X					
3. High degree of competition	X					
4. Indirect/substitute products/services						
Severe	X	X				
Moderate		X	X			
B. Nature of Target Market						
1. High degree of client/customer loyalty			X			
C. Stage of Each Product/Service Life Cycle						
1. Development	X	X				
2. Growth	X		X			
3. Maturity			X			
4. Decline			X			
Internal Factors						
D. Quality of Products/Services						
1. High Quality		X				
2. Low Quality or Average	X					
E. Capacity of Operations						
1. Unused capacity	X					
2. Full capacity		X				
F. Financial Position of Organization						
1. In debt	X					
2. Losing money	X					

G. Degree of Potential Customer Behavior Desired by Management
  1. Awareness of product/service
  2. Familiarity with product/service
  3. Understanding of product/service
  4. Action to buy product/service

H. Revenue Strategy Desired by Management
  1. Maximize revenues
  2. Minimize revenues
  3. Increase revenues

I. NPO Organizational Objectives Desired by Management
  1. Profit
  2. Growth
  3. Maintenance of market share
  4. Customer service
  5. Improved image
  6. Survival of organization
  7. Others

J. Other Survival Factors

Overall Evaluation and Prescription:

discussed are the major ones. The key factors depend on the overall situation facing the NPO.

A guide for making this type of decision or for evaluating the present message strategy is suggested in Figure 16.6.

Media Selection

The selection of various media for promotion purposes becomes a strategic decision for the marketing administrator of an NPO. There are many alternatives to choose from — notably, personal selling, public speaking, telephones, newspapers, direct mail, magazines, point-of-purchase displays, newsletters, billboards, special promotions, handbills, radio, television, and others. Each of these varied media has specific factors that provide advantages in promoting a NPO's services. What are some of these factors?

The first factor is the target market geographical exposure desired by the administrator. Various media appeal to local, regional, and/or national target markets. For example, the local target market can be reached fairly easily by point-of-purchase displays, billboards, handbills, and public speaking. Regional exposure results from using newspapers, television, radio, and regional magazines. National exposure is gained through direct mail, magazines, newsletters, and television. Obviously, several media offer exposure to all three markets — local, regional, and national.

The appeal of the message — that is, whether the message appeals to sight, sound, action, or other senses — is a major factor in determining the media to be used. For example, an appeal to sight suggests personal selling, public speaking, newspapers, magazines, direct mail, newsletters, billboards, handbills, and television. An appeal to sound would suggest personal selling, public speaking, telephones, and radio. An appeal to action would suggest personal selling, public speaking, and television. A further concept that should be considered is that of reinforcement, a psychological principle which suggests that a message that is reinforced by more than one sense is probably going to be more effective than one that appeals to only one sense.

Another factor is the type of message desired — a persuasive, informative, or reminder message. For example, persuasive messages would require a personal selling medium, along with telephones, direct mail, and special promotions. An informative message would suggest public speaking, newspapers, direct mail, magazines, point-of-purchase displays, newsletters, billboards, handbills, radio, and television. Reminder types would suggest public speaking, newspapers, direct mail, newsletters, billboards, special promotions, and handbills.

The cost of each medium also plays a role in media selection. Those media that have high costs attached to them are personal selling, public speaking, telephones, magazines, billboards, special promotions, and television. Those media that are associated with low costs are newspapers, direct mail, point-

Figure 16.7
Media Selection

Media Alternatives	Target Market Exposure Desired	Appeal of Message to Senses	Type of Message Desired	Cost of Medium	Time-liness of the Medium
1. Personal Selling	Local Special	Sight Sound Action	Persuasive	High	Excellent
2. Public Speaking	Local Special	Sight Sound Action	Informative Reminder	High	Excellent
3. Telephones	Local Regional National Special	Sound	Persuasive	High	Excellent
4. Newspapers	Local Regional	Sight	Informative Reminder	Low	Excellent
5. Direct Mail	Regional National Special	Sight	Informative Reminder Persuasive	Low	Excellent
6. Magazines	Regional National Special	Sight	Informative	High	Fair
7. Point-of-Purchase Displays	Local	Sight	Informative	Low	Good
8. Newsletters	Local Regional National Special	Sight	Informative Reminder	Low	Excellent
9. Billboards	Local	Sight	Informative Reminder	High	Fair
10. Special Promotions	Local	Sight	Reminder Informative Persuasive	High	Excellent
11. Handbills	Local	Sight	Informative Reminder	Low	Excellent
12. Radio	Local Regional	Sound	Informative	Low	Good
13. Television	Regional National	Sight Sound Action	Informative	High	Good

14. Other Media

Note: The personal philosophy of the administrator might also play a role in media selection.

Overall Evaluation and Prescription:

of-purchase displays, newsletters, handbills, and radio. One of the subfactors to be considered is the cost of the medium divided by the number of people reached by that medium.

The timeliness of each medium is another factor to be considered. When timing is of critical importance, then various media take on significance. For example, excellent timeliness suggests personal selling, public speaking, telephones, newspapers, direct mail, newsletters, special promotion, and handbills.

These factors can be combined into a guideline to be used by an NPO administrator in deciding what type of media to use or in evaluating the media actually used by an NPO (see Figure 16.7).

A pertinent problem facing NPO administrators is how to allocate the costs of various media to the target market geographical exposure desired. A suggestion as to how this problem might be handled follows.

Suppose an NPO has a number of clients in various states:

	No.	%
Illinois	4,000	40
Indiana	3,000	30
Michigan	2,000	20
Wisconsin	1,000	10
Total	10,000	100

Further suppose that the NPO has $20,000 to spend on promoting its services. On the basis of previous factors and judgments, the NPO wishes to spend the $20,000 on various media as follows:

Television	$8,000	Appeal to sound, sight,
Radio	4,000	and action; persuasion
Newspapers	2,000	
Magazines	1,000	
Specials	2,000	Appeal to sight; infor-
Direct Mail	1,000	mative; timely
Newsletters	1,000	
Billboards	1,000	
	$20,000	

The NPO administrator could set up a matrix as follows:

Media Allocation	Illinois 40%	Indiana 30%	Michigan 20%	Wisconsin 10%	Total 100%
Television	$3,200	$2,400	$1,600	$ 800	$ 8,000
Radio	1,600	1,200	800	400	4,000
Newspapers	800	600	400	200	2,000
Magazines	400	300	200	100	1,000
Specials	800	600	400	200	2,000
Direct Mail	400	300	200	100	1,000
Newsletters	400	300	200	100	1,000
Billboards	$ 400	$ 300	$ 200	$ 100	$ 1,000
Totals	$8,000	$6,000	$4,000	$2,000	$20,000

Geographic Exposure Desired

With the allocation of media to the geographic exposure desired, the NPO could then break down each of the media in each of the states into specific television stations, newspapers, radio stations, magazines, and so forth to set up a specific budget for promotion expenses.

The next chapter deals with the other variables in the market mix strategy for NPOs.

17

Market Mix Strategies — Place, Personnel, and Pecuniary

PLACE STRATEGIES

There are at least two fundamental place strategy decisions (and possibly others) facing an NPO. One involves the use of middlemen in the channels of distribution to get the NPO's products/services to the right place, and the other involves the actual place or site where the NPO's products/services are consumed.

Channel of Distribution Strategies

Place is important in marketing strategy because if time and place utility are not combined in order to give the client possession utility, a service has little usefulness even though it possesses form utility.

One aspect of place strategy sets up an ideal channel of distribution in order to facilitate the movement of the NPO's product/service to the ultimate client in the target market. The place strategy of an NPO selling directly to the consumer or user gives the NPO the advantage of being in close contact with its clients/customers. The close contact allows the NPO to be more sensitive to changes in the clients' attitudes, interests, and opinions — their psychographics — and to be in a better position to make prompt adjustments in its services, promotion, price, personnel, and financial strategies.

However, the major disadvantage of being in close contact with the clients/customers through a complete, direct channel of distribution is the large amount of financial resources associated with performing all the marketing functions in distributing the NPO's products/services to its clients. These large amounts of capital usually force an NPO with limited financial resources to turn over part of the job of distribution to wholesalers, retailers, and other middlemen who can do the job more effectively than the NPO can. Whatever the situation, an NPO must determine its channel strategy.

Channels of distribution resemble road maps, showing the routes of the goods and services from the producer through the various middlemen who help the product along the channel to the ultimate consumer. Much like a cross-country trip, there are several routes that goods can travel, depending on the classification of the goods and services that an NPO produces. For example, if an NPO produces a good, that good is either a consumer good or an industrial good. A consumer good is one that is delivered to the ultimate personal consumer in such a form that it may be used or consumed without further commercial processing. An industrial good, on the other hand, is one that requires further processing in order to produce a finished product. Some NPOs produce consumer goods, and there also may be some NPOs that produce industrial goods.

Whether consumer or industrial goods, there are usually four different channels for distributing them from producer to consumer or user:

1. Direct — from producer to consumer/user
2. Retailers — from producer to retailer to consumer/user
3. Single Wholesaler — from producer to wholesaler to retailer to consumer/user
4. Multiple Wholesalers — from producer to large wholesaler to small wholesaler to retailer to consumer/user

These channels may be depicted as follows:

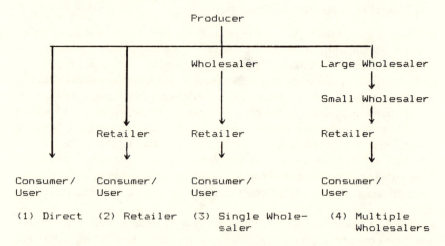

As can be seen, the number of middlemen (wholesalers and retailers) can be quite numerous if the target market is geographically dispersed, or the number may be quite small if a direct channel is used. What are the factors to be considered in selecting the proper channels of distribution for an NPO?

The first is the nature of the clients/customers in the target market. For example, the geographic dispersion usually affects the channel selected in the sense that usually the more highly concentrated the consumers/users are geographically, the more direct the channel of distribution is and the fewer the middlemen that are required. The wider the geographic dispersion, the more middlemen are required.

If an NPO's clients/customers purchase a large volume of the NPO's goods/services, this would suggest more direct contact and fewer middlemen in the channel. On the other hand, if the NPO's clientele are small-volume clients — that is, they purchase only small amounts of the products/services — this would suggest more middlemen in the channel.

The nature of the NPO's products/services is another major factor. If the good is an industrial one, that would suggest fewer middlemen and a more direct channel. If the good is a consumer one, that would suggest more middlemen in the channel since consumers are more numerous and more geographically widespread than are industrial users.

If the good is highly technical, there would probably be fewer middlemen in the channel since wholesalers and retailers do not usually have the expertise to perform technical selling and repair work.

If the good is of high value because of its scarcity, this would suggest a more direct channel with fewer middlemen. If it is a low-value good, then more middlemen would probably be required.

If the good is perishable, then a more direct channel and fewer middlemen would be required.

If the NPO's output is a service, as opposed to a good, then a more direct channel and fewer middlemen would be required. The nature of a service suggests that it is produced and consumed at practically the same time and place, thereby cutting out middlemen in the channel. On the other hand, if the NPO's output is a good, as opposed to a service, then probably it would have to be stored and transported, requiring more middlemen. Most NPOs are concerned with producing services rather than goods.

If the managers of an NPO desire various degrees of market exposure, then this would have a bearing on the channel of distribution. Three degrees of market exposure are usually recognized: (1) intensive exposure, (2) selective exposure, and (3) exclusive exposure. Intensive exposure through distribution channels refers to the sale of a product or service through many responsible and suitable wholesalers and retailers in order to get a wide exposure of the product or service to as many clients/customers as possible. Intensive exposure requires a channel with many middlemen. Selective exposure refers to the use of only those wholesalers and retailers who will do the best job of distributing the products/services. Exclusive exposure refers to the distribution of the products/services through only one wholesaler or retailer in a given market area. Such would suggest very few middlemen in the channel.

An external factor that would influence the channels of distribution is the structure of market. For example, if the NPO is in a monopsony situation (one buyer for the NPO's services), then such a factor would suggest a direct channel. If the NPO is in an oligopsony situation (only a few buyers), then this factor would also suggest a fairly direct channel with few middlemen.

Internal organizational factors also play a role in the selection of channels of distribution. For example, if the NPO does not have the necessary financial resources, it must rely on middlemen to facilitate the movement of its products/services to the ultimate consumer/user. Likewise, the lack of qualified and trained sales personnel affects the number of middlemen in the channel. If an NPO does not have the required personnel, it must rely on other middlemen.

Just plain tradition also plays a role in channel selection. Sometimes "That's the way we've always done it" is a factor in channel selection. Whatever factors are facing an NPO, situational guidelines are suggested for an NPO marketing administrator to consider in deciding on a channel or channels and/or in evaluating existing channels of distribution (see Figure 17.1).

A further note about channels is necessary. The channels normally have been thought of as one way — from the NPO to the ultimate consumer. However, such is not always the case. For example, an educational organization normally says, "Here we are, student. You come to us if you want an education." Or a hospital says, "Here we are, patient. You come to us if you want care and cure of your illness." The direction of the channel is reversed because of the production orientation of the educational institution and the hospital. If a true marketing orientation is practiced, then the NPO should extend its services to its clients/customers rather than having them come to the NPO.

Retailers and wholesalers may be replaced by other agencies or organizations when we speak of channels for certain types of NPOs. For example, the channel of distribution by which a patient takes advantage of hospital services is from the patient to the doctor who serves as a middleman in admitting a patient to the hospital. Sometimes an additional middleman is thrust into the path of a patient who wants to enter the hospital — that is, the insurance company. Consequently, a common channel is from patient (ultimate consumer) to doctor (middleman) to insurance company (middleman) to hospital (producer). Each NPO has its own situational factors suggesting the number and types of middlemen in its single channel, and sometimes multiple channels, of distribution.

Specific Site Location Strategy

Another crucial decision for many NPOs is where to locate the specific site for producing and distributing its services. Several factors need to be considered in site location.

Of significant importance are the target market characteristics. For example, the NPO should be located where there is an increasing population, if

Figure 17.1
Strategic Decision: Number of Middlemen in the Channel of Distribution

Theoretical Situational Factors	Number of Middlemen in Channel of Distribution	Describe Actual Factors & Situation	Evaluation Strength/ Weakness	Prescribe
A. Service-Market Match Factors				
1. Nature of Clients/Customers				
If there is a wide geographic dispersion, then	more			
If there is a geographic concentration, then	few--more direct			
If there are large volume clients/customers, then	few--more direct			
If there are small volume clients/customers, then	more			
2. Nature of Product/Services				
If industrial, then	few--more direct			
If consumer, then	more			
If technical, then	few--more direct			
If high value, then	few--more direct			
If low value, then	more			
If perishable, then	few--more direct			
If a service, then	few--more direct			
If a good, then	more			
B. Managerial Factors				
1. Market Exposure Desired by Management				
If intensive, then	more			
If selective, then	few			
If exclusive, then	few			
C. External Factors				
1. Market Structure				
If in a monopsony situation, then	few--more direct			
If in a oligopsony situation, then	few--more direct			
D. Internal Factors				
If there is a lack of money, then	more			
If there is a lack of personnel, then	more			
E. Others				

Overall Evaluation and Possible Prescription:

possible. If not, then it should be located where there is enough population to support the services offered. And, of course, the NPO should be located near its target market. These three factors — expanding market, large market, and nearness to market — are probably the key ones in specific site selection.

Complementary business and industry factors should also be considered. For example, are there a substantial number of businesses and industries (in addition to population) to help support the NPO? Is there an upward trend in community payrolls? Is there diversity in the businesses and industries in the area? Are these businesses and industries stable enough to support the NPO? The local chamber of commerce would be a good source of information to answer these questions.

Supporting services should also be a consideration in the site location decision. For example, are banking services available? Transportation services? Governmental services? Labor supplies? Materials and equipment supplies? Other necessary support services?

Rent is another factor. If the NPO rents space, a number of subfactors need to be considered in deciding whether to rent in a high-rent area or a low-rent area. For example, high rents could be paid if the NPO's products/services have a low gross margin and a high inventory turnover rate. If the products/services appeal to a transient market, are of high value compared with bulk, feature low prices per unit, are convenience goods/services in nature, have to be featured in window displays, or have other relevant characteristics, then a high-rent area should be considered.

On the other hand, if the NPO's products/services have a high gross margin and a low inventory turnover rate, then a low-rent area might be appropriate. Furthermore, if much space is needed for storage and/or display, the products/services are of low value compared with bulk, they are shopping goods, and they have a number of loyal customer/clients, then a low-rent area should be considered.

Parking is another location factor. Does the site provide sufficient parking spaces? And does the site allow easy access?

Traffic flows are important. Is the site near adequate automobile traffic? How about adequate pedestrian traffic? Near complementary services traffic?

Proper zoning is another factor to be considered. Is the site zoned for residential, commercial, and/or industrial uses?

There may be other factors important to an NPO, such as the general atmosphere of the site. However, the ones discussed are the major ones.

A site guideline, Figure 17.2, might be used for either decision-making or evaluation purposes by NPO administrators.

SALES PERSONNEL STRATEGIES

Since an NPO has to "sell" goods and services (mainly services), a basic strategy has to be formulated and integrated into the overall NPO objectives as to what type of salesperson to use in selling each of the services (and goods). Three alternatives face NPO administrators regarding types of sales personnel. The first is the creative salesperson — the type of person who aggressively seeks out people to become clients/customers of the NPO. He/she is sometimes called an order getter. The second is the service salesperson — the type who is usually capable of taking or servicing orders. In fact, sometimes he/she is called an order taker. The third type is the supportive salesperson — the type

Figure 17.2
Strategic Decision: Specific Site Location

Theoretical Situational Factors —————→ Describe Actual Factors & Site Situation —→ Evaluation Strength/ Weakness ——→ Prescribe

1. Target Market Characteristics
   1.1 Expanding market?
   1.2 Large market?
   1.3 Nearness to market?
   1.4 Others

2. Complementary Businesses and Industries
   2.1 Substantial number of businesses and industries?
   2.2 Upward trend in community payroll?
   2.3 Diversified businesses?
   2.4 Stable businesses and industries?
   2.5 Others

3. Supporting Services Available
   3.1 Banking services?
   3.2 Transportation?
   3.3 Governmental?
   3.4 Labor supply?
   3.5 Materials and equipment?
   3.6 Others?

4. Rental Factors
   4.1 High-rent area appropriate?
   4.2 Low-rent area appropriate?
   4.3 (See subfactors) in text

5. Parking
   5.1 Sufficiency?
   5.2 Easy access?
   5.3 Others

6. Traffic Flows
   6.1 Near adequate automobile traffic?
   6.2 Pedestrian traffic?
   6.3 Complementary services traffic?
   6.4 Others

7. Zoning Laws
   7.1 Commercial
   7.2 Industrial
   7.3 Residential
   7.4 Others

8. General Atmosphere

9. Others

Overall evaluation and prescription:

who performs missionary work or technical work on the services/goods offered by the NPO. He/she is sometimes called an order helper.

Not all selling situations call for all three types of sales personnel. For example, if an NPO wants to sell itself to the general public or to a possible donor of funds who is wavering in his/her support of the NPO, a creative sales approach would be most appropriate. On the other hand, if various drinks or other concession products are to be sold to a captive audience — for example, during intermission at a symphony concert — then order takers or service sales personnel would be most appropriate. Consequently, the question usually arises as to what situational factors are to be considered in determining the proper sales personnel strategy.

One fundamental factor is the nature of the NPO's products/services to be sold. If the product/service is a consumer one — for example, a convenience or shopping or specialty good — a different strategy might be used than if it is an industrial good or service. A convenience good/service is one that is by nature a staple, an impulse purchase, or an emergency purchase. As such, it would require some service-type sales personnel to sell it. Shopping goods, on the other hand, require a creative salesperson to sell them. A specialty good/service requires some special effort to sell or is out of the ordinary. As such, it would require creative-type sales personnel. If the good or service is a new consumer good, perhaps missionary and supportive sales personnel would be needed. If the good/service is normally unsought by a consumer, then a creative salesperson is needed.

If the product or service is an industrial one, then usually a combination of creative and supportive personnel is needed. If a major installation (such as land, a building, or major equipment, whether standard or custom-made) is to be sold, then a combination of creative and supportive salespersons is needed. The same is true for accessory equipment.

The sale of raw materials, component parts, supplies, and other industrial services would normally require a combination of creative and service personnel — probably a creative salesperson to sell initially and a service person to take succeeding orders.

Another major factor in determining the types of sales personnel to be used is the nature of the buyer. Selling to an industrial buyer usually requires salesmanship of the highest order. Here both creative and supportive personnel would be needed. Selling to retailers and wholesalers would dictate both creative and service types of personnel. Sales to the ultimate consumer would also require both creative and service sales personnel.

A further factor is the stage of the product/service in its life cycle. If in the development stage, then missionary and creative sales personnel are needed. If in the growth stage, then creative and supportive sales personnel are appropriate. If in either the maturity or the decline stage, then only service sales personnel are necessary.

These factors may be analyzed in a sales personnel strategy situation (see Figure 17.3) by comparing the actual situation factors to good, sound theory and then evaluating the strengths and weaknesses of the NPO for each of the various products/services it sells.

PECUNIARY STRATEGIES

Probably the last strategic decision to be made for the market mix strategies is how to finance the sale of the NPO's products or services. The question

Figure 17.3
Strategy: To Determine Appropriate Sales Personnel

Theoretical Situational Factors	Alternative Types of Sales Personnel Needed	Describe Actual Situation Factors and Types of Sales Personnel	Strength/ Weakness	Prescription
1. Consumer goods/ services				
1.1 Convenience				
1.11 Staple	Service			
1.12 Impulse	Service			
1.13 Emergency	Service			
1.2 Shopping	Creative			
1.3 Specialty	Creative			
1.4 New good/service	Supportive & Missionary			
1.5 Unsought	Creative			
2. Industrial goods				
2.1 Installations	Creative & Supportive			
2.2 Major equipment	Creative & Supportive			
2.3 Accessory equipment	Creative & Service			
2.4 Raw materials	Creative & Service			
2.5 Component parts	Creative & Service			
2.6 Supplies	Creative & Service			
3. Nature of buyer				
3.1 Industrial buyer	Creative & Supportive			
3.2 Wholesaler and retailer	Creative & Service			
3.3 Ultimate consumer	Creative & Service			
4. Product life cycle				
4.1 Development	Missionary & Creative			
4.2 Growth	Creative & Supportive			
4.3 Maturity	Service			
4.4 Decline	Service			
5. Others				

Overall evaluation and prescription:

usually revolves around the decision whether to sell for cash on the barrel head or whether to sell on credit, using various forms such as layaway, installments, 30-day open charge accounts, or the like. Various factors influence such a strategic marketing/financial decision.

The objectives desired by the NPO administrators are the important factors. For example, if the administrators desire to increase revenues from the sale of the goods/services, then it is wise to sell on credit—all forms of it.

Credit sales usually increase the client/customer's willingness to buy. Further, if the administrators desire to stress client/customer service, using credit as a client convenience, then it is wise to sell on credit.

The nature of the NPO's products/services will also affect the decision. If the product is repossessable, then an NPO can usually sell on credit. The characteristics of the product will usually determine repossessability, such as whether the product is a durable good, a tangible good, a good with high value, or a luxury good. On the other hand, if the NPO offers a service, it should probably not be sold on credit unless other factors are present.

A major factor is the degree of creditworthiness of the NPO's clients/customers. If the clientele is wealthy, then credit can be offered. The C's of credit — character, capacity, capital, collateral, and conditions — have to be possessed by the NPO's clients if the NPO wants to use credit as a tool for customer convenience. If the clientele does not have a high degree of creditworthiness, then it is wise to sell only for cash.

The cost of granting credit is another factor to be considered. The costs of credit should be lower than the benefits to be derived if the NPO wishes to use credit to increase its revenues. Typical costs to be considered are (1) the external costs of borrowing working capital (the interest cost); (2) the costs of maintenance, including salaries, materials, and the overhead costs of granting credit; and (3) the cost of bad debts. If the costs are less than the marginal revenues gained by offering credit, then the NPO could use credit for its clientele.

Another factor is the availability of a cash flow to finance the accounts receivable necessary to offer credit. If sufficient cash flow is not available, then the offering of credit is not a wise choice. Accounts receivable require available cash to finance the credit accounts until they are collected. An NPO should have the necessary cash if credit is to be used.

There may be other factors, but the preceding are the major ones. They may be used as a guideline to help NPO administrators make a strategic decision as to whether to offer credit or use cash to finance sales (see Figure 17.4).

THE RELATIVE IMPORTANCE OF VARIOUS MARKETING STRATEGIES

The seven variables (target market, product/service, price, promotion, place, personnel, and pecuniary strategies) have to be combined to form a market mix. Which ones are more important than others? Which ones should an NPO push more heavily than others? The answer, of course, depends on the situation facing the organization.

Normally, the service-market match strategy would suggest that the product/service is the most important factor. Without a product/service, marketing would not be necessary. On the other hand, a product/service without a

Figure 17.4
Strategic Decision: Whether To Use Credit Or Cash To Finance the Sale

Theoretical Situational Factors	Alternatives				Describe Actual Situational Factors	Evaluation Strength/Weakness	Prescription
	Use Cash	Use Credit Open Account	Layaway	Installment			
1. Objectives Desired by Administrators							
1.1 If increased revenues are desired, then use	X	X	X	X			
1.2 If client/customer service is desired, then use	X	X	X	X			
2. Nature of the Products/Services							
2.1 If products are repossessable, then (durable, tangible, high value, luxury)		X	X	X			
2.2 If services are offered, then (unless other factors)	X						
3. Creditworthiness of Clientele							
3.1 If clientele are credit-worthy, then		X	X	X			
3.2 If not, then	X						
4. Costs of Credit							
4.1 If costs of credit are greater than marginal revenues, then	X						
5. Availability of Cash Flow							
5.1 If cash flow is available to finance accounts receivable, then	X	X	X	X			
5.2 If not, then	X						
6. Other factors							

Overall evaluation and prescription:

market has nothing to gain. Consequently, logic would tell us that both the product/service and the target market are the two most important variables. But what if competing organizations also have an excellent service-market match strategy? Which variables take on significance? Is price more important than promotion? Is place more important than personnel? And so forth.

The answer as to the relative importance of the market mix variables can be found by querying the NPO's clients as to what they perceive the relative importance to be. A scaling device may be administered to a sample of the clients to get their perceptions of the degrees of importance. (The administrators may also rank their perceptions and compare theirs with those of the clients to see if any "gaps" appear.) Once the perceptions of the clients are known, then the NPO administrators can allocate resources accordingly.

The following is an example of an attempt by symphony orchestra administrators to determine the relative importance of their marketing variables by surveying clients who attended their concerts. (No attempt was made to determine the perceptions of non-attendees, although such information might also be useful.)

The board of directors, the executive director, and a random sample of 24 patrons were asked to fill out a survey of the relative importance of variables affecting patron attendance at the concerts of the symphony orchestra. Each person was asked to rank the variables on a scale of one to seven (with seven indicating that the variable was most important and one indicating least important). The results were depicted on four graphs.

An analysis and an interpretation were made. Following are the 13 variables listed in order of importance by the 24 patrons, the 15 board members, and the executive director. (See Graph 17.4 for a pictorial presentation.)

Patrons	Board Members	Director
1. Guest artists	1. To support the arts	1. Right promotional information
2. Musical talent of performers	2. Musical talent of performers	1. Atmosphere
3. Available location	3. Selection of music	2. Availability of parking
4. Selection of music	4. Guest artists	2. Selection of music
5. To support the arts	5. Right promotional information	2. Available location
6. Time of performance	6. Atmosphere	2. Personal image/ status
7. Atmosphere	7. Time of performance	2. Musical talent of performers
8. Availability of parking	8. Available location	2. Time of performance
9. Price of ticket	9. Availability of parking	3. Price of ticket
10. Right promotional information	10. Price of ticket	3. Guest artists
11. Social factors	11. Social factors	4. To support the arts
12. Personal image/ status	12. Personal image/ status	4. Social factors
13. Concessions	13. Concessions	5. Concessions

It was interesting to note that the guest artists were rated by the patrons as being the most important variable. The board rated this variable as fourth, and the executive director rated it way down on his list.

The price was rated ninth by the patrons, tenth by the board members, and way down by the director, suggesting that price is not too important a variable.

The place was rated third by the patrons, eighth by the board, and tied for

Graph 17.1
Factors Affecting Patron Attendance of the Northwest Arkansas Symphony Orchestra — Patrons

Please rank each of these factors by placing an "X" in one of the spaces provided, with 7 indicating the factor is very important regarding your attendance and 1 being not very important at all.

		MEAN							
1.	Guest Artist	6.04	1	2	3	4	5	6	7
2.	Musical Talent	6.00	1	2	3	4	5	6	7
3.	Available Location	5.71	1	2	3	4	5	6	7
4.	Selection of Music	5.71	1	2	3	4	5	6	7
5.	To Support the Arts	5.58	1	2	3	4	5	6	7
6.	Time of Performance	5.46	1	2	3	4	5	6	7
7.	Atmosphere	4.83	1	2	3	4	5	6	7
8.	Availability of Parking	4.83	1	2	3	4	5	6	7
9.	Price of Tickets	4.25	1	2	3	4	5	6	7
10.	Right Promotional Information	3.63	1	2	3	4	5	6	7
11.	Social Factors	2.54	1	2	3	4	5	6	7
12.	Personal Image	1.92	1	2	3	4	5	6	7
13.	Concessions	1.25	1	2	3	4	5	6	7

Graph 17.2
Factors Affecting Patron Attendance of the Northwest Arkansas Symphony Orchestra — Board of Directors

Please rank each of these factors by placing an "X" in one of the spaces provided, with 7 indicating the factor is very important regarding your attendance and 1 being not very important at all.

		MEAN	1	2	3	4	5	6	7
1.	Support of the Arts	6.07						X	
2.	Musical Talent	5.27					X		
3.	Selection of Music	5.20					X		
4.	Guest Artists	5.13					X		
5.	Right promotional information	4.87				X			
6.	Atmosphere	4.86				X			
7.	Time of Performance	4.33				X			
8.	Available Location	4.27				X			
9.	Available Parking	4.20				X			
10.	Price of Ticket	3.60			X				
11.	Social Factors	3.27			X				
12.	Personal Image	2.20		X					
13.	Concessions	1.73	X						

second by the director. Parking was rated in the middle, as was atmosphere (except by the director).

The product — the guest artists, the musical talent, music selection — was rated high by both the patrons and the board members.

Other interpretations could be made, but it was obvious that there was a gap between the patrons and the director as to the relative importance of the marketing mix variables, suggesting some changes in the marketing strategy.

Graph 17.3
Factors Affecting Patron Attendance of the Northwest Arkansas
Symphony Orchestra — Executive Director

Please rank each of these factors by placing an "X" in one of the
spaces provided, with 7 indicating the factor is very important regarding
your attendance and 1 being not very important at all.

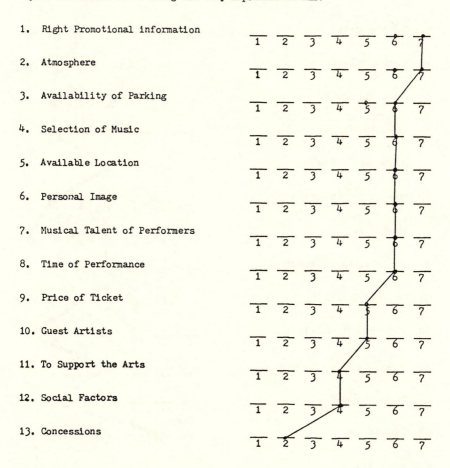

1. Right Promotional information

2. Atmosphere

3. Availability of Parking

4. Selection of Music

5. Available Location

6. Personal Image

7. Musical Talent of Performers

8. Time of Performance

9. Price of Ticket

10. Guest Artists

11. To Support the Arts

12. Social Factors

13. Concessions

Such a survey could be made fairly easily by most NPOs to determine the
relative importance of the marketing variables in the marketing mix.

SUMMARY

Channels of distribution are part of a place strategy, and a number of factors
need to be considered in determining the number of middlemen (the length

Graph 17.4
Factors Affecting Patron Attendance of the Northwest Arkansas Symphony Orchestra—Comparison of Patrons, Board of Directors, and Executive Director

Please rank each of these factors by placing and "X" in one of the spaces provided, with 7 indicating the factor is very important regarding your attendance and 1 being not very important at all.

1. Guest Artists

2. Musical Talent

3. Available Location

4. Selection of Music

5. To Support the Arts

6. Time of Performance

7. Atmosphere

8. Availability of Parking

9. Price of Ticket

10. Right Promotional Information

11. Social Factors

12. Personal Image

13. Concessions

Solid line = Patrons
Bold line = Executive Director
Dotted line = Board Members

of the channel) in a channel of distribution. Further, specific site selection factors help to determine the appropriate location for an NPO's products/ services.

An analysis must also be made of the factors involved in determining the types of sales personnel to be used in selling the NPO's products/services.

The NPO must choose the appropriate combination of order getters, order takers, and order helpers.

The last strategy in the marketing mix is the pecuniary strategy — that is, whether to sell on credit and/or for cash. The factors that influence this decision include the creditworthiness of the NPO's clients/customers.

Finally, some attempt could be made to determine the relative importance of the marketing mix variables (product, price, promotion, place, personnel, and pecuniary factors) to determine which ones to emphasize. A way to evaluate the variables is suggested as an example.

Evaluation of Marketing Mix Strategies

   I. You are asked to make an analysis of the NPO's perception of its services as viewed by marketing.
      A. Consider all the factors of differentiation, design, packaging, atmosphere, branding, and so on.
      B. Gather evidence and back up the factors with facts.
      C. Evaluate and prescribe.
  II. If the NPO markets public goods/services,
      A. Make an analysis of whether they are pure public or quasi-public goods/services.
      B. Make an analysis of externalities from various perspectives.
      C. Determine pricing strategy.
         1. Use the guidelines suggested.
         2. Make it factual.
      D. Evaluate and prescribe.
 III. If the NPO markets non-public goods/services, make an analysis of the NPO's pricing strategy.
      A. Use the guidelines.
      B. Gather facts.
      C. Evaluate and prescribe.
  IV. Make an analysis of promotion/publicity strategies.
      A. Use the guidelines for
         1. Content analysis.
         2. Type of message.
         3. Media selection.
      B. Gather the facts.
      C. Evaluate and prescribe.
      D. Allocate the promotion dollars.
         1. See the suggested guidelines.
   V. Make an analysis of place strategies.
      A. Use the channels of distribution guidelines.
      B. Use the specific site location guidelines.
      C. Gather the facts.
      D. Evaluate and prescribe.
  VI. Make an analysis of the sales personnel strategies.
      A. Use the guidelines.

B. Gather the facts.

C. Evaluate and prescribe.

VII. Make an analysis of the NPO's cash/credit terms.

A. Use the guidelines.

B. Gather the facts.

C. Evaluate and prescribe.

VIII. Determine the relative importance of the marketing mix strategies.

A. See the example.

B. Make graphs comparing managers' perceptions and clients' perceptions.

C. Evaluate and prescribe.

IX. Evaluate and prescribe for the market mix.

18

Personnel Objectives and Related Strategies

Most non-profit organizations are very labor intensive; that is, a great deal of personal work is involved in creating the services that the NPO provides for its clientele. For example, in a typical hospital more than 50 percent of the total expenses of administering the hospital are labor expenses — most notably, wages, salaries, fringe benefits, consulting fees, and other personnel expenses. The same labor intensiveness is characteristic of educational institutions, churches, governmental units, and the many other kinds of NPOs. As a result, the personnel functions of an NPO take on added significance for their administrators. What objectives and what strategies are beneficial in administering the employee resources of an NPO?

Whether an NPO is large and has a personnel department or whether it is small and does not have a separate personnel department, the fundamental personnel functions have to be performed by someone — by the chief executive, his/her assistant, or a personnel department. The personnel functions are fairly universal in that they exist and someone has to make them work.

Any manager is a "personnel manager" in that he/she manages personnel to achieve the objectives of the organization. Many administrators state that of all the factors that affect the success of a non-profit organization, none is more vital than the people involved within and outside the organization. When an NPO sets up a special department to help the line and service and staff functions manage the human resources (both operative and managerial) of an NPO, we have what is commonly known as the personnel department or the employee relations department. These names refer to a special service department, the chief objective of which is to serve the other functions by helping solve people problems.

Personnel administration is a specialized function with the general objective of helping managers acquire and maintain both operative and managerial work forces. Once the overall mission and related objectives and strategies have been formulated, they have to be integrated into the personnel function, the chief role of which is to provide the human, or employee and managerial, resources for the accomplishment of employee and managerial personal ob-

jectives and organizational objectives. To do this effectively, there has to be
an exchange between the NPO and its employees and managers as to the
benefits and burdens each one provides to each other. Just what does the
NPO expect from its human resources, and what do the employees and
managers expect from the NPO?

In the first place, most NPOs want their people to contribute to the
productivity of the organization. They want people to work hard. They also
want them to be loyal to the NPO. They want people to be stable and at the
same time flexible enough to adapt to changing situations. They want people
to contribute their time and talents and be ready, willing, and able to help the
NPO achieve its objectives of client service, growth, image, survival, and so on.

In exchange for contributing their productivity, time, talents, loyalty, readiness, willingness, and abilities, employees and managers generally want to
satisfy some of their personal needs, which include physiological, safety,
acceptance, recognition, and self-actualization needs. In the exchange process
of satisfying organizational needs and personal needs, the personnel department has to integrate its various functions into the overall NPO objectives
and related strategies which have been formulated by the administrators of
the NPO.

CLIENT SERVICE AND RELATED
PERSONNEL FUNCTIONS

If client service and the resulting service-market match strategies have been
formulated, then it becomes the job of the administrators to find and train
the marketing personnel (order getters, order takers, and order helpers), the
production personnel (of which there are many types), and the managers
necessary to produce and sell the NPO's services to satisfy client needs.

The functions performed by most personnel departments have become
fairly standardized when it comes to acquiring workers. The most obvious
ones are analyzing jobs, recruiting, interviewing, testing, and hiring. Before
an NPO can acquire personnel, it must know what its various general strategies are—that is, whether the NPO is planning to grow, to cut costs, to
maintain continuity, and so forth. These overall strategies help to determine
anticipated production requirements, marketing efforts, backlogs of services,
personnel turnover, and other variables that affect personnel planning in
terms of how many and what types of personnel are needed and when to
acquire them.

Analysis of positions is fundamental to acquiring people. Someone has to
determine what the position functions are and what requirements a person
must meet to perform the functions. A position description is an outgrowth
of a position analysis. The position description spells out the objectives, the
functions to be performed, the relationship of the position to other positions,
and the working conditions of the position.

Next, the position specifications are prepared which describe the special qualifications of the person who has the potential capabilities to fill the position. The specifications include information about education, experience, special skills, and other requirements. Thus, the first step in acquiring either operative or managerial personnel is to make a position analysis, followed by a position description and a position specification.

PERSONNEL STRATEGIES TO ACQUIRE MANAGERIAL PERSONNEL

We know that there are at least four types of managers/executives/employees who could fill the position of a top manager who is concerned with getting organizational objectives accomplished: (1) the work horse, (2) the star, (3) the problem child, and (4) the deadwood. Experience suggests that 80 percent of an organization's managers are work horses — the 10-, 12- and 14-hour-a-day managers who thrive as workaholics. About 10 percent are the stars who shine in their positions. Another 10 percent are the problem children who have executive potential, but for one reason or another are not top performers. Finally, the deadwood managers are usually retired or transferred or put out to pasture.

These four types may be conceptualized on a matrix with axes for executive potential (from low to high) and executive performance (from low to high). The high performers are involved in accomplishing innovative objectives, the middle performers are involved in problem-solving objectives, and the low performers are involved in regular or normal objectives. This scheme is depicted on Figure 18.1.

The strategy would be to match the type of manager with the various service-market matches of the organization (as shown in Figure 18.2). The star managers would be put in charge of the NPO's star service-market matches, or perhaps they could be put in charge of the problem service-market matches. The work horses would be matched with the cash cows. Such a strategy would have to be preceded by various steps — most notably, preparation of the position analysis, the position description, and the position specifications.

Another approach to managerial selection is that formulated by Fred Fiedler, a social psychologist, who has suggested that the position specifications for an effective manager in a small active work group should consist of at least four situational factors: (1) the manager's leadership style, (2) the leader-member relations, (3) the task or job structure, and (4) the position power of the leader.[1]

Fiedler has conducted empirical research about leadership effectiveness on at least 1,000 small groups over a period of 30 years and has found that there is a relationship between effectiveness in managing and these four situational factors. He first has to determine whether a manager has a task-motivated or

Figure 18.1
Employee/Manager Resource Portfolio

```
                             High

                    P ·
      Innovative    e ·    Work           ·        Stars        ·
      Objectives    r ·    Horses         ·                     ·
                    f ·                   ·                     ·
      Problem       o ·           80%     ·         10%         ·
      Solving       r ·                   ·
      Objectives    m ·                   ·                     ·
                    a ·    Dead           ·        Problem      ·
                    n ·    Wood           ·        Children     ·
      Regular       c ·                   ·                     ·
      Objectives    e ·                   ·         10%         ·
                      ·                   ·                     ·

                         Low            Potential           High
```

Source: George Odiorne, former professor of management, University of Massachusetts, now retired. Used by permission.

a relationship-motivated style of leadership. Either style is effective, depending on the other three factors; that is, both task-motivated and relationship-motivated leaders are effective, depending on the various situational factors. Neither style is more effective than the other, but their effectiveness depends on situational factors or is situationally determined.

For example, Fiedler has found that a task-motivated leader performs very well in what he calls high-control situations. These types of situations are characterized by (1) good leader-member relations, (2) a structured task, and (3) a generally high degree of position power. Therefore, the position specifications for the selection of an effective manager for a small active group would depend on at least the four factors that Fiedler has researched. Fiedler would specify that a task-motivated leader in a high-control situation should have considerate and supportive behavior, which would result in a good performance. Generally poor performance in a high-control situation would be associated with leader behavior that is somewhat autocratic, aloof, self-centered, and seemingly concerned with task, but with poor results.

In a moderate-control situation, the four factors would generally be described as (1) a moderate degree of leader-member relations, (2) a moderately structured task, (3) a moderate degree of position power, and (4) a relationship-motivated leader. These four situational variables would be associated with a behavior pattern of being considerate with people, being open (not closed), and using a participative style. The performance would be good. A poor performance in a moderate-control situation would be specified by Fiedler as managerial behavior that is tense and task-focused with poor results.

Figure 18.2
Personnel Management Portfolio Strategy

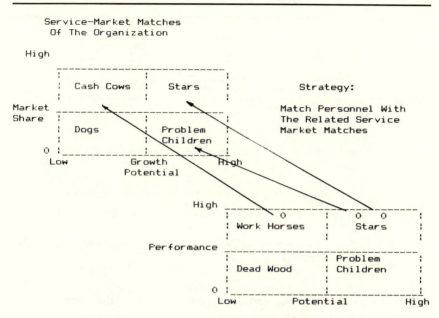

Source: George Odiorne, former professor of management, University of Massachusetts, now
    retired. Used by permission.

In a low-control situation, (1) the leader-member relations would be poor,
(2) an unstructured task (a low degree of task structure) would appear, (3) the
position power would be low, and (4) the leadership style would be task-
motivated, if good performance is desired. The specified behavior of a good
performer would be directive, task focused, and serious. A poor performer in
a low-control situation would be anxious, tentative, and overly concerned
with interpersonal relations, with a resulting poor performance.

In summary, Fiedler's position specifications might be spelled out as
shown in Table 18.1.

BREAK-EVEN OBJECTIVES AND RELATED
PERSONNEL STRATEGIES

Since breaking even or perhaps making a small profit is an objective, the
personnel function's role is to reduce or minimize, if possible, the personnel
costs and at the same time increase productivity through a wide variety of
personnel strategies. Training, for example, leads to lower costs through
greater skills on the part of both employees and managers. The basic ra-

Table 18.1
Summary of Leadership Styles, Behavior, and Performance
in Three Types of Situations

LEADER TYPE	HIGH-CONTROL SITUATION	MODERATE-CONTROL SITUATION	LOW-CONTROL SITUATION
Relationship Motivated Leader	Behavior: Somewhat autocratic, aloof and self-centered. Seemingly concerned with task.	Behavior: Considerate, open and participative.	Behavior: Anxious, tentative, overly concerned with interpersonal relations.
	Performance: Poor	Performance: Good	Performance: Poor
Task-Motivated Leader	Behavior: Considerate, and supportive.	Behavior: Tense, task-focused.	Behavior: Directive, task-focused, serious.
	Performance: Good	Performance: Good	Performance: Relatively good

Source: Fred Fiedler, Martin Chemers, and Linda Mahar, *Improving Leadership Effectiveness* (New York: John Wiley, 1977).

tionale for such a training strategy again is found in the learning curve concept (see Figure 18.3).

Obviously, the time it takes to increase productivity and to reduce expenses varies with the positions involved, but the rationale is sound.

When employees or managers quit, labor turnover, and the increased costs associated with it, is the result. The higher expenses associated with interviewing, testing, and hiring often result. In addition, training costs are repeated, and more importantly, productivity is lost because of high labor turnover and absenteeism. How can labor turnover be reduced?

By turning to the research that Frederick Herzberg, a social scientist, has conducted, we can suggest the causes of labor turnover and then prescribe what to do about them. Herzberg, through a series of interviews with managers and employees, has found that two sets of factors affect employee and managerial behavior. His two-factor theory suggests that the hygiene factors consist of company policy and administration, supervision, salary, interpersonal relations, and working conditions.[2] These hygiene factors are associated with negative feelings toward the job. The motivational factors, on the other hand, are associated with positive feelings toward the job. These include achievement, recognition, the work itself, responsibility, and advancement. They are the motivators for increased productivity.

The motivational factors are called *satisfiers*, while the hygiene factors are called *dissatisfiers*.[3] The dissatisfiers are the ones that are associated with labor turnover. That is, when managers and employees are dissatisfied with salary, or working conditions, or supervision, or company policy and administration,

Figure 18.3
The Learning Curve Applied To Employee Costs
and Productivity Through Training Programs

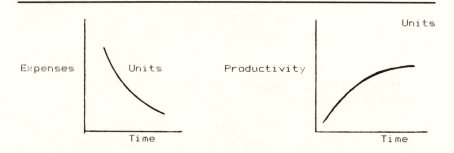

they will quit and try to find another job. If those negative factors are present in an employment situation, then the chances are good that labor turnover will be high.

Of course, it must be remembered that the negative feelings associated with the dissatisfiers have to be relative; for example, salary is relative to other people and/or to other positions in other NPOs. The relativity as perceived by the individual will determine to a large degree whether a factor engenders negative feelings. When it does, the dissatisfier will become a factor in or cause of labor turnover.

Obviously, it becomes a manager's job to identify those negative hygiene factors and make a decision as to what to do about them. Some type of cost/benefit analysis would have to be made to determine whether to change the factors to reduce turnover or whether to hire different people.

GROWTH OBJECTIVES AND RELATED
PERSONNEL STRATEGIES

If an NPO is pursuing a growth strategy, one of the actions it must take is to forecast personnel needs to support such a strategy. This personnel forecast is concerned not only with numbers of employees and managers needed, but also with employee/managerial skills, experience, and, where necessary, training requirements. Managers must be available who are ready, willing, and able to provide leadership in growth situations.

Personnel forecasts regarding quantities needed are usually associated with revenue forecasts and production forecasts. For example, if revenues are forecasted to grow, that means the numbers of production, marketing, and financial personnel will also grow. A useful ratio is that of revenues divided by the number of personnel. For example, if it takes one marketing person per $100,000 of revenues, then it becomes fairly easy to forecast the number of marketing personnel needed. In like fashion, the number of production and financial personnel needed per $100,000 of revenues could be determined.

And the ratio of managers to personnel might be used to determine the number of managers needed. Other analyses would have to be made to determine types, experience, and education levels.

Once a personnel forecast is available, then it becomes the task of personnel to recruit, train, and perform other related functions. Here again the position analyses, position descriptions, and position specifications take on added significance.

OTHER ORGANIZATIONAL OBJECTIVES AND RELATED PERSONNEL STRATEGIES

If maintenance of market share is an organizational objective and if the NPO has formulated an overall strategy based on the product life cycle, then it behooves the personnel function to determine the right types of marketing personnel needed. For example, during the development and growth stages, order getters would be most appropriate, with missionary people needed during development stage. The maturity and decline stages would suggest order takers. These types have to be recruited, trained, and paid in light of the situational factors facing the NPO. The managerial personnel needed would be the work horses for mature service lines and the stars for growth.

If the survival of the NPO is an objective, then the personnel function has to consider at least two strategies: (1) an executive and employee development program and (2) an executive succession program with a "two-deep" organizational structure. Survival requires that there be, for example, a plan or strategy to ensure that top managers will be replaced as needed because of retirement, accident, resignation, death, or other causes. This fundamental need calls for a well-thought-out plan of executive development, including identification of managers in the organization as potential candidates for promotion or for transfer to various functions in the organization or to various strategic organizational units. The executive development plan should be geared individually for each manager.

The primary purpose of the individual development plan is to permit formulation of specific training and development activities for each manager after assessing his/her strengths and weaknesses. This individual plan has to be related to specific goals which have been spelled out in light of the strategies developed.

The NPO's total executive development program can be determined by having the personnel officer or administrator compile a summary report of all the individual training projections outlined in each manager's development plan. The overall training needs can thus be identified, and specific training methods can be spelled out. These might include coaching, on-the-job training, seminars, individual courses to be taken, and a host of other possibilities.

The individual and organizational development plans are tools that assist each manager in using his/her talents to further both organizational and personal objectives. However, a word of caution is needed. A manager has to exercise care in identifying individual development needs and prescribing courses of action; training and personal development cannot be considered a panacea for inadequate performance that results from other organizational factors, such as improper selection, placement, or organization structure, or

Table 18.2
Individual Development Program
(For the Forthcoming Year)

Description of Individual's Development Needs	Plan for Training and Development of Individual Based on Prescribed Need (Methods and Sources)	Proposed Dates To		Date Completed
		Begin	Complete	
Development Plan of Action for Current Position				
1. Needs further development in marketing techniques	1. Enroll in evening or correspondence course on "Principles of Salesmanship"	Jan 1	Oct 1	
2. Needs to expand knowledge of NPO services offered	2. Attend the next training session	Next scheduled meeting preferably first half of year		
3. Needs to expand knowledge of the revisions to "A" service including application and specification	3. Recommend that the NPO develop a training course	Begin as soon as possible	July 1	
4. Telephone operating expenses have been higher than average	4. (a) Review information on practices relating to economical operations of the telephone	Jan 1	Mar 1	
	(b) Discussion with telephone company relative to efficient operation of telephone	Jan 1	Dec 31	
Development Plan of Action For Promotion Preparation				
1. In preparing for marketing management, needs to learn principles of supervision	1. Read three books on marketing management and management from library	Feb 1	Dec 31	
2. Should develop knowledge of executive officer's functions	2. (a) Counseling sessions with executive officer	Jan 1	Dec 31	
	(b) Provide vacation relief for executive officer	June 1	June 22	

from other personal factors, such as attitude, ability, readiness, and willingness to perform. Further, the needs of executives are much too complex to permit the use of highly standardized training methods. Their needs are so varied that the use of only group training methods would not be adequate. An example of a proposed plan is shown in Table 18.2.

The two-deep strategy, copied from the military, can be used in organization structuring by always training and developing someone to take over each key managerial position. This strategy can be implemented by coaching, on-the-job training, relief training when the incumbent manager is out of town, and other training methods.

Other organizational objectives require the personnel function to integrate its activities into the overall strategies. For example, if the NPO wants to improve its industry's position, the personnel function has to make sure that both managers and employees hold offices in industry trade associations.

If improvement of the NPO's image is an overall strategy, then the personnel function has to make sure that officers and key employees hold offices in professional and community organizations.

If improving the quality of life is an organizational objective, then administrators have to integrate personnel strategies to assist schools and colleges, support open housing for its employees, support regional and city planning for the community welfare, support mass transportation systems for its employees' benefit, support arts and cultural activities, support medical facilities in each community, support recreation facilities for the community, and implement other quality of life strategies that involve the NPO's managers and employees.

PERSONNEL STRATEGIES TO ACHIEVE PERSONAL OBJECTIVES

The reciprocity concept, as discussed earlier, suggests that employees and managers have personal objectives that are exchanged for organizational objectives. The underlying theory for attainment of those personal objectives is Maslow's hierarchy of needs.[4] He lists those needs in the following priority order:

1. Physiological needs
2. Safety needs
3. Belongingness and love needs
4. Esteem needs
5. Self-actualization needs

Maslow suggests that these needs are satisfied in the order of priority listed. However, when a need is satisfied, it no longer becomes a motivator (Herzberg's two-factor theory is an application of Maslow's need hierarchy).

The priority does not mean that there are no exceptions, nor does it mean that once a need is satisfied, it can be ignored. But Maslow's theory does mean that organizations can follow certain personnel strategies to help both the person and the organization accomplish their respective objectives.

One of the first personal objectives of employees of an NPO is that of satisfactory pay. A key strategic decision that has to be made is whether to pay above, at, or below the community pay level. What situational factors affect such a decision?

If getting the best person for a position is important to an administrator, the theory would suggest that above-market pay should be offered. Higher pay could also be offered to compensate for the NPO's unfavorable location or poor working conditions. If the administrator is pressured by clients to hire an eminent person, then above-market pay should be considered.

If the NPO is subject to poor working conditions, has a poor location for employment, or is subject to other unfavorable employment conditions, then good theory would suggest that above-market pay levels would have to prevail. All these factors plus the desire to get the best would favor higher than average pay.

However, if the administrator does not want salary to be the main factor in attracting personnel and does want to rely on other factors, then good theory would suggest paying at the market.

If only mediocre personnel are needed for the NPO, good theory suggests that below-market or at-market pay would be appropriate. Further, if a large supply of personnel is available, theory would suggest below-market pay. Likewise, if a person is locked into a situation for personal reasons, an administrator might want to pay below or at the market.

Other situational factors may affect the decision, but the ones mentioned can be summarized in a guideline to help determine this key personnel strategy (see Figure 18.4).

Another personal objective desired by most people is working reasonable hours. For managers the time spent on the job is not set by laws such as the Fair Labor Standards Act which sets the normal working week for employees at 40 hours and requires an hourly pay rate of $1\frac{1}{2}$ times the regular rate for hours worked in excess of 40 hours. Managers often work 50–60 hours a week with no overtime pay. A fairly new strategy for some NPOs is the 4-day, 10-hour-day plan. Further, some NPOs are allowing their employees to choose a flexible hourly plan; that is, they can work whenever they want as long as they put in the required number of hours.

Reasonable working conditions is another personal objective. For example, employee washrooms, locker rooms, dining rooms, and recreational rooms are acceptable. Safety programs are sought. Proper ventilation and space are sought. The Occupational Safety and Health Act now requires acceptable working conditions. Job restructuring is another strategy that may be used to provide reasonable working conditions.

Figure 18.4
Key Personnel Decision: Proper Pay Strategy

Theoretical Situational Factors	Pay Alternatives			Describe Actual Situational Factors and Actual Pay	Compare Actual to Theory and Evaluate	Prescription
	Above Market	At Market	Below Market			
1. If there is a desire to get the best, then	X					
2. If there is a desire to offset an unfavorable location, then	X					
3. If poor working conditions are to be off-set then	X					
4. If other employment conditions are not favorable, then	X					
5. If a high quality product/service is desired, then	X					
6. If the NPO desires to neutralize salary as a competitive factor (rely on other factors), then		X				
7. If the NPO needs only mediocre personnel, then		X	X			
8. If there is a large supply of personnel available, then			X			
9. If personnel are locked in for personal reasons, then		X	X			
10. Other factors?						

Overall Evaluation and Possible Prescription:

Job security is another personal objective of most workers. Such strategies as guaranteed annual wages, last hired–first fired policies, and employee grievance systems have been employed to help people achieve their personal objective of job security.

Fringe benefits are sought by most people. Such strategies as hospitalization plans, life insurance programs, job disability plans, pension plans, day care plans, job-related moving expense reimbursement plans, and others are used to give people a degree of security in their working lives.

Job training becomes a personal objective for most workers. On-the-job and off-the-job training strategies are commonly sought. Special retraining because of automation, computer technology, and relocation has been accepted as a viable strategy. Special remedial training in spelling, English, arithmetic, reading, and other fundamental skills is often used as a personnel strategy for underprivileged and uneducated personnel.

Most people desire fair treatment relative to other people in the organization. Strategies such as employee and managerial grievance plans have been integrated into organization procedures to ensure fair treatment. Special strategies, now required by the Civil Rights Acts, have made fair and equal treatment, regardless of race, creed, color, age, and sex, more of a reality. Further, fairness in pay plans has been implemented through the use of job evaluation methods — the factor-comparison method, job ranking systems, and others — which scale pay rates according to the skills needed, responsibility, effort, and working conditions of each job. Equal pay for equal work is a common strategy used by organizations.

Adequate information is another personal objective. Newspapers, bulletin boards, public address systems, and other one-way media are used to provide information.

Two-way communication can be implemented by suggestion systems, open meetings, employee counseling, exit interviews, and other forms of interaction where an exchange of information gives people feelings of security and belonging — two of their fundamental needs, according to Maslow.

Personal recognition is a fundamental need of most people. The organization can help workers realize this personal objective through various strategies such as making awards to both employees and managerial personnel. Further, a conscious strategy of recognizing personal differences in outstanding performance by giving perquisites is another strategy.

Good supervision is another need that people have. Varying leadership styles are needed, according to varying situations, to properly supervise people. Fiedler's contingency approach to leadership is probably the preferred strategy to use, although there are other strategies that might be used.

Interpersonal relations on the job are important to most people because they have to deal with others. However, some jobs by their very nature do not require much contact with others. These types of jobs require special people to fill them.

Job responsibility is another personal objective desired by most people. Responsibility necessitates being recognized by other people and being needed by the NPO. Job restructuring and job enlargement are common strategies for creating additional responsibility for people.

Interesting work itself is sought by most workers. Job redesign and job rotation are common strategies used to create work that is interesting, although it must be admitted that some people resist these two strategies.

Opportunity for advancement is another personal objective for most people. This objective can be partially implemented by such strategies as training and development programs, job enlargement, job improvement by structuring jobs in a career path, job rotation, special minority advancement strategies, formal education, and vertical and horizontal promotions.

Self-actualization is a rather personal objective that relatively few people can achieve in their lifetimes, particularly by working in an organization. However, there are some people who can and do become what they are potentially capable of becoming, particularly in professional jobs.

A review of Herzberg's theory would suggest that the hygiene factors are concerned with the lower-level needs of Maslow's need hierarchy — that is, pay, working conditions, supervision, company policy and administration, and, to some extent, interpersonal relations. All of these are necessary for people to work, but they are not the motivators; they are the dissatisfiers.

The satisfiers and productivity factors — achievement, recognition, the work itself, responsibility, and advancement — are concerned with Maslow's higher-level needs. These are the personal needs that turn people into productive personnel who accomplish the NPO objectives of creating productivity, working hard, being stable and flexible, being loyal, and being ready, willing, and able to accomplish the NPO's fundamental mission — creating services to satisfy its clientele — and the related objectives of growth, image, survival, and an improved quality of life for society.

EVALUATION OF PERSONNEL STRATEGIES

If an NPO wants to determine the effectiveness of the objective-related exchanges between the organization and its personnel, as suggested by the reciprocity theory, it might evaluate its personnel strategies using the summary in Figure 18.5.

SUMMARY

Evaluation of Personnel Strategies

I. Does the NPO have a program to acquire personnel?
   A. Make position analyses.
      1. Position descriptions
      2. Position specifications

Figure 18.5
Summary of Personnel Strategies

I. Do Personnel Contribute the
    Following to the NPO?
    A. Productivity
    B. Hard Work
    C. Loyalty
    D. Stability
    E. Flexibility
    F. Ability
    G. Readiness
    H. Willingness
    I. Others

II. In Exchange, Does the NPO
    Pursue the Following Strategies
    to Help Personnel Accomplish Their
    Personal Objectives?
    A. Satisfactory Pay
        1. Above the market
        2. At the market
        3. Below the market
    B. Reasonable Hours
        1. Obey government laws
        2. 4-day, 10-hour-day
            workweek
        3. Flexible hours
        4. Others
    C. Working Conditions
        1. Washrooms, locker rooms,
            dining rooms, and
            recreational rooms
        2. Safety programs
        3. Ventilation, space
        4. Job restructuring, if
            necessary
        5. OSHA standards
        6. Others
    D. Job Security
        1. Guaranteed pay
        2. Last hired, first fired
        3. Grievance system
        4. Others
    E. Fringe Benefits
        1. Hospitalization
        2. Life insurance
        3. Disability insurance
        4. Pensions
        5. Day care
        6. Others
    F. Training and Development
        1. On-the-job
        2. Off-the-job
        3. Special retraining
        4. Special remedial training
        5. Others

Figure 18.5 (continued)

```
                                            Evaluation
                                  Strength/    Don't    Needs
                                  Weakness     Know     More
                                  ----------------------Work

    G.  Fair Treatment
        1.  Grievance plan
        2.  Civil Rights Acts
            a.  race
            b.  creed
            c.  color
            d.  age
            e.  sex
            f.  others
        3.  Job evaluation
        4.  Equal pay for equal work
        5.  Others
    H.  Adequate Information
        1.  Newsletter
        2.  Bulletin board
        3.  PA system
        4.  Others
    I.  Two-Way Communication
        1.  Suggestion system
        2.  Open meetings
        3.  Counseling
        4.  Exit interviews
        5.  Others
    J.  Recognition
        1.  Awards
        2.  Recognitions of outstanding
            performance
        3.  Perquisites
        4.  Others
    K.  Supervision
        1.  Proper leadership styles
        2.  Fiedler's methods
        3.  Others
    L.  Interpersonal Relations
    M.  Job Responsibility
        1.  Restructuring, if necessary
        2.  Job enlargement, if necessary
        3.  Others
    N.  Interesting Work
        1.  Job redesign
        2.  Job rotation
        3.  Others
    O.  Opportunity for Advancement
        1.  Training and development
        2.  Job enlargement
        3.  Job designs for career path
        4.  Job rotation
        5.  Special minority advancement
        6.  Formal education
        7.  Vertical promotions
        8.  Horizontal promotions
        9.  Others
    P.  Self Actualization Strategies
    Q.  Herzberg's Two-Factor Theory
        1.  Satisfiers
        2.  Dissatisfiers
    R.  Other Strategies
```

Figure 18.5 (continued)

```
                                            Evaluation
                                    Strength/  Don't   Needs
                                    Weakness   Know    More
                                    _____Work
```

III. Does the Personnel Function
     Integrate Its Strategies into
     an Overall Organization Mission
     and Related Objectives?
     A. Client Service
        1. Perform position analyses
        2. Have position descriptions
        3. Have position specifications
        4. Acquire correct
           1. Marketing personnel
           2. Production personnel
           3. Other personnel
           4. Executive personnel
              a. Portfolio types
              b. Supervisory types
           5. Others
     B. Breakeven or Minimal Profit
        1. Minimize/reduce personnel
           costs
        2. Training
        3. Reducing labor turnover
           a. Herzberg's factors
        4. Others
     C. Growth
        1. Personnel forecasts
        2. Recruiting
        3. Hiring
        4. Orientation
        5. Training
        6. Others
     D. Maintenance of Market Share
        1. Life cycle stages
        2. Others
     E. Survival
        1. Executive and employee
           training and development
        2. Two-deep organization
           structure
        3. Others
     F. Improving Industry Position
        1. Hold offices in trade
           associations
        2. Others
     G. Image
        1. Hold office in community
           organizations
        2. Hold office in professional
           organizations
        3. Others
     H. Quality of Life
        1. Asistance to schools and
           colleges
        2. Support open housing
        3. Support regional and city
           planning
        4. Support mass transit
        5. Support art and cultural
           programs

Figure 18.5 (continued)

```
                                              Evaluation
                                        Strength/  Don't   Needs
                                        Weakness   Know    More
                                        ---------------------Work
            6.   Support medical facilities
            7.   Support recreation
            8.   Others
       I.   Other Organizational Objectives
            1.   Related strategies

 IV.   Is There an Equitable Exchange Between
       Personnel and the Organization?
            A.   Yes?
            B.   No?

 V.    If No, Who Holds The Upper Hand?
            A.   The organization
            B.   Personnel


Overall Evaluation and Possible Prescriptions:
```

    B. Get some examples to determine if they state
       1. Objectives.
       2. Functions.
       3. Authority.
       4. Responsibility.
       5. Accountability.
       6. Relationships.
    C. Evaluate and prescribe.
  II. Is there an equitable exchange between the NPO and its employees?
    A. Are employees satisfied?
    B. Is the NPO satisfied?
    C. If not, who holds the upper hand?
 III. What types of high-level managerial personnel does the NPO have?
    A. Work horses
    B. Stars
    C. Problem children
    D. Deadwood
    E. Is there a proper match between the types of managerial personnel and the service-market match?
       1. Is a work horse matched with a cash cow?
       2. Is a star matched with a problem child or a star?
    F. Evaluate and prescribe.
 IV. Do lower-level managerial personnel match with the situation, as proposed by Fiedler?
    A. What types of managerial personnel does the NPO have?
       1. Relationship-motivated
       2. Task-motivated

B. Do they fit the situational factors?
   1. Leader-member relations
   2. Task structure
   3. Position power
C. Give some evidence of the leader-situation match.
D. Evaluate and prescribe.
V. What about employee turnover? How much is there?
   A. Why do employees leave?
   B. Apply Herzberg's theory.
      1. Motivational factors
      2. Hygiene factors
VI. Evaluate the personnel strategies.
   A. Use the Personnel Strategies evaluation above as the basic guide.
   B. Gather facts.
   C. Evaluate and prescribe.

Notes

1. Fred Fiedler, Martin Chemers, and Linda Mahar, *Improving Leadership Effectiveness* (New York: John Wiley, 1977), 136.

2. Frederick Herzberg, *Work and the Nature of Man* (New York: Thomas Y. Crowell Company, 1966), 71–92.

3. Ibid.

4. Abraham Maslow, *Motivation and Personality*, 2d ed. (New York: Harper and Row, 1970).

19

Personnel Strategies for Volunteers

An obvious difference between not-for-profit and for-profit organizations is the extensive use of volunteer workers in the not-for-profit sector. Volunteer work can be seen everywhere: in hospitals, in churches, in schools, in civic clubs, in cultural organizations, and wherever NPOs operate. And to top it off, volunteers work at the board level, the CEO level, the supervisory level, and the operative level. Many NPOs could not exist without them.[1]

TRENDS THAT AFFECT VOLUNTEERISM

Probably a major reason for the use of volunteers is the recent decline in government funding of NPOs. If funds are not available to hire regular employees, then obviously one strategy is to seek volunteer help. And that's what NPOs have done.

Another trend is the increased concern of businesses with improving the quality of life for society. One strategy for doing this is for businesses to volunteer their executives and employees to help NPOs. Corporate giving is a response to give back to the community, of which NPOs are a part, some resources in exchange for the community's providing resources to business. Various example programs exist: adopt-a-school, loaned executives, serving on NPO boards, and participating in the United Fund, Community Chest, and other organizations. By volunteering its resources, a business gains positive public relations.

The two trends of decreased government funding and increased business giving are responsible, in part, for the third trend — more people volunteering their services. Those volunteers consist of not only older people but also young people. Why? People have more discretionary time. They are retiring earlier than before, and they are living longer with more time to give. Young people see volunteering as a possible career exploration and perhaps as a way to express their idealism.

Because they have a greater need for volunteers, NPOs are now competing for them. Therefore, a strategy is needed to market the NPO to attract the services of volunteers. The increased use of volunteers creates a high visibility in the media. Volunteer activities usually make the news in the papers and on television. The NPO's image can be enhanced by such visibility.

And, finally, there is a growing expectation among volunteers that volunteer-based programs will be effectively managed. When people volunteer, they do not want to waste their time and talent. If that occurs, volunteer turnover increases, the NPO's image suffers, and accomplishment of the mission is diminished.

REASONS FOR VOLUNTEERING

Why do people volunteer to work for NPOs? Probably for the same reasons that non-volunteers do — that is, to satisfy some of their personal needs. More specifically, people have expectations such as the following: (1) recognition, (2) socialization, (3) personal growth, (4) opportunity for leadership, (5) outlet for creativity and use of talents, (6) work experience, (7) classroom credit, and (8) possible career exploration. If these needs are present, then the NPO has to adopt strategies to help volunteers meet these needs. If not, turnover will exist because volunteers can easily stop working and seek commitments elsewhere.

STRATEGIES FOR DEALING WITH VOLUNTEERS

Usually an NPO with many volunteers places the volunteer staff under the direction of a separate organizational administrator who is set apart from the permanently employed people. This dual relationship may create problems, as when a volunteer trustee also works as a volunteer staff worker, or when a volunteer staff worker has a reporting relationship separate from that of the executive director. Despite the parallel structure, some NPOs make the system work because a volunteer staff has unique problems. The key is to have the permanent CEO and the chief volunteer administrator work together as a team, rather than in a superior-subordinate relationship. This is easier said than done. The organization has to adapt to both sets of employees — the volunteer and the non-volunteer — to accomplish its mission.

The planning function should accommodate the volunteers. For example, the volunteer board members, paid staff, volunteers, and client/members have to participate together in the strategy development phases of an NPO. Further, there should be a separate budget item for volunteer workers and written position descriptions for all volunteers, spelling out duties, objectives, authority, and relationships.

Recruiting volunteers is not a haphazard job. The volunteer administrator needs to know how many and what types of people are needed, costs of recruiting (including brochures), and the methods of recruiting.

Orientation sessions should be held for volunteers to let each one know about the mission and related strategies of the NPO.

Placement of a volunteer is crucial. The volunteer should be placed on the basis of the time commitments he/she can make relative to the needs of the

NPO. Normally, the time commitment of each volunteer is limited. Consequently, placement is fundamental to both the NPO and the volunteer.

Pre-service and in-service training is usually necessary to fulfill the requirements of the NPO and to meet the needs of the volunteer. Satisfaction on the job is crucial to the volunteer who wants to feel that his/her services are necessary to accomplish the mission.

Supervisory support is necessary for each volunteer. He/she wants the oversight of someone who is organized, who can communicate well, who can delegate, who can negotiate, and who will evaluate the volunteer's efforts fairly.

Record keeping is helpful. For example, the following types of records are useful: (1) application; (2) work performed, including hours worked; (3) training attended; (4) type of work; and (5) miscellaneous records.

Recognition of work is needed. This recognition can come in different forms — letters of recognition, appointments as a supervisory training leader, parties, banquets, special lounges, and so forth.

Evaluation of volunteers' work and performance, both quantity and quality, is crucial. Even an MBO system can be used to advantage with volunteers.

The program for volunteers can be evaluated by the NPO to determine its strengths and weaknesses, as shown in Figure 19.1.

SPECIAL REWARDS FOR VOLUNTEERS

Although volunteering to accomplish the NPO's mission may be a reward in itself, it may not be enough to sustain the commitments of volunteers. Therefore, a reward system needs to be integrated into the personnel strategies for volunteers. Furthermore, a continuing need for rewards has to exist for the NPO to be successful in using the services of volunteers to accomplish its mission.

For volunteer employees, the following forms of rewards are suggested:

1. Lapel pins
2. Uniforms
3. Membership cards
4. Plaques
5. Trophies
6. Press releases
7. Award dinners
8. Personal phone calls
9. Handwritten letters

The importance of a modest reward cannot be overstated. Very seldom does a volunteer turn down a public award. A reward system satisfies one of the basic needs of a volunteer — that is, recognition for work performed.

Figure 19.1
Personnel Strategies for Volunteers

	Strength/	Don't	Needs
Strategy	Weakness	Know	Work

A. Does the NPO know why people volunteer?

B. Does the NPO have a separate person in charge of volunteers, reporting directly to the board?

C. Do the volunteers participate in policy and strategy?

D. Is there a special budgetary unit for volunteers?

E. Is there a special program for recruiting volunteers, together with job descriptions?

F. Are volunteers placed properly in jobs to accomplish the mission?

G. Are time commitments of the volunteers fulfilled?

H. Is there a pre-service and in-service training program for volunteers?

I. Is there supervisory support for volunteers?

J. Are records kept of volunteer activities?

K. Are volunteers recognized for their activities?

L. Is there a program of evaluation of volunteers?

Overall Evaluation and Possible Prescription:

The volunteer trustee has special needs. The NPO can give the trustee access to the public through press releases. Such an action provides the trustee with a sense of power. Further, the NPO can suggest that the trustee have an opportunity to rub shoulders with community leaders, which eventually may pay off with tangible rewards. Whatever forms the rewards may take, they are fundamental to the success of the NPO.

PERSONNEL PRACTICES IN VOLUNTARY NPOS

In one of the first research studies done on voluntary NPOs, William F. Crittenden found some interesting relationships between personnel factors and NPO performance. Using a data base of 300 NPOs with a variety of statistical tests (canonical correlations, Pearson product moment regressions, factor analyses, and others), Crittenden found among other factors that a relationship existed between the sex of the administrator and the administrator's number of years of business management experience. Female administrators of NPOs generally were found to have little or no managerial experience in the profit sector, while male administrators generally were found to have some business management experience. Such a finding suggests that the interaction between the profit sector and the non-profit sector may exist for male administrators and not for female administrators. Of course, females may not have infiltrated the male-dominated administrative positions despite the fairly recent feminist movement.[2]

What few female administrators there were, were more likely to use committees than males were.

In addition, Crittenden found that there was a relationship between the age of members and the NPO's expressive tendencies. Those organizations that stressed internal objectives and internal activities for their members were found to have a large proportion of members under 20 years of age. Such a finding would indicate that younger members may be interested in belonging to NPOs that have objectives and activities directed primarily toward the satisfaction of members (Boy Scouts, Girl Scouts, YMCA, YWCA, for example) rather than toward external activities. Those NPOs wanting to attract younger members should promote the benefits and activities to members rather than external objectives, particularly in their production and marketing functions.[3]

Crittenden also found that practices in the profit sector are generalizable to those in the non-profit sector, particularly those exhibiting instrumental tendencies; for example, those personnel practices used by profit-making organizations could and are being followed by NPOs with externally oriented objectives and performances.[4]

PERFORMANCE MEASURES OF NPOS

In profit organizations, performance criteria usually measure results in financial terms. Even though financial measures do not really measure all aspects of how well the organization satisfies the needs of its resource contributors, the measures of financial efficiency and profitability are fairly well accepted. However, profitability measures often are inappropriate, irrelevant, and/or unavailable for voluntary NPOs.

Since the basic proposition has been established that an NPO exists to satisfy the needs of its resource contributors, some types of measurements are needed to determine how well the NPO satisfies its clients/customers, members, managers, employees, suppliers, government, and other contributors. One possible way to measure client/customer need satisfaction, discussed in relation to the service-market match strategy, is to use a modified semantic differential as the measurement tool. The semantic differential could be similarly applied to the members, managers, employees, suppliers, and other resource contributors.

Since each NPO has multiple objectives which often conflict with each other (because different resource contributors have differing perceptions of what satisfies their needs), there is not a single measure of performance applicable to all NPOs. The most common one, which the author espouses, is that an NPO is effective if it satisfies its *key* resource contributors so that they continue to support the NPO. Some crude measures of performance might be used to quantify the satisfaction of key contributors.

For example, if the *key* contributors to a voluntary NPO consist of its members, managers, financial donors, and others, then some quantitative measures might be utilized to determine NPO effectiveness relative to its direct and indirect competition for resources. The annual percentage change in revenues and other monetary contributions (from any source) is one measure of performance that might be used. This measure should reflect the level of satisfaction (or dissatisfaction) as perceived by its members, clients/customers, government, donors, and other possible revenue sources.

Another similar measure might be the annual percentage change in active volunteer membership. Logically, volunteer members and potential members would increase or decrease their involvement as they perceive the organization to presently or potentially be more effective or ineffective.

The annual percentage change in services or products offered might be used to measure the satisfaction or dissatisfaction level of the NPO's client/customer base and even its membership base. An increase or decrease in services offered logically would have a positive or negative impact on the clients/members since the larger or smaller the number of the services offered, the greater or lesser the possibility of meeting each individual's needs.

For determining managerial and employee effectiveness, an NPO might use measures of turnover, absenteeism, attitudes, grievances, tardiness, and the like.

Other measures of performance could be constructed for the NPO's suppliers, government, community, creditors, and society in general if they are the *key* resource contributors. The measures selected should be used to allow for the uniqueness of the voluntary NPO.

THE RELATIONSHIP BETWEEN PERSONNEL ACTIVITIES AND NPO PERFORMANCE

As suggested by Crittenden's research, there is a contingency or situational relationship among various personnel activities and NPO performance. For example, in an organizational environment that has older members and a volunteer, or low-paid, administrator, with an emphasis on a total scope of

Figure 19.2
Relationship of Personnel Activities and Performance Measures

Theoretical Situational Factors	Alternative Performance Measures	Describe Actual Situation	Compare and Evaluate	Prescribe
1. If a NPO is concerned with instrumental, external objectives and If the administrator is highly paid and If its members are female volunteers and If the NPO has low expressive tendencies and If it is involved in subjective planning and If there is a deemphasis on planning contraints, and If the majority of its members are 20-59 years of age, then	1. High percentage change in the number of voluntary members and 1.1 High positive percentage change in the number of service offerings and 1.2 Negative change in the level of funding received			
2. If a NPO is concerned with expressive, internally oriented objectives and activities and If a large proportion of its members are under 20 years of age and If the administrator is highly paid and If there is a low degree of administrative informality, then	High positive percentage change of funding received.			
3. If the NPO has older members and If the administrator is low paid and is a volunteer and If a total scope of planning is used, then	High degree of administrator satisfaction			

planning, these variables will lead to higher levels of need satisfaction for administrators.[5]

Another relationship exists in that in an externally oriented instrumental organization with a highly paid administrator, a large female volunteer membership with low expressive tendencies, and a large proportion of members in the 20–59 age bracket, with an emphasis on subjective planning and a de-emphasis on constraints, such variables will aid in recruiting additional volunteers and will also increase the number of services and activities offered, while adversely affecting the level of funds received. These findings would suggest that a possible tradeoff might exist between the performance measures of funding levels and additional services and an increase in members.[6]

Another situational relationship is found in those organizations that are low in instrumental tendencies, are high in expressive tendencies, have a large proportion of members under 30 years of age, and have a high-paid administrator with a low degree of administrative informality. All these variables are associated with a high positive percentage of change in the levels of funding received.[7]

The preceding relationships may be summarized in a situational matrix, as shown in Figure 19.2. This matrix may be used to evaluate the personnel practices and performance measures of voluntary NPOs by comparing the actual personnel practices to the theoretical situational factors and then possibly prescribing changes in the personnel functions.

SUMMARY

This chapter has suggested various volunteer personnel strategies for the organization. These strategies are designed to accomplish the objectives of the typical NPO that is heavily volunteer-labor-intensive and relies on its volunteer employees/helpers to accomplish its major mission of providing services for its clientele.

Evaluation of Volunteerism

If an NPO has a fairly large number of volunteer workers, the following evaluation should be made.

1. Determine, if possible, the reasons for volunteering.
   a. Ask the volunteers.
   b. In light of the answers, is the NPO pursuing the correct strategies?
2. Does the NPO pursue the following strategies in dealing with volunteers?
   a. Separate person in charge of volunteers
   b. Participation by volunteers in strategy/policy
   c. Special budget for volunteers
   d. Job descriptions
   e. Recruiting

    f. Proper placement
    g. Time commitments
    h. Training
    i. Supervisory support
    j. Records
    k. Recognition
    l. Evaluation
3. Do volunteers receive special rewards?
    a. What kinds?
    b. Continuous program?
    c. For workers?
    d. trustees?
4. Does the voluntary NPO follow the strategies suggested in Crittenden's dissertation?
5. Evaluate and prescribe.

Notes

1. For an excellent discussion of volunteerism, see Israel Unterman and Richard H. Davis, *Strategic Management of Not-For-Profit Organizations* (New York: Praeger, 1984); in particular, see Chapter 8 by Judy Rauner.

2. Research on voluntary NPOs was conducted by William F. Crittenden, "An Investigation of Strategic Planning in Voluntary Non-profit Organizations" (Ph.D. diss., University of Arkansas, 1982).

3. Ibid.

4. Ibid.

5. Ibid.

6. Ibid.

7. Ibid.

20

Financial Strategies

Once the NPO's overall mission and related strategies have been formulated (for example, service-market match, profitability, growth, image, maintenance of market share, and survival), these strategies have to be integrated into the finance function of the NPO. The finance function's key role is to provide cash flows to help the NPO accomplish its mission and related objectives. Cash flows from (1) internal sources of profits and retained earnings and (2) external creditors and donors provide the financial wherewithal so necessary for the NPO to carry out its basic mission.

RECIPROCITY BETWEEN THE NPO AND ITS CAPITAL PROVIDERS

There has to be a high degree of reciprocity between the NPO and its external sources of capital — namely, the creditors who lend capital to the NPO and the donors who provide funds to start the NPO and to keep it going. Both the donors and the creditors have to perceive an equitable exchange of their capital for other benefits that they expect to receive in return for their investments.

ASSET GROWTH AND RELATED SHORT-TERM CASH FLOW STRATEGIES

A positive cash flow has to exist if the NPO wishes its assets to grow. One strategy to achieve this is to use other people's money (OPM) rather than the NPO's money to finance asset growth, without paying interest on OPM.

"Free debt" is widely used; that is, assets are lent to the organization by short-term creditors as long as the organization meets the creditors' payment schedules (usually 30 days or longer). The free debt ratio is calculated by dividing the non-interest-bearing liabilities (usually current liabilities, but not always) by the total assets. Usually about one-fourth of the total assets are in the form of free debt. They are worth monitoring closely. To keep the ratio high, the strategy is to not pay until the terms demand the NPO to do so. But it is not wise to pay late because suppliers will then charge interest and perceive the NPO as a poor credit risk, which does not create a good image for the NPO in the eyes of its creditors.

Another suggested short-term strategy is to capitalize on the float created by suppliers who are slow in cashing the NPO's checks.

On the other hand, the NPO should be aggressive in billing and collecting its accounts receivable. Billing accounts receivable early (before the client receives the services) is a strategy that some clients will often accept in return for price discounts. A favorable cash flow will result.

MARKET SHARE AND GROWTH AND RELATED CASH FLOW STRATEGIES

The Boston Consulting Group (BCG), under the leadership of Bruce Henderson, has developed a cash flow strategy based on "the product portfolio." BCG's contention is that an organization should have a portfolio of services with different market shares and different growth rates.[1] A natural cash flow strategy is created by such a portfolio of services. High-growth services require large cash inflows, while low-growth services should generate extra cash flows. Both kinds are needed. For example, a hospital has a portfolio of services, as does a collegiate athletic program. An educational institution also has a portfolio of "self-sustaining auxiliary enterprises." Other types of NPOs may have several services with different growth rates and market shares.

BCG lays out four rules that determine the cash flow of a service.

1. Margins and cash flow generated are a function of market share. High margins and high market share go together, explained by the experience curve.
2. Growth requires cash input to finance additional assets. That cash required to maintain market share is a function of growth rates.
3. High market share usually is either earned or bought. If bought, additional investment is needed.
4. No market can grow indefinitely. The payoff from growth is cash that cannot be reinvested in that service.

BCG has developed the portfolio matrix shown below.

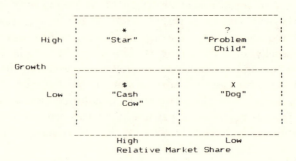

Services with a high market share and slow growth are cash cows. They generally produce large amounts of cash in excess of the reinvestment required to maintain market share. BCG suggests that the excess cash flow should not be reinvested in cash cows.

Services with a low market share and slow growth are dogs. They may show an accounting profit, but the profit must be reinvested to maintain market share, with no excess cash flow. The service is relatively worthless as a cash flow generator, except in liquidation.

All services, according to BCG, eventually become cash cows or dogs. The value of a service depends on whether it obtains a leading share of the market before its growth slows down.

A low market share and high growth indicates the problem children. They almost always require far more cash flow than they generate. If cash is not supplied, they die. Even if they are allocated cash, if they only maintain market share, they still become dogs if their growth stops. The low market share and the high growth are liabilities unless the product/service becomes a leader. The problem child requires very large cash flows that it cannot generate itself.

A "star" is a product/service with a high market share and high growth. It may show profits, but may not always generate all of its own cash. If it remains a leader, it will generate cash when its growth slows and its reinvestment requirements diminish. It eventually will become a cash cow with cash throwoff for reinvestment elsewhere.

The portfolio is worthwhile, says BCG.[2] Every organization needs services that generate cash and services that need cash. And if it has problem children, they need cash.

If a firm has a balanced portfolio of services, it can capitalize on them.

- Stars have a high share and high growth which provide assurance for the future.
- Cash cows supply funds for that future growth.
- Hopefully problem children will be converted into stars with added cash flows.
- "Dogs" are not necessary.

Cash flow strategies follow from the BCG portfolio.

FUND RAISING

Long-term and short-term cash flows are constant problems for an NPO because (1) no long-term sources of capital are provided by the owners and (2) the NPO is not set up to make profits from which short-term capital is provided. As a result, the NPO has to rely on donations from people and organizations that have an "interest" in the basic mission of the NPO. This interest provides a possible source of capital when the NPO seeks gifts in campaigns, usually yearly, and sometimes in special campaigns to help fund the deficits of the NPO.

The Importance of Image

Fund-raising campaigns are successful when the image of the NPO is favorable in the minds of possible donors. Image is crucial to fund raising. If potential donors in the community have never heard of the NPO, there is not much chance of securing gifts. As a result, there is a need to pursue the strategies suggested to maintain an image: (1) provide excellent services, (2) have a positive attitude on the part of managers, employees, and members, (3) have television and radio coverage, (4) maintain good press relations, (5) make an image survey, (6) have well-groomed employees and administrators, (7) hold offices in professional organizations, (8) support community projects, (9) stress beauty in the NPO's surroundings, and (10) others.

Organization for Fund Raising

Who should be involved with fund raising? Normally, at least four organizational units are jointly concerned with securing gifts: (1) the board of directors, (2) the executive director, (3) the development committee, and (4) the development officer.

The members of the board have the ultimate responsibility for securing financial resources for the NPO. In fact, raising money is probably a key function of the board and a key reason for selecting board members who have access to financial resources.

The executive director or CEO is often the recognized leader for the NPO in the community. He/she is usually the spokesperson for the organization. Further, the CEO is the person who is responsible for determining the financial resources needed and who presents the financial needs to the board for approval and action.

The chairman of the board usually appoints a member of the board to chair the fund-raising activities. A committee is then selected, consisting of business executives, wealthy patrons of the NPO, and representatives of various community members whose services are needed to aid in fund raising (e.g., advertising agencies, printing firms, and so forth). In addition, geographic representation of community leaders is necessary to ensure peer solicitations in a broadly based fund-raising campaign.

The development officer is responsible for developing a plan and executing it, working with the board, the CEO, and the development committee.

The Steps Involved in Fund Raising

The basic marketing concepts would be suggested in raising money. The first step would be concerned with the services provided by the NPO. Each member of the board or sales representative of the NPO must gain knowledge about the organization's mission and strategies in order to accomplish them.

The next step would be to get a commitment from the board member or sales representative to the NPO's basic mission. It is difficult to raise money if the board member does not have a deep commitment to the organization.

Third, the board members have to identify the target market. They do this by furnishing the development officer with a list of all their professional, school, church, and social affiliated peers. A similar list from the member's spouse would help. With this list, the development officer would be able to chart a target market for board members and sales representatives to call on. Sometimes the amount of the financial donation would be suggested for each target donor. Further, time limits might be suggested.

Then each potential donor would be contacted to cultivate his/her interest and to acquaint the donor with the mission of the NPO. At this stage, it is imperative that the donor's needs be interpreted so as to select the appropriate tactic to pursue to get a donation.

A follow-up step is needed to provide the donor with information about the NPO.

Finally, the donor is asked to contribute. Usually a peer request is made; that is, "Peers give to peers when asked." Letters need to be sent thanking the donor. Some type of reward is necessary to reinforce the donor's giving.

FINANCIAL RATIO ANALYSIS

The financial officer of an NPO can make an evaluation of the financial position and financial operations of the organization by using a financial ratio analysis. A note of caution: Not every NPO can easily be financially evaluated by the ratios applicable to all. Every NPO may have to use different ratios, unique to its operations. And to be effective, the ratios should be compared over time to determine trends and be compared with those of similar organizations to determine effectiveness.

An example of a hospital's financial ratio analysis will illustrate some of the ratios that might be applicable to other NPOs. The chief financial officer of the hospital presented the following report to the board of directors.

"If we are to plan for the future, we need to keep two objectives in mind. First, we are here to serve our patients in whatever scenario is best. Second, we must keep ourselves financially strong enough to be able to serve our resource contributors.

"There are a number of superficial ways to determine whether we are doing well financially. Do we have cash in the bank? Are we in the black? Is it necessary for our prices to be higher than those of others? Are we having to borrow? Whereas each of these is important, it must be understood that the question of 'enough' is not addressed and that the measures above are only outward indications of the deeper forces that drive them.

"The following financial analysis takes a glimpse at these deeper forces.

There are some definite 'victories' for us and some confirmed problems. The fact that problems exist pressures an overperformance of other indicators. These problems are necessary to know as we gear up for future activity.

"Basically, we are going to stress our return on equity indicator. Our rate of growth must be matched by our return on equity. If we plan to add assets to grow faster than we can earn equity, borrowing must be contemplated. If our return on equity exceeds our growth rate, funds gather cobwebs waiting to be put to work.

"Four types of pressures will form the equity product. If all four function in harmony, we are said to be 'viable.' If any of the four is weak, the other activities must pick up the slack. The four active pressures are (1) operating margins, (2) asset efficiencies, (3) non-operating revenues, and (4) asset leverage."

After laying the groundwork, the chief financial officer presented a series of ratios in graphic form, accompanied by a brief interpretation of the ratio.

Return on Equity (High Is Good)

"This is the single most important ratio. It defines the amount of net income earned per dollar of equity or, alternatively, the rate at which equity grew during the years. Since capital formation is the single most important issue, growth of equity capital is a key objective. Real future growth may well be constrained by the hospital's failure to accumulate new capital.

$$\frac{\text{Excess of Revenues over Expenses}}{\text{Fund Balance}} = \text{Return on Equity}$$

"Our hospital has had a 13 percent growth rate in recent years.

	Our Hospital	HCA
This year	13.5%	16.0%
Last year	13.5	15.5
2 years ago	13.8	13.7
3 years ago	17.0	16.8
4 years ago	17.2	17.2
5 years ago	13.5	13.9
6 years ago	7.0	17.0
7 years ago	6.0	16.0

"HCA had comparable ratios.

"Especially during the last two years, the real growth is emphasized as opposed to the inflated growth of four and five years ago.

"Our rate of growth is strong because of the high mark-up ratios and excellent operating margins. However, on the negative side, our asset utilization is pretty poor. Factors affecting the return on equity favorably should be (1) high operating margins, (2) high asset turnover, (3) high non-operating revenues, and (4) low equity financing. Each of these will be discussed.

Operating Margin (High Is Good)

"Extremely important to capital formation and a good return on equity is the operating margin: net operating income divided by total operating revenue. High values indicate good operating profits. This is the test of a hospital's profitability used predominantly today.

"It is important to note that a good operating margin is not by itself always sufficient to guarantee survival. Older facilities, highly leveraged facilities, poorly used assets, and heavy working-capital users require relatively higher levels of profit to maintain their organizational integrity.

	Our Hospital	HCA
Last year	6.2%	7.6%
2 years ago	5.9	5.8
3 years ago	5.0	5.4
4 years ago	6.5	6.2
5 years ago	4.9	5.9
6 years ago	1.7	6.0
7 years ago	1.0	6.1

"Our operating margin contributed heavily toward its return on equity. Our margin closely paralleled that of HCA and excels in the industry. This is made possible largely by an excellent mark-up ratio, but it is depressed somewhat by a higher than usual deductible ratio.

Mark-Up Ratio (Up Is Good)

"This ratio measures the relationship between prices and expenses: gross revenues divided by operating expenses. A value of 1.2 means you have a spread of 20 percent from cost to billed revenue. This spread is affected two ways — by reduced cost and/or by increased prices.

	Our Hospital	HCA
This year	1.34	1.23
Last year	1.33	1.20
2 years ago	1.28	1.19
3 years ago	1.26	1.22
4 years ago	1.27	1.25
5 years ago	1.25	1.23
6 years ago	1.15	1.22
7 years ago	1.14	1.21

"Since our hospital excels in this measure, operating margins are good. By itself, however, one cannot judge whether it is too high or too low. For example, if the deductible ratio is high, a high mark-up ratio is necessary to produce the desired operating margin.

Deductible Ratio (Down Is Good)

"This ratio defines that portion of operating revenues not collected. We cannot lose sight of the fact that a 20 percent mark-up is no good if you have a 20 percent deductible ratio. The ratio is calculated as follows: allowances for bad debts divided by gross patient revenues.

"Usually this ratio moves in the same direction as the mark-up ratio does. However, under the prospective payment system, this parallel will no longer be mandated.

	Our Hospital	HCA
This year	1.9%	1.1%
Last year	2.0	1.0
2 years ago	1.7	1.0
3 years ago	1.7	1.1
4 years ago	1.7	1.1
5 years ago	1.8	1.1
6 years ago	1.2	1.1
7 years ago	1.2	1.0

"High days in accounts receivable will reduce the deductible ratio because the accounts are not charged off to bad debts. Conversely, rapid bad debt chargeoffs increase the deductible ratio. There is evidence that this occurred last year, with days in patient accounts receivable dropping sharply and the deductible ratio blipping upward. However, it is forecasted that this will stabilize this year.

"In summary, the high deductibles are pressuring the mark-up ratios upward. It should be understood that prospective payment systems may change the opposites. Most certainly, as prices increase, bad debts increase. But, whereas in the past, high mark-up ratios created high deductibles, under prospective payment, one will not necessarily follow the other. Our hospital has good operating margins not so much because of our prices, but because of our maintenance of costs. However, the sole use of costs as a margin creator will eventually have its limitation.

Asset Efficiency: Total Asset Turnover (High Is Good)

"This measure, total operating revenue divided by total assets, indicates the overall effectiveness of asset efficiency. How we use what we have is very important to our return on equity."

"This ratio measures the dollars of revenue generated per dollar of investment. Investments in this case are all that you own. Increasing this ratio is vital to our return on equity. Low turnover ratios usually point toward over-investment for the pattern of utilization.

	Our Hospital	HCA
This year	.67	.89
Last year	.68	.94
2 years ago	.71	.82
3 years ago	.65	.65
4 years ago	.61	.70
5 years ago	.52	.80

"Our hospital suffers in this measure. Because the problem is very significant in that this ratio is below the national median (1.1 to 1.2), the mark-up ratio had to be raised to compensate.

"In determining the reason for the low asset turnover rating, several analyses are possible: (1) fixed asset turnover, (2) average age of the plant, (3) current asset turnover, (4) days cash on hand ratio, (5) days in patient accounts receivable, and (6) inventory ratio.

Fixed Asset Turnover (High Is Good)

"This ratio is calculated as follows: total operating revenue divided by net fixed assets.

	Our Hospital	HCA
This year	.87	.94
Last year	.87	.93
2 years ago	.91	.92
3 years ago	.91	.91
4 years ago	.80	.97
5 years ago	.62	1.00
6 years ago	.55	.96
7 years ago	.45	.95

"You will note that our hospital is poor in this measure, falling far below the industry median (1.9 to 2.1). Given that overinvestment is part of the problem, age of the plant is another. An older plant will tend to have a higher ratio than a new plant will. Usually, older plants, though generally less efficient, are pretty well crammed and cramped for space. When new plants are built, the tendency is to hedge against need for future space, this being poorly utilized (like ours).

Average Age of Plant (Lower Values Tend to Decrease Asset Turnover)

"This ratio is calculated as follows: depreciation allowance divided by depreciation expense.

	Our Hospital	HCA
This year	5.6 years	3.9 years
Last year	5.0	3.8
2 years ago	4.9	3.7
3 years ago	4.8	3.6
4 years ago	4.7	3.9
5 years ago	4.0	3.8
6 years ago	3.4	3.6
7 years ago	3.8	3.8

"The median industry average is eight years. Hospitals with a high age value should critically examine their profitability position. High values usually mean replacement is imminent, necessitating heavy financial needs. A history of profitability will enhance prospects for long-term credit when replacement is necessary.

Current Asset Turnover (Higher Is Better)

"This measure (total operating revenue divided by current assets) compares the currently invested or receivable dollars we have against our operating revenues. It is an old question, but a good one: How much current asset margin is needed to produce good revenue? The lower the investment, the more likely it is that the turnover will be higher and the dollars will be working efficiently. There is a break-over point at which current dollars will become too scarce for the bills to be paid. This is why I have indicated that a higher (rather than a high) ratio would be good.

	Our Hospital	HCA
This year	2.8	4.7
Last year	2.9	5.3
2 years ago	3.0	5.3
3 years ago	2.9	3.9
4 years ago	2.8	3.9
5 years ago	3.0	4.0
6 years ago	2.8	4.1
7 years ago	2.5	4.2

"It is surprising to note that our hospital does poorly in managing our current assets. Unlike the poor values for fixed assets, conceptually we should be able to do something about putting our current assets to work. If this could happen, it would be easier to maintain an appropriate return on equity, taking some of the pressure off our operating margins.

"To diagnose the problem, we will look at (1) the days cash on hand ratio, (2) the days in patient accounts receivable, and (3) the inventory ratio.

Days Cash on Hand (Lower Is Better)

"Days cash on hand simply defines the average number of days in cash expenses available at the present time (cash plus securities multiplied by 365 divided by total operating expenses less depreciation). High values are usually indicators of a highly liquid position. Hospitals not funding depreciation should have a high value in this measure.

	Our Hospital	HCA
Last year	47 days	9 days
2 years ago	36	8
3 years ago	34	9
4 years ago	36	9
5 years ago	30	12
6 years ago	25	5
7 years ago	20	18

"The presumption here is that our excess cash should be put to work. But care should be taken to observe the average payment period ratio which indicates how quickly bills are paid. (This ratio will be discussed later.)

Days in Patient Accounts Receivable (Low Is Good)

"This ratio is calculated as follows: net patient accounts receivable multiplied by 365 divided by net patient services revenue.

	Our Hospital	HCA
This year	68 days	62 days
Last year	68	74
2 years ago	77	73
3 years ago	79	64
4 years ago	78	62
5 years ago	75	58
6 years ago	76	65
7 years ago	82	52

"It is obvious that except in recent years we have done poorly in this measure. However, two occurrences happened to change this stalled position: (1) we are now more fully automated and (2) we changed office managers last year. I somehow believe that these two moves were significant. Three years ago bugs in the computer system blocked improvement. Now fully operational, the system is producing collectible data.

Inventory Ratio (High Is Good)

"This ratio measures inventory investment in relation to operating revenue — that is, total operating revenue divided by inventory. In theory, a storeroom should contain stock sufficient to avoid disruption of service. A high investment would accomplish this objective, but would leave dollars inactive on the shelves.

	Our Hospital	HCA
This year	66	42
Last year	67	39
2 years ago	62	38
3 years ago	41	31
4 years ago	41	28
5 years ago	30	30
6 years ago	31	29
7 years ago	42	30

"Though better in recent years, we are operating at industry minimum levels of 60+ days. Improvements are still out there to be made.

"It should be noted that besides changing administrative leadership two years ago, the function for inventory was automated. These were two important factors in improving this ratio.

Summary of Asset Efficiency

"Our poor showing in terms of using vested dollars has put pressure on our operating margins. It seems that there are a few things we can do to increase our asset efficiency:

1. Raise our income per square foot by initiating new income-producing services to occupy our vacant spaces.
2. Use our excess cash more wisely.
3. Continue to work accounts receivable toward the median level.
4. Reduce our inventory investment.

Non-Operating Revenue

"Our non-operating revenues are fairly static. In summary, we have not developed these non-patient sources, except for keeping funds invested. In order to relieve the pressure now being exerted on the operating margins, this source should be pursued.

Leverage

"The final set of ratios to be examined includes those having to do with debt encumbrances and debt coverage. The term *leverage* means to use your assets to generate new capital. To say an asset is heavily leveraged usually means that it is heavily encumbered. Encumbrance is usually entered into to increase the equity balance beyond that which is assembled through operating income.

Equity Financing Ratio (High Is Good)

"This ratio (fund balance divided by total assets) measures the proportion of total assets financed from operations. High values are usually favorable and imply that future borrowings are possible. A low value would dictate examination of the ratio on liquidity. If liquid ratios are low because of heavy indebtedness, refinancing is in order.

	Our Hospital	HCA
This year	.52	.43
Last year	.48	.42
2 years ago	.45	.38
3 years ago	.44	.25
4 years ago	.38	.29
5 years ago	.35	.36
6 years ago	.31	.28
7 years ago	.28	.31

"Fortunately our ratio is improving. More than half of our current assets are financed through operations. Our goal should be to improve this ratio, suggesting that we develop a leverage capability when it is needed in the future.

Fixed Asset Financing Ratio (Low Is Good)

"This ratio (long-term debt divided by net fixed assets) usually fluctuates in the reverse of the equity financing ratio. It measures the encumbrance on fixed assets. A low value usually means that no payment problems exist on current indebtedness and that leverage is available on existing value.

	Our Hospital	HCA
This year	.50	.75
Last year	.54	.74
2 years ago	.60	.73
3 years ago	.62	.72
4 years ago	.68	.62
5 years ago	.74	.52
6 years ago	.74	.61
7 years ago	.73	.63

"Our hospital values rest in a strong position. The debt service coverage ratio and the times interest ratio should be examined as further valuation of this measure.

Current Asset Ratio (High Could Be Good)

"This ratio (current assets divided by current liabilities) should determine whether current debt service is burdensome. If current values are high, it is likely that debt restructuring is not necessary.

"However, it should be pointed out that a heavily skewed liquid position could indicate that investments are in place, but not productive. Since our hospital's values are fairly high, we are in danger of such an occurrence.

	Our Hospital	HCA
This year	2.9	1.2
Last year	2.3	1.3
2 years ago	2.5	1.3
3 years ago	2.7	1.1
4 years ago	2.7	1.0
5 years ago	2.6	1.2
6 years ago	3.0	1.3
7 years ago	3.2	1.3

"To further evaluate, we need to look at the average payment period.

Average Payment Period Ratio (Medium Is Good)

"This ratio (current liabilities multiplied by 365 divided by total operating expenses minus depreciation) measures the lapsed time before current liabilities are paid.

"It is ideal to register a high current asset ratio along with a medium ratio value for paying bills. But such a combination will not really assist in improving your return on equity.

	Our Hospital	HCA
This year	60 days	74 days
Last year	62	73
2 years ago	57	71
3 years ago	53	70
4 years ago	56	77
5 years ago	63	71
6 years ago	47	68
7 years ago	43	67

"Current asset values must be lowered by putting liquid assets to work, but only to the point that leverage payment ratios are not forced upward.

Debt Service Coverage Ratio (High Is Good)

"This ratio is calculated as follows: net income plus depreciation plus interest expense divided by debt principal plus interest. It measures our ability to pay long-term debts.

	Our Hospital	HCA
This year	2.9	1.0
Last year	2.8	.9
2 years ago	3.0	.8
3 years ago	2.9	.7
4 years ago	2.8	1.5
5 years ago	2.5	1.0
6 years ago	2.8	1.7
7 years ago	3.5	2.3

"We are a little below the industry median (2.8–2.9), but well ahead of HCA.

Times Interest Earned Ratio (Up Is Good)

"This measure evaluates the income available to pay the interest on debt. It is calculated as follows: excess of revenues over expenses plus interest expense divided by interest expense.

	Our Hospital	HCA
This year	3.8 times	2.1 times
Last year	3.1	2.0
2 years ago	3.0	1.8
3 years ago	3.0	1.6

	Our Hospital	HCA
4 years ago	2.8	2.2
5 years ago	2.1	2.1
6 years ago	1.4	2.1
7 years ago	1.8	2.2

"Our hospital demonstrates a capability to pay interest. The ratios also suggest that added leverage would drop this value to unacceptable levels since the industry median is 3.0.

Long-Term Debt to Equity (Low Is Good)

"This ratio (long-term debt divided by fund balance) measures the relative importance of long-term debts in the hospital's permanent capital structure. High values indicate that hospitals have used debt financing to acquire their assets, and such high values are described as leveraged assets. High values carry the risk of having the financial reports viewed unfavorably. However, it should likewise be said that low values do not guarantee a favorable review, especially if low values are accompanied by low debt coverage ratios.

	Our Hospital	HCA
This year	.7	1.1
Last year	.9	1.1
2 years ago	1.0	1.3
3 years ago	1.1	2.0
4 years ago	1.3	1.5
5 years ago	1.8	1.0
6 years ago	2.0	1.5
7 years ago	2.2	1.5

"In our hospital's case, a favorable trend is down, associated with favorable debt service coverage and favorable times interest earned ratios. This situation indicates improved capability to leverage assets, should the need arise. However, care should be taken to continue to use operating funds to finance asset purchases.

Cash Flow to Total Debt (High Is Good)

"This ratio (cash flow divided by total debt) is the last measure concerning leverage. It is an important indicator of financial solvency. Cash flow is used (1) to increase working capital to meet bills and payroll, (2) to replace and augment equipment, and (3) to retire debt. These activities cannot be put off. Therefore, the hospital must demonstrate its capability to cover its total debt.

	Our Hospital	HCA
This year	.28	.12
Last year	.24	.10
2 years ago	.22	.09
3 years ago	.20	.08
4 years ago	.18	.10
5 years ago	.13	.14
6 years ago	.10	.14
7 years ago	.05	.13

"By looking at the figures, it is easy to see why Peat, Marwick was so concerned seven years ago. At that time, our hospital could not have remained solvent. However, there is no doubt that the problem has been dealt with.

Leverage Summary

"Basically, our hospital is showing average coverage ratios and improving equity financing ratios. These factors are extremely important if borrowing is contemplated.

"It should be understood that demonstrated ability to control debt rests with history rather than with promises. That history is being developed right now, so our hospital should continue to strive to show a favorable trend in this area because lending agencies rely heavily upon this record.

Conclusion

"We have measured four influences on our hospital's return on equity. We have found that

1. The operating margin is excellent, and
2. The assets are not overly encumbered and leveraged.

"These two factors indicate that credit may be available if leverage is needed. However, we also found that

3. The non-operating revenues are stagnant, and
4. We use out assets very poorly.

"It would seem, therefore, that if our organization is to be balanced and viable, we must concentrate on the deficiencies. Otherwise, the pressure for continued reliance on mark-up ratio performance will force the gap between prices and costs to continue to widen — a concept the hospital's publics will not support.

"Specifically, we should search for a way to place excess working capital to work, earning revenues and forming operating (or equity) capital. Allowing it to sit around drawing cobwebs does not fulfill our missional objective. We must continue to reduce our inventories. No matter what the situation may be, some items can be stricken from the shelves. Perhaps we should seriously study whether a 95 percent fill rate is too high — perhaps some requisitions need not be answered in the immediate time frame. We should search for new revenue products within our walls as well as without. Simply expanding an already existing service will not serve to use our assets more efficiently. Doing these things will improve our asset efficiency ratios and, if we accomplish this, will improve our return on equity.

"Specifically, we must improve our non-operating income through controlled outside business functions including a foundation. Non-operating and/or non-reported income will become increasingly important in the coming months and years.

"Let us not forget what all this is for. It is to form capital or, in other words, to maintain a return on equity commensurate with the desired rate of growth. If our desired growth rate is not matched by equity, leveraged assets will result, and the advantages we enjoy will not be available in future years."

SUMMARY

There has to be reciprocity between the long-term creditors and donors and the NPO if favorable financial relations are to exist. Since there are no owners, long-term creditors are a major source of capital, and their relationships with the NPO should be cultivated.

Short-term cash flows are crucial to an NPO, as are long-term cash flows. Various tactics and strategies must be used to obtain such cash flows.

Many NPOs have to raise funds by having donors make contributions, and the steps suggested here for fund raising should prove useful.

Further, various financial ratios can be used to measure the financial health of a NPO. These ratios, discussed in detail using as an example the ratios in a hospital, may be adapted by other NPOs.

Evaluation of Financial Strategies

I. Describe the short-term and long-term cash flow tactics and strategies used by the NPO.
   A. Use the guidelines suggested.
   B. Evaluate and prescribe, if appropriate.
II. If the NPO has to raise funds, describe how it does so.
   A. Use the guidelines suggested.
   B. Evaluate and prescribe, if appropriate.

III. Make a financial ratio analysis of the NPO.
    A. Use appropriate ratios, adapted to the NPO.
        1. Compare over time.
        2. Compare with those of other NPOs.
    B. Evaluate and prescribe, if appropriate.

21

Accounting

Generally accepted accounting principles (GAAPs) for profit organizations have been formulated by the accounting profession. However, the formulation of GAAP for non-profit organizations has progressed much more slowly than it has for profit organizations. Some progress has been made with the recent *Statement of Financial Accounting Concepts No. 4* dealing with "Objectives of Financial Reporting by Nonbusiness Organizations," dated December 1980. To quote from the highlights:

• This Statement focuses on organizations that have predominantly nonbusiness characteristics that heavily influence the operations of the organization.

—— The major distinguishing characteristics of nonbusiness organizations include: a) receipts of significant amounts of resources from resource providers who do not expect to receive either repayment or economic benefits proportionate to resources provided, b) operating purposes that are primarily other than to provide goods or services at a profit or profit equivalent, and c) absence of defined ownership interests that can be sold, transferred, or redeemed, or that convey entitlement to a share of a residual distribution of resources in the event of liquidation of the organization.

—— These characteristics result in certain types of transactions that are infrequent in business enterprises, such as contributions and grants, and in the absence of transactions with owners.

—— The line between nonbusiness organizations and business enterprises is not always sharp since the incidence and relative importance of those characteristics in any organization are different. This suggests that, for purposes of developing financial reporting objectives, a spectrum of organizations exists ranging from those with clearly dominant nonbusiness characteristics to those with wholly business characteristics.

. . . .

—— Examples of organizations that clearly fall within the focus of this Statement include most human service organizations, churches, foundations, and some other organizations, such as those private nonprofit hospitals and nonprofit schools that receive a significant portion of their financial resources from sources other than the sale of goods and services.

—— Borderline cases may exist where organizations possess some of the distinguishing characteristics but not others. Examples are those private non-profit hospitals and nonprofit schools that may receive relatively small amounts of contributions and grants but finance their capital needs largely from the proceeds of debt issues and their operating needs largely from service charges.

• The objectives in this Statement stem from the common interests of those who provide resources to nonbusiness organizations in the services those organizations provide and their continuing ability to provide services.

• Nonbusiness organizations generally have no single indicator of performance comparable to a business enterprise's profit. Thus, other indicators of performance usually are needed.

• The performance of nonbusiness organizations generally is not subject to the test of direct competition in markets to the extent that business enterprises are.

—— Other kinds of controls introduced to compensate for the lesser influence of markets are a major characteristic of their operations and affect the objectives of their financial reporting. Controls, such as formal budgets and donor restrictions on the use of resources, give managers a special responsibility to endure compliance. Information about departures from those mandates is important in assessing how well managers have discharged their stewardship responsibilities.

• The objectives in this Statement apply to general purpose external financial reporting by nonbusiness organizations.

—— The objectives stem primarily from the needs of external users who generally cannot prescribe the information they want from an organization.

—— In addition to information provided by general purpose external financial reporting, managers and, to some extent, governing bodies need a great deal of internal accounting information to carry out their responsibilities in planning and controlling activities. That information and information directed at meeting the specialized needs of users having the power to obtain the information they need are beyond the scope of this Statement.

• The objectives of financial reporting are affected by the economic, legal, political and social environment in which financial reporting takes place.

—— The operating environments of nonbusiness organizations and business enterprises are similar in many ways. Both nonbusiness organizations and business enterprises produce and distribute goods and services and use scarce resources in doing so.

—— Differences between nonbusiness organizations and business enterprises arise in the ways they obtain resources. Noneconomic reasons are commonly factors in decisions to provide resources to particular nonbusiness organizations.

• The objectives also are affected by the characteristics and limitations of the kind of information that financial reporting can provide.

—— The information provided by financial reporting is primarily financial in nature: It is generally quantified and expressed in units of money. However, quantified information expressed in terms other than units of money and nonquantified information may be needed to understand the significance of information expressed in units of money or to help in assessing the performance of a nonbusiness organization.

—— The information provided by financial reporting pertains to individual reporting entities, often results from approximate rather than exact measures, largely reflects the effects of transactions and events that have already happened, is but one source of information needed by those who make decisions about nonbusiness organizations, and is provided and used at a cost.
- The objectives state that:
  —— Financial reporting by nonbusiness organizations should provide information that is useful to present and potential resource providers and other users in making rational decisions about the allocation of resources to those organizations.
  —— Financial reporting should provide information to help present and potential resource providers and other users in assessing the services that a nonbusiness organization provides and its ability to continue to provide those services.
  —— Financial reporting should provide information that is useful to present and potential resource providers and other users in assessing how managers of a nonbusiness organization have discharged their stewardship responsibilities and about other aspects of their performance.
  —— Financial reporting should provide information about the economic resources, obligations, and net resources of an organization, and the effects of transactions, events, and circumstances that change resources and interests in those resources.
  —— Financial reporting should provide information about the performance of an organization during a period. Periodic measurement of the changes in the amount and nature of the net resources of a nonbusiness organization and information about the service efforts and accomplishments of an organization together represent the information most useful in assessing its performance.
  —— Financial reporting should provide information about how an organization obtains and spends cash or other liquid resources, about its borrowing and repayment of borrowing, and about other factors that may affect an organization's liquidity.
  —— Financial reporting should include explanations and interpretations to help users understand financial information provided.[1]

ACCOUNTING PRINCIPLES AND REPORTING PRACTICES FOR CERTAIN NPOS

To implement the objectives of financial reporting for NPOs, the American Institute of Certified Public Accountants (AICPA) has issued a *Statement of Position 78-10, Accounting Principles and Reporting Practices for Certain Nonprofit Organizations.* In this statement, the AICPA proposes certain standards for an NPO to follow if it wishes to abide by generally accepted accounting principles. Certain standards have been issued for hospitals (1972), colleges and universities (1973), voluntary health and welfare organizations (1974), and state and local governments (1974). However, many other types of NPOs are not covered by these standards. The *Statement 78-10* proposes the following:[2]

.002 This statement of position is issued to recommend financial accounting principles and reporting practices for nonprofit organizations not covered by existing guides that prepare financial statements in conformity with generally accepted accounting principles. This statement is not intended to supersede or amend any of the listed guides. For numerous nonprofit organizations, complex accounting may be neither practical nor economical, and reporting based on cash receipts and disbursements or some other basis may be adequately informative. Under those circumstances, special-purpose financial reports should be prepared.

. . . .

.005 This statement of position applies to all nonprofit organizations not covered by the AICPA industry audit guides listed in paragraph .001, other than those types of entities that operate essentially as commercial businesses for the direct economic benefit of members or stockholders. Examples of the latter category are employee benefit and pension plans, mutual insurance companies, mutual banks, trusts, and farm cooperatives. Although this list is not all-inclusive, the following organizations are among those covered by this statement:

Cemetery organizations
Civic organizations
Fraternal organizations
Labor unions
Libraries
Museums
Other cultural institutions
Performing arts organizations
Political parties
Private and community foundations
Private elementary and secondary schools
Professional associations
Public broadcasting stations
Religious organizations
Research and scientific organizations
Social and country clubs
Trade associations
Zoological and botanical societies

. . . .

.007 Some have contended that the division has not sufficiently considered the costs and efforts involved in implementing its recommendations – especially for smaller organizations. Some organizations may believe that special-purpose reports prepared on a basis other than generally accepted accounting principles better serve their needs – especially in light of the relationship between costs and benefits; these recommendations do not preclude such organizations from continuing to use appropriate special-purpose reports.

USERS OF FINANCIAL STATEMENTS

.008 A wide variety of persons and groups are interested in the financial statements of nonprofit organizations. Among the principal groups are a) contributors to the organization, b) beneficiaries of the organization, c) the organization's trustees or directors, d) employees of the organization, e) governmental units, f) the organization's creditors and potential creditors, and g) constituent organizations.

.009 A principal purpose of a nonprofit organization's financial statements is to communicate the ways resources have been used to carry out the organization's objectives. It requires reporting the nature and amount of available resources, the uses made of the resources, and the net change in fund balances during the period. In addition while adequate measures of program accomplishment generally are not available in the context of present financial statements, the financial statements should identify the organization's principal programs and their costs. A third aspect of financial reporting for nonprofit organizations is disclosure of the degree of control exercised by donors over use of resources. A fourth aspect is that the financial statements of a nonprofit organization should help the reader evaluate the organization's ability to carry out its fiscal objectives.

.010 The division has prepared this statement of the position based on the foregoing concepts as a guide to preparing financial statements to be used primarily by persons outside the management of the organization. It recognizes that financial statements prepared for use by management or members of the governing board often require more detail than is prescribed in this statement.

THE ACCRUAL BASIS OF ACCOUNTING

In accounting, revenue is recognized when it is earned, rather than when the cash is collected. Likewise, expenses may be incurred when the funds are committed, rather than when the required cash is paid. These definitions reflect the accrual basis of accounting, as contrasted with the cash basis. *Statement 78-10* amplifies on the accrual concept as follows:

.011 The accrual basis of accounting is widely accepted as providing a more appropriate record of all an entity's transactions over a given period of time than the cash basis of accounting. The cash basis or any basis of accounting other than the accrual basis does not result in a presentation of financial information in conformity with generally accepted accounting principles. Accordingly, financial statements of nonprofit organizations represented as being in conformity with generally accepted accounting principles should be prepared using the accrual basis of accounting.[3]

.012 For example, under accrual basis accounting, goods and services purchased should be recorded as assets or expenses at the time the liabilities arise, which is normally when title to the goods passes or when the services are received. Encumbrances representing outstanding purchase orders and other commitments for materials or services not yet received are not liabilities as of the reporting date and should not be reported as expenses nor included in liabilities on the balance sheet. However, significant commitments should be disclosed in the notes to the financial statements, and an organization may designate in its balance sheet the portion of the fund balance so committed.

.013 For numerous nonprofit organizations, complex accounting procedures may be neither practical nor economical, and reporting based essentially on cash receipts and disbursements may be adequately informative. If financial statements prepared on the cash basis are not materially different from those prepared on the accrual basis, the independent auditor may still be able to conclude that the statements are presented in conformity with generally accepted accounting principles. Otherwise, cash basis financial statements should be considered to be special purpose financial statements and should be reported on accordingly.

FUND ACCOUNTING FOR NPOS

Since NPOs have no owners per se, the concept of fund balance must be substituted for owners' equity. Fund accounting is another GAAP that is practiced by NPOs. *Statement 78-10* says:

.014 Many nonprofit organizations receive resources restricted for particular purposes. To facilitate observance of limitations, the accounts are often maintained using fund accounting, by which resources are classified for accounting and reporting purposes into funds associated with specified activities or objectives. Each fund is a separate accounting entity with a self-balancing set of accounts for recording assets, liabilities, fund balance, and changes in the fund balance. Although separate accounts are maintained for each fund, the usual practice in preparing financial statements is to group funds that have similar characteristics.

.015 The division believes that reporting on a fund accounting basis may be helpful where needed to segregate unrestricted from restricted resources. If an organization has restricted resources and elects not to report on a fund accounting basis, the financial statements should disclose all material restrictions and observe the specific requirements indicated in paragraphs .016 through .041, "Basic Financial Statements."

BASIC FINANCIAL STATEMENTS

.016 The basic financial statements, including related notes, of nonprofit organizations covered by this statement are —

Balance sheet

Statement of activity

Statement of changes in financial position

.017 The balance sheet is intended to present financial position. The statement of activity, including changes in fund balances, is intended to present results of operations. However, when it is intended that the financial statements present both financial position and results of operations, all three statements listed in paragraph .016 should be presented.

.018 Although the division has identified the basic financial statements to be prepared, for the most part, it does not prescribe specific titles or formats. Each organization should develop the statement formats most appropriate to its needs in conformity with the principles discussed in this statement. . . .

Balance Sheet

.019 The balance sheet should summarize the assets, liabilities, and fund balances of the organization.

.020 An organization's unrestricted fund balance represents the net amount of resources available without restriction for carrying out the organization's objectives. Those resources include amounts designated by the board for specific purposes, undesignated amounts, and, frequently, amounts invested in operating plant. While the balance sheet may set forth amounts designated for a program or other purposes, the total of all unrestricted fund balances, other than amounts shown in a plant fund, as discussed in paragraph .022, should be shown and labeled on the balance sheet.

.021 Current restricted resources and resources restricted for future acquisition of fixed assets should be reported in the balance sheet as deferred revenue until the restrictions are met. Other restricted resources such as endowment funds should be reflected separately in the fund balance section of the balance sheet. If significant, the nature of the restrictions on fund balances and deferred revenues should be described in the notes to the financial statements.

.022 Many organizations use a separate fund to account for the investments in operating plant, art collections, rare books and manuscripts, and similar items. The sources of the funds used to acquire those assets often are a combination of unrestricted and restricted funds. It may not be clear whether assets purchased with restricted funds continue to bear the original donor restrictions. While the division believes an organization should indicate whether the fund balances are restricted or unrestricted, that may not be possible for the plant fund. Thus, the plant fund may be reported separately or combined with either the unrestricted or restricted funds, as appropriate.

.023 Many organizations covered by this statement have only unrestricted funds. Those organizations should classify their assets as current, fixed, and other long-term assets and should classify their liabilities as current and long-term. To be classified as "current," the assets generally should be realizable and the liabilities payable within a normal operating cycle; however, if there is no normal operating cycle or the operating cycle is less than one year, all assets expected to be converted to cash or other liquid resources within one year and all liabilities to be liquidated within one year should be classified as current.

.024 Other organizations have both unrestricted and restricted funds. Frequently, the fund classifications themselves adequately disclose the current and long-term nature of the assets and liabilities. If not, a classified balance sheet should be presented.

Statement of Activity

.025 Throughout this statement of position the term *statement of activity* identifies the financial statement that reports the support, revenue, capital or nonexpendable additions, and functional expense categories. The statement might carry a different title, such as *statement of support, revenue, expense, capital additions, and changes in fund balances,* or simply *statement of changes in fund balances.* The statement of activity should include the activity for the period and a reconciliation between the beginning and ending fund balances. However, an organization may prepare two separate statements: a statement of activity and a statement of changes in fund balances. Changes in fund balances should include the excess or deficiency of revenue and support over expenses after capital additions for the period, adjustments to reflect changes in the carrying amount of certain marketable securities and other investments, as discussed in paragraph .080, and the additions and deductions of interfund transfers.

.026 The division has considered the diverse practices used to report details of financial activity. It has concluded that variations in format and presentation are appropriate, provided that the statement of activity shows the major sources and amounts of revenue and support, as well as the principal sources and amounts of additions to plant, endowment, and other capital funds. This does not prohibit an organization from reporting revenue and expenses separately from sources of support in its financial statements.

.027 Nonprofit organizations derive revenue from a variety of sources – dues, sale of services, ticket sales, investment income, and so forth – but they are often not sufficient to cover the cost of providing services. Many organizations, therefore, solicit support to enable them to fulfill their program objectives. Such support may be obtained from individuals, and other entities.

.028 Certain contributions cannot be spent currently for program or supporting services because of donor or legal restrictions and have many of the characteristics of "capital." Such items include gifts, grants, and bequests to endowment, plant, and loan funds restricted either permanently or for a period of time by parties outside the organization. Those items also include investment income that has been restricted by donors and gains or losses on investments held in such funds that must be added to the principal.[4] The accounting standards division has concluded that disclosure of those items would be useful, and they should be differentiated from items that are available for current operations. Captions such as "capital additions," or "nonexpendable additions," should be used.

.029 Capital additions do not include restricted gifts, grants, bequests, or gains on the sale of assets that can be used for current activities even though the contributions have been deferred until the organization incurs an expense that satisfies the terms of the restriction, nor do they include unrestricted amounts that the board designates as nonexpendable. See paragraphs .054 through .062 for a further discussion on current restricted gifts, grants, bequests, and other income.

.030 While there is wide diversity of practice, the division concluded that an "excess" line-item caption in the statement of activity is useful. Although the purpose of the organizations covered by this statement is not to make "profits" as this term is generally used, nonprofit entities can survive only if they have support, revenue, and other additions equal to or in excess of expenses. This measure is an important indicator of financial health and is therefore of interest to management, members of the governing board, donors, beneficiaries, and other users of the financial statements. Accordingly the statement of activity should report the excess (deficiency) of revenues and support over expenses for the period.

.031 If financial activities include capital additions, there should be *two* clearly labeled "excess" line-item captions, such as "excess (deficiency) of revenue and support over expenses before capital additions" and "excess (deficiency) of revenue and support over expenses after capital additions" (alternative wording may be used).

Statement of Changes in Financial Position

.032 The statement of changes in financial position provides a summary of available resources and their use during the period.

.033 Many nonprofit organizations obtain their resources from contributions, borrowed money, investment income, and so forth. The statement of changes in financial position provides the user with information about both the methods of financing programs and activities and the use and investment of resources during the period.

.034 The statement of changes in financial position should summarize all changes in financial position, including capital additions, changes in deferred support and revenue, and financing and investing activities.

Other Types of Fund Classifications

.035 Rather than using the traditional fund accounting classifications, some organizations prefer using classifications such as expendable and nonexpendable or unrestricted and restricted in their financial statements. Such classifications are appropriate provided that all the required disclosures indicated in paragraphs .016 and .041 are met.

Columnar v. Layered Presentation

.036 The practice of presenting data by major fund groups has evolved to emphasize meaningful distinctions between the types of unrestricted and restricted resources for which an organization is accountable. Many organizations report financial position and results of activities in a multicolumn format. Others report their financial statements in a layered or "pancake" format, and still others report certain data in a columnar format and other data in a layered format. Each organization should develop the statement format most appropriate to its needs to conform with the principles discussed in this statement of position.

Totals of All Funds

.037 Some organizations present their financial statements (either in columnar or layered format) only by major fund groups without showing totals of all funds. They do not consider totals of all funds to be meaningful and sometimes consider such totals to be misleading because of restrictions on the use of certain resources; however, other organizations, believing that totals are meaningful, present details by major fund groups and totals of all funds in one or more of their statements.

.038 Certain organizations present financial statements showing only the totals of all funds and do not show the major fund groups. Organizations do that if they do not establish separate funds for reporting purposes, if the financial information concerning particular funds is not significant, or if such information can be adequately set forth in other ways in the statements or the notes.

.039 Financial statements in columnar format lend themselves to presenting totals of all funds. Financial statements presented in layered format lend themselves to fund group presentations with comparative data for the preceding period.

.040 The presentation of totals of all fund groups in all financial statements is preferable, although not required. In presenting such totals, the specifics of the major fund groups should also be provided, and care should be taken to assure that the captions are not misleading and that adequate information is provided concerning interfund borrowings and important restrictions on the uses of resources.

Comparative Financial Statements

.041 Although it is not required, financial statements of the current period should be presented on a comparative basis with financial statements for one or more prior reporting periods. If multicolumn financial statements are presented for the current period, some organizations prefer to present only summarized, total-all-funds information (in a single column) for each of the prior periods because of space limitations and to avoid the confusion that a second set of multicolumn statements might cause. However, where it is intended to present financial statements of the prior periods as well as the current period in accordance with generally accepted accounting principles, care must be taken that there is sufficient disclosure in the summarized data and in the supporting notes.

SOURCES OF REVENUES FOR THE NPO

Since NPOs rely heavily on gifts, grants, donations, and other non-traditional sources of revenue, as compared to profit organizations, *Statement 78-10* addresses at length the sources of revenues for an NPO.

REVENUE, SUPPORT, AND CAPITAL ADDITIONS

.050 The statement of activity should report revenue, support, and capital additions. Revenue and support are discussed under "Statement of Activity," paragraphs .025 through .031.

Capital Additions

.051 Capital additions include nonexpendable gifts, grants, and bequests restricted by donors to endowment, plant, or loan funds either permanently or for extended periods of time. Capital additions also include legally restricted investment income and gains or losses on investments held in such funds that must be added to the principal. Capital additions do not include donor-restricted gifts for program or supporting services.

.052 Capital additions that are restricted for acquisition of plant assets should be treated as deferred capital support in the balance sheet until they are used for the indicated purpose. Once used, these amounts should be reported as capital additions in the statement of activity.

.053 Some organizations may prefer to use the caption "nonexpendable additions" instead of "capital additions." As previously noted, that or other wording is acceptable.

Current Restricted Gifts, Grants, Bequests, and Other Income

.054 Current restricted gifts, grants, bequests, and other income provide expendable resources that have been restricted by donors, grantors, or other outside parties to the purposes for which they may be used. Such restrictions usually involve written assertions expressed in restrictive language by one party to the other. Amounts received from appeals for restricted funds by solicitation letter, radio, television, newspaper, and so forth are generally deemed to be restricted according to the nature of the appeal.

. . . .

.062 . . . current restricted gifts, grants, bequests, and other income should be accounted for as revenue and support in the statement of activity to the extent that expenses have been incurred for the purpose specified by the donor or grantor during the period. The balances should be accounted for as deferred revenue or support in the balance sheet outside the fund balance section until the restrictions are met. The specific language in the donative instrument or grant award should govern whether restrictions have been met. Recognition of expenses that satisfy donor restrictions results in recognition of equivalent amounts of revenue or support in that period.

Unrestricted Gifts, Grants, and Bequests

.063 Unrestricted gifts, grants, and bequests should be reported in the unrestricted fund in the statement of activity above the caption "excess (deficiency) of revenue and support over expenses before capital additions."

Pledges

.064 Pledges an organization can legally enforce should be recorded as assets and reported at their estimated realizable values. In determining these values, such matters as the donee organization's past collection experience, the credit standing of the donor and other matters affecting the collectibility of the pledges should be considered.

.065 The estimated realizable amount of pledges should be recognized as support in the period designated by the donor. If the period designated by the donor extends beyond the balance sheet date, the pledge should be accounted for as deferred support in the balance sheet. In the absence of a specified support period, the net estimated realizable amount of pledges scheduled to be received over a future period should be assumed to be support for that period and should be accounted for as deferred support in the balance sheet.

.066 Pledges for fixed assets should also be recorded in the balance sheet at their estimated realizable values and reported in the statement of activity as provided in paragraph .052.

Donated and Contributed Services

.067 The nature and extent of donated or contributed services received by organizations vary and range from the limited participation of many individuals in fund-raising activities to active participation in the organization's service program. Because it is difficult to place a monetary value on such services, their values are usually not recorded. The accounting standards division believes that those services should not be recorded as an expense.

. . . .

.070 Notes to the financial statements should disclose the methods used by the organization in valuing, recording, and reporting donated or contributed services and should distinguish between donated or contributed services for which values have and have not been recorded.

Donated Materials and Facilities

.071 Donated materials and facilities, if significant in amount, should be recorded at their fair value, provided the organization has a clearly measurable and objective basis for determining the value. If the materials are such that values cannot reasonably be determined, such as clothing, furniture, and so forth, which vary greatly in value depending on condition and style, they should not be recorded as contributions. If donated materials pass through the organization to its charitable beneficiaries, and the organization serves only as an agent for the donors, the donation should not be recorded as a contribution. The recorded value of the use of contributed facilities should be included as revenue and expense during the period of use.

Investment Income and Gains and Losses

.072 Unrestricted investment income (interest and dividends) from all funds should be reported as revenue in the statement of activity when it is earned. All unrestricted gains and losses on investments of unrestricted and current restricted funds should also be reported in the statement of activity before the excess (deficiency) of revenue and support over expenses before capital additions. See paragraphs .077 through .082 for a discussion of the carrying amount of investments and the bases of reporting gains and losses.

. . . .

.074 Traditionally, nonprofit organizations have accounted for income yield (dividends, interest, rents, royalties, and so forth) as revenues available for current purposes and have excluded from that category capital gains on investment transactions of the endowment fund.

. . . .

Subscription and Membership Income

.084 Subscriptions and revenues derived from the performance of services or the sale of goods should be recognized as revenue in the periods in which they are provided. Revenue derived from membership dues should be recognized by the organization over the period to which the dues relate. Nonrefundable initiation and life membership fees should be recognized as revenue in the period the fees are receivable, if future dues or fees can reasonably be expected to cover the cost of the future services; otherwise, the fees should be amortized to future periods based on average membership duration, life expectancy, or other appropriate methods. However, if items such as dues, assessments, and nonrefundable initiation fees are in substance contributions and services are not to be provided to the member, they should be recognized as revenue and support in the periods in which the organization is entitled to them.

EXPENSE ACCOUNTING FOR NPOS

Since many NPOs have expenses greater than revenues, resource providers keep a wary eye on expenses in order to ask questions about the cost of doing business. Consequently, *Statement 78-10* addresses some concepts regarding expenses.

Functional Classification of Expenses

.085 Organizations that receive significant support in the form of contributions from the general public should summarize the cost of providing various services or other activities on a functional basis in the statement of activity. (For purposes of this paragraph, the accounting standards division believes that organizations receiving support from federated fund-raising or similar organizations are deemed to have received support from the general public.) Organizations receiving no significant support from such contributors are encouraged to report on a functional basis but may choose to summarize expenses on another basis (such as natural classifications) that would be considered useful to readers of the statement of activity. If expenses are not reported on a functional basis, the notes should contain a description of the basic programs of the organization. The remainder of this section is for those organizations that report expenses on a functional basis.

.086 The functional classifications should include specific program services that describe the organization's service activities and supporting services, such as management and general and fund-raising.

.087 The statement of activity should present costs separately for each significant program and supporting activity. Program activities are those directly related to the purposes for which the organization exists. Supporting activities do not relate directly to the purposes for which the organization exists. Fund raising, membership development, and unallocated management and general expense are three examples of supporting activities that should be reported separately.

.088 An organization may also present as supplementary information a schedule of functional expenses by object classification, that is, classifying expenses by type rather than function, such as salaries, employee-benefit expenses, and purchased services.

Program Services

.089 Functional reporting classifications for program services vary according to the nature of the service rendered. For some organizations, a single functional reporting classification may be adequate to portray the program service provided. In most cases, however, several separate and identifiable services are provided, and in such cases, expenses for program services should be reported by the type of service function or group of functions. The purposes of the various functions should be clearly described, and each functional classification should include all of the applicable service costs.

.090 Some local organizations remit a portion of their receipts to an affiliated state or national organization. The amount to be paid to the affiliates should be reported as either an expense or a deduction from total support and revenue in the statement of activity. The appropriate treatment depends on the arrangements: A reporting organization that is, in effect, a collecting agent for the state or national organization, such as local organizations that are required to remit a fixed percentage of all contributions, should report the remittance as a deduction from total support and revenue; other organizations should report the remittance as a program expense.

Management and General Costs

.091 Management and general costs are those not identifiable with a single program or fund-raising activity but are indispensable to the conduct of those activities and to an organization's existence, including expenses for the overall direction of the organization's general board activities, business management, general recordkeeping, budgeting, and related purposes. Costs of overall direction usually include the salary and expenses of the chief officer of the organization and his staff. However, if such staff spend a portion of their time directly supervising program services or categories of supporting services, their salaries and expenses should be prorated among those functions. The costs of disseminating information to inform the public of the organization's "stewardship" of contributed funds, announcements concerning appointments, the annual report, and so forth, should likewise be classified as management and general expenses.

Fund-Raising and Other Supporting Services

.092 Fund-raising costs are incurred in inducing others to contribute money, se-curities, time, materials, or facilities for which the contributor will receive no direct economic benefit. They normally include the costs of personnel, occupancy, main-taining mailing lists, printing, mailing, and all direct and indirect costs of soliciting, as well as the cost of unsolicited merchandise sent to encourage contributions. The cost of such merchandise should be disclosed. Fund-raising costs paid directly by a con-tributor should be reported as support and as fund-raising expenses.

.093 Some organizations hold special fund-raising events, such as banquets, din-ners, theater parties, and so forth, in which the donor receives a direct benefit (for example, a meal or theater ticket). Some organizations sell merchandise as a fund-raising technique. The costs of such merchandise or direct benefits are not considered fund-raising costs and should be applied against gross proceeds received from the person receiving such direct benefit. The costs of such merchandise or direct benefit costs should be disclosed.

.094 A growing number of users of financial statements are seeking financial infor-mation that will enable them to evaluate fund-raising costs. A single functional report-ing classification ordinarily is adequate to portray the fund-raising activity; however, other organizations may believe that reporting total public support and total fund-raising expense does not provide adequate information for a useful evaluation because the organizations conduct a number of fund-raising activities with widely varying relationships. For those organizations, it may be appropriate to report fund-rais-ing costs and the corresponding support obtained separately for each type of fund-raising function, either in the statement of activity or in the notes. The various fund-raising functions should be adequately described and should include all of the applicable costs. The total of all fund-raising activities should be disclosed whether the entity reports expenses on a functional or some other basis.

.095 Fund-raising efforts made in one year, such as those made to obtain bequests or to compile a mailing list of prospective contributors, often result in contributions that will be received in future years. Some have advocated deferring the costs of such fund-raising efforts until the period in which the contributions are expected to be received. Although there may be valid reasons to consider deferring those costs, the accounting standards division is concerned with the difficulty of assessing their ulti-mate recovery and the possibility of misstating the fund-raising cost relationships. Accordingly, fund-raising costs should be expensed when incurred. However, if pledges or restricted contributions that have already been received are recorded as deferred revenue and support, related fund-raising costs, if specifically identifiable with the contributions, may also be deferred if it is clear that the contributor intended that the contribution could be used to cover such costs. Similarly, costs incurred in the acquisition of literature, materials, and so forth, that will be used in connection with a fund-raising drive to be conducted in a succeeding period should be deferred to that period.

.096 Costs incurred in the solicitation of grants from foundations or governments and cost of membership development in bona fide membership organizations should be shown as separate categories of supporting expenses. If the membership fee in-cludes an element of contribution, the costs of membership development should be allocated between development and fund raising.

.097 If an organization combines the fund-raising function with a program function (for example, a piece of educational literature with a request for funds), the costs should be allocated to the program and fund-raising categories on the basis of the use made of the literature, as determined from its content, the reasons for its distribution, and the audience to whom it is addressed.

Allocation of Costs That Pertain to Various Functions

.098 In some larger organizations, individual functions are performed by separate departments, with expenses classified by types within each department. Many other organizations incur items of cost that apply to more than one functional purpose. For those organizations, it may be necessary to allocate the cost among functions. Examples include salaries of persons who perform more than one type of service, rental of a building used for various program services, management and general expenses, and expenses of fund raising activities.

.099 The salaries of employees who perform duties relating to more than one function, as well as all other expenses pertaining to more than one function, should be allocated to the separate functional categories according to procedures that determine, as accurately as possible, the portion of the cost related to each function.

.100 A reasonable allocation of an organization's functional expenses may be made on a variety of bases, and costs that have been allocated to programs and supporting services should be disclosed in the notes to the financial statements. It is not the intention of this statement to require organizations to undertake extensive detailed analyses and computations aimed at making overly meticulous allocations. The division recognizes that meaningful financial statements can often be prepared using estimates and overall computations when appropriate. . . .

Grants

.101 Organizations that make grants to others should record grants as expenses and liabilities at the time recipients are entitled to them. That normally occurs when the board approves a specific grant or when the grantee is notified.

.102 Some grants stipulate that payments are to be made over a period of several years. Grants payable in future periods subject only to routine performance requirements by the grantee and not requiring subsequent review and approval for continuance of payment should be recorded as expenses and liabilities when the grants are first made. However, if the grant instrument specifically states that the grantor reserves the right to revoke the grant regardless of the performance of the grantee, unpaid grants should not be recorded. Grants subject to periodic renewal should be recorded as expenses and liabilities at renewal with a disclosure of the remaining commitment in the notes to the financial statements.

Tax Allocation

.103 Certain organizations are subject to a federal excise tax on investment income or to federal and state income taxes on certain unrelated business income. If timing differences exist between the income base for tax and financial reporting purposes, interperiod allocation of tax should be made.

Transfers

.104 Allocations of resources among fund groups are neither revenues nor expenses of the related funds and should be distinguished from support and revenues that increase the total resources available to fulfill the objectives of an organization. Therefore, interfund transfers, including board-designated transfers of gains under the total-return concept, should be reported as changes in fund balances under the caption "fund balance beginning of the period." Transfers required under contractual arrangements with third parties should be separately disclosed. Transfers required as a result of the expiration of a term endowment fund also should be separately disclosed.

VALUATION OF FIXED ASSETS AND DEPRECIATION

One topic of continuing controversy is whether NPOs should use depreciation accounting for long-term assets. It would seem plausible to record the depreciation expense for exhaustible assets inasmuch as the cost of wearing out or using up an asset is an actual expense. *Statement 78-10* addresses the issues of depreciation accounting as follows:

Fixed Assets

.105 Nonprofit organizations should capitalize purchased fixed assets at cost. Donated fixed assets should be recorded at their fair value at the date of the gift. Organizations that have not previously capitalized their fixed assets should do so retroactively. If historical costs are unavailable for assets already in service, another reasonable basis may be used to value the assets. Other bases might be cost-based appraisals, insurance appraisals, replacement costs, or property tax appraisals adjusted for market. However, an alternative basis should be used only if historical cost information is unavailable and only to establish a value at the date an organization adopts this statement of position. Subsequent additions should be recorded at cost, or fair value for donated assets. The basis of valuation and the amount of any assets pledged to secure outside borrowing should be disclosed in the financial statements.

Depreciation[5]

.106 In Accounting Terminology Bulletin No. 1, *Review and Resume*, the AICPA Committee on Terminology defined *depreciation accounting* as a means of allocating the cost or other carrying value of tangible capital assets to expense over their useful lives:

> *Depreciation accounting* is a system of accounting which aims to distribute the cost or other basic value of tangible capital assets, less salvage (if any), over the estimated useful life of the unit (which may be a group of assets) in a systematic and rational manner. It is a process of allocation, not valuation. *Depreciation for the year* is the portion of the total charge under such a system that is allocated to the year. Although the allocation may properly take into account occurrences during the year, it is not intended to be a measurement of the effect of all such occurrences.

.107 Exhaustible fixed assets should be depreciated over their estimated useful lives. The relative effort being expended by one organization compared with others and the allocation of the efforts to various programs of the organization are indicated, in part, by cost determinations. Depreciation of fixed assets used in providing such services is relevant as an element of that cost. Although depreciation can be distinguished from most other elements of cost in that it requires no current equivalent cash outlay, recognition of depreciation as a cost is not optional. Most assets used in providing services are both valuable and exhaustible. Thus, a cost is associated with the use of exhaustible assets whether they are owned or rented, acquired by gift or by purchase or used by a business or a nonprofit organization.

.108 Assets that are not exhaustible, such as landmarks, monuments, cathedrals, or historical treasures, need not be depreciated. Structures used primarily as houses of worship need not be depreciated.

.109 An organization may receive grants, allocations, or reimbursements from other organizations on the basis of the cost associated with its program and support-ing services. Recording depreciation as an element of cost does not indicate that it necessarily should be included in the base on which grants, allocations, or reimburse-ments will be determined: whether the base includes or excludes depreciation depends on the agreement or understanding reached between the two organizations.

.110 The amount of depreciation provided on assets carried at historical cost and the amount, if any, provided on assets carried on a basis other than historical cost should be disclosed.

.111 Depreciation accounting is sometimes confused with funding replacements. The means of replacing fixed assets and the degree to which replacements should be funded currently are financing decisions to be made by the governing board and do not directly affect the current costs of providing program or supporting services. Depreciation accounting is designed to determine and present those costs, not to provide replacement funds.

.112 Retroactive adjustments should be made to reflect accumulated depreciation as of the date an organization adopts this statement of position. For this purpose, the determination of asset lives should be based on a combination of the period from acquisition to the adoption date, plus estimated remaining life based on the current condition and planned use of the assets. When an organization records fixed assets using one of the "current value" methods referred to in paragraph .105, it is not necessary to disclose accumulated depreciation that would have been recorded had cost-based data been available.

ILLUSTRATIVE FINANCIAL STATEMENTS

Statement 78-10 has several examples of financial statements for such NPOs as (1) an independent school, (2) a cemetery organization, (3) a country club, (4) a library, (5) a museum, (6) a performing arts organization, (7) a private foundation, (8) a public broadcasting station, (9) a religious organization, (10) a research and scientific organization, (11) a trade association, (12) a union, and (13) a zoological and botanical society. The reader is urged to consult *Statement 78-10* for examples of financial statements, complete with foot-notes, for these types of NPOs.

NPOs are urged to develop formats that are appropriate for their particu-lar situations, but following the concepts suggested in this chapter. The GAAPs have been researched by the accounting profession and are suggested as standards for NPOs.

ANNUAL AUDIT

Each NPO should have an annual independent audit of its financial transactions. Such an audit adds a touch of credibility to the NPO which is vitally necessary to maintain an image. The audit may be used to answer the questions of the users of the financial statements — the managers, the employees, the board, the NPO's creditors and potential creditors, the major resource contributors, and others who may have an interest in the affairs of the NPO.

Further, the NPO may wish to issue an annual report to the public about the stewardship of the board and managers. Such a report also adds credibility to the NPO and helps to maintain a good image.

NPOs may even wish to have their own internal auditors to examine their financial affairs.

INTERNAL FINANCIAL REPORTS FOR MANAGERIAL PURPOSES

Although this chapter is primarily concerned with the GAAPs of external financial statements, most NPOs use internal financial reports for the managerial purposes of planning and control. For example, the board of directors may review monthly or quarterly cash position reports, showing cash received, cash spent, and cash balances. Another common report is the financial budget which comparing actual revenues and expenses with budget estimates. Special financial reports may also be prepared, and are usually found in the board minutes. These internal reports are very useful for managers who plan NPO financial affairs and evaluate past activities.

Accounting serves as a useful tool for NPO executives in administering the affairs of the organization.

Evaluation of Accounting Concepts in the NPO's Financial Statements

I. Get copies of the financial statements of the NPO you are evaluating.
   A. If the NPO is part of another NPO and uses a cash basis, special purpose financial reports should be used.
   B. If the NPO is an independent, self-supporting entity, then evaluate their financial statements according the GAAPs in the chapter, as presented in *Statement of Position 78-10, Accounting Principles and Reporting Practices for Certain Nonprofit Organizations*, December 31, 1978.
   C. Who are the users of financial statements?
   D. Accrual basis vs. cash basis vs. mixed?
   E. Fund accounting?
   F. Basic financial statements prepared?
      1. Balance sheet
      2. Statement of activity
      3. Statement of changes in financial position

    G. Annual audit by CPA?

    H. Fund classifications?

    I. Columnar vs. layered presentation?

    J. Comparative financial statements?

    K. Revenue, support, and capital additions?

    L. Functional classification of expenses?

    M. Management and general costs?

    N. Fund-raising expenses?

    O. Allocation of costs to functions?

    P. Allocation of resources from other funds?

    Q. Depreciation?

    R. Specialized GAAPs for an NPO?

    S. Annual report?

    T. Internal audit?

    U. Evaluate and prescribe, if appropriate.

II. If the NPO uses various financial statements for internal managerial purposes, obtain copies, if possible.

    A. Cash statements

    B. Budgets

    C. Special reports

    D. Evaluate their usefulness and prescribe, if appropriate.

Notes

1. For a complete discussion of FASB Concepts *Statement No. 4*, see the December 1980 document *Objectives of Financial Reporting by Nonbusiness Organizations*, copyright by the Financial Accounting Standards Board, 401 Merritt 7, Norwalk, Connecticut, 06856 USA (203-847-0700). Copies of the complete document are available from the FASB.

2. The numbered paragraphs quoted in this chapter were taken from *Statements of Position of the Accounting Standards Division*, particularly Section, 10, 250, *Statement of Position 78-10, Accounting Principles and Reporting Practices for Certain Non-Profit Organizations*. Copyright © 1978 by the American Institute of Certified Public Accountants, Inc. Reprinted with permission.

3. Some organizations keep their books on a cash basis throughout the period and, through adjustment at the end of the period, prepare statements on the accrual basis. The requirement is only that the financial statements be presented on the accrual basis and not that the books be kept on that basis throughout the period.

4. The division does not suggest that gains on the sales of restricted assets are legally restricted or that they cannot be used at the discretion of the organization. Those are legal questions that depend on applicable law, donor intent, or both.

5. The concepts of depreciation have been reinforced by FASB Statement No. 93 *Recognition of Depreciation by Not-for-Profit Organizations*, dated August 1987. However, there has been some movement toward excepting governmental non-profit organizations from depreciating assets.

PART IV
Implementation of Strategies

Once strategies have been formulated and integrated into the functional areas, the managers have to implement them. Various functions have to be performed—namely, (1) planning for their implementation, (2) acquiring resources, (3) organizing these resources, (4) coordinating their efforts, and (5) evaluating the results. These managerial functions describe a managerial system. The system, combined with a leadership style, forms the organizational culture, which may be described as "here's the way we do things around here." The culture is a key to executing or carrying out the strategy.

22

Strategic Change Implementation

Strategic change management becomes necessary when certain strategic determinants create turbulence or uncertainty for the non-profit organization. The necessity for change hopefully will be perceived and acted on by the administrators in the NPO who will have to mobilize their people resources to deal with the uncertainty. Because strategic change is large-scale change affecting the whole NPO, it usually is triggered by large-scale uncertainty, most frequently in the form of a threat or an opportunity.

ADMINISTERING STRATEGIC CHANGE

Organizational change has been defined by Edgar Schein as the induction of new patterns of action, belief, and attitudes among substantial segments of a population. Strategic change refers to non-routine, non-incremental, and discontinuous change that alters the overall direction and orientation of the NPO. Administered change refers to the actions of the NPO's administrators in managing the uncertainty caused when the determinants of strategy are changed. The process of strategic change occurs when various threats or opportunities are perceived by the chief executive officer and board who decide on a different mission or related objectives.[1]

Change is caused by various triggers, including at least four: (1) external environmental changes, such as increased competition, recession, scarcity of resources, increased demand, technological developments, new laws, changes in political parties, changes in consumption patterns and life styles of people, and several other forces, as discussed previously; (2) internal environmental changes, such as changes of the guard in terms of executive directors and disagreements over the means of production, marketing, financial control, and personnel; (3) changes in mission and related objectives, such as disagreements among board members and the CEO about the types and importance of the service-market match and related strategies regarding growth, market share, and others; and (4) changes in the philosophical beliefs of the CEO and the shared values of the people in the organization.

A trigger usually causes a strategic gap; that is, the NPO desires to be in a different state from where it is now. These gaps are perceived by various comparisons such as those suggested by George F. Wieland and Robert A. Ullrich:[2]

1. A gap caused by historical comparisons between current performance and past performance (productivity ratios may worsen over time)
2. A gap caused by planning comparisons of current performance against future projections (when a CEO wants to grow from $1 million in revenues to $5 million in revenues in five years)
3. A gap caused by extraorganizational comparisons with NPOs in the same industry (market share comparisons in competitive situations)
4. A gap caused by scientific comparisons (where the NPO is compared to theoretical predictions)
5. A gap caused by the CEO's expectations (being a status quo executive director does not create visibility for a CEO who wants to make a name for himself/herself)

These gaps are usually created by a CEO's perception of the external environmental factors or the internal environmental factors. Karl Weick has pointed out that the human being creates the various environments to which the organization then adapts. Thus, the human actor does not react to the environment; he "enacts" it. The CEO's perception of the environment (both external and internal) is a representation as he/she sees it.[3]

When the CEO perceives an environmental gap, he/she usually formulates a strategy to close that gap. Once the strategy is formulated and various decisions have been made to integrate the strategy into the various operative functional areas, then comes the time to implement the strategy.

Implementation involves the function of executing or carrying out the strategy. The execution phase involves the performance of managerial functions which eventually are translated into the internal organizational culture, which may be described as "here's the way we do things around here."

THE CULTURE OF THE NPO
AND STRATEGY IMPLEMENTATION

Culture is a major determinant of how to implement strategies. It comes about when members of an NPO deal with common problems, tasks, and objectives and, in so doing, try various functions, certain of which become firmly established and are transmitted to successive generations as the culture.

Culture exists in an NPO when there are shared values that are accepted by most of the NPO members and are supported by those members. Those values are usually determined by the CEO's philosophy, which becomes the managerial system of the NPO. The shared values of the CEO and the managerial system determine the internal organizational culture of the NPO.

Culture is a rather fuzzy concept because it is difficult to measure, it is intangible, and it is a fairly recently recognized concept. However, it can be seen, heard, and felt by managers who deal with strategy implementation. Moreover, care has to be taken to separate the contents of culture from the media of culture. The contents of culture concern the core values of the NPO, usually the mission and the related managerial functions and systems which are most often influenced by the CEO's values or beliefs. The forms by which these values are transmitted are special jargon, stories, symbols, rituals, and role models. Sometimes the core values are expressed and reinforced by slogans of the organization. The contents may be transmitted by planning systems, information systems, organizational structure systems, task systems, human resource systems, and others.

Types of Cultures

Organizational cultures may be classified in a variety of ways, but a general way is to classify them as organic, mechanistic, or mixed organic-mechanistic.

A Mechanistic Culture

T. Burns and G. M. Stalker called a rule-regulated culture mechanistic and characterized it as follows: tasks are narrowly defined, specialized, and differentiated; people should perform only those narrow tasks; there is unity of command — one boss only; a rigid hierarchy of authority exists; detailed job descriptions are provided; behavior is governed by superiors; only top managers see the overall picture; and communication is along vertical lines — top down. The measures taken to design such a mechanistic culture include time and motion studies, job analyses, job descriptions, control systems, and formal organization charts — all designed to increase organizational efficiency.[4]

An Adaptive Organic Culture

Research by social psychologists suggested that the mechanistic culture had dehumanizing and dysfunctional consequences. They felt that the mechanistic culture was too authoritarian, was unresponsive to employee needs, could not adapt too well to uncertainty, and was taking too much of a toll on organizational members.

The organic culture is characterized by the following: democratic leaders are very effective; employees are effective when they can participate in decision making; communication is effective when there is trust, openness, and honesty; individuals derive satisfaction from working in groups; and the role of the manager is to develop cohesive groups by participation of the members of the group.

Burns and Stalker characterized the organic culture as having a network structure of control, authority, and communication; continual adjustment of tasks by interacting with others; commitment to the whole organization, rather than just one part; lateral as well as vertical communication; communication of advice rather than orders; lack of formal job definitions; and sanctions derived from peers and superiors.[5]

Mechanistic and Organic Cultures Compared

Burns and Stalker found that both types of cultures are compatible with effectiveness, depending on environmental factors. Porter, Lawler, and Hackman found that mechanistic cultures are effective when members are inexperienced or unskilled; when members do not have high self-esteem and strong needs for achievement, autonomy, and self-actualization; when technologies are not rapidly changing, irregular, and unplanned; and when environments are not dynamic and complex.[6] Organic cultures are effective when there is authority based on knowledge, when people are committed to tasks over loyalty to people, when there is high uncertainty and irregular and unplanned technologies, and when tasks prescribe people networks that are complex and not formalized.[7]

Both types of cultures are effective in implementing strategies, depending on the factors of the situation facing the NPO. But what are these situational factors that determine which type of culture — organic or mechanistic — is most compatible with strategic implementation?

External Environmental Factors

James Thompson suggested that organizations are driven to seek predictability and control in the environment and thus to reduce uncertainty.[8] Jeffrey Pfeffer and Gerald Salancik have suggested that there are dimensions that are related to uncertainty.[9] For example, organizational concentrations of power to control economic outcomes would suggest a degree of certainty for the organization. A monopoly position in the market would ensure a relatively high degree of certainty for the organization, thus suggesting a mechanistic culture. Moreover, uncertainty is reduced in oligopoly situations. But intense competition would allow for a great deal of uncertainty, suggesting organic cultures.

The availability of critical resources for the organization is another factor that affects the degree of uncertainty facing the organization. An environment with scarce resources such as labor, capital, raw materials, and energy would suggest an uncertain environment; an organization would have to respond with an organic culture. But with plenty of resources available to it, an organization would not have to worry about getting them and could carry out its strategy with a mechanistic culture.

The demand for the organization's products and services would also be a factor. If the demand is constantly increasing, there will not be too much pressure to change from a mechanistic type to an organic one. However, if the demand is dropping, there will be concern for doing something about it, causing a degree of uncertainty for the establishment of an organic culture.

The demand, availability of resources, and state of the competition are all indicators of economic instability, causing either mechanistic or organic cultures to exist.

In addition, there are other external environmental factors to consider, such as political-legal uncertainty, technological uncertainty, socio-cultural trends causing uncertainty, and ethical-religious factors. Those that are certain, predictable, and stable would favor a mechanistic type, while those that are unstable and not predictable would suggest an organic type.

Finally, a mechanistic culture would be associated with products/services that are established and proved and not changed over time, while an organic culture would be associated with organizational products/services that are new and developing.

DETERMINING THE RELATIONSHIP OF THE EXTERNAL ENVIRONMENT, THE STRATEGY, THE LEADERSHIP STYLE, THE MANAGEMENT SYSTEM, THE INTERNAL CULTURE ON THE NPO'S PERFORMANCE

In this section we are trying to determine the effect of several variables on the implementation of the NPO's strategies. More specifically, does the external environment affect the characteristics of strategies? Do the strategies affect the leadership style which in turn affects the management system which in turn affects the internal organization culture? Do these variables, in turn, affect the performance of the NPO? To do so, the CEO of the NPO is asked to determine scores, based on his/her perception, of the various factors and to plot these scores on a situational contingency tree.

External Environment Scores

As an NPO executive you are asked to give your perceptions of the external environmental factors facing your NPO. Circle the number that you believe is closest to the condition that exists in your organization.

```
1.  How would you describe the competitive environment facing your
    NPO?

        Little          1  2  3  4  5  6        Much
        competition                             competition

2.  How would you describe the external availability of resources for
    your NPO?

        Plentiful       1  2  3  4  5  6        Scarce
        resources                               resources

3.  How would you describe the demand for your services/products?

        Increasing      1  2  3  4  5  6        Decreasing
        demand                                  demand
```

4. Considering the competitive environment, the availability of
    resources, and the demand for your services (all together), how
    would you describe the external environment facing your NPO?

Favorable	1	2	3	4	5	6	Unfavorable
Stable	1	2	3	4	5	6	Unstable
Friendly	1	2	3	4	5	6	Hostile
Certain	1	2	3	4	5	6	Uncertain
Predictable	1	2	3	4	5	6	Unpredictable

    Add your scores for Questions 1-4, and divide by eight to get an
average. An average of 1 to 2.5 would suggest a favorable
environment; a 2.6 to 4.5 score would suggest a mixed environment, and
4.6 to 6 would suggest an unfavorable environment; be prepared to plot
your score on a situational contingency tree (to be discussed later).

Strategies Affecting Implementation

1. How would you describe the overall core strategies of your NPO?

Unchanging	1	2	3	4	5	6	Dynamic
Safe	1	2	3	4	5	6	Risky
Not competitive	1	2	3	4	5	6	Competitive
Passive	1	2	3	4	5	6	Active
Inflexible	1	2	3	4	5	6	Flexible

    Add your scores, and divide to get an average (1-2.5 static,
2-4.5 mixed; 4.6-6 dynamic). Be prepard to plot your score on the
situational contingency tree.

Leadership Style of the Top Management

1. Please characterize the leadership style of top management.

        Non-participative 1   2   3   4   5   6   Participative

2. How would you describe the philosophy of top management?

        Conservative   1 2 3 4 5 6   Liberal

3. Regarding decision making, do you think your NPO is ...

        Centralized   1 2 3 4 5 6   Decentralized

4. In describing the communications flow, do you consider it...

        Mainly   1 2 3 4 5 6   Both vertical
        vertical   and horizontal

5. Describe the contents of the communications from upper-level
    management. Do you consider it to...

        Consist mainly 1 2 3 4 5 6   Consist mainly
        of decisions   of information
        and direction

6. How are the opinions of personnel regarded by your NPO?

        Ignored   1 2 3 4 5 6   Valued

7. How committed are your personnel?

        Slightly   1 2 3 4 5 6   Highly
        committed   committed

    Add your scores, and get an average (1-2.5 directive; 2.6-4.5
mixed; 4.6-6.0 participative).

Tasks Affecting Systems of Management

    The leadership style and values of top managers will affect the management system (top down, mixed, bottom up).

1.   How would you describe the tasks of the NPO?

Simple and routine	1	2	3	4	5	6	Complex and non-routine
Independently performed	1	2	3	4	5	6	Highly inter-dependent
Standardized	1	2	3	4	5	6	Tailor-made
Structured	1	2	3	4	5	6	Unstructured

    Add your scores, and get an average.

Planning and Management System

1.   When thinking about the objectives of your NPO, which of the following tends to describe those objectives?

Objectives are used as very specific guidelines for employee behavior	1	2	3	4	5	6	Objectives are used as general guidelines for employee behavior

2.   In your opinion, would you say that the NPO's budget is...

Used as a control device	1	2	3	4	5	6	Used as a planning device

3.   Would you say that planning is...

Formal	1	2	3	4	5	6	Informal

    Add your scores, and get an average.

Acquiring Resources

1.   Our NPO in acquiring resources (both human and financial)...

Has very little difficulty in acquiring them	1	2	3	4	5	6	Has a great deal of difficulty

2.   Do you consider the resources (both human and other) of your NPO to be...

Strong	1	2	3	4	5	6	Weak

    Add the two, and get an average.

Organization Structure

1.   When thinking about the organizational structure of your NPO, would you say there are...

Many hierarchical levels	1	2	3	4	5	6	Few hierarchical levels

2.   What type of committees are used by your NPO?

Standing committees	1	2	3	4	5	6	Temporary committees

3. How would you describe the organizational control?

```
    We rely on        1  2  3  4  5  6        We rely on
    written policy,                           oral policies,
    rules, and                                rules, and
    regulations                               regulations
    Add your scores, and get an average.
```

Coordination Procedures

1. In describing your NPO's communications flow, do you consider it...

```
    Mainly vertical  1  2  3  4  5  6        Both horizontal
                                             and vertical
```

2. Regarding your organization, does it consist of...

```
    Many hierarchical  1  2  3  4  5  6      Few hierarchical
    levels                                   levels
```

3. Regarding communications from top management, it consists mainly of...

```
    Decisions and    1  2  3  4  5  6        Information
    directives
```

4. How would you describe the coordination procedures?

```
    We rely on        1  2  3  4  5  6        We rely on
    written                                   oral policy
    policy and                                and procedures
    procedures
```

5. Regarding people interaction in the NPO, there is a...

```
    Low need for      1  2  3  4  5  6        High need for
    people                                    people
    interaction                               interaction
```

6. Regarding information processing, there is a...

```
    Low need         1  2  3  4  5  6         High need
    to process                                to process
    information                               information
```

7. Regarding coordination devices, there is a...

```
    Need for         1  2  3  4  5  6         Need for
    simple                                    complex
    coordination                              coordination
    devices                                   devices
```

8. Regarding committees to coordinate thought, we use...

```
    Very few         1  2  3  4  5  6         Several
    committees                                committees
```

    Add the scores, and get an average.

Control and Evaluation Systems

1. Would you say that control measures are...

```
    Specific         1  2  3  4  5  6         General
    measures                                  measures
```

2.   Regarding goals of the NPO for employees...

They are used   1 2 3 4 5 6   They are used
as very specific   as general
guidelines   guidelines

3.   Describe your perception of management control.

Tight   1 2 3 4 5 6   Loose

Add your scores, and get an average.

Values and Implementation

1.   Regarding communications within the NPO...

There is closed,   1 2 3 4 5 6   There is open,
distrustful   trustful
communication   communication
among people   among people

2.   Regarding values within the organization, there is...

Little capacity   1 2 3 4 5 6   Large capacity
for incongruent   for incongruent
values and   values and
ideologies   ideologies
within the   within the
organization   organization

Add the scores, and get an average.

Combining the Various Managerial Functions into Systems Score

Fill in the average scores from the preceding functions:

Tasks   -------
Planning   -------
Acquiring   -------
Organization   -------
Coordination   -------
Control   -------
Values   -------
        Total   -------

Add the scores, and get an average. If the average is 1 to 2.5,
the management system is a top down one; if 2.6 to 4.5, the system is
a mixed one; if 4.6 to 6, the management system is a bottom up one.

Determination of Organizational Culture

Add the total average scores for leadership and management
system.

                         Score
Leadership   -------
System   -------
Culture (Total)   -------

If the total score is 1 to 2.5, the internal organization culture
is a mechanistic one; if 2.6 to 4.5, the culture is a mixed one; if
4.6 to 6, the culture is an organic one.

Performance Measure of the NPO

Determine an appropriate performance measure for the NPO. If possible, use a five-year average performance measure. Compare it to other similar NPOs.

The following is a partial situational contingency tree. (You are asked to fill in the blanks with the scores you have accumulated).

Partial Situational Contingency Tree

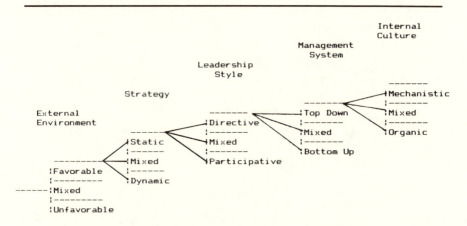

Example:	This tree is designed for an NPO that has a favorable external environment, a static strategy, a directive leadership style, a top-down management system, a mechanistic culture, and some performance measure.
Instructions:	Design a tree based on the scores you have obtained.
Conclusion:	Reach a conclusion as to whether the implementation is successful, unsuccessful, or partially so, based on your performance measure.

Partial Situational Contingency Tree

Another example:	This tree is designed for an NPO that has an unfavorable external environment, a dynamic strategy, a participative leadership style, a bottom-up management system, an organic culture, and some performance measure.
Instructions:	Design a tree based on the scores you have obtained.
Conclusion:	Reach a conclusion as to whether the implementation is successful, unsuccessful, or partially so, based on your performance measure.

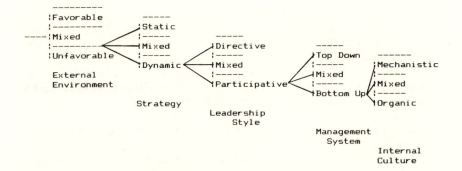

Partial Situational Contingency Tree

Another example: This tree is designed for an NPO that has a mixed external environment, a static strategy, a participative leadership style, a bottom-up management system, an organic culture, and some performance measure.

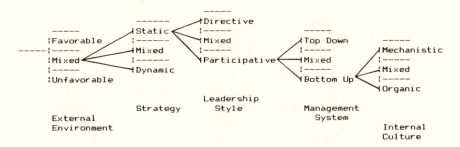

Instructions: Using the three examples given, design a tree to fit the scores you have computed.

Conclusion: Reach a conclusion as to whether the implementation is successful, unsuccessful, or partially so, based on your performance measure.

Notes

1. Edgar Schein, *Organizational Psychology*, 2d ed., (Englewood Cliffs, N.J.: Prentice Hall, 1970).

2. George A. Wieland and Robert A. Ullrich, *Organizations: Behavior, Design and Change*, (Homewood, Ill.: Irwin, 1976), Ch. 15.

3. Karl E. Weick, *The Social Psychology of Organizing*, 2d ed., (Reading, Mass.: Addison Wesley, 1979), 131.

4. T. Burns and G. M. Stalker, *The Management Innovation*, (London: Tavistock, 1961), 5–6.

5. Ibid.

6. Lyman W. Porter, Edward E. Lawler, V. Richard Hackman, *Behavior in Organizations*, (New York: McGraw-Hill, 1975), Ch. 8.

7. Burns and Stalker, 125.

8. James D. Thompson, *Organizations in Action*, (New York: McGraw-Hill, 1969).

9. Jeffrey Pfeffer and Gerald Salancik, "Organizational Decision Making as a Political Process," *Administrative Science Quarterly* (1974): 135–51.

References

Burns, T., and G. Stalker. *The Management of Innovation*. London: Tavistock Press, 1961.

Chandler, A. D., Jr. *Strategy and Structure*. Cambridge, Mass.: MIT Press, 1962.

Etzioni, A. *A Comparative Analysis of Complex Organizations*. New York: Free Press, 1968.

Fayol, Henri. *General and Industrial Management*. New York: Pitman, 1949.

Homans, George. *The Human Group*. New York: Harcourt, Brace, 1950.

Katz, D., and R. L. Kahn. *The Social Psychology of Organizations*. New York: Wiley, 1978.

Krech, D., R. S. Crutchfield, and E. L. Ballachey. *The Individual in Society*. New York: McGraw-Hill, 1962.

Lewin, Kurt. *Contributions to Psychological Theory*. Durham, N.C.: Duke University Press, 1938.

Likert, Rensis. *New Patterns of Management*. New York: McGraw-Hill, 1961.

McGregor, D. *The Human Side of Enterprise*. New York: McGraw-Hill, 1960.

March, J. G., and H. A. Simon. *Organizations*. New York: John Wiley & Sons, 1958.

Merton, R. K. *Social Theory and Social Structure*. Glencoe, Ill.: Free Press, 1957.

Peters, Thomas. "Management Systems: The Language of Organizational Character and Competence." *Organizational Dynamics* (Summer 1980):3–26.

Pfeffer, J., and G. Salancik. *The External Control of Organizations*. New York: Harper & Row, 1978.

Porter, Lyman, E. E. Lawler, and J. R. Hackman. *Behavior in Organizations*. New York: McGraw-Hill, 1975.

Roethlisberger, F. J., and W. J. Dickson. *Management and the Worker*. Cambridge, Mass.: Harvard University Press, 1939.

Schein, Edgar H. *Organizational Psychology*, 2d ed. Englewood Cliffs, N.J.: Prentice-Hall, 1970.

Taylor, Frederick. *The Principles of Scientific Management*. New York: Harper, 1913.

Thompson, J. D. *Organizations in Action*. New York: McGraw-Hill, 1967.

Tichy, Noel M. *Managing Strategic Change*. New York: John Wiley & Sons, 1983.

Urwick, Lyndall F. *The Elements of Administration*. New York: Harper, 1943.

Weber, Max. *The Theory of Social and Economic Organizations*, ed. T. Parsons. New York: Oxford University Press, 1947.

Weick, Karl E. *The Social Psychology of Organizing*. 2d ed. Reading, Mass.: Addison-Wesley, 1979.

Index

About the Author

ROBERT D. HAY is University Professor of Management at the University of Arkansas, Fayetteville. He is a nationally recognized case researcher, a member of many professional organizations, and has published numerous articles and books, including *Sports Law for Educational Institutions* (Quorum, 1988).